Praise for Plan B

"Lester Brown tells us how to build a more just world and save the planet . . . in a practical, straightforward way. We should all heed his advice."   —President Bill Clinton

". . . a far-reaching thinker."   —*U.S. News & World Report*

"It's exciting . . . a masterpiece!"   —Ted Turner

"In tackling a host of pressing issues in a single book, *Plan B 2.0* makes for an eye-opening read."

—*Times Higher Education Supplement*

"Lester Brown should receive a Nobel Peace Prize for his new book."   —*The Herald Mexico*

"A great book which should wake up humankind!"

—Klaus Schwab, World Economic Forum

"Lester R. Brown, one of the world's preeminent ecoeconomists . . . has a solution for dealing with the threat . . . Plans must be periodically revised and refined, which Brown has done with insight and foresight in this volume."   —*Ode*

". . . a highly readable and authoritative account of the problems we face from global warming to shrinking water resources, fisheries, forests, etc. The picture is very frightening. But the book also provides a way forward."

—Clare Short, British Member of Parliament

"Lester R. Brown gives concise, but very informative, summaries of what he regards as the key issues facing civilization as a consequence of the stress we put on our environment . . . a valuable contribution to the ongoing debate."   —*The Ecologist*

continued . . .

PLAN B 3.0

OTHER NORTON BOOKS
BY LESTER R. BROWN

*Plan B 2.0: Rescuing a Planet
Under Stress and a
Civilization in Trouble*

*Outgrowing the Earth: The Food
Security Challenge in an Age
of Falling Water Tables and
Rising Temperatures*

*Plan B: Rescuing a Planet
Under Stress and a
Civilization in Trouble*

The Earth Policy Reader
with Janet Larsen and
Bernie Fischlowitz-Roberts

*Eco-Economy: Building an
Economy for the Earth*

State of the World 1984
through *2001*
annual, with others

Vital Signs 1992 through *2001*
annual, with others

Beyond Malthus
with Gary Gardner
and Brian Halweil

The World Watch Reader 1998
editor with Ed Ayres

Tough Choices

Who Will Feed China?

Full House
with Hal Kane

Saving the Planet
with Christopher Flavin
and Sandra Postel

Building a Sustainable Society

Running on Empty
with Colin Norman
and Christopher Flavin

The Twenty-Ninth Day

In the Human Interest

Earth Policy Institute® is a nonprofit environmental research organization
providing a plan for building a sustainable future. It seeks to reach a global
constituency through the media and the Internet. In addition to the Plan B
series, the Institute issues four-page *Plan B Updates* that assess progress in
implementing Plan B. All of these can be downloaded at no charge from
the EPI Web site.

Web site: www.earthpolicy.org

PLAN B 3.0

Mobilizing to Save Civilization

Lester R. Brown

EARTH POLICY INSTITUTE

W · W · NORTON & COMPANY

NEW YORK   LONDON

The text of this book is composed in Sabon. Composition by Elizabeth Doherty; manufacturing by Courier Westford.

ISBN 978-0-393-06589-3 (cloth) 978-0-393-33087-8 (pbk)

W. W. Norton & Company, Inc., 500 Fifth Avenue, New York, N.Y. 10110
www.wwnorton.com

W. W. Norton & Company Ltd., Castle House, 75/76 Wells Street, London W1T 3QT

1 2 3 4 5 6 7 8 9 0

Contents

Contents

Preface

When Elizabeth Kolbert was interviewing energy analyst Amory Lovins for a profile piece in the *New Yorker*, she asked him about thinking outside the box. Lovins responded, "There is no box." There is no box. That is the spirit embodied in Plan B.

Perhaps the most revealing difference between *Plan B 2.0* and *Plan B 3.0* is the change of the subtitle from "Rescuing a Planet Under Stress and a Civilization in Trouble" to simply "Mobilizing to Save Civilization." The new subtitle better reflects both the scale of the challenge we face and the wartime speed of the response it calls for.

Our world is changing fast. When *Plan B 2.0* went to press two years ago, the data on ice melting were worrying. Now they are scary.

Two years ago, we knew there were a number of failing states. Now we know that number is increasing each year. Failing states are an early sign of a failing civilization.

Two years ago there was early evidence that the potential for expanding oil production was much less than officially projected. Now, we know that peak oil could be on our doorstep. Two years ago oil was $50 a barrel. As of this writing in late 2007, it is over $90 a barrel.

In *Plan B 2.0*, we speculated that if we continued to build ethanol distilleries to convert grain into fuel for cars, the price of grain would move up toward its oil-equivalent value. Now that the United States has enough distilleries to convert one fifth of its grain crop into fuel for cars, this is exactly what is happening. Corn prices have nearly doubled. Wheat prices have more than doubled.

Two years ago, we reported that in five of the last six years world grain production had fallen short of consumption. Now, it has done so in seven of the past eight years, and world grain stocks are dropping toward all-time lows.

As the backlog of unresolved problems grows, including continuing rapid population growth, spreading water shortages, shrinking forests, eroding soils, and grasslands turning to desert, weaker governments are breaking down under the mounting stress. If we cannot reverse the trends that are driving states to failure, we will not be able to stop the growth in their numbers.

Some of the newly emerging trends—such as the coming decline in world oil production, the new stresses from global warming, and rising food prices—could push even some of the stronger states to the breaking point.

On the economic front, China has now overtaken the United States in consumption of most basic resources. By 2030, when its income per person is projected to match that in the United States today, China will be consuming twice as much paper as the world currently produces. If in 2030 the country's 1.46 billion people have three cars for every four people, U.S. style, China will have 1.1 billion cars. And it will be consuming 98 million barrels of oil per day, well above current world production.

The western economic model—the fossil-fuel-based, automobile-centered, throwaway economy—is not going to work for China. If it doesn't work for China, it won't work for India or the other 3 billion people in developing countries who are also dreaming the American dream. And in an increasingly integrated world economy, where we all depend on the same grain, oil, and steel, it will not work for industrial countries either.

The challenge for our generation is to build a new economy, one that is powered largely by renewable sources of energy, that has a highly diversified transport system, and that reuses and recycles everything. And to do it with unprecedented speed.

Continuing with business as usual (Plan A), which is destroying the economy's eco-supports and setting the stage for dangerous climate change, is no longer a viable option. It is time for Plan B.

There are four overriding goals in *Plan B 3.0*: stabilizing climate, stabilizing population, eradicating poverty, and restoring the earth's ecosystems. At the heart of the climate-stabilizing initiative is a detailed plan to cut carbon dioxide emissions 80 percent by 2020 in order to hold the global temperature rise to a minimum. The climate initiative has three components: raising energy efficiency, developing renewable sources of energy, and expanding the earth's forest cover both by banning deforestation and by planting billions of trees to sequester carbon.

We are in a race between tipping points in nature and our political systems. Can we phase out coal-fired power plants before the melting of the Greenland ice sheet becomes irreversible? Can we gather the political will to halt deforestation in the Amazon before its growing vulnerability to fire takes it to the point of no return? Can we help countries stabilize population before they become failing states?

The United States appears to be approaching a political tipping point as opposition builds to the construction of new coal-fired power plants. A fast-spreading nationwide campaign has led several states, including California, Texas, Florida, Kansas, and Minnesota, to refuse construction permits or otherwise restrict construction.

With this movement gaining momentum, it may be only a matter of time before it expands to embrace the phasing out of existing coal-fired power plants. The question is, Will this happen soon enough to avoid dangerous climate change?

In *Plan B 2.0*, we talked about the enormous potential of renewable sources of energy, especially wind power. Since then we've seen proposed projects to generate electricity from such resources on a scale never seen with fossil fuel power plants. For example, the state of Texas is coordinating a vast expansion of wind farms that will yield up to 23,000 megawatts of new electrical generating capacity, an amount equal to 23 coal-fired power plants.

Two years ago, the notion of plug-in gas-electric hybrid cars was little more than a concept. Today five leading automobile manufacturers are moving to market with plug-in hybrids, with the first ones expected in 2010.

We have the technologies to restructure the world energy economy and stabilize climate. The challenge now is to build the political will to do so. Saving civilization is not a spectator sport. Each of us has a leading role to play.

When we published the original *Plan B* four years ago, we noticed that some 600 individuals ordered a copy of the book and then came back and ordered 5, 10, 20 or 50 copies for distribution to friends, colleagues, and political and opinion leaders. With *Plan B 2.0*, this number jumped to more than 1,500 individuals and organizations that were bulk buying and distributing the book.

We call these distributors our Plan B Team. Ted Turner, who distributed some 3,600 copies to heads of state, cabinet members, Fortune 500 CEOs, the U.S. Congress, and the world's 672 other billionaires, was designated Plan B team captain.

This book can be downloaded without charge from our Web site. Permission for reprinting or excerpting portions of the manuscript can be obtained from Reah Janise Kauffman at Earth Policy Institute.

And finally, there is not anything sacred about Plan B. It is our best effort to lay out an alternative to business as usual, one that we hope will help save our civilization. If anyone can come up with a better plan, we will welcome it. The world needs the best plan possible.

Lester R. Brown
October 2007

Earth Policy Institute
1350 Connecticut Ave. NW
Suite 403
Washington, DC 20036

Phone: (202) 496-9290
Fax: (202) 496-9325
E-mail: epi@earthpolicy.org
Web: www.earthpolicy.org

For additional information on the topics discussed in this book, see www.earthpolicy.org.

PLAN B 3.0

1

Entering a New World

During the late summer of 2007, the news of accelerating ice melting arrived at a frenetic pace. In early September, the *Guardian* in London reported, "The Arctic ice cap has collapsed at an unprecedented rate this summer, and levels of sea ice in the region now stand at a record low." Experts were "stunned" by the loss of ice, as an area almost twice the size of Britain disappeared in a single week.[1]

Mark Serreze, a veteran Arctic specialist with the U.S. National Snow and Ice Data Center, said: "It's amazing. If you asked me a couple of years ago when the Arctic could lose all of its ice, then I would have said 2100, or 2070 maybe. But now I think that 2030 is a reasonable estimate."[2]

A few days later, the *Guardian*, reporting from a symposium in Ilulissat, Greenland, said that the Greenland ice cap is melting so fast that it is triggering minor earthquakes as pieces of ice weighing several billion tons each break off the ice sheet and slide into the sea. Robert Corell, chairman of the Arctic Climate Impact Assessment, reported that "we have seen a massive acceleration of the speed with which these glaciers are moving into the sea. The ice is moving at 2 meters an hour on a front 5 kilometers [3 miles] long and 1,500 meters deep."[3]

Corell said that when flying over the Ilulissat glacier he had "seen gigantic holes (moulins) in it through which swirling masses of melt water were falling." This melt water lubricates the surface between the glacier and the land below, causing the glacier to flow faster into the sea. Veli Kallio, a Finnish scientist who had been analyzing the earthquakes, said they were new to northwest Greenland and showed the potential for the entire ice sheet to break up and collapse.[4]

Corell noted that the projected rise in sea level during this century of 18–59 centimeters (7–23 inches) by the Intergovernmental Panel on Climate Change was based on data that were two years old. He said that some scientists now believe the increase could be as much as 2 meters.[5]

In late August, a *Reuters* story began with "a thaw of Antarctic ice is outpacing predictions by the U.N. climate panel and could in the worst case drive up world sea levels by 2 meters (6 feet) by 2100, a leading expert said." Chris Rapley, head of the British Antarctic Survey said, "The ice is moving faster both in Greenland and in the Antarctic than the glaciologists had believed would happen."[6]

Several months earlier, scientists had reported that the Gangotri glacier, the principal glacier that feeds the Ganges River, is melting at an accelerating rate and could disappear entirely in a matter of decades. The Ganges would become a seasonal river, flowing only during the monsoon season.[7]

Glaciers on the Tibet-Qinghai Plateau that feed the Yellow and Yangtze rivers are melting at 7 percent a year. Yao Tandong, one of China's leading glaciologists, believes that at this rate, two thirds of these glaciers could disappear by 2060.[8]

These glaciers in the Himalayas and on the Tibet-Qinghai Plateau feed all the major rivers of Asia, including the Indus, Ganges, Mekong, Yangtze, and Yellow Rivers. It is the water from these rivers that irrigates the rice and wheat fields in the region.

We are crossing natural thresholds that we cannot see and violating deadlines that we do not recognize. Nature is the time keeper, but we cannot see the clock. Among the other environmental trends undermining our future are shrinking forests, expanding deserts, falling water tables, collapsing fisheries, disappearing species, and rising temperatures. The temperature increases bring crop-withering heat waves, more-destructive storms, more-intense droughts, more forest fires, and, of course, ice melting.

We can see from ice melting alone that our civilization is in trouble. If the Greenland ice sheet melts, sea level rises 7 meters (23 feet). If the West Antarctic Ice Sheet breaks up, and many scientists think it could go before Greenland, it adds another 5 meters to the increase, for a total of 12 meters (39 feet).[9]

The International Institute for Environment and Development has studied the likely effects of a 10-meter (33-foot) rise. Their 2007 study projected more than 600 million refugees from rising seas. More people than currently live in the United States and Western Europe combined would be forced to migrate inland to escape the rising waters.[10]

Now that we are belatedly recognizing these trends and the need to reverse them, time is running out. We are in a race between tipping points in the earth's natural systems and those in the world's political systems. Which will tip first? Will we reach the point where the melting of the Greenland ice sheet is irreversible? Or will we decide to phase out coal-fired power plants fast enough to avoid this wholesale ice melting?

A rise in temperature to the point where the earth's ice sheets and glaciers melt is only one of many environmental tipping points needing our attention. While the earth's temperature is rising, water tables are falling on every continent. Here the challenge is to raise water use efficiency and stabilize population before water shortages become life-threatening.[11]

Population growth, which contributes to all the problems discussed here, has its own tipping point. Scores of countries have developed enough economically to sharply reduce mortality but not yet enough to reduce fertility. As a result, they are caught in the demographic trap—a situation where rapid population growth begets poverty and poverty begets rapid population growth. In this situation, countries eventually tip one way or the other. They either break out of the cycle or they break down.

Over the last few decades, the world has accumulated a growing number of unresolved problems, including those just mentioned. As the stresses from these unresolved problems accumulate, weaker governments are beginning to break down, leading to what are now commonly referred to as failing states.

Failing states are an early sign of a failing civilization. The countries at the top of the lengthening list of failing states are not particularly surprising. They include, for example, Iraq, Sudan, Somalia, Chad, Afghanistan, the Democratic Republic of the Congo, and Haiti. And the list grows longer each year, raising a disturbing question: How many failing states will it take before civilization itself fails? No one knows the answer, but it is a question we must ask.[12]

A Massive Market Failure

When Nicholas Stern, former chief economist at the World Bank, released his ground-breaking study in late 2006 on the future costs of climate change, he talked about a massive market failure. He was referring to the failure of the market to incorporate the climate change costs of burning fossil fuels. The costs, he said, would be measured in the trillions of dollars. The difference between the market prices for fossil fuels and the prices that also incorporate their environmental costs to society are huge.[13]

The roots of our current dilemma lie in the enormous growth of the human enterprise over the last century. Since 1900, the world economy has expanded 20-fold and world population has increased fourfold. Although there were places in 1900 where local demand exceeded the capacity of natural systems, this was not a global issue. There was some deforestation, but overpumping of water was virtually unheard of, overfishing was rare, and carbon emissions were so low that there was no serious effect on climate. The indirect costs of these early excesses were negligible.[14]

Now with the economy as large as it is, the indirect costs of burning coal—the costs of air pollution, acid rain, devastated ecosystems, and climate change—can exceed the direct costs, those of mining the coal and transporting it to the power plant. As a result of neglecting to account for these indirect costs, the market is undervaluing many goods and services, creating economic distortions.[15]

As economic decisionmakers—whether consumers, corporate planners, government policymakers, or investment bankers—we all depend on the market for information to guide us. In order for markets to work and economic actors to make sound decisions, the markets must give us good information, including the full cost of the products we buy. But the market is giving us bad information, and as a result we are making bad decisions—so bad that they are threatening civilization.

The market is in many ways an incredible institution. It allocates resources with an efficiency that no central planning body can match and it easily balances supply and demand. The market has some fundamental weaknesses, however. It does not incorporate into prices the indirect costs of producing goods. It does not value nature's services properly. And it does not respect the sustainable yield thresholds of natural systems. It also favors the near term over the long term, showing little concern for future generations.

One of the best examples of this massive market failure can be seen in the United States, where the gasoline pump price in mid-2007 was $3 per gallon. But this price reflects only the cost of discovering the oil, pumping it to the surface, refining it into gasoline, and delivering the gas to service stations. It overlooks the costs of climate change as well as the costs of tax subsidies to the oil industry (such as the oil depletion allowance), the burgeoning military costs of protecting access to oil in the politically unstable Middle East, and the health care costs for treating respiratory illnesses from breathing polluted air.[16]

Based on a study by the International Center for Technology Assessment, these costs now total nearly $12 per gallon ($3.17 per liter) of gasoline burned in the United States. If these were added to the $3 cost of the gasoline itself, motorists would pay $15 a gallon for gas at the pump. In reality, burning gasoline is very costly, but the market tells us it is cheap, thus grossly distorting the structure of the economy. The challenge facing governments is to restructure tax systems by systematically incorporating indirect costs as a tax to make sure the price of products reflects their full costs to society and by offsetting this with a reduction in income taxes.[17]

Another market distortion became abundantly clear in the summer of 1998 when China's Yangtze River valley, home to nearly 400 million people, was wracked by some of the worst flooding in history. The resulting damages of $30 billion exceeded the value of the country's annual rice harvest.[18]

After several weeks of flooding, the government in Beijing

announced a ban on tree cutting in the Yangtze River basin. It justified this by noting that trees standing are worth three times as much as trees cut: the flood control services provided by forests were far more valuable than the lumber in the trees. In effect, the market price was off by a factor of three.[19]

This situation has occasional parallels in the commercial world. In the late 1990s Enron, a Texas-based energy trading corporation, may have appeared on the cover of more business magazines than any other U.S. company. It was spectacularly successful. The darling of Wall Street, it was the seventh most valuable corporation in the United States in early 2001. Unfortunately, when independent auditors began looking closely at Enron in late 2001 they discovered that the company had been leaving certain costs off the books. When these were included, Enron was worthless. Its stock, which had traded as high as $90 a share, was suddenly trading for pennies a share. Enron was bankrupt. The collapse was complete. It no longer exists.[20]

We are doing today exactly what Enron did. We are leaving costs off the books, but on a far larger scale. We focus on key economic indicators like economic growth and the increase in international trade and investment, and the situation looks good. But if we incorporate all the indirect costs that the market omits when setting prices, a very different picture emerges. If we persist in leaving these costs off the books, we will face the same fate as Enron.

Today, more than ever before, we need political leaders who can see the big picture, who understand the relationship between the economy and its environmental support systems. And since the principal advisors to government are economists, we need economists who can think like ecologists. Unfortunately they are rare. Ray Anderson, founder and chairman of Atlanta-based Interface, a leading world manufacturer of industrial carpet, is especially critical of economics as it is taught in many universities: "We continue to teach economics students to trust the 'invisible hand' of the market, when the invisible hand is clearly blind to the externalities and treats massive subsidies, such as a war to protect oil for the oil companies, as if the subsidies were deserved. Can we really trust a blind invisible hand to allocate resources rationally?"[21]

Environment and Civilization

To understand our current environmental dilemma, it helps to look at earlier civilizations that also got into environmental trouble. Our early twenty-first century civilization is not the first to face the prospect of environmentally induced economic decline. The question is how we will respond.

As Jared Diamond points out in his book *Collapse*, some of the early societies that were in environmental trouble were able to change their ways in time to avoid decline and collapse. Six centuries ago, for example, Icelanders realized that overgrazing on their grass-covered highlands was leading to extensive soil loss from the inherently thin soils of the region. Rather than lose the grasslands and face economic decline, farmers joined together to determine how many sheep the highlands could sustain and then allocated quotas among themselves, thus preserving their grasslands. The Icelanders understood the consequences of overgrazing and reduced their sheep numbers to a level that could be sustained. Their wool production and woolen goods industry continue to thrive today.[22]

Not all societies have fared as well as the Icelanders. The early Sumerian civilization of the fourth millennium BC had advanced far beyond any that had existed before. Its carefully engineered irrigation system gave rise to a highly productive agriculture, one that enabled farmers to produce a food surplus, supporting formation of the first cities. Managing Sumer's irrigation system required a sophisticated social organization. The Sumerians had the first cities and the first written language, the cuneiform script.[23]

By any measure it was an extraordinary civilization, but there was an environmental flaw in the design of its irrigation system, one that would eventually undermine its food supply. The water that backed up behind dams built across the Euphrates was diverted onto the land through a network of gravity-fed canals. As with most irrigation systems, some irrigation water percolated downward. In this region, where underground drainage was weak, this slowly raised the water table. As the water climbed to within inches of the surface, it began to evaporate into the atmosphere, leaving behind salt. Over time, the accumulation of salt on the soil surface lowered the land's productivity.[24]

As salt accumulated and wheat yields declined, the Sumerians shifted to barley, a more salt-tolerant plant. This postponed Sumer's decline, but it was treating the symptoms, not the cause, of their falling crop yields. As salt concentrations continued to build, the yields of barley eventually declined also. The resultant shrinkage of the food supply undermined this once-great civilization. As land productivity declined, so did the civilization.[25]

Archeologist Robert McC. Adams has studied the site of ancient Sumer on the central floodplain of the Euphrates River, an empty, desolate area now outside the frontiers of cultivation. He describes how the "tangled dunes, long disused canal levees, and the rubble-strewn mounds of former settlement contribute only low, featureless relief. Vegetation is sparse, and in many areas it is almost wholly absent....Yet at one time, here lay the core, the heartland, the oldest urban, literate civilization in the world."[26]

The New World counterpart to Sumer is the Mayan civilization that developed in the lowlands of what is now Guatemala. It flourished from AD 250 until its collapse around AD 900. Like the Sumerians, the Mayans had developed a sophisticated, highly productive agriculture, this one based on raised plots of earth surrounded by canals that supplied water.[27]

As with Sumer, the Mayan demise was apparently linked to a failing food supply. For this New World civilization, it was deforestation and soil erosion that undermined agriculture. Changes in climate may also have played a role. Food shortages apparently triggered civil conflict among the various Mayan cities as they competed for something to eat. Today this region is covered by jungle, reclaimed by nature.[28]

The Icelanders crossed a political tipping point that enabled them to come together and limit grazing before grassland deterioration reached the point of no return. The Sumerians and Mayans failed to do so. Time ran out.

Today, our successes and problems flow from the extraordinary growth in the world economy over the last century. The economy's annual growth, once measured in billions of dollars, is now measured in the trillions. Indeed, just the growth in the output of goods and services in 2007 exceeded the total output of the world economy in 1900.[29]

While the economy is growing exponentially, the earth's natural capacities, such as its ability to supply fresh water, forest products, and seafood, have not increased. A team of scientists led by Mathis Wackernagel concluded in a 2002 study published by the U.S. National Academy of Sciences that humanity's collective demands first surpassed the earth's regenerative capacity around 1980. Today, global demands on natural systems exceed their sustainable yield capacity by an estimated 25 percent. This means we are meeting current demands by consuming the earth's natural assets, setting the stage for decline and collapse.[30]

In our modern high-tech civilization, it is easy to forget that the economy, indeed our existence, is wholly dependent on the earth's natural systems and resources. We depend, for example, on the earth's climate system for an environment hospitable to agriculture, on the hydrological cycle to provide us with fresh water, and on long-term geological processes to convert rocks into the soil that has made the earth such a biologically productive planet.

There are now so many of us placing such heavy demands on the earth that we are overwhelming its natural capacities to meet our needs. The earth's forests are shrinking. Each year overgrazing converts vast areas of grassland into desert. The pumping of underground water exceeds natural recharge in countries containing half the world's people, leaving many without adequate water as their wells go dry.[31]

Each of us depends on the products and services provided by the earth's ecosystems, ranging from forest to wetlands, from coral reefs to grasslands. Among the services these ecosystems provide are water purification, pollination, carbon sequestration, flood control, and soil conservation. A four-year study of the world's ecosystems by 1,360 scientists, the Millennium Ecosystem Assessment, reported that 15 of 24 primary ecosystem services are being degraded or pushed beyond their limits. For example, three quarters of oceanic fisheries, a major source of protein in the human diet, are being fished at or beyond their limits, and many are headed toward collapse.[32]

Tropical rainforests are another ecosystem under severe stress, including the vast Amazon rainforest. Thus far roughly 20 percent of the rainforest has been cleared either for cattle ranching or soybean farming. Another 22 percent has been weakened by logging and road building, letting sunlight reach the forest floor, drying it out, and turning it into kindling. When it reaches this point, the rainforest loses its resistance to fire and begins to burn when ignited by lightning strikes.[33]

Scientists believe that if half the Amazon is cleared or weakened, this may be the tipping point, the threshold beyond which the rainforest cannot be saved. We will have crossed the tipping point, with consequences that will reverberate around the world. Amazonian ecologist Philip Fearnside says "with every tree that falls, we increase the probability that the tipping point will arrive." Geoffrey Lean, summarizing the findings of a symposium on the Amazon in the *Independent*, says that the alternatives to a rainforest in the Amazon would be "dry savannah at best, desert at worst."[34]

Daniel Nepstad, an Amazon-based senior scientist from the Woods Hole Research Center, sees a future of "megafires" sweeping through the drying jungle. He notes that the carbon stored in the Amazon's trees equals roughly 15 years of human-induced carbon emissions in the atmosphere. If we reach this tipping point we will have triggered yet another climate feedback, taken another step that could help seal our fate as a civilization.[35]

The excessive pressures on a given resource typically begin in a few countries and then slowly spread to others. Nigeria and the Philippines, once net exporters of forest products, are now importers. Thailand, now largely deforested, has banned logging. So has China, which is turning to Siberia and to the few remaining forested countries in Southeast Asia, such as Myanmar and Papua New Guinea, for the logs it needs.[36]

A similar situation exists with fisheries. At first only a few fisheries were under excessive pressure, mostly in the North Sea, off the east coast of North America, and off the coast of East Asia. Now with fishing fleets replete with factory processing ships and modern technologies, overfishing is the rule, not the exception. In the absence of intervention, the decline in scores of fisheries will culminate in collapse. Some, such as the cod fishery off the coast of Newfoundland and the Atlantic tuna fishery, may never recover. The Chilean sea bass fishery in the Southern Ocean and the sturgeon fishery in the Caspian Sea may also be approaching the point of no return.[37]

As wells go dry, as grasslands are converted into desert, and as soils erode, people are forced to migrate elsewhere, either within their country or across national boundaries. As the earth's natural capacities at the local level are exceeded, the declining economic possibilities generate a flow of environmental refugees.

While the continuing erosion of the economy's environmental support systems has convinced environmentalists, natural scientists, and others of the need to restructure the global economy, many others are not yet convinced. What is happening in China may change their minds.

China: Why the Existing Economic Model Will Fail

For almost as long as I can remember we have been saying that the United States, with 5 percent of the world's people, consumes a third or more of the earth's resources. That was true. It is no longer true. Today China consumes more basic resources than the United States does.[38]

Among the key commodities such as grain, meat, oil, coal, and steel, China consumes more of each than the United States except for oil, where the United States still has a wide (though narrowing) lead. China uses a third more grain than the United States. Its meat consumption is nearly double that of the United States. It uses three times as much steel.[39]

These numbers reflect national consumption, but what would happen if consumption per person in China were to catch up to that of the United States? If we assume that China's economy slows from the 10 percent annual growth of recent years to 8 percent, then in 2030 income per person in China will reach the level it is in the United States today.[40]

If we also assume that the Chinese will spend their income more or less as Americans do today, then we can translate their income into consumption. If, for example, each person in China consumes paper at the current American rate, then in 2030 China's 1.46 billion people will need twice as much paper as is produced worldwide today. There go the world's forests.[41]

If we assume that in 2030 there are three cars for every four people in China, as there now are in the United States, China will have 1.1 billion cars. The world currently has 860 million cars. To provide the needed roads, highways, and parking lots, China would have to pave an area comparable to what it now plants in rice.[42]

By 2030 China would need 98 million barrels of oil a day. The world is currently producing 85 million barrels a day and may never produce much more than that. There go the world's oil reserves.[43]

What China is teaching us is that the western economic model—the fossil-fuel-based, automobile-centered, throwaway economy—is not going to work for China. If it does not work for China, it will not work for India, which by 2030 may have an even larger population than China. Nor will it work for the other 3 billion people in developing countries who are also dreaming the "American dream." And in an increasingly integrated global economy, where we all depend on the same grain, oil, and steel, the western economic model will no longer work for the industrial countries either.[44]

The overriding challenge for our generation is to build a new economy—one that is powered largely by renewable sources of energy, that has a much more diversified transport system, and that reuses and recycles everything. We have the technology to build this new economy, an economy that will allow us to sustain economic progress. Can we build it fast enough to avoid a breakdown of social systems?

Mounting Stresses, Failing States

States fail when national governments lose control of part or all of their territory and can no longer ensure the personal security of their people. When governments lose their monopoly on power, law and order begin to disintegrate. When they can no longer provide basic services such as education, health care, and food security, they lose their legitimacy. A government in this position may no longer be able to collect enough revenue to finance effective governance. Societies can become so fragmented that they lack the cohesion to make decisions.

Failing states often degenerate into civil war. As warring groups vie for power, they become a threat to neighboring countries when internal conflict spills over national borders. They provide possible training grounds for international terrorist groups, as in Afghanistan, Iraq, and Somalia, or they become sources of drugs, as in Myanmar (formerly Burma) or Afghanistan (with the latter accounting for 92 percent of the world's opium supply in 2006). Because they lack functioning health care services, weakened states can become a source of infectious disease, as Nigeria has for polio.[45]

In failed states, where governments are no longer in control, power is typically assumed by other elements in society. In Afghanistan, it is local warlords; in Somalia, tribal chiefs; in Haiti, street gangs. New governing groups may also include drug rings or organized crime.

In the past, governments have been concerned by the concentration of too much power in one state, as in Nazi Germany, Imperial Japan, and the Soviet Union. But today it is failing states that provide the greatest threat to global order and stability. As *Foreign Policy* magazine notes, "World leaders once worried about who was amassing power; now they worry about the absence of it."[46]

The U.S. Central Intelligence Agency estimates the number of failing states at 20 or so. The British government's international development arm has identified 46 so-called fragile states. The World Bank focuses its attention on 35 low-income countries under stress, which it also describes as fragile states.[47]

The most systematic ongoing effort to analyze failed and failing states is one undertaken jointly by the Fund for Peace and the Carnegie Endowment for International Peace, which is updated annually and published in each July/August issue of *Foreign Policy*. This invaluable service, which draws on thousands of information sources worldwide, is rich with insights into the changes that are under way in the world and, in a broad sense, where the world is heading.[48]

In this analysis, countries are graded on 12 social, economic, political, and military indicators, with scores that range from 1 to 10. Scores for each indicator are aggregated into a single country indicator: the Failed States Index. A score of 120, the maximum, means that a society is failing totally by every measure.[49]

In the first *Foreign Policy* listing, based on data for 2004 and published in 2005, 7 countries had scores of 100 or more. In 2005 this increased to 9 countries, and in 2006 it was 12—nearly doubling in two years. This short trend is far from definitive, but both the rise in country scores near the top and the near doubling of countries with scores of 100 or higher suggest that state failure is increasing.[50]

Most of the top 10 countries in 2006 (see Table 1–1) were

near the top of the list in the two preceding years. In reviewing the data for 2006, *Foreign Policy* noted that "few encouraging signs emerged in 2006 to suggest the world is on a path to greater peace and stability." The one bright spot was the improvement in Liberia, which moved from ninth in 2004, on the verge of state failure, to twenty-seventh in 2006. When Liberia, after years of turmoil, held an election that brought Ellen Johnson-Sirleaf to the presidency in late 2005, it restored both a measure of political stability and hope for the country's future.[51]

Ranking on the Failed States Index is closely linked with key demographic and environmental indicators. Of the top 20 failing states, 17 have rapid rates of population growth, many of

Table 1–1. *Top 20 Failing States, 2006*

Rank	Country	Score
1	Sudan	113.7
2	Iraq	111.4
3	Somalia	111.1
4	Zimbabwe	110.1
5	Chad	108.8
6	Ivory Coast	107.3
7	Democratic Republic of the Congo	105.5
8	Afghanistan	102.3
9	Guinea	101.3
10	Central African Republic	101.0
11	Haiti	100.9
12	Pakistan	100.1
13	North Korea	97.7
14	Burma	97.0
15	Uganda	96.4
16	Bangladesh	95.9
17	Nigeria	95.6
18	Ethiopia	95.3
19	Burundi	95.2
20	Timor-Leste	94.9

Source: Fund for Peace and Carnegie Endowment for International Peace.

them expanding at close to 3 percent a year or 20-fold per century. In 5 of these 17 countries, women have an average of nearly seven children each. Viewed in terms of the demographic transition, these 17 countries are caught in the demographic trap. They have progressed far enough economically to reduce mortality but not far enough to create the economic and social conditions for fertility decline.[52]

In all but 6 of the top 20 failing states, at least 40 percent of the population is under 15. Such a large share of young people often signals future political instability. Young men, lacking employment opportunities, often become disaffected, making them ready recruits for insurgency movements.[53]

Not surprisingly, there is also often a link between the degree of state failure and the destruction of environmental support systems. In a number of countries on the list—including Sudan, Somalia, and Haiti—deforestation, grassland deterioration, and soil erosion are widespread. The countries with fast-growing populations are also facing a steady shrinkage of both cropland and water per person. After a point, as rapid population growth, deteriorating environmental support systems, and poverty reinforce each other, the resulting instability makes it difficult to attract investment from abroad. Even public assistance programs from donor countries are often phased out as the security breakdown threatens the lives of aid workers, forcing their withdrawal.

State failure is not neatly contained by national boundaries. It often spreads to neighboring countries, much as the genocide in Rwanda spilled over into the Democratic Republic of the Congo, eventually drawing several other countries into the war that claimed some 3.9 million lives in the Congo over several years. More recently, the killings in Darfur have spread into Chad.[54]

As the number of failing states grows, dealing with various international crises becomes more difficult. Actions that may be relatively simple in a healthy world order of functioning nation states, such as controlling the spread of infectious diseases, could become difficult or impossible in a world with many disintegrating states. Even maintaining international flows of raw materials could become a challenge. At some point, spreading political instability could disrupt global economic progress,

suggesting that we need to address the causes of state failure
with a heightened sense of urgency.

A Civilizational Tipping Point

In recent years there has been a growing concern over thresholds
or tipping points in nature. For example, scientists worry about
when the shrinking population of an endangered species will
fall to a point from which it cannot recover. Marine biologists
are concerned about the point where overfishing will trigger the
collapse of a fishery.

We know there were social tipping points in earlier civilizations, points at which they were overwhelmed by the forces
threatening them. For instance, at some point the irrigation-
related salt buildup in their soil overwhelmed the capacity of the
Sumerians to deal with it. With the Mayans, there came a time
when the effects of cutting too many trees and the associated
loss of topsoil were simply more than they could manage.[55]

The social tipping points that lead to decline and collapse
when societies are overwhelmed by a single threat or by simultaneous multiple threats are not always easily anticipated. As a
general matter, more economically advanced countries can deal
with new threats more effectively than developing countries
can. For example, while governments of industrial countries
have been able to hold HIV infection rates among adults under
1 percent, many developing-country governments have failed to
do so and are now struggling with much higher infection rates.
This is most evident in some southern African countries, where
up to 20 percent or more of adults are infected.[56]

A similar situation exists with population growth. While
populations in nearly all industrial countries except the United
States have stopped growing, rapid growth continues in nearly
all the countries of Africa, the Middle East, and the Indian subcontinent. Nearly all of the 70 million people being added to
world population each year are born in countries where natural
support systems are already deteriorating in the face of excessive population pressure, in the countries least able to support
them. In these countries, the risk of state failure is growing.[57]

Some issues seem to exceed even the management skills of
the more advanced countries, however. When countries first
detected falling underground water tables, it was logical to

expect that governments in affected countries would quickly raise water use efficiency and stabilize population in order to stabilize aquifers. Unfortunately, not one country—industrial or developing—has done so. Two failing states where over-pumping and security-threatening water shortages loom large are Pakistan and Yemen.

Although the need to cut carbon emissions has been evident for some time, not one country—industrial or developing—has succeeded in becoming carbon-neutral. Thus far this has proved too difficult politically for even the most technologically advanced societies. Could rising carbon dioxide levels in the atmosphere prove to be as unmanageable for our early twenty-first century civilization as rising salt levels in the soil were for the Sumerians in 4000 BC?

Another potentially severe stress on governments is the coming decline in oil production. Although world oil production has exceeded new oil discoveries by a wide margin for more than 20 years, only Sweden and Iceland actually have anything that remotely resembles a plan to effectively cope with a shrinking supply of oil.[58]

This is not an exhaustive inventory of unresolved problems, but it does give a sense of how their number is growing as we fail to solve existing problems even as new ones are being added to the list. The risk is that these accumulating problems and their consequences will overwhelm more and more governments, leading to widespread state failure and eventually the failure of civilization.

Analytically, the challenge is to assess the effects of mounting stresses on the global system. These stresses are perhaps most evident in their effect on food security, which was the weak point of many earlier civilizations that collapsed. Several converging trends are making it difficult for the world's farmers to keep up with the growth in food demand. Prominent among these are falling water tables, the growing conversion of cropland to nonfarm uses, and more extreme climate events, including crop-withering heat waves, droughts, and floods. As a result, world grain production has fallen short of consumption in seven of the last eight years, dropping world grain stocks to their lowest level in 34 years. Corn prices nearly doubled and wheat prices nearly tripled between late 2005 and late 2007.[59]

Just when it seemed that things could not get much worse, the United States, the world's breadbasket, is planning to double the share of its grain harvest going to fuel ethanol—from 16 percent of the 2006 crop to 30 percent or so of the 2008 crop. With this enormous growth in the U.S. capacity to convert grain into fuel, the world price of grain is moving up toward its oil-equivalent value. This ill-conceived U.S. effort to reduce its oil insecurity has helped drive world grain prices to all-time highs, creating unprecedented world food insecurity. Under this stress, still more states may fail.[60]

State failure can come quickly—and often unexpectedly. In looking back at earlier civilizations, it was often a single environmental trend that led to their demise. But countries today are facing several simultaneously, some of which reinforce each other. The earlier civilizations such as the Sumerians and Mayans were often local, rising and falling in isolation from the rest of the world. In contrast, we will either mobilize together to save our global civilization, or we will all be potential victims of its disintegration.

Plan B—A Plan of Hope

Plan B is shaped by what is needed to save civilization, not by what may currently be considered politically feasible. Plan B does not fit within a particular discipline, sector, or set of assumptions.

Implementing Plan B means undertaking several actions simultaneously, including eradicating poverty, stabilizing population, and restoring the earth's natural systems. It also involves cutting carbon dioxide emissions 80 percent by 2020, largely through a mobilization to raise energy efficiency and harness renewable sources of energy.

Not only is the scale of this save-our-civilization plan ambitious, so is the speed with which it must be implemented. We must move at wartime speed, restructuring the world energy economy at a pace reminiscent of the restructuring of the U.S. industrial economy in 1942 following the Japanese attack on Pearl Harbor. The shift from producing cars to planes, tanks, and guns was accomplished within a matter of months. One of the keys to this extraordinarily rapid restructuring was a ban on the sale of cars, a ban that lasted nearly three years.[61]

We face an extraordinary challenge, but there is much to be upbeat about. All the problems we face can be dealt with using existing technologies. And almost everything we need to do to move the world economy back onto an environmentally sustainable path has already been done in one or more countries.

We see the components of Plan B—the alternative to business as usual—in new technologies already on the market. On the energy front, for example, an advanced-design wind turbine can produce as much energy as an oil well. Japanese engineers have designed a vacuum-sealed refrigerator that uses only one eighth as much electricity as those marketed a decade ago. Gas-electric hybrid automobiles, getting nearly 50 miles per gallon, are twice as efficient as the average car on the road.[62]

Numerous countries are providing models of the various components of Plan B. Denmark, for example, today gets 20 percent of its electricity from wind and has plans to push this to 50 percent. Some 60 million Europeans now get their residential electricity from wind farms. By the end of 2007, some 40 million Chinese homes will be getting their hot water from rooftop solar water heaters. Iceland now heats close to 90 percent of its homes with geothermal energy. In so doing, it has virtually eliminated the use of coal for home heating.[63]

With food, India—using a small-scale dairy production model that relies almost entirely on crop residues as a feed source—has more than quadrupled its milk production since 1970, overtaking the United States as the world's leading milk producer. The value of India's dairy production now exceeds that of its rice harvest.[64]

Fish farming advances in China, centered on the use of an ecologically sophisticated carp polyculture, have made this the first country where fish farm output exceeds the oceanic catch. Indeed, the 32 million tons of farmed fish produced in China in 2005 was equal to roughly a third of the world's oceanic fish catch.[65]

We see what a Plan B world could look like in the reforested mountains of South Korea. Once a barren, almost treeless country, the 65 percent of South Korea now covered by forests has checked flooding and soil erosion, returning environmental health and stability to the Korean countryside.[66]

The United States—which over the last two decades retired

one tenth of its cropland, most of it highly erodible, and shifted to conservation tillage practices—has reduced soil erosion by 40 percent. At the same time, the nation's farmers expanded the grain harvest by more than one fifth.[67]

Some of the most innovative leadership has come from cities. Curitiba, Brazil, a city of 1 million people, began restructuring its transport system in 1974. Since then its population has tripled, but its car traffic has declined by 30 percent. Amsterdam has developed a diverse urban transport system, where nearly 40 percent of all trips within the city are taken by bicycle. Paris has a transport diversification plan that also includes a prominent role for the bicycle and is intended to reduce car traffic by 40 percent. London is relying on a tax on cars entering the city center to attain a similar goal.[68]

Not only are new technologies becoming available, but some of these technologies can be combined to create entirely new outcomes. Gas-electric hybrid cars with an enhanced battery and a plug-in capacity, combined with investment in wind farms feeding cheap electricity into the grid, permit most daily driving to be done with electricity, and at a cost equivalent of less than $1-a-gallon gasoline. In much of the world, domestic wind energy can be substituted for imported oil.[69]

The challenge is to build a new economy and to do it at wartime speed before we miss so many of nature's deadlines that the economic system begins to unravel. This introductory chapter is followed by five chapters outlining the principal environmental, demographic, and economic challenges facing civilization. Then there are seven chapters that outline Plan B, the roadmap of where the world needs to go and how to get there.

Our civilization is in trouble because of trends we ourselves have set in motion. The good news is that momentum is building in efforts to reverse damaging environmental trends. Just to cite one example, in early 2007 Australia announced that it would ban incandescent light bulbs by 2010, replacing them with highly efficient compact fluorescents that use only one fourth as much electricity. Canada quickly followed with a similar initiative. Europe, the United States, and China are expected to do the same soon. The world may be approaching a tipping point on a political initiative that can drop world electricity use by nearly 12 percent, enabling us to close 705 coal-fired power plants. This "ban the bulb" movement could become the first major win in the battle to stabilize climate.[70]

Participating in the construction of this enduring new economy is exhilarating. So is the quality of life it will bring. We will be able to breathe clean air. Our cities will be less congested, less noisy, less polluted, and more civilized. A world where population has stabilized, forests are expanding, and carbon emissions are falling is within our grasp.

I

A Civilization in Trouble

2

Deteriorating Oil and Food Security

The twentieth century was the oil century. In 1900, the world produced 150 million barrels of oil. In 2000, it produced 28 billion barrels, an increase of more than 180-fold. This was the century in which oil overtook coal to become the world's leading source of energy.[1]

The fast-growing supply of cheap oil led to an explosive worldwide growth in food production, population, urbanization, and human mobility. In 1900, only 13 percent of us lived in cities. Today half of us do. The world grain harvest quadrupled during the last century. Human mobility exploded as trains, cars, and planes began moving people at a pace and over distances scarcely imaginable when the century began.[2]

Today, we are an oil-based civilization, one that is totally dependent on a resource whose production will soon be falling. Since 1981, the quantity of oil extracted has exceeded new discoveries by an ever-widening margin. In 2006, the world pumped 31 billion barrels of oil but discovered fewer than 9 billion barrels of new oil. World reserves of conventional oil are in a free fall, dropping every year.[3]

Discoveries of conventional oil total roughly 2 trillion barrels, of which 1 trillion have been extracted so far, with another trillion barrels to go. By themselves, however, these numbers miss a central point. As Michael Klare notes, the first trillion barrels was easy oil, "oil that's found on shore or near to shore; oil close to the surface and concentrated in large reservoirs; oil produced in friendly, safe, and welcoming places." The other half, Klare notes, is tough oil, "oil that's buried far offshore or deep underground; oil scattered in small, hard-to-find reservoirs; oil that must be obtained from unfriendly, politically dangerous, or hazardous places."[4]

At some point in the not-so-distant future, world oil production will peak and turn downward. When it does so, it will be a seismic event. The only world we have known is one where oil production is rising. In this new world, where oil production is no longer expanding, one country can get more oil only if another gets less.

We are witnessing a fundamental shift in the relationship between oil and food, one that has been in the making for several decades. From 1950 to 1972, a bushel of wheat could be traded for a barrel of oil on the world market. The price of each during that period was remarkably stable, averaging just under $2 per bushel of wheat and per barrel of oil. Since then, oil prices have climbed. In late 2007, even with the recent run-up in wheat prices, it took eight bushels of wheat to buy one barrel of oil.[5]

Agricultural analysts have long been concerned about the effect of the coming rise in oil prices on food production costs, but now the price gap is so wide that the United States is starting to convert grain into fuel for cars. When the price of oil rises above $60 a barrel, it becomes highly profitable to do this. An estimated 16 percent of the U.S. grain harvest was converted into automotive fuel in 2006. For the 2008 harvest, the figure could be close to 30 percent.[6]

The line between the food and energy economies is becoming blurred as the two begin to merge. As a result, the world price of grain is now moving up toward its oil price equivalent. If the food value of a commodity is less than its fuel value, the market will move it into the energy economy.

The Coming Decline of Oil

When the price of oil climbed above $50 a barrel in late 2004, public attention began to focus on the adequacy of world oil supplies—and specifically on when production would peak and begin to decline. There was no consensus on this issue, but several prominent analysts now believe that the oil peak is imminent.[7]

Various approaches are used to analyze the oil prospect. Oil companies, oil consulting firms, and national governments rely heavily on computer models to project future oil production and prices. As with any such model, the results vary widely, depending on the quality of data and the assumptions fed into them.

Another approach uses the reserves/production relationship to gain a sense of future production trends. This was pioneered in 1956 by the legendary M. King Hubbert, a geologist with Shell Oil and later with the U.S. Geological Survey. Given the nature of oil production, Hubbert theorized that the time lag between the peaking of new discoveries and production was predictable. Noting that the discovery of new reserves in the United States had peaked around 1930, he predicted that U.S. oil production would peak in 1970. He hit it right on the head. As a result of this example and other more recent country experiences, his basic model is now used by many oil analysts.[8]

A third approach separates the world's principal oil-producing countries into three groups: those where production is falling, those where production is still rising, and those that appear to be on the verge of a downturn. Of the leading oil producers, output appears to have peaked in a dozen or so and to still be clearly rising in nine.[9]

Among the post-peak countries are the United States, which peaked at 9.6 million barrels a day in 1970, dropping to 5.1 million barrels a day in 2006, a decline of 47 percent; Venezuela, where production also peaked in 1970; and the two North Sea oil producers, the United Kingdom and Norway, where production peaked in 1999 and 2000, respectively.[10]

The pre-peak countries are dominated by Russia, now the world's biggest oil producer, having eclipsed Saudi Arabia in 2006. Other countries with substantial potential for increasing production are Canada, largely because of its tar sands, and

Kazakhstan, which is developing the large Kashagan oil field in the Caspian Sea. The other pre-peak countries are Algeria, Angola, Brazil, Nigeria, Qatar, and the United Arab Emirates. Libya, which is now producing 1.7 million barrels a day, plans to double its output to over 3 million barrels a day, close to the 3.3 million it produced in 1970.[11]

The next group are countries that appear to be nearing a period of production decline, including Saudi Arabia, Mexico, and China. The biggest question mark among the major oil producers is Saudi Arabia. Saudi officials claim that the country can produce far more oil. But the Ghawar oil field that has supplied half of Saudi oil output is 50 years old and is believed by many analysts to be in its declining years. With the crown jewel of world oil fields and other older Saudi fields largely depleted, it remains to be seen whether pumping from new fields will be sufficient to more than offset the loss from the old ones. Somewhat ominously, Saudi oil production data for the first eight months of 2007 show output of 8.37 million barrels per day, a 6-percent drop from the 8.93 million barrels per day of 2006. If Saudi Arabia does not move much above its current level, which I suspect may be the case, then peak oil is on our doorstep.[12]

In Mexico, the second-ranking supplier of oil to the United States after Canada, production apparently peaked in 2004 at 3.4 million barrels per day. Geologist Walter Youngquist notes that Cantarell, the country's dominant oil field, is now in steep decline, and this could make Mexico an oil importer by 2015. China, producing slightly more than Mexico, may also be approaching its peak year. The question is, will production actually increase enough in the pre-peak countries to offset the declines under way in the post-peak countries?[13]

Another clue to the oil production prospect is the actions of the major oil companies themselves. Although oil prices have risen well above $50 a barrel, there have not been any dramatic increases in exploration and development. This suggests that the companies agree with the petroleum geologists who say that 95 percent of all the oil in the world has already been discovered. "The whole world has now been seismically searched and picked over," says independent geologist Colin Campbell. "Geological knowledge has improved enormously in the past 30 years and it is almost inconceivable now that major fields remain to be found." The bottom line is that the oil reserves of major companies are shrinking yearly.[14]

Sadad al-Husseini, former head of exploration and production at Aramco, the Saudi national oil company, pointed out in an interview that new oil output coming online had to be sufficient to cover both estimated annual growth in world demand of 2 million barrels a day and the annual decline in production from older fields of over 4 million barrels a day. "That's like a whole new Saudi Arabia every couple of years," Husseini said. "It's not sustainable."[15]

The geological evidence suggests that world oil production will be peaking sooner rather than later. Matt Simmons, a prominent oil investment banker, says in reference to new oil fields: "We've run out of good projects. This is not a money issue...if these oil companies had fantastic projects, they'd be out there [developing new fields]." Kenneth Deffeyes, a highly respected geologist and former oil industry employee now at Princeton University, said in his 2005 book, *Beyond Oil*, "It is my opinion that the peak will occur in late 2005 or in the first few months of 2006." Walter Youngquist and A.M. Samsam Bakhtiari of the Iranian National Oil Company both projected that oil would peak in 2007.[16]

It is quite possible that Deffeyes, Youngquist, and Bakhtiari are close to the mark. The International Energy Agency (IEA) reports that world oil production in 2005 of 84.39 million barrels per day rose to 85.01 million barrels per day in 2006. For the first nine months in 2007 output averaged 84.75 million barrels per day, slightly less than in 2006. Whether output in the last three months of the year will rise enough to take the annual output above the 2006 level remains to be seen as of this writing. Whether it does or not, there is a clear loss of momentum in production growth that, in the face of rising oil demand, will almost certainly translate into higher oil prices in the near term.[17]

Yet another way of assessing the oil prospect is simply to look at the age of the major oil fields. Of the top 20 fields ever discovered in terms of oil reserves, 18 were discovered between 1917 (Bolivar in Venezuela) and 1968 (Shaybah in Saudi Arabia). The 2 more recent discoveries, Cantarell in Mexico and East Baghdad Field in Iraq, were discovered during the 1970s, but

none have come since then. Even Kashagan, the only large find
in recent decades, misses making the all-time top 20. With so
many of the largest oil fields aging and in decline, offsetting this
with new discoveries or stepped-up production at existing fields
using more advanced extraction technologies will become
increasingly difficult.[18]

If 2006 does turn out to be the historical peak in world oil
production, and if the output trend follows a bell-shaped curve,
one where the shape of the curve on the ascending and descend-
ing sides is more or less symmetrical (as with the classic Hubbert's Peak curve), then we can use the recent historical trend to
estimate the likely future trend. In recent decades, politics and
prices influenced oil production levels, but we may now be moving into an era of aging oil fields where geology will largely
determine   production   trends

Based on this, to project oil production from the peak year
2006 to 2020 we simply go back 14 years, to 1992. Output that
year averaged 67 million barrels per day. It then climbed to 85
million barrels per day in 2006, an increase of 18 million barrels
per day. If the production decline is symmetrical, then output
per day in 2020 would again be 67 million barrels, a drop of 21
percent. Assuming a 1.1 percent annual rate of world population growth from 2006 to 2020, for a total growth of 16 percent,
oil supply per person would drop by a staggering 32 percent in
just 14 years. In stark contrast to this projection of 67 million
barrels per day in 2020, based on the Hubbert's Peak curve, the
IEA is projecting world oil output in 2020 at 106 million barrels
per day.[19]

If production did peak in 2006 and if future production does
follow the Hubbert curve, what are the options? One is to look
for oil in even more remote places. Some of the estimated 5 percent of conventional oil not yet discovered may be in the Arctic.
With the prospect of an ice-free Arctic Ocean within a few
decades, countries bordering the Arctic are beginning to think
about oil exploration within the region. Looking for oil in the
polar region will raise scores of geopolitical issues, including
who controls what parts of the Arctic and what environmental
regulations should cover the development of any oil discovered
there.

Aside from conventional petroleum, which can easily be

pumped to the surface, vast amounts of oil are stored in tar sands and can be produced from oil shale. The Athabasca tar sand deposits in Alberta, Canada, may total 1.8 trillion barrels. Only about 300 billion barrels of this may be recoverable, however. Venezuela also has a large deposit of extra heavy oil, estimated at 1.2 trillion barrels. Perhaps a third of it can be readily recovered.[20]

Oil shale concentrated in Colorado, Wyoming, and Utah in the United States holds large quantities of kerogen, an organic material that can be converted into oil and gas. In the late 1970s the United States launched a major effort to develop the oil shale on the western slope of the Rocky Mountains in Colorado. When oil prices dropped in 1982, the oil shale industry collapsed. Exxon quickly pulled out of its $5-billion Colorado project, and the remaining companies soon followed suit. Since extracting oil from shale requires several barrels of water for each barrel of oil produced, water scarcity may limit its revival.[21]

The one project that is moving ahead is the tar sands project in Canada's Alberta Province. Launched in the early 1980s, it is now producing 1.4 million barrels of oil a day, enough to meet nearly 7 percent of current U.S. oil needs. This tar sand oil is not cheap, however, and it wreaks environmental havoc on a vast scale.[22]

Producing oil from tar sands is highly carbon-intensive. Heating and extracting the oil from the sands relies on the extensive use of natural gas, production of which has already peaked in North America. As peak oil analyst Richard Heinberg notes, "Currently, two tons of sand must be mined in order to yield one barrel of oil." The net energy yield is low. Walter Youngquist notes, "It takes the equivalent of two out of each three barrels of oil recovered to pay for all the energy and other costs involved in getting the oil from the oil sands."[23]

Thus although these reserves of oil in tar sands and shale may be vast, gearing up for production is a costly, climate-disrupting, time-consuming process. At best, the development of tar sands and oil shale is likely only to slow the coming decline in world oil production.[24]

One of the influences on oil production in the years immediately ahead that is most difficult to measure is the emergence of what I call a "depletion psychology." Once oil companies or oil-exporting countries realize that output is about to peak, they will begin to think seriously about how to stretch out their remaining reserves. As it becomes clear that even a moderate cut in production can double world oil prices, the long-term value of their oil will become much clearer.

The Oil Intensity of Food

Modern agriculture depends heavily on the use of fossil fuels. Most tractors use gasoline or diesel fuel. Irrigation pumps use diesel fuel, natural gas, or coal-fired electricity. Fertilizer production is also energy-intensive. Natural gas is used to synthesize the basic ammonia building block in nitrogen fertilizers. The mining, manufacture, and international transport of phosphates and potash all depend on oil.[25]

Efficiency gains can help reduce agriculture's dependence on oil. In the United States, the combined direct use of gasoline and diesel fuel in farming fell from its historical high of 7.7 billion gallons (29.1 billion liters) in 1973 to 4.2 billion in 2005—a decline of 45 percent. Broadly calculated, the gallons of fuel used per ton of grain produced dropped from 33 in 1973 to 12 in 2005, an impressive decrease of 64 percent.[26]

One reason for this achievement was a shift to minimum- and no-till cultural practices on roughly two fifths of U.S. cropland. But while U.S. agricultural fuel use has been declining, in many developing countries it is rising as the shift from draft animals to tractors continues. A generation ago, for example, cropland in China was tilled largely by draft animals. Today much of the plowing is done with tractors.[27]

Fertilizer accounts for 20 percent of U.S. farm energy use. Worldwide, the figure may be slightly higher. As the world urbanizes, the demand for fertilizer climbs. As people migrate from rural areas to cities, it becomes more difficult to recycle the nutrients in human waste back into the soil, requiring the use of more fertilizer. Beyond this, the growing international food trade can separate producer and consumer by thousands of miles, further disrupting the nutrient cycle. The United States, for example, exports some 80 million tons of grain per year—grain that contains large quantities of basic plant nutrients: nitrogen, phosphorus, and potassium. The ongoing export of these nutrients would slowly drain the inherent fertility from U.S. cropland if the nutrients were not replaced.[28]

Irrigation, another major energy claimant, is requiring more energy worldwide as water tables fall. In the United States, close to 19 percent of farm energy use is for pumping water. And in some states in India where water tables are falling, over half of all electricity is used to pump water from wells. Some trends, such as the shift to no-tillage, are making agriculture less oil-intensive, but rising fertilizer use, the spread of farm mechanization, and falling water tables are having the opposite effect.[29]

Although attention commonly focuses on energy use on the farm, agriculture accounts for only one fifth of the energy used in the U.S. food system. Transport, processing, packaging, marketing, and kitchen preparation of food are responsible for the rest. The U.S. food economy uses as much energy as the entire economy of the United Kingdom.[30]

The 14 percent of energy used in the food system to move goods from farmer to consumer is equal to two thirds of the energy used to produce the food. And an estimated 16 percent of food system energy use is devoted to canning, freezing, and drying food—everything from frozen orange juice concentrate to canned peas.[31]

Food staples such as wheat have traditionally moved over long distances by ship, traveling from the United States to Europe, for example. What is new is the shipment of fresh fruits and vegetables over vast distances by air. Few economic activities are more energy-intensive.[32]

Food miles—the distance that food travels from producer to consumer—have risen with cheap oil. At my local supermarket in downtown Washington, D.C., the fresh grapes in winter typically come by plane from Chile, traveling almost 5,000 miles. One of the most routine long-distance movements of fresh produce is from California to the heavily populated U.S. East Coast. Most of this produce moves by refrigerated trucks. In assessing the future of long-distance produce transport, one writer observed that the days of the 3,000-mile Caesar salad may be numbered.[33]

Packaging is also surprisingly energy-intensive, accounting for 7 percent of food system energy use. It is not uncommon for the energy invested in packaging to exceed that in the food it contains.[34]

The U.S. farmer gets about 20 percent of the consumer food dollar. And for some products, the figure is much lower. As one analyst has observed, "An empty cereal box delivered to the grocery store would cost about the same as a full one."[35]

The most energy-intensive segment of the food chain is the kitchen. Much more energy is used to refrigerate and prepare food in the home than is used to produce it in the first place. The big energy user in the food system is the kitchen refrigerator, not the farm tractor. While oil dominates the production end of the food system, electricity dominates the consumption end. With higher energy prices, the modern food system that evolved when oil was cheap will not survive as it is now structured.[36]

The Changing Food Prospect

The world grain harvest has more than tripled since 1950, climbing from 630 million to 2 billion tons. The most rapid growth came between 1950 and 1973, when the grain harvest doubled. In 23 years, farmers expanded the grain harvest by as much as during the 11,000 preceding years, from the beginning of agriculture until 1950.[37]

The mid-twentieth century marked an abrupt transition point in world agriculture as the frontiers of agricultural settlement largely disappeared. Prior to then, increases in the harvest came largely from expanding the cropped area, as farmers moved from valley to valley and eventually from continent to continent. Yield increases were typically so slow as to be imperceptible within a human life span. In contrast, since 1950 four fifths of the world grain harvest growth has come from raising land productivity, with much of the rise dependent on oil.[38]

Between 1950 and 1990, the systematic application of science to agriculture helped raise grain yields from less than 1.1 tons per hectare to close to 2.5 tons. Grainland productivity worldwide increased 2.1 percent a year. Since 1990, however, the rise has slowed to 1.2 percent a year. By 1990, most of the easy steps to raise grain yields had already been taken.[39]

The growth in land productivity since 1950 was driven by three trends: a near-tripling of the world irrigated area, a 10-fold growth in world fertilizer use, and the rapid dissemination of high-yielding varieties that centered on hybrid corn in the United States and the high-yielding dwarf wheats and rices in Asia.[40]

While world grain production has expanded continuously, it has slowed in recent decades, falling below the growth in world population after 1984. As a result, grain production per person peaked in 1984 at 342 kilograms, dropping to 302 kilograms in 2006. A 12-percent drop in the grain harvested per person could be expected to lead to a dramatic increase in world hunger, but it did not. The number of hungry people in the world, which was greatly reduced from 1950 to 1984, continued to decline until the late 1990s before turning upward.[41]

The fall in grain production per person did not automatically translate into more hunger because of the enormous growth in the world soybean harvest—from 68 million tons in 1984 to 222 million tons in 2007. The growing use of soybean meal, the high-protein meal left after the oil is extracted, as a supplement to grain in livestock, poultry, and fish rations both substituted for some of the grain used for feed and greatly increased the efficiency with which the grain itself was converted into animal protein. Feed rations containing roughly four fifths grain and one fifth soybean meal are now standard fare in livestock, poultry, and fish feeding. This allowed the global diet to improve even as the grain supply per person was declining.[42]

Originally domesticated by farmers in central China some 5,000 years ago, the soybean now occupies a dominant position in world agriculture. The growth in soybean production has been meteoric. In both Brazil and Argentina, soybean production took off after 1980. By 2005 the soybean harvest in each country was rivaling or exceeding the grain harvest. By 1990, more U.S. land was planted to soybeans than to wheat.[43]

In the end, however, the world food prospect depends heavily on the expansion of the "big three" grains—wheat, rice, and corn. In seven of the last eight years, world grain production has fallen short of consumption, dropping world carryover stocks of grain to their lowest level in 34 years. The world's farmers—already struggling to expand fast enough to feed 70 million more people each year and to allow billions of low-income consumers to move up the food chain—are now being further challenged by the exploding demand for grain to produce fuel ethanol for cars.[44]

Farmers are facing new constraints as they attempt to meet record growth in the demand for grain. While the irrigated area was growing throughout the last half-century, supplies of irrigation water in this new century are beginning to shrink in some countries as wells go dry and scarce water is diverted to cities. And for the first time, harvests in large countries like China are being reduced by water shortages. This is most evident with wheat, produced mainly in the more arid northern half of China, where water tables are falling and wells are going dry. China's wheat harvest peaked in 1997 at 123 million tons and has now dropped to scarcely 100 million tons, a fall of nearly 20 percent.[45]

The wildcard in the food prospect is climate change. Crop ecologists estimate that for each 1-degree-Celsius rise in temperature above the norm during the growing season, we can expect a 10-percent decline in grain yields. With higher global temperatures, we can expect more extreme weather events, including more-destructive floods and more-intense droughts.[46]

Putting further pressure on farmers is the conversion of cropland to nonfarm uses. This is gaining momentum in many parts of the world, particularly in countries with urban sprawl, such as the United States, and in densely populated, rapidly industrializing countries like China. From the central valley of California to the Yangtze River basin in China, construction of homes, factories, roads, highways, and parking lots is devouring some of the world's most productive farmland.

Cars and People Compete for Crops

For most of the 25 years after 1978, when the crop-based fuel ethanol program was launched in the United States, investment in distilleries was modest, trickling along well below the radar screen. Then oil prices jumped above $60 a barrel in 2005, pushing U.S. gasoline prices to over $3 a gallon. Suddenly investments in corn-based distilleries became hugely profitable, unleashing an investment frenzy. Investment in U.S. ethanol distilleries, once dependent on the ethanol subsidy of 51¢ per gallon, was now driven primarily by surging oil prices. By mid-2007 the capacity of plants under construction slightly exceeded that of all plants built since the crop-based fuel ethanol program began. Stated otherwise, when these plants are completed, the grain used in ethanol production will double.[47]

The United States eclipsed Brazil as the world's leading ethanol producer in 2005. While Brazil uses sugarcane as the feedstock, U.S. distillers use grain—mostly corn. The estimated 81 million tons of the 2007 U.S. corn harvest used to produce 8.3 billion gallons of ethanol represents one fifth of the country's entire grain harvest, but it will supply less than 4 percent of its automotive fuel.[48]

Brazil, the world's largest sugar producer and exporter, is now converting half of its sugarcane harvest into fuel ethanol. With 10 percent of the world's sugar harvest going into ethanol, the price of sugar is rising. Cheap sugar may now be history.[49]

In Europe, the emphasis is on producing biodiesel. In 2006, the European Union (EU) produced 1.2 billion gallons of biodiesel from vegetable oil, mostly in Germany and France, and 417 million gallons of ethanol, most of it distilled from grain in France, Spain, and Germany. To meet its goal of obtaining 10 percent of its automotive fuel from plant-based sources, the EU is increasingly turning to palm oil imported from Indonesia and Malaysia, a trend that is leading to the clearing of rainforests for oil palm plantations. The Netherlands, concerned about the impact this could have, is reconsidering its import of palm oil for biodiesel production.[50]

In Asia, China converted some 4 million tons of grain—mostly corn—into ethanol in 2006. In India, as in Brazil, ethanol is produced largely from sugarcane. Malaysia and Indonesia are investing heavily in oil palm plantations and new biodiesel refineries.[51]

Production of corn, now the world's dominant feed grain as well as the leading ethanol feedstock, overtook wheat roughly a decade ago. In 2006, the world corn harvest exceeded 700 million tons, wheat was just under 600 million tons, and rice was 420 million tons. The "big three" account for 85 percent of the 2-billion-ton world grain harvest.[52]

The U.S. corn production is huge, accounting for 40 percent of the global harvest and two thirds of world corn exports. The corn harvest of Iowa, the leading corn-producing state, exceeds the entire grain harvest of Canada.[53]

Iowa is also the epicenter of ethanol distillery construction. Robert Wisner, Iowa State University economist, reports that the state's demand for corn from processing plants that were operating, under construction, or being planned as of late 2006 totaled 2.7 billion bushels. Yet even in a good year the state harvests only 2.2 billion bushels. As distilleries compete for grain also used to feed livestock and poultry, Iowa could become a corn-deficit state—with no corn to export to the rest of the world.[54]

What happens to the U.S. corn crop is obviously of concern to the entire world. Leading importers like Japan, Egypt, and Mexico will be particularly affected by any reduction in U.S. corn exports.

As the share of the U.S. grain harvest going to ethanol distilleries escalates, it is driving up food prices worldwide. In September 2007, the price of corn was nearly double that of two years earlier. Wheat prices had more than doubled, reaching historic highs. Soybean prices were up by more than half.[55]

The countries initially hit by rising food prices were those where corn is a staple food. In Mexico, one of more than 20 countries with a corn-based diet, the price of tortillas in early 2007 was up by 60 percent. Angry Mexicans in crowds of up to 75,000 took to the streets in protest, forcing the government to institute price controls on tortillas. In the summer of 2007, Italian consumers organized pasta boycotts to protest soaring prices. Meanwhile, the British were worrying about rising bread prices.[56]

From an agricultural vantage point, the world's appetite for crop-based fuels is insatiable. The grain required to fill an SUV's 25-gallon tank with ethanol just once will feed one person for a whole year. If the entire U.S. grain harvest were to be converted to ethanol, it would satisfy at most 18 percent of U.S. automotive fuel needs.[57]

Historically the food and energy economies were separate. But with so many ethanol distilleries now being built to convert grain into fuel, the two are merging. In this new situation the world price of grain is moving up toward its oil-equivalent value. If the fuel value of grain exceeds its food value, the market will simply move the commodity into the energy economy. If the price of oil jumps to $100 a barrel, the price of grain will follow it upward. If oil goes to $120, grain will follow. The price of grain is now keyed to the price of oil.

The emerging competition between the owners of the

world's 860 million automobiles and the 2 billion poorest people is uncharted territory for humanity. Suddenly the world is facing a moral and political issue that has no precedent: Should we use grain to fuel cars or to feed people? The average income of the world's automobile owners is roughly $30,000 a year; the 2 billion poorest people earn on average less than $3,000 a year. The market says, Let's fuel the cars.[58]

The risk is that rising grain prices will lead to chaos in world grain markets and to food riots in low- and middle-income countries that import grain. One likely consequence is more failing states as governments that are unable to provide food security lose legitimacy. The resulting political instability could disrupt global economic progress. At that point, it would not be merely the price of food but the Nikkei Index and the Dow Jones Industrials that would be affected by the massive diversion of grain to the production of automotive fuel.

Although there are no alternatives to food for people, there are alternatives to using food-based fuels. For example, the 4 percent of U.S. automotive fuel currently supplied from ethanol could be achieved several times over—and at a fraction of the cost—simply by raising auto fuel-efficiency standards by 20 percent.[59]

Another way to reduce the fuel needed for cars is to shift to highly efficient gas-electric hybrid plug-in cars. (See Chapter 12.) This would allow motorists to do short-distance driving, such as the daily commute, with electricity. If wind rich countries such as the United States, China, and those in Europe invest heavily in wind farms to feed cheap electricity into the grid, cars could run primarily on wind energy—and at the gasoline equivalent of less than $1 a gallon.[60]

While it makes little sense to use food crops to fuel cars if it drives up food prices, there is the option of producing automotive fuel from fast-growing trees, switchgrass, prairie grass mixtures, or other cellulosic materials, which can be grown on wasteland. The technologies to convert these cellulosic materials into ethanol exist, but the cost of producing cellulosic ethanol is still more than double that of grain-based ethanol. More research is needed.[61]

Another option that is fast gaining attention is the use of wasteland to produce jatropha. This four-foot woody shrub bears inedible golf ball–sized fruit with seeds containing oil that can be turned into biodiesel. In addition to being a drought-resistant, low-maintenance shrub with a 50-year lifespan, jatropha requires little fertilizer or water.[62]

The Indian State Railway has planted 7.5 million jatropha plants along rail lines in that country and uses the oil in its diesel-powered locomotives. The government has identified 11 million hectares of wasteland that can be used for this shrub. One of the early enthusiasts, O. P. Singh, a horticulturalist for India's Ministry of Railways, says that one day "every house will have jatropha."[63]

Jatropha diesel can be produced for $43 per barrel, a price comparable to that of sugarcane-based ethanol but well below that of other biofuels. Companies that process vegetable oils are offering farmers in India long-term, fixed-price contracts for their harvest of jatropha seeds. A U.K. biodiesel company, D1 Oils, has already planted 150,000 hectares of jatropha in Swaziland, Zambia, and South Africa. A Dutch firm, BioKing, is developing plantings in Senegal. China is also considering large-scale production of jatropha.[64]

The World Beyond Peak Oil

Few countries are planning for a reduction in oil use. Indeed, the projections by both the International Energy Agency and the U.S. Department of Energy expect world oil consumption to go from roughly 85 million barrels or so a day at present to close to 120 million barrels a day by 2030. How did they come up with these rosy forecasts? Apparently they focused primarily on demand and then simply assumed that the needed supply would be forthcoming. To use the words of Thomas Wheeler, editor of the *Alternative Press Review*, many analysts and leaders are simply "oblivious to the flashing red light on the earth's fuel gauge."[65]

Even though peak oil may be imminent, most countries are counting on much higher oil consumption in the decades ahead. Indeed, they are building automobile assembly plants, roads, highways, parking lots, and suburban housing developments as though cheap oil will last forever. Thousands of large jet airliners are being delivered with the expectation that air travel and freight will expand indefinitely. Yet in a world of falling oil production, no country can use more oil unless another uses less.[66]

Darrin Qualman, Director of Research for the National Farmer's Union of Canada says, "The problem isn't simply Peak Oil.... The problem is the combination of Peak Oil and an economic system in which ... 'no one is in control.' Ours is a system where it is no one's job to look past next year's profits, to take stock of how this year's production might affect next decade's weather, ...where we become ever more dependent on energy despite the fact that no one is keeping an eye on the fuel gauge."[67]

Some segments of the global economy will be affected more than others simply because some are more oil-intensive. Among these are the automobile, food, and airline industries. Stresses within the U.S. auto industry are already evident. General Motors and Ford, both trapped in a heavy reliance on sales of gas-hogging sport utility vehicles, have seen investment analysts reduce their corporate bonds to junk bond status.[68]

Modern cities are another product of the oil age. From the first cities, which took shape in Mesopotamia some 6,000 years ago, until 1900, urbanization was, with a few exceptions, a slow, barely perceptible process. When the last century began, there were only a few cities with a million people. Today there are more than 400 such cities, and 20 mega-cities have 10 million or more residents.[69]

The metabolism of cities depends on concentrating vast amounts of food, water, and materials and then dispersing the resulting garbage and human waste. This takes vast amounts of energy. With the limited range and capacity of horse-drawn wagons, it was difficult to create large cities. Trucks running on cheap oil changed all that.

As cities grow ever larger and as nearby landfills reach capacity, garbage must be hauled longer distances to disposal sites. With oil prices rising and available landfills receding ever further from the city, garbage disposal becomes increasingly oil-dependent. At some point, many throwaway products may be priced out of existence.

Cities will be affected by the coming decline in oil production, but it is the suburbs that will take the big hit. People living in poorly designed suburbs, in the sprawl of housing developments, are often isolated geographically from their jobs and shops, forced to use a car even to get a loaf of bread.

Suburbs have created a commuter culture, with the daily roundtrip commute taking, on average, close to an hour a day in the United States. Although Europe's cities were largely mature before the onslaught of the automobile, those in the United States, a much younger country, were shaped by the car. While city limits are rather clearly defined in Europe, and while Europeans only reluctantly convert productive farmland into housing developments, Americans have few qualms about this because of a residual frontier mentality and because cropland was long seen as a surplus commodity.[70]

This unsightly, aesthetically incongruous sprawl of suburbs and strip malls is not limited to the United States. It is found in Latin America, in Southeast Asia, and increasingly in China. Flying from Shanghai to Beijing provides a good view of the sprawl of buildings, including homes and factories, that is following new roads and highways. This is in sharp contrast to the tightly built villages that shaped residential land use for millennia in China.

Shopping malls and huge discount stores, symbolized in the public mind by Wal-Mart, were all subsidized by artificially cheap oil. Isolated by high oil prices, sprawling suburbs may prove to be ecologically and economically unsustainable. Thomas Wheeler observes, "There will eventually be a great scramble to get out of the suburbs as the world oil crisis deepens and the property values of suburban homes plummet."[71]

The food sector will be affected in two ways. Food will become more costly as higher oil prices drive up production and transport costs. As oil costs rise, diets will be altered as people move down the food chain and as they consume more local, seasonally produced food. Diets will thus become more closely attuned to local products and more seasonal in nature.

Air transport, both passenger travel and freight, will suffer as jet fuel prices climb, simply because fuel is the biggest airline operating expense. Although industry projections show air passenger travel growing by some 5 percent a year for the next decade, this seems highly unlikely. Cheap airfares may soon become history.[72]

Air freight may be hit even harder, perhaps leading at some point to an absolute decline. One of the early casualties of rising fuel costs could be the use of jumbo jets to transport fresh produce from the southern hemisphere to industrial countries during the northern winter. The price of fresh produce out of season may simply become prohibitive.

During the century of cheap oil, a vast automobile infrastructure was built in industrial countries, and its maintenance now requires large amounts of energy. The United States, for example, has 2.6 million miles of paved roads, covered mostly with asphalt, and 1.4 million miles of unpaved roads to maintain even if world oil production is falling.[73]

National political leaders seem reluctant to face the coming downturn in oil and to plan for it even though it will become one of the great fault lines in world economic history. Trends now taken for granted, such as rapid urbanization and globalization, could be slowed almost overnight as oil becomes scarce and costly. Economic historians writing about this period may routinely distinguish between before peak oil (BPO) and after peak oil (APO).

Developing countries will be hit doubly hard as still-expanding populations collide with a shrinking oil supply to steadily reduce oil use per person. Without a rapid restructuring of the energy economy, such a decline could quickly translate into a fall in living standards, with those of the poorest falling below survival levels. If the United States, which burns more gasoline than the next 20 countries combined, can sharply reduce its use of oil, this could buy the world time for a smoother transition to the post-petroleum era.[74]

The peaking of world oil production raises questions more difficult than any since civilization began. Will world population growth survive a continuing decline in world oil production? How will a shrinking oil supply be allocated among countries? By the market? By negotiated international agreements? By war? Can civilization itself survive the stresses associated with falling oil production at a time when food prices are rising and the stresses from climate change are mounting? And the list goes on.

Food Insecurity and Failing States

During the concluding half of the last century, the world was making steady progress in reducing hunger, but during the transition into the new century, the tide began to turn. In February

2007, James Morris, head of the U.N. World Food Programme (WFP), announced that 18,000 children are now dying each day from hunger and related causes. For perspective, this loss of young lives in one day is almost five times U.S. combat deaths in Iraq through four years of fighting. Although these huge numbers of dying children may be an abstraction, each represents a young life ended far too soon.[75]

There are many ways of measuring hunger. The U.N. Food and Agriculture Organization (FAO) calculates the number of hungry people based on food intake. FAO data say the long-term trend in reducing hunger is encouraging, but not the recent trend. The number of people in developing countries who are hungry and malnourished, which declined from 960 million in 1970 to 800 million in 1996, has turned upward, reaching 830 million in 2003.[76]

Projections by Ford Runge and Benjamin Senauer of the University of Minnesota four years ago showed the number of hungry and malnourished people decreasing to 625 million by 2025. But an update of these projections in early 2007 that took into account the effect of the massive diversion of grain to ethanol distilleries on world food prices shows the number of hungry people climbing instead of decreasing—to 1.2 billion by 2025.[77]

One of the manifestations of a sharp rise in grain prices is a correspondingly sharp drop in food assistance. Since the budgets of food aid agencies are set a year or more ahead, a rise in food prices shrinks food assistance. For example, the United States, by far the largest food aid donor, saw the price of a ton of food aid in 2007 climb to $611, up from $363 per ton in 2004. In the absence of supplemental appropriations, food aid will drop by 40 percent. Key recipients, like Ethiopia, Afghanistan, and the Sudan, will be hit hard.[78]

Working together, the FAO and WFP each year release an assessment of crop and food conditions that lists the countries in dire need of food assistance. In May 2007, a total of 33 countries with a combined population of 763 million were on this list. Of these, 17 were in need of external food assistance because of recent civil strife and conflict. Many of these countries are on the top 20 list of failing states, including Afghanistan, Burundi, Côte d'Ivoire, the Democratic Republic of the Congo, Guinea, Pakistan, Somalia, Sudan, and Zimbabwe. The bottom line is that political insecurity and food insecurity often go hand-in-hand.[79]

The countries on WFP's food emergency lists are mostly societies trapped between lowered mortality and continuing high-levels of fertility. In this situation, which leads to state failure if permitted to continue indefinitely, agricultural development is often interrupted by a decline in personal security that makes it difficult to maintain technical support for farmers and to sustain timely flows of seed and fertilizer.

With failing states and declining personal security, it is difficult even to operate food relief programs. WFP head James Morris, discussing the food relief operation in early 2007 in Sudan's Darfur region, where violence and insecurity are rampant, says, "Our convoys are attacked almost daily. We had a driver killed there at the end of last year. Our convoys coming through Chad from Libya are always at risk." In failed and failing states, food relief, however sorely needed, is not always assured. And sometimes even though people are starving, it is simply not possible to reach them with food.[80]

There are many threats to future food security, including falling water tables and rising temperatures, but the most immediate threat may be the diversion of an ever-larger share of the U.S. grain harvest into the production of fuel for cars. Only the U.S. government can intervene to restrict this diversion and avoid life-threatening rises in world grain prices.

3

Rising Temperatures and Rising Seas

Civilization has evolved during a period of remarkable climate stability, but this era is drawing to a close. We are entering a new era, a period of rapid and often unpredictable climate change. The new climate norm is change.

In the spring of 2007, while giving a lecture at Kyoto University, I noted that there had been a remarkable shift during the decade since the Kyoto Protocol was negotiated. In 1997, climate change was discussed in the future tense. Today we discuss it in the present tense. It is no longer something that may happen. It is happening now.

Today not only do we know that the earth is getting warmer, but we can begin to see some of the effects of higher temperatures. Mountain glaciers are melting almost everywhere. Himalayan glaciers that feed the rivers that irrigate the rice fields of China and the wheat fields of India are fast disappearing.[1]

The attention of climate scientists is turning to the melting ice sheets of Greenland and West Antarctica. If we cannot cut carbon emissions quickly enough to save these, then sea level will rise 12 meters (39 feet). Many of the world's coastal cities will be under water; over 600 million coastal dwellers will be forced to move.[2]

The destructive effects of higher temperatures are visible on many fronts. Crop-withering heat waves have lowered grain harvests in key food-producing regions in recent years. In 2002, record-high temperatures and drought reduced grain harvests in India, the United States, and Canada, dropping the world harvest 90 million tons, or 5 percent below consumption. The record-setting 2003 European heat wave contributed to a world harvest that again fell short of consumption by 90 million tons. Intense heat and drought in the U.S. Corn Belt in 2005 contributed to a world grain shortfall of 34 million tons.[3]

Such intense heat waves also take a direct human toll. In 2003, the searing heat wave that broke temperature records across Europe claimed more than 52,000 lives in nine countries. Italy alone lost more than 18,000 people, while 14,800 died in France. More than 18 times as many people died in Europe in this heat wave as died during the terrorist attacks on the World Trade Center on September 11, 2001.[4]

The insurance industry is painfully aware of the relationship between higher temperatures and storm intensity. As weather-related damage claims have soared, the last few years have brought a drop in earnings and a flurry of lowered credit ratings for insurance companies as well as the reinsurance companies that insure them.[5]

Companies using historical records as a basis for calculating insurance rates for future storm damage are realizing that the past is no longer a reliable guide to the future. This is a problem not only for the insurance industry but for all of us. We are altering the earth's climate, setting in motion trends we do not always understand with consequences we cannot anticipate.

Rising Temperature and Its Effects

Scientists at the Goddard Institute for Space Studies of the National Aeronautics and Space Administration (NASA) gather data from a global network of some 800 climate-monitoring stations to measure changes in the earth's average temperature. Their direct measurements go back to 1880.[6]

Since 1970, the earth's average temperature has risen by 0.6 degrees Celsius, or 1 degree Fahrenheit. Meteorologists note

50   PLAN B 3.0

that the 23 warmest years on record have come since 1980. And the seven warmest years since recordkeeping began in 1880 have come in the last nine years. Four of these—2002, 2003, 2005, and 2006—were years in which major food-producing regions saw their crops wither in the face of record temperatures.[7]

The amount of carbon dioxide (CO_2) in the atmosphere has risen substantially since the start of the Industrial Revolution, growing from 277 parts per million (ppm) to 384 ppm in 2007. The annual rise in the atmospheric CO_2 level, one of the world's most predictable environmental trends, is the result of the annual discharge into the atmosphere of 7.5 billion tons of carbon from burning fossil fuels and 1.5 billion tons from deforestation. The current annual rise is nearly four times what it was in the 1950s, largely because of increased emissions from burning fossil fuels. As more CO_2 accumulates in the atmosphere, temperatures go up.[8]

Against this backdrop of record increases, the projections that the earth's average temperature will rise 1.1–6.4 degrees Celsius (2.0–11.5 degrees Fahrenheit) during this century seem all too possible. These projections are the latest from the Intergovernmental Panel on Climate Change (IPCC), the body of more than 2,500 scientists from around the world that in 2007 released a consensus report affirming humanity's role in climate change.[9]

The IPCC-projected rise in temperature is a global average. In reality, the rise will be very uneven. It will be much greater over land than over oceans, in the high northern latitudes than over the equator, and in the continental interiors than in coastal regions.[10]

Higher temperatures diminish crop yields, melt the snow/ice reservoirs in the mountains that feed the earth's rivers, cause more-destructive storms, increase the area affected by drought, and cause more frequent and destructive wildfires.

In a paper presented at the American Meteorological Society's annual meeting in San Diego, California, in January 2005, a team of scientists from the National Center for Atmospheric Research reported a dramatic increase in the land surface affected by drought over the last few decades. The area experiencing very dry conditions expanded from less than 15 percent of the earth's total land area in the 1970s to roughly 30 percent by 2002. The scientists attributed part of the change to a rise in temperature and part to reduced precipitation, with high temperatures becoming progressively more important during the latter part of the period. Lead author Aiguo Dai reported that most of the drying was concentrated in Europe and Asia, Canada, western and southern Africa, and eastern Australia.[11]

Researchers with the U.S. Department of Agriculture's Forest Service, drawing on 85 years of fire and temperature records, reported in August 2004 that even a 1.6-degree-Celsius rise in summer temperature could double the area of wildfires in the 11 western states.[12]

Ecosystems everywhere will be affected by higher temperatures, sometimes in ways we cannot easily predict. The 2007 IPCC report notes that a rise in temperature of 1 degree Celsius will put up to 30 percent of all species at risk of extinction. The Pew Center on Global Climate Change sponsored a meta-study analyzing some 40 scientific reports that link rising temperature with changes in ecosystems. Among the many changes reported are spring arriving nearly two weeks earlier in the United States, tree swallows nesting nine days earlier than they did 40 years ago, and a northward shift of red fox habitat that has it encroaching on the Arctic fox's range. Inuits have been surprised by the appearance of robins, a bird they have never seen before. Indeed, there is no word in Inuit for "robin."[13]

The National Wildlife Federation (NWF) reports that if temperatures continue to rise, by 2040 one out of five of the Pacific Northwest's rivers will be too hot for salmon, steelhead, and trout to survive. Paula Del Giudice, Director of NWF's Northwest Natural Resource Center, notes that "global warming will add an enormous amount of pressure onto what's left of the region's prime cold-water fish habitat."[14]

Douglas Inkley, NWF Senior Science Advisor and senior author of a report to The Wildlife Society, notes, "We face the prospect that the world of wildlife that we now know—and many of the places we have invested decades of work in conserving as refuges and habitats for wildlife—will cease to exist as we know them, unless we change this forecast."[15]

The Crop Yield Effect

Agriculture as it exists today has been shaped by a climate system that has changed little over farming's 11,000-year history. Crops were developed to maximize yields in this long-standing climatic regime. As the temperature rises, agriculture will be increasingly out of sync with its natural environment. Nowhere is this more evident than in the relationship between temperature and crop yields.

Since crops in many countries are grown at or near their thermal optimum, even a relatively minor increase during the growing season of 1 or 2 degrees Celsius can shrink the grain harvest in major food-producing regions, such as the North China Plain, the Gangetic Plain of India, and the U.S. Corn Belt.[16]

Higher temperatures can reduce or even halt photosynthesis, prevent pollination, and lead to crop dehydration. Although the elevated concentrations of atmospheric CO_2 that raise temperature can also raise crop yields, the detrimental effect of higher temperatures on yields overrides the CO_2 fertilization effect for the major crops.

In a study of local ecosystem sustainability, Mohan Wali and his colleagues at Ohio State University noted that as temperature rises, photosynthetic activity in plants increases until the temperature reaches 20 degrees Celsius (68 degrees Fahrenheit). The rate of photosynthesis then plateaus until the temperature hits 35 degrees Celsius (95 degrees Fahrenheit), whereupon it begins to decline, until at 40 degrees Celsius (104 degrees Fahrenheit), photosynthesis ceases entirely.[17]

The most vulnerable part of a plant's life cycle is the pollination period. Of the world's three food staples—rice, wheat, and corn—corn is particularly vulnerable. In order for corn to reproduce, pollen must fall from the tassel to the strands of silk that emerge from the end of each ear of corn. Each of these silk strands is attached to a kernel site on the cob. If the kernel is to develop, a grain of pollen must fall on the silk strand and then journey to the kernel site. When temperatures are uncommonly high, the silk strands quickly dry out and turn brown, unable to play their role in the fertilization process.

The effects of temperature on rice pollination have been studied in detail in the Philippines. Scientists there report that the pollination of rice falls from 100 percent at 34 degrees Celsius to near zero at 40 degrees Celsius, leading to crop failure.[18]

High temperatures can also dehydrate plants. While it may take a team of scientists to understand how temperature affects rice pollination, anyone can tell that a wilted cornfield is suffering from heat stress. When a corn plant curls its leaves to reduce exposure to the sun, photosynthesis is reduced. And when the stomata on the underside of the leaves close to reduce moisture loss, CO_2 intake is reduced, thereby restricting photosynthesis. At elevated temperatures, the corn plant, which under ideal conditions is so extraordinarily productive, goes into thermal shock.

Within the last few years, crop ecologists in several countries have been focusing on the precise relationship between temperature and crop yields. One of the most comprehensive of these studies was conducted at the International Rice Research Institute (IRRI) in the Philippines. A team of eminent crop scientists using crop yield data from experimental field plots of irrigated rice confirmed the rule of thumb emerging among crop ecologists—that a 1-degree Celsius rise in temperature above the norm lowers wheat, rice, and corn yields by 10 percent. The IRRI finding was consistent with those of other recent research projects. The scientists concluded that "temperature increases due to global warming will make it increasingly difficult to feed Earth's growing population."[19]

Two scientists in India, K. S. Kavi Kumar and Jyoti Parikh, assessed the effect of higher temperatures on wheat and rice yields. Basing their model on data from 10 sites, they concluded that in north India a 1-degree Celsius rise in mean temperature did not meaningfully reduce wheat yields, but a 2-degree rise lowered yields at almost all the sites. When they looked at temperature change alone, a 2-degree Celsius rise led to a decline in irrigated wheat yields ranging from 37 percent to 58 percent. When they combined the negative effects of higher temperature with the positive effects of CO_2 fertilization, the decline in yields among the various sites ranged from 8 percent to 38 percent. For a country projected to add 500 million people by midcentury, this is a troubling prospect.[20]

Reservoirs in the Sky

Snow and ice masses in mountains are nature's freshwater reservoirs—nature's way of storing water to feed rivers during the dry season. Now they are being threatened by the rise in temperature. Even a 1-degree rise in temperature in mountainous regions can markedly reduce the share of precipitation falling as snow and boost that coming down as rain. This in turn increases flooding during the rainy season and reduces the snowmelt that flows into rivers.

Beyond this, the glaciers that feed rivers during the dry season are melting. Some have disappeared entirely. Nowhere is the melting of glaciers of more concern than in Asia, where 1.3 billion people depend for their water supply on rivers originating in the Himalayan Mountains and the adjacent Tibet-Qinghai Plateau.[21]

India's Gangotri Glacier, which supplies 70 percent of the water to the Ganges, is not only melting, it is doing so at an accelerated rate. If this melting continues to accelerate, the Gangotri's life expectancy will be measured in decades and the Ganges will become a seasonal river, flowing only during the rainy season. For the 407 million Indians and Bangladeshis who live in the Ganges basin, this could be a life-threatening loss of water.[22]

In China, which is even more dependent than India on river water for irrigation, the situation is particularly challenging. Chinese government data show the glaciers on the Tibet-Qinghai Plateau that feed both the Yellow and Yangtze Rivers are melting at 7 percent a year. The Yellow River, whose basin is home to 147 million people, could experience a large dry-season flow reduction. The Yangtze River, by far the larger of the two, is threatened by the disappearance of glaciers as well. The basin's 369 million people rely heavily on rice from fields irrigated with Yangtze River water.[23]

Yao Tandong, a leading Chinese glaciologist, predicts that two thirds of China's glaciers could be gone by 2060. "The full-scale glacier shrinkage in the plateau region," Yao says, "will eventually lead to an ecological catastrophe."[24]

Other Asian rivers that originate in this rooftop of the world include the Indus, with 178 million people in its basin in India and Pakistan; the Brahmaputra, which flows through Bangladesh; and the Mekong, which waters Cambodia, Laos, Thailand, and Viet Nam.[25]

In Africa, Tanzania's snow-capped Kilimanjaro may soon be snow- and ice-free. Ohio State University glaciologist Lonnie Thompson's studies of Kilimanjaro show that Africa's tallest mountain lost 33 percent of its ice field between 1989 and 2000. He projects that its snowcap could disappear entirely by 2015. Nearby Mount Kenya has lost 7 of its 18 glaciers. Local rivers fed by these glaciers are becoming seasonal rivers, generating conflict among the 2 million people who depend on them for water supplies during the dry season.[26]

Bernard Francou, research director for the French government's Institute of Research and Development, believes that 80 percent of South American glaciers will disappear within the next 15 years. For countries like Bolivia, Ecuador, and Peru, which rely on glaciers for water for household and irrigation use, this is not good news.[27]

Peru, which stretches some 1,600 kilometers along the vast Andean mountain range and which is home to 70 percent of the earth's tropical glaciers, is in trouble. Some 22 percent of its glacial endowment, which feeds the many Peruvian rivers that supply water to the cities in the semi-arid coastal regions, has disappeared. Lonnie Thompson reports that the Quelccaya Glacier in southern Peru, which was retreating by 6 meters per year in the 1960s, is now retreating by 60 meters annually.[28]

Many of Peru's farmers irrigate their wheat and potatoes with the river water from these disappearing glaciers. During the dry season, farmers are totally dependent on irrigation water. For Peru's 28 million people, shrinking glaciers will eventually mean a shrinking food supply.[29]

Lima, a city of 7 million people, gets most of its water from three rivers high in the Andes, rivers that are fed partly by glacial melt. While the glaciers are melting, the river flows are above normal, but once they are gone, the river flows will drop sharply, leaving Lima with severe water shortages.[30]

In many agricultural regions, snow and ice masses are the leading source of irrigation and drinking water. In the southwestern United States, for instance, the Colorado River—the region's primary source of irrigation water—depends on snowfields in the Rockies for much of its flow. California, in addition to depending heavily on the Colorado, also relies on snowmelt from the Sierra Nevada in the eastern part of the state. Both the Sierra Nevada and the coastal range supply irrigation water to California's Central Valley, the world's fruit and vegetable basket.[31]

Preliminary results of an analysis of rising temperature

effects on three major river systems in the western United States—the Columbia, the Sacramento, and the Colorado—indicate that the winter snow pack in the mountains feeding them will be dramatically reduced and that winter rainfall and flooding will increase.[32]

With a business-as-usual energy policy, global climate models project a 70-percent reduction in the amount of snow pack for the western United States by mid-century. A detailed study of the Yakima River Valley, a vast fruit-growing region in Washington state, conducted by the U.S. Department of Energy's Pacific Northwest National Laboratory shows progressively heavier harvest losses as the snow pack shrinks, reducing irrigation water flows.[33]

Agriculture in the Central Asian countries of Afghanistan, Kazakhstan, Kyrgyzstan, Tajikistan, Turkmenistan, and Uzbekistan depends heavily on snowmelt from the Hindu Kush, Pamir, and Tien Shan mountain ranges for irrigation water. Nearby Iran gets much of its water from the snowmelt in the 5,700-meter-high Alborz Mountains between Tehran and the Caspian Sea.[34]

The snow and ice masses in the world's leading mountain ranges and the water they store are taken for granted simply because they have been there since before agriculture began. Now that is changing. If we continue raising the earth's temperature, we risk losing the reservoirs in the sky on which cities and farmers depend.

Melting Ice and Rising Seas

Ice melting in mountainous regions not only affects river flows, it also affects sea level rise. On a larger scale, the melting of the earth's two massive ice sheets—Antarctica and Greenland—could raise sea level enormously. If the Greenland ice sheet were to melt, it would raise sea level 7 meters (23 feet). Melting of the West Antarctic Ice Sheet would raise sea level 5 meters (16 feet). But even just partial melting of these ice sheets will have a dramatic effect on sea level rise. Senior scientists are noting that the IPCC projections of sea level rise during this century of 18 to 59 centimeters are already obsolete and that a rise of 2 meters during this time is within range.[35]

Assessing the prospects for the Greenland ice sheet begins

with looking at the warming of the Arctic region. A 2005 study, *Impacts of a Warming Arctic*, concluded that the Arctic is warming almost twice as fast as the rest of the planet. Conducted by the Arctic Climate Impact Assessment (ACIA) team, an international group of 300 scientists, the study found that in the regions surrounding the Arctic, including Alaska, western Canada, and eastern Russia, winter temperatures have already climbed by 3-4 degrees Celsius (4–7 degrees Fahrenheit) over the last half-century. Robert Corell, chair of ACIA, says this region "is experiencing some of the most rapid and severe climate change on Earth."[36]

In testimony before the U.S. Senate Commerce Committee, Sheila Watt-Cloutier, an Inuit speaking on behalf of the 155,000 Inuits who live in Alaska, Canada, Greenland, and the Russian Federation, described their struggle to survive in the fast-changing Arctic climate as "a snapshot of what is happening to the planet." She called the warming of the Arctic "a defining event in the history of this planet." And she went on to say "the Earth is literally melting."[37]

The ACIA report described how the retreat of the sea ice has devastating consequences for polar bears, whose very survival may be at stake. A subsequent report indicated that polar bears, struggling to survive, are turning to cannibalism. Also threatened are ice-dwelling seals, a basic food source for the Inuit.[38]

Since this 2005 report, there is new evidence that the problem is worse than previously thought. A team of scientists from the National Snow and Ice Data Center and the National Center for Atmospheric Research, which has compiled data on Arctic Ocean summer ice melting from 1953 to 2006, concluded that the ice is melting much faster than climate models had predicted. They found that from 1979 to 2006 the summer sea ice shrinkage accelerated to 9.1 percent a decade. In 2007, Arctic sea ice shrank some 20 percent below the previous record set in 2005. This suggests that the sea could be ice-free well before 2050, the earliest date projected by the IPCC in its 2007 report. Arctic scientist Julienne Stroeve observed that the shrinking Arctic sea ice may have reached "a tipping point that could trigger a cascade of climate change reaching into Earth's temperate regions."[39]

Reinforcing this concern is a recent study by Joséfino

Comiso, a senior scientist at NASA's Goddard Space Flight Center. Comiso reported for the first time that even the winter ice cover in the Arctic Ocean shrank by 6 percent in 2005 and again in 2006. This new development, combined with the news that the sea ice cover is thinning, provides further evidence that the ice is not recovering after its melt season, meaning that summer ice in the Arctic Ocean could disappear much sooner than earlier thought possible.[40]

Walt Meier, a researcher at the U.S. National Snow and Ice Data Center who tracks the changes in Arctic sea ice, views the winter shrinkage with alarm. He believes there is "a good chance" that the Arctic tipping point has been reached. "People have tried to think of ways we could get back to where we were. We keep going further and further in the hole, and it's getting harder and harder to get out of it." Some scientists now think that the Arctic Ocean could be ice-free in the summer as early as 2030.[41]

Scientists are concerned that "positive feedback loops" may be starting to kick in. This term refers to a situation where a trend already under way begins to reinforce itself. Two of these potential feedback mechanisms are of particular concern to scientists. The first, in the Arctic, is the albedo effect. When incoming sunlight strikes the ice in the Arctic Ocean, up to 70 percent of it is reflected back into space. Only 30 percent is absorbed as heat. As the Arctic sea ice melts, however, and the incoming sunlight hits the much darker open water, only 6 percent is reflected back into space and 94 percent is converted into heat. This may account for the accelerating shrinkage of the Arctic sea ice and the rising regional temperature that directly affects the Greenland ice sheet.[42]

If all the ice in the Arctic Ocean melts, it will not affect sea level because the ice is already in the water. But it will lead to a much warmer Arctic region as more of the incoming sunlight is absorbed as heat. This is of particular concern because Greenland lies largely within the Arctic Circle. As the Arctic region warms, the island's ice sheet—up to 1.6 kilometers (1 mile) thick in places—is beginning to melt.[43]

The second positive feedback mechanism also has to do with ice melting. What scientists once thought was a fairly simple linear process—that is, a certain amount at the surface of an ice sheet melts each year, depending on the temperature—is now seen to be much more complicated. As the surface ice begins to melt, some of the water filters down through cracks in the glacier, lubricating the surface between the glacier and the rock beneath it. This accelerates the glacial flow and the calving of icebergs into the surrounding ocean. The relatively warm water flowing through the glacier also carries surface heat deep inside the ice sheet far faster than it would otherwise penetrate by simple conduction.[44]

Several recent studies report that the melting of the Greenland ice sheet is accelerating. A study published in *Science* in September 2006 reported that the rate of ice melt on the vast island has tripled over the last several years. That same month a University of Colorado team published a study in *Nature* indicating that between April 2004 and April 2006 Greenland lost ice at a rate 2.5 times that of the preceding two years. In October 2006, a team of NASA scientists reported that the flow of glaciers into the sea was accelerating. Eric Rignot, a glaciologist at NASA's Jet Propulsion Laboratory, said, "None of this has been predicted by numerical models, and therefore all projections of the contribution of Greenland to sea level [rise] are way below reality."[45]

At the other end of the earth, the 2-kilometer-thick Antarctic ice sheet, which covers a continent about twice the size of Australia and contains 70 percent of the world's fresh water, is also beginning to melt. Ice shelves that extend from the continent into the surrounding seas are starting to break up at an alarming pace.[46]

In May 2007, a team of scientists from NASA and the University of Colorado reported satellite data showing widespread snow-melt on the interior of the Antarctic ice sheet over an area the size of California. This melting in 2005 was 900 kilometers inland, only about 500 kilometers from the South Pole. Konrad Steffen, one of the scientists involved, observed, "Antarctica has shown little to no warming in the recent past with the exception of the Antarctic Peninsula, but now large regions are showing the first signs of the impacts of warming."[47]

The ice shelves surrounding Antarctica are formed by the flow of glaciers off the continent into the surrounding sea. This flow of ice, fed by the continuous formation of new ice on land

and culminating in the breakup of the shelves on the outer
fringe and the calving of icebergs, is not new. What is new is the
pace of this process. When Larsen A, a huge ice shelf on the east
coast of the Antarctic Peninsula, broke up in 1995, it was a sig-
nal that all was not well in the region. Then in 2000, a huge iceberg nearly the size of Connecticut—11,000 square kilometers,
or 4,250 square miles—broke off the Ross Ice Shelf.[48]

After Larsen A broke up, it was only a matter of time, given
the rise in temperature in the region, before neighboring Larsen
B would do the same. So when the northern part of the Larsen
B ice shelf collapsed into the sea in March 2002, it was not a
total surprise. At about the same time, a huge chunk of ice
broke off the Thwaites Glacier. Covering 5,500 square kilometers, this iceberg was the size of Rhode Island.[49]

Even veteran ice watchers are amazed at how quickly the disintegration is occurring. "The speed of it is staggering," said Dr.
David Vaughan, a glaciologist at the British Antarctic Survey,
which has been monitoring the Larsen Ice Shelf closely. Along
the Antarctic Peninsula, in the vicinity of the Larsen Ice Shelf,
the average temperature has risen 2.5 degrees Celsius over the
last five decades.[50]

When ice shelves already largely in the water break off from
the continental ice mass, this does not have much direct effect
on sea level per se. But without the ice shelves to impede the
flow of glacial ice, typically moving 400–900 meters a year, the
flow of ice from the continent could accelerate, leading to a
thinning of the ice sheet on the edges of the Antarctic continent.
If this were to happen, sea level would rise accordingly.[51]

The International Institute for Environment and Development (IIED) has analyzed the effect of a 10-meter rise in sea
level, providing a sense of what the melting of the world's
largest ice sheets could mean. The IIED study begins by pointing out that 634 million people live along coasts at or below 10
meters above sea level, in what they call the Low Elevation
Coastal Zone. This massive vulnerable group includes one
eighth of the world's urban population.[52]

One of the countries most vulnerable is China, with 144 million potential climate refugees. India and Bangladesh are next,
with 63 and 62 million respectively. Viet Nam has 43 million vulnerable people, and Indonesia, 42 million. Others in the top 10

include Japan with 30 million, Egypt with 26 million, and the United States with 23 million.[53]

The world has never seen such a massive potential displacement of people. Some of the refugees could simply retreat to higher ground within their own country. Others—facing extreme crowding in the interior regions of their homeland—would seek refuge elsewhere. Bangladesh, already one of the world's most densely populated countries, would face a far greater concentration: in effect, 62 million of its people would be forced to move in with the 97 million living on higher ground. Would a more sparsely populated country like the United States be willing to accommodate an influx of rising-sea refugees while it was attempting to relocate 23 million of its own citizens?[54]

Not only would some of the world's largest cities, such as Shanghai, Kolkata, London, and New York, be partly or entirely inundated, but vast areas of productive farmland would also be lost. The rice-growing river deltas and floodplains of Asia would be covered with salt water, depriving Asia of part of its food supply. This loss of prime farmland would parallel the loss of river water as Himalayan glaciers disappear.[55]

In the end, the question is whether governments are strong enough to withstand the political and economic stress of relocating large numbers of people while suffering losses of housing and industrial facilities. The relocation is not only an internal matter, as a large share of the displaced people will want to move to other countries. Can governments withstand these stresses, or will more and more states fail?

More-Destructive Storms

Rising seas are not the only threat that comes with elevated global temperatures. Higher surface water temperatures in the tropical oceans mean more energy radiating into the atmosphere to drive tropical storm systems, leading to more-destructive storms. The combination of rising seas, more powerful storms, and stronger storm surges can be devastating.[56]

Just how devastating this combination can be became evident in late August 2005, when Hurricane Katrina came onshore on the U.S. Gulf Coast near New Orleans. In some Gulf Coast towns, Katrina's powerful 28-foot-high storm surge did not leave a single structure standing. New Orleans survived the initial hit but was flooded when the inland levees were breached and water covered everything in large parts of the city except for the rooftops, where thousands of people were stranded. Even in August 2006, a year after the storm had passed, the most damaged areas of the city remained without water, power, sewage disposal, garbage collection, or telecommunications.[57]

With advance warning of the storm and official urging to evacuate coastal areas, 1 million or so evacuees fled northward into Louisiana or to neighboring states of Texas and Arkansas. Of this total, some 290,000 have not yet returned home and will likely never do so. These storm evacuees are the world's first large wave of climate refugees.[58]

Katrina was the most financially destructive hurricane ever to make landfall anywhere. It was one of eight hurricanes that hit the southeastern United States in 2004 and 2005. As a result of the unprecedented damage, insurance premiums have doubled, tripled, and even in some especially vulnerable situations gone up 10-fold. This enormous jump in insurance costs is lowering coastal real estate values and driving people and businesses out of highly exposed states like Florida.[59]

The devastation caused by Katrina was not an isolated incident. In the fall of 1998, Hurricane Mitch—one of the most powerful storms ever to come out of the Atlantic, with winds approaching 200 miles per hour—hit the east coast of Central America. As atmospheric conditions stalled the normal northward progression of the storm, some 2 meters of rain were dumped on parts of Honduras and Nicaragua within a few days. The deluge collapsed homes, factories, and schools, leaving them in ruins. It destroyed roads and bridges. Seventy percent of the crops and much of the topsoil in Honduras were washed away—topsoil that had accumulated over long stretches of geological time. Huge mudslides destroyed villages, burying some local populations.[60]

The storm left 11,000 dead. Thousands more, buried or washed out to sea, were never found. The basic infrastructure—the roads and bridges in Honduras and Nicaragua—was largely destroyed. President Flores of Honduras summed it up this way: "Overall, what was destroyed over several days took us 50 years to build." The damage from this storm, exceeding the annual gross domestic product of the two countries, set their economic development back by 20 years.[61]

In 2004, Japan experienced a record 10 typhoons (hurricanes) that collectively caused $10 billion worth of losses. During the same season, Florida was hit by 4 of the 10 most costly hurricanes in U.S. history. These 4 hurricanes together generated insurance claims of $22 billion.[62]

Against this backdrop, insurance companies and reinsurance companies are finding it difficult to calculate a safe level of premiums, since the historical record traditionally used to calculate insurance fees is no longer a guide to the future. For example, the number of major flood disasters worldwide has grown over the last several decades, increasing from 6 major floods in the 1950s to 26 in the 1990s.[63]

Insurers are convinced that with higher temperatures and more energy driving storm systems, future losses will be even greater. They are concerned about whether the industry can remain solvent under this onslaught of growing damages. So, too, is Moody's Investors Service, which has several times downgraded the creditworthiness of some of the world's leading reinsurance companies over the last six years.[64]

Thomas Loster, a climate expert at Munich Re, a leading reinsurance company, says the overall balance of natural catastrophes is now "dominated by weather-related disasters, many of them exceptional and extreme. We need to stop this dangerous experiment humankind is conducting on the Earth's atmosphere."[65]

Munich Re has published a list of natural disasters with insured losses of $1 billion or more. The first one came in 1983, when Hurricane Alicia struck the United States, racking up $1.5 billion in insured losses. Of the 58 natural catastrophes with $1 billion or more of insured losses recorded through the end of 2006, 3 were earthquakes, including the devastating 2004 earthquake-related Asian tsunami; the other 55 were weather-related—storms, floods, hurricanes, or wildfires. During the 1980s, there were 3 such events; during the 1990s, there were 26; and between 2000 and 2006 alone there were 26.[66]

Prior to Hurricane Katrina, the two largest events in terms of total damage were Hurricane Andrew in 1992, which took down 60,000 homes and racked up $30 billion worth of damage, and the flooding of China's Yangtze River basin in 1998, which also cost an estimated $30 billion, a sum comparable to the value of China's rice harvest. Part of the growing damage toll is due to greater urban and industrial development in coastal areas and river floodplains. But part is due to more-destructive storms.[67]

In the West, the regions most vulnerable to more powerful storms currently are the Atlantic and Gulf Coasts of the United States and the Caribbean countries. In the East, it is East and Southeast Asia, including China, Japan, the Philippines, Taiwan, and Viet Nam, that are likely to bear the brunt of the powerful storms crossing the Pacific. In the Bay of Bengal, Bangladesh and the east coast of India are particularly vulnerable.

Western Europe, traditionally experiencing a heavily damaging winter storm perhaps once in a century, had its first winter storm to exceed $1 billion in 1987—one that caused $3.7 billion of destruction, $3.1 billion of which was covered by insurance. Since then, Western Europe has had nine major winter storms with insured losses ranging from $1.3 billion to $5.9 billion.[68]

As the climate changes, more extreme weather events are expected. Andrew Dlugolecki, a consultant on climate change and its effects on financial institutions, notes that damage from atmospherically related events has increased by roughly 10 percent a year. "If such an increase were to continue indefinitely," he notes, "by 2065 storm damage would exceed the gross world product. The world obviously would face bankruptcy long before then." Few double-digit annual growth trends continue for several decades, but Dlugolecki's basic point is that climate change can be destructive, disruptive, and very costly.[69]

If we allow the climate to spin out of our control, we risk huge financial costs. In a late 2006 report, former World Bank chief economist Nicholas Stern projected that the long-term costs of climate change could exceed 20 percent of gross world product (GWP). By comparison, the near-term costs of cutting greenhouse gas emissions to stabilize climate, which Stern estimates at 1 percent of GWP, would be a bargain.[70]

Cutting Carbon 80 Percent by 2020

In 2004, Stephen Pacala and Robert Socolow at Princeton University published an article in *Science* that showed how annual carbon emissions from fossil fuels could be held at 7 billion tons instead of rising to 14 billion tons over the next 50 years, as would occur with business as usual. The goal of Pacala, an ecologist, and Socolow, an engineer, was to prevent atmospheric CO_2 concentrations, then near 375 ppm, from rising above 500 ppm.[71]

They described 15 ways, all using proven technologies, that by 2054 could each cut carbon emissions by 1 billion tons per year. Any seven of these options could be used together to prevent an increase in carbon emissions through 2054. Pacala and Socolow further theorize that advancing technology would allow for annual carbon emissions to be cut to 2 billion tons by 2104, a level that can be absorbed by natural carbon sinks in land and oceans.[72]

The Pacala/Socolow conceptualization has been extraordinarily useful in helping to think about how to cut carbon emissions. During the three years since the article was written, the urgency of acting quickly and on a much larger scale has become obvious. We also need now to go beyond the conceptual approach that treats all potential methods of reducing carbon emissions equally and concentrate on those that are most promising.

Researchers such as James Hansen, a leading climate scientist at NASA, believe that global warming is accelerating and may be approaching a tipping point, a point at which climate change acquires a momentum that makes it irreversible. They think we may have a decade to turn the situation around before this threshold is crossed. I agree.[73]

We often hear descriptions of what we need to do in the decades ahead or by 2050 to avoid "dangerous climate change," but we are already facing this. Two thirds of the glaciers that feed the Yellow and Yangtze rivers of China will disappear by 2060 if even the current 7 percent annual rate of melting continues. Glaciologists report that the Gangotri glacier, which supplies 70 percent of the ice melt that feeds the Ganges River during the dry season, could disappear entirely in a matter of decades.[74]

What could threaten world food security more than the melting of the glaciers that feed the major rivers of Asia during the dry season, the rivers that irrigate the region's rice and wheat fields? In a region with half the world's people, this potential loss of water during the dry season could lead not just to hunger but to starvation on an unimaginable scale.

Asian food security would take a second hit because its rice-growing river deltas and floodplains would be under water. The World Bank tells us that a sea level rise of only 1 meter would inundate half of the riceland in Bangladesh. While a 1-meter rise in sea level will not happen overnight, what is worrisome is that if ice melting continues at today's rates, at some point such a rise in sea level will no longer be preventable. The melting that would cause this is not just what may happen if the earth's temperature rises further; this is something that is starting to happen right now with the current temperature.[75]

As summer neared an end in 2007, reports from Greenland indicated that the flow of glaciers into the sea had accelerated beyond anything glaciologists had thought possible. Huge chunks of ice weighing several billion tons each were breaking off and sliding into the sea, causing minor earthquakes as they did so.[76]

With melt-water lubricating the surface between the glaciers and the rocks on which they rested, ice flows were accelerating, flowing into the ocean at a pace of 2 meters an hour. This accelerated flow, along with the earthquakes, shows the potential for the entire ice sheet to break up and collapse.[77]

Beyond what is already happening, the world faces a risk that some of the feedback mechanisms will begin to kick in, further accelerating the warming process. Scientists who once thought that the Arctic Ocean could be free of ice during the summer by 2100 now see it occurring by 2030. Even this could turn out to be a conservative estimate.[78]

This is of particular concern to scientists because of the albedo effect, where the replacement of highly reflective sea ice with darker open water greatly increases heat absorbed from sunlight. This, of course, has the potential to further accelerate the melting of the Greenland ice sheet.

A second feedback loop of concern is the melting of permafrost. This would release billions of tons of carbon, some as methane, a potent greenhouse gas with a global warming effect per ton 25 times that of carbon dioxide.[79]

The risk facing humanity is that climate change could spiral out of control and it will no longer be possible to arrest trends such as ice melting and rising sea level. At this point, the future of civilization would be at risk.

This combination of melting glaciers, rising seas, and their effects on food security and low-lying coastal cities could overwhelm the capacity of governments to cope. Today it is largely weak states that begin to deteriorate under the pressures of mounting environmental stresses. But the changes just described could overwhelm even the strongest of states. Civilization itself could begin to unravel under these extreme stresses.

In contrast to Pacala and Socolow's goal of holding carbon emissions constant until 2054, in Plan B we propose an all-out effort to cut net carbon dioxide emissions 80 percent by 2020. Our goal is to prevent the atmospheric CO_2 concentration from exceeding 400 ppm, thus limiting the future rise in temperature.[80]

This is an extraordinarily ambitious undertaking. It means, for example, phasing out all coal-fired power plants by 2020 while greatly reducing the use of oil. This is not a simple matter.

We can, however, make this shift using currently available technologies. The three components of this carbon-cutting effort are halting deforestation while planting trees to sequester carbon (see Chapter 8), raising energy efficiency worldwide (see Chapter 11), and harnessing the earth's renewable sources of energy (see Chapter 12). Plan B calls for using the most energy-efficient technologies available for lighting, for heating and cooling buildings, and for transportation. It calls for an ambitious exploitation of the earth's solar, wind, and geothermal energy sources. It means, for example, a wholesale shift to plug-in hybrid cars, running them largely on wind-generated electricity.

Plan B includes a wholesale restructuring of the world energy economy with a wartime sense of urgency, much as the U.S. restructured its industrial economy in a matter of months at the beginning of World War II. (See Chapter 13.) The stakes in World War II were high, but they are far higher today. What is at issue now is whether we can mobilize fast enough to save our global civilization.

4

Emerging Water Shortages

Africa's Lake Chad, once a landmark for astronauts circling the earth, is now difficult for them to locate. Surrounded by Cameroon, Chad, Niger, and Nigeria—all countries with fast-growing populations—the lake has shrunk 96 percent in 40 years. The region's soaring demand for irrigation water coupled with declining rainfall is draining dry the rivers and streams that feed the lake. As a result, Lake Chad may soon disappear entirely, its whereabouts a mystery to future generations.[1]

The shrinkage of Lake Chad is not unique. The world is incurring a vast water deficit—one that is largely invisible, historically recent, and growing fast. Because the deficit comes largely from aquifer overpumping, it is often discovered only when wells go dry.

This global water deficit is the result of demand tripling over the last half-century. The drilling of millions of irrigation wells has pushed water withdrawals beyond recharge rates, in effect leading to groundwater mining. The failure of governments to limit pumping to the sustainable yield of aquifers means that water tables are now falling in countries that contain more than half the world's people, including the big three grain producers—China, India, and the United States.[2]

Beyond these traditional sources of water insecurity, climate change is now affecting water supplies. Rising temperatures are boosting evaporation rates, altering rainfall patterns, and melting the glaciers that feed rivers during the dry season. As the glaciers melt, they are threatening to convert perennial rivers such as the Ganges in India and the Yellow in China into seasonal rivers, increasing both water and food insecurity. With the earth's climate system and its hydrological cycle so intertwined, any changes in climate will alter the hydrological cycle.[3]

Among the more visible manifestations of water scarcity are rivers running dry and lakes disappearing. A politics of water scarcity is emerging between upstream and downstream claimants both within and among countries. Water scarcity is now crossing borders via the international grain trade. Countries that are pressing against the limits of their water supply typically satisfy the growing need of cities and industry by diverting irrigation water from agriculture and then importing grain to offset the loss of productive capacity.

The link between water and food is strong. We each drink on average nearly 4 liters of water per day in one form or another, while the water required to produce our daily food totals at least 2,000 liters—500 times as much. This helps explain why 70 percent of all water use is for irrigation. Another 20 percent is used by industry, and 10 percent goes for residential purposes. With the demand for water growing in all three categories, competition among sectors is intensifying, with agriculture almost always losing. While most people recognize that the world is facing a future of water shortages, not everyone has connected the dots to see that this also means a future of food shortages.[4]

Water Tables Falling

Scores of countries are overpumping aquifers as they struggle to satisfy their growing water needs. Most aquifers are replenishable, but not all are. When most of the aquifers in India and the shallow aquifer under the North China Plain are depleted, the maximum rate of pumping will be automatically reduced to the rate of recharge.

Fossil aquifers, however, are not replenishable. For these— the vast U.S. Ogallala aquifer, the deep aquifer under the North China Plain, or the Saudi aquifer, for example—depletion brings pumping to an end. Farmers who lose their irrigation water have the option of returning to lower-yield dryland farming if rainfall permits. But in more arid regions, such as in the southwestern United States or the Middle East, the loss of irrigation water means the end of agriculture.

Falling water tables are already adversely affecting harvests in some countries, including China, which rivals the United States as the world's largest grain producer. A groundwater survey released in Beijing in August 2001 revealed that the water table under the North China Plain, an area that produces over half of the country's wheat and a third of its corn, is falling fast. Overpumping has largely depleted the shallow aquifer, forcing well drillers to turn to the region's deep aquifer, which is not replenishable.[5]

The survey reported that under Hebei Province in the heart of the North China Plain, the average level of the deep aquifer was dropping nearly 3 meters (10 feet) per year. Around some cities in the province, it was falling twice as fast. He Qingcheng, head of the groundwater monitoring team, notes that as the deep aquifer is depleted, the region is losing its last water reserve—its only safety cushion.[6]

His concerns are mirrored in a World Bank report: "Anecdotal evidence suggests that deep wells [drilled] around Beijing now have to reach 1,000 meters [more than half a mile] to tap fresh water, adding dramatically to the cost of supply." In unusually strong language for a Bank report, it foresees "catastrophic consequences for future generations" unless water use and supply can quickly be brought back into balance.[7]

The U.S. Embassy in Beijing reports that wheat farmers in some areas are now pumping from a depth of 300 meters, or nearly 1,000 feet. Pumping water from this far down raises pumping costs so high that farmers are often forced to abandon irrigation.[8]

Falling water tables, the conversion of cropland to nonfarm uses, and the loss of farm labor in provinces that are rapidly industrializing are combining to shrink China's grain harvest. The wheat crop, grown mostly in semiarid northern China, is particularly vulnerable to water shortages. After peaking at 123 million tons in 1997, the harvest has fallen, coming in at 105 million tons in 2007, a drop of 15 percent.[9]

The World Bank study indicates that China is mining underground water in three adjacent river basins in the north—those of the Hai, which flows through Beijing and Tianjin; the Yellow; and the Huai, the next river south of the Yellow. Since it takes 1,000 tons of water to produce one ton of grain, the shortfall in the Hai basin of nearly 40 billion tons of water per year (1 ton equals 1 cubic meter) means that when the aquifer is depleted, the grain harvest will drop by 40 million tons—enough to feed 120 million Chinese.[10]

As serious as water shortages are in China, they are even more serious in India, where the margin between food consumption and survival is so precarious. To date, India's 100 million farmers have drilled 21 million wells, investing some $12 billion in wells and pumps. In a survey of India's water situation, Fred Pearce reported in the *New Scientist* that "half of India's traditional hand-dug wells and millions of shallower tube wells have already dried up, bringing a spate of suicides among those who rely on them. Electricity blackouts are reaching epidemic proportions in states where half of the electricity is used to pump water from depths of up to a kilometer."[11]

In Tamil Nadu, a state with more than 62 million people in southern India, wells are going dry almost everywhere. According to Kuppannan Palanisami of Tamil Nadu Agricultural University, falling water tables have dried up 95 percent of the wells owned by small farmers, reducing the irrigated area in the state by half over the last decade. As a result, many farmers have returned to dryland farming.[12]

As water tables fall, well drillers are using modified oil-drilling technology to reach water, going as deep as 1,000 meters in some locations. In communities where underground water sources have dried up entirely, all agriculture is rain-fed and drinking water must be trucked in. Tushaar Shah, who heads the International Water Management Institute's groundwater station in Gujarat, says of India's water situation, "When the balloon bursts, untold anarchy will be the lot of rural India."[13]

India's grain harvest, squeezed both by water scarcity and the loss of cropland to non-farm uses, has plateaued since 2000. This helps explain why India reemerged as a leading wheat importer in 2006. A 2005 World Bank study reports that 15 percent of India's food supply is produced by mining groundwater.

Stated otherwise, 175 million Indians are fed with grain produced with water from irrigation wells that will soon go dry.[14]

As water tables fall, the energy required for pumping rises. In both India and China, the rising electricity demand from irrigation is satisfied largely by building coal-fired power plants.[15]

In the United States, the U.S. Department of Agriculture (USDA) reports that in parts of Texas, Oklahoma, and Kansas—three leading grain-producing states—the underground water table has dropped by more than 30 meters (100 feet). As a result, wells have gone dry on thousands of farms in the southern Great Plains, forcing farmers to return to lower-yielding dryland farming. Although this mining of underground water is taking a toll on U.S. grain production, irrigated land accounts for only one fifth of the U.S. grain harvest, compared with close to three fifths of the harvest in India and four fifths in China.[16]

For the seven states that draw on Colorado River water—Arizona, California, Colorado, Nevada, New Mexico, Utah, and Wyoming—the USDA survey shows an irrigated area decline in each from 1997 to 2002. In the two leading irrigation states, California and Colorado, the area dropped by 2 percent and 24 percent respectively. The 2007 survey will likely show further shrinkage in irrigated area.[17]

Pakistan, a country with 164 million people that is growing by 3 million per year, is also mining its underground water. In the Pakistani part of the fertile Punjab plain, the drop in water tables appears to be similar to that in India. Observation wells near the twin cities of Islamabad and Rawalpindi show a fall in the water table between 1982 and 2000 that ranges from 1 to nearly 2 meters a year.[18]

In the province of Balochistan, which borders Afghanistan, water tables around the capital, Quetta, are falling by 3.5 meters per year. Richard Garstang, a water expert with the World Wildlife Fund and a participant in a study of Pakistan's water situation, said in 2001 that "within 15 years Quetta will run out of water if the current consumption rate continues."[19]

The water shortage in Balochistan is province-wide. Sardar Riaz A. Khan, former director of Pakistan's Arid Zone Research Institute in Quetta, reports that six basins have exhausted their groundwater supplies, leaving their irrigated lands barren.

Khan expects that within 10–15 years virtually all the basins outside the canal-irrigated areas will have depleted their groundwater supplies, depriving the province of much of its grain harvest.[20]

Future irrigation water cutbacks as a result of aquifer depletion will undoubtedly reduce Pakistan's grain harvest. Country-wide, the harvest of wheat—the principal food staple—is continuing to grow, but more slowly than in the past.[21]

Iran, a country of 71 million people, is overpumping its aquifers by an average of 5 billion tons of water per year, the water equivalent of one third of its annual grain harvest. Under the small but agriculturally rich Chenaran Plain in northeastern Iran, the water table was falling by 2.8 meters a year in the late 1990s. New wells being drilled both for irrigation and to supply the nearby city of Mashad are responsible. Villages in eastern Iran are being abandoned as wells go dry, generating a flow of "water refugees."[22]

Saudi Arabia, a country of 25 million people, is as water-poor as it is oil-rich. Relying heavily on subsidies, it developed an extensive irrigated agriculture based largely on its deep fossil aquifer. After several years of supporting wheat prices at five times the world market level, the government was forced to face fiscal reality and cut the subsidies. Its wheat harvest dropped from a high of 4.1 million tons in 1992 to 2.7 million tons in 2007, a drop of 34 percent.[23]

Craig Smith writes in the *New York Times,* "From the air, the circular wheat fields of this arid land's breadbasket look like forest green poker chips strewn across the brown desert. But they are outnumbered by the ghostly silhouettes of fields left to fade back into the sand, places where the kingdom's gamble on agriculture has sucked precious aquifers dry." Some Saudi farmers are now pumping water from wells that are 4,000 feet deep, nearly four fifths of a mile or 1.2 kilometers.[24]

A 1984 Saudi national survey reported fossil water reserves at 462 billion tons. Half of that, Smith reports, has probably disappeared by now. This suggests that irrigated agriculture could last for another decade or so and then will largely vanish.[25]

In neighboring Yemen, a nation of 22 million, the water table under most of the country is falling by roughly 2 meters a year

as water use outstrips the sustainable yield of aquifers. In western Yemen's Sana'a Basin, the estimated annual water extraction of 224 million tons exceeds the annual recharge of 42
million tons by a factor of five, dropping the water table 6
meters per year. World Bank projections indicate the Sana'a
Basin—site of the national capital, Sana'a, and home to 2 million people—may be pumped dry by 2010.[26]

In the search for water, the Yemeni government has drilled
test wells in the basin that are more than a mile deep—depths
normally associated with the oil industry—but they have failed
to find water. Yemen must soon decide whether to bring water
to Sana'a, possibly by pipeline from coastal desalting plants, if
it can afford it, or to relocate the capital. Either alternative will
be costly and potentially traumatic.[27]

With its population growing at 3 percent a year and with
water tables falling everywhere, Yemen is fast becoming a
hydrological basket case. With its grain production falling by
two thirds over the last 20 years, Yemen now imports four fifths
of its grain supply. Living on borrowed water and borrowed
time, Yemen ranks twenty-fourth on *Foreign Policy*'s list of failing states.[28]

Israel, even though it is a pioneer in raising irrigation water
productivity, is depleting both of its principal aquifers—the
coastal aquifer and the mountain aquifer that it shares with
Palestinians. Because of severe water shortages, Israel has
banned the irrigation of wheat. Conflicts between Israelis and
Palestinians over the allocation of water are ongoing.[29]

In Mexico—home to a population of 107 million that is projected to reach 132 million by 2050—the demand for water is
outstripping supply. Mexico City's water problems are well
known. Rural areas are also suffering. In the agricultural state
of Guanajuato, the water table is falling by 2 meters or more a
year. In the northwestern state of Sonora, farmers once pumped
water from the Hermosillo aquifer at a depth of 35 feet. Today
they pump from more than 400 feet. At the national level, 51
percent of all the water extracted from underground is from
aquifers that are being overpumped.[30]

Since the overpumping of aquifers is occurring in many
countries more or less simultaneously, the depletion of aquifers
and the resulting harvest cutbacks could come at roughly the

same time. And the accelerating depletion of aquifers means this day may come soon, creating potentially unmanageable food scarcity.

Rivers Running Dry

While falling water tables are largely hidden, rivers that are drained dry or reduced to a trickle before they reach the sea are highly visible. Two rivers where this phenomenon can be seen are the Colorado, the major river in the southwestern United States, and the Yellow, the largest river in northern China. Other large rivers that either run dry or come close to doing so during the dry season are the Nile, the lifeline of Egypt; the Indus, which supplies most of Pakistan's irrigation water; and the Ganges in India's densely populated Gangetic basin. Many smaller rivers have disappeared entirely.[31]

As the world's demand for water has tripled over the last half-century and as the demand for hydroelectric power has grown even faster, dams and diversions of river water have drained many rivers dry. As water tables have fallen, the springs that feed rivers have gone dry, reducing river flows.[32]

Since 1950, the number of large dams, those over 15 meters high, has increased from 5,000 to 45,000. Each dam deprives a river of some of its flow. Engineers like to say that dams built to generate electricity do not take water from the river, only its energy, but this is not entirely true since reservoirs increase evaporation. The annual loss of water from a reservoir in arid or semiarid regions, where evaporation rates are high, is typically equal to 10 percent of its storage capacity.[33]

The Colorado River now rarely makes it to the sea. With the states of Colorado, Utah, Arizona, Nevada, and California depending heavily on the Colorado's water, there is little, if any, water left when it reaches the Gulf of California. This excessive demand for water is destroying the river's ecosystem, including its fisheries.[34]

A similar situation exists in Central Asia. The Amu Darya—which, along with the Syr Darya, feeds the Aral Sea—is now drained dry by Uzbek and Turkmen cotton farmers upstream. With the flow of the Amu Darya cut off, only the diminished flow of the Syr Darya keeps the Aral Sea from disappearing entirely.[35]

China's Yellow River, which flows some 4,000 kilometers through five provinces before it reaches the Yellow Sea, has been under mounting pressure for several decades. It first ran dry in 1972, and since 1985 it has often failed to reach the sea.[36]

The Nile, site of another ancient civilization, now barely makes it to the sea. Water analyst Sandra Postel notes in *Pillar of Sand* that before the Aswan Dam was built, some 32 billion cubic meters of water reached the Mediterranean each year. After the dam was completed, however, increasing irrigation, evaporation, and other demands reduced its discharge to less than 2 billion cubic meters.[37]

Pakistan, like Egypt, is essentially a river-based civilization, heavily dependent on the Indus. This river, originating in the Himalayas and flowing southwestward to the Indian Ocean, not only provides surface water, it also recharges aquifers that supply the irrigation wells dotting the Pakistani countryside. In the face of growing water demand, it too is starting to run dry in its lower reaches. With a population of 164 million that is projected to reach 292 million by 2050, Pakistan is in political trouble, ranking twelfth on the 2007 list of failing states.[38]

In Southeast Asia, the flow of the Mekong is being reduced by the dams being built on its upper reaches by the Chinese. The downstream countries, including Cambodia, Laos, Thailand, and Viet Nam—countries with 172 million people—complain about the reduced flow of the Mekong, but this has done little to curb China's efforts to exploit the power and the water in the river.[39]

The same problem exists with the Tigris and Euphrates Rivers, which originate in Turkey and flow through Syria and Iraq en route to the Persian Gulf. This river system, the site of Sumer and other early civilizations, is being overused. Large dams erected in Turkey and Iraq have reduced water flow to the once "fertile crescent," helping to destroy 80 percent of the vast wetlands that formerly enriched the delta region.[40]

In each of the river systems just discussed, virtually all the water in the basin is being used. Inevitably, if people upstream get more water, those downstream will get less. Allocating water among competing interests, within and among societies, is part of an emerging politics of resource scarcity.

Lakes Disappearing

As river flows are reduced or even eliminated entirely and as water tables fall from overpumping, lakes are shrinking and in some cases disappearing. As my colleague Janet Larsen notes, the lakes that are disappearing are some of the world's best known—including Lake Chad in Central Africa, the Aral Sea in Central Asia, and the Sea of Galilee (also known as Lake Tiberias).[41]

Reuters reporter Megan Goldin writes that "walking on the Sea of Galilee is a feat a mere mortal can accomplish," as a result of its receding shores. When I first saw the Jordan River as it enters Israel from Syria, its fragility was obvious. Indeed, in many places it would be called a creek. And yet it has the primary responsibility for supplying water to the Sea of Galilee, which it enters at the north end and exits on the south end. It then continues southward some 105 kilometers before emptying into the Dead Sea.[42]

With the Jordan's flow further diminished as it passes through Israel, the Dead Sea is shrinking even faster than the Sea of Galilee. Over the past 40 years, its water level has dropped by some 25 meters (nearly 80 feet). It could disappear entirely by 2050.[43]

Of all the shrinking lakes and inland seas, none has gotten as much attention as the Aral Sea. Its ports, once centers of commerce, are now abandoned, looking like the ghost mining towns of the American West. Once one of the world's largest freshwater bodies, the Aral has lost four fifths of its volume since 1960. Ships that once plied its routes are now stranded in the sand of the old seabed—with no water in sight.[44]

The seeds for the Aral Sea's demise were sown in 1960, when Soviet central planners in Moscow decided the region embracing the Syr Darya and Amu Darya basins would become a vast cotton bowl to supply the country's textile industry.[45]

As cotton planting expanded, so too did the diversion of water from the two rivers that fed the Aral Sea. And as the sea shrank, the salt concentrations climbed until the fish died. The thriving fishery that once yielded 50,000 tons of seafood per year disappeared, as did the jobs on the fishing boats and in the fish processing factories.[46]

With the 65-billion-cubic-meter annual influx of water from

the two rivers now down to 1.5 billion cubic meters a year, the prospect for restoring the sea is not good, though some local successes have been recorded. With the sea's shoreline now up to 250 kilometers (165 miles) from the original port cities, there is a vast area of exposed seabed. Each day the wind lifts thousands of tons of sand and salt from the dry seabed, distributing the airborne particles on the surrounding grasslands and croplands, reducing their fertility.[47]

At a 1990 Soviet Academy of Sciences conference on the future of the Aral Sea, there was an aerial tour for foreign guests. Flying in what seemed to be a World War II-vintage single-engine biplane a few hundred feet above the dry, salt-covered seabed, I noted that it looked like the surface of the moon. There was no vegetation, no sign of life, only total desolation.

The disappearance of lakes is perhaps most pronounced in China. In western China's Qinhai province, through which the Yellow River's main stream flows, there were once 4,077 lakes. Over the last 20 years, more than 2,000 have disappeared. The situation is far worse in Hebei Province, which surrounds Beijing. With water tables falling throughout this region, Hebei has lost 969 of its 1,052 lakes.[48]

Population is also outgrowing the water supply in Mexico. Lake Chapala, the country's largest, is the primary source of water for Guadalajara, which is home to 4 million people. Expanding irrigation in the region has reduced water volume in the lake by 80 percent.[49]

Lakes are disappearing on every continent and for the same reasons: excessive diversion of water from rivers and overpumping of aquifers. No one knows exactly how many lakes have disappeared over the last half-century, but we do know that thousands of them now exist only on old maps.

Farmers Losing to Cities

Water tensions among countries are more likely to make the headlines, but it is the jousting for water between cities and farms within countries that preoccupies local political leaders. The economics of water use do not favor farmers in this competition, simply because it takes so much water to produce food. For example, while it takes only 14 tons of water to make a ton of steel worth $560, it takes 1,000 tons of water to grow a ton of wheat worth $200. In countries preoccupied with expanding the economy and creating jobs, agriculture becomes the residual claimant.[50]

Many of the world's largest cities are located in watersheds where all available water is being used. Cities in such watersheds, such as Mexico City, Cairo, and Beijing, can increase their water consumption only by importing water from other basins or taking it from agriculture. Increasingly the world's cities are meeting their growing needs by taking irrigation water from farmers. Among the U.S. cities doing so are San Diego, Los Angeles, Las Vegas, Denver, and El Paso.[51]

The competition between farmers and cities for underground water resources is intensifying throughout India. Nowhere is this more evident than in Chennai (formerly Madras), a city of 7 million on the east coast of south India. As a result of the city government's inability to supply water for some of the city's residents, a thriving tank-truck industry has emerged that buys water from farmers and hauls it to the city's thirsty residents.[52]

For farmers surrounding the city, the price of water far exceeds the value of the crops they can produce with it. Unfortunately, the 13,000 tankers hauling the water to Chennai are mining the underground water resources. Water tables are falling and shallow wells have gone dry. Eventually even the deeper wells will go dry, depriving these communities of both their food supply and their livelihood.[53]

Chinese farmers along the Juma River downstream from Beijing discovered in 2004 that the river had suddenly stopped flowing. A diversion dam had been built near the capital to take river water for Yanshan Petrochemical, a state-owned industry. Although the farmers protested bitterly, it was a losing battle. For the 120,000 villagers downstream from the diversion dam, the loss of water could cripple their ability to make a living from farming.[54]

Literally hundreds of cities in other countries are meeting their growing water needs by taking the water that farmers count on. In western Turkey, for example, the historic city of Izmir now relies heavily on well fields (a network of wells connected by pipe) from the neighboring agricultural district of Manisa.[55]

In the U.S. southern Great Plains and Southwest, where

virtually all water is now spoken for, the growing water needs of cities and thousands of small towns can be satisfied only by taking water from agriculture. A monthly publication from California, *The Water Strategist*, devotes several pages to a listing of water sales that took place in the western United States during the preceding month. Scarcely a working day goes by without another sale. A University of Arizona study of over 2,000 of these water transfers from 1987 to 2005 reported that at least 8 out of 10 were by individual farmers or irrigation districts to cities and municipalities.[56]

Colorado has one of the world's most active water markets. Fast-growing cities and towns in a state with high immigration are buying irrigation water rights from farmers and ranchers. In the upper Arkansas River basin, which occupies the southeastern quarter of the state, Colorado Springs and Aurora (a suburb of Denver) have already bought water rights to one third of the basin's farmland. Aurora has purchased rights to water that was once used to irrigate 9,600 hectares (23,000 acres) of cropland in the Arkansas valley.[57]

Far larger purchases are being made by cities in California. In 2003, San Diego bought annual rights to 247 million tons (200,000 acre-feet) of water from farmers in the nearby Imperial Valley—the largest farm-to-city water transfer in U.S. history. This agreement covers the next 75 years. In 2004, the Metropolitan Water District, which supplies water to 18 million southern Californians in several cities, negotiated the purchase of 137 million tons of water per year from farmers for the next 35 years. Without irrigation water, the highly productive land owned by these farmers is wasteland. The farmers who are selling their water rights would like to continue farming, but city officials are offering far more for the water than the farmers could possibly earn by irrigating crops.[58]

Whether it is outright government expropriation, farmers being outbid by cities, or cities simply drilling deeper wells than farmers can afford, the world's farmers are losing the water war. They are faced with not only a shrinking water supply in many situations but also a shrinking share of that shrinking supply. Slowly but surely, fast-growing cities are siphoning water from the world's farmers even as they try to feed some 70 million more people each year.[59]

Scarcity Crossing National Borders

Historically, water scarcity was a local issue. It was up to national governments to balance water supply and demand. Now this is changing as scarcity crosses national boundaries via the international grain trade. Since it takes 1,000 tons of water to produce one ton of grain, as noted earlier, importing grain is the most efficient way to import water. Countries are, in effect, using grain to balance their water books. Similarly, trading in grain futures is in a sense trading in water futures.[60]

After China and India, there is a second tier of smaller countries with large water deficits—Algeria, Egypt, Mexico, and Pakistan. Algeria, Egypt, and Mexico already import much of their grain. With its population outgrowing its water supply, Pakistan too may soon turn to world markets for grain.[61]

The Middle East and North Africa—from Morocco in the west through Iran in the east—has become the world's fastest-growing grain import market. The demand for grain is driven both by rapid population growth and by rising affluence, much of the latter from the export of oil. With virtually every country in the region pressing against its water limits, the growing urban demand for water can be satisfied only by taking irrigation water from agriculture.[62]

Egypt, with some 75 million people, has become a major importer of wheat in recent years, vying with Japan—traditionally the leading wheat importer—for the top spot. It now imports close to 40 percent of its total grain supply, a dependence that reflects a population that is outgrowing the grain harvest produced with the Nile's water. Algeria, with 34 million people, imports well over half of its grain.[63]

Overall, the water required to produce the grain and other farm products imported into the Middle East and North Africa last year approached the annual flow of the Nile River at Aswan. In effect, the region's water deficit can be thought of as another Nile flowing into the region in the form of imported food.[64]

It is often said that future wars in the Middle East will more likely be fought over water than oil, but in reality the competition for water is taking place in world grain markets. The countries that are financially the strongest, not necessarily those that are militarily the strongest, will fare best in this competition.

Knowing where grain deficits will be concentrated tomorrow requires looking at where water deficits are developing today. Thus far, the countries importing much of their grain have been smaller ones. Now we are looking at fast-growing water deficits in both China and India, each with more than a billion people.[65]

As noted earlier, overpumping is a way of satisfying growing food demand that virtually guarantees a future drop in food production when aquifers are depleted. Many countries are in essence creating a "food bubble economy"—one in which food production is artificially inflated by the unsustainable mining of groundwater. At what point does water scarcity translate into food scarcity?

David Seckler and his colleagues at the International Water Management Institute, the world's premier water research group, summarized this issue well: "Many of the most populous countries of the world—China, India, Pakistan, Mexico, and nearly all the countries of the Middle East and North Africa— have literally been having a free ride over the past two or three decades by depleting their groundwater resources. The penalty for mismanagement of this valuable resource is now coming due and it is no exaggeration to say that the results could be cata- strophic for these countries and, given their importance, for the world as a whole."[66]

Since expanding irrigation helped triple the world grain har- vest from 1950 to 2000, it comes as no surprise that water loss- es can shrink harvests. With water for irrigation, many countries are in a classic overshoot-and-decline mode. If coun- tries that are overpumping do not move quickly to raise water use efficiency and stabilize water tables, then an eventual drop in food production may be inevitable.[67]

Water Scarcity Yields Political Stresses

We typically measure well-being in economic terms, in income per person, but water well-being is measured in cubic meters or tons of water per person. A country with an annual supply of 1,700 cubic meters of water per person is well supplied with water, able to comfortably meet agricultural, industrial, and res- idential needs. Below this level, stresses begin to appear. When water supply drops below 1,000 cubic meters per person, people face scarcity. Below 500 cubic meters, they face acute scarcity. At this level people are suffering from hydrological poverty—living without enough water to produce food or, in some cases, even for basic hygiene.[68]

The world's most severe water stresses are found in North Africa and the Middle East. While Morocco and Egypt have fewer than 1,000 cubic meters per person per year, Algeria, Tunisia, and Libya have fewer than 500. Some countries, including Saudi Arabia, Yemen, Kuwait, and Israel, have less than 300 cubic meters per person per year. A number of sub-Saharan countries are also facing water stress, including Kenya and Rwanda.[69]

While national averages indicate an adequate water supply in each of the world's three most populous countries—China, India, and the United States—regions within these countries also suffer from acute water shortages. Water is scarce throughout the northern half of China. In India, the northwestern region suffers extreme water scarcity. For the United States, the southwestern states from Texas to California are experiencing acute water shortages.[70]

Although the risk of international conflict over water is real, so far there have been remarkably few water wars. Water tensions tend to build more within societies, particularly where water is already scarce and population growth is rapid. Recent years have witnessed conflicts over water in scores of countries. Perhaps the most common of these is the competition described earlier between cities and farmers, particularly in countries like China, India, and Yemen. In other countries the conflicts are between tribes, as in Kenya, or between villages, as in India and China, or upstream and downstream water users, as in Pakistan or China. In some countries local water conflicts have led to violence and death, as in Kenya, Pakistan, and China.[71]

In Pakistan's arid southwest province of Balochistan, water tables are falling everywhere as a fast-growing local population swelled by Afghan refugees is pumping water far faster than aquifers can recharge. The provincial capital of Quetta, as noted earlier, is facing a particularly dire situation. Naser Faruqui, a researcher at Canada's International Development Research Centre, describes the situation facing Quetta: "With over a million people living there now, many of whom are Afghan refugees, the possibility of confrontation over decreasing water resources, or even mass migration from the city, is all too real."[72]

Not far to the west, Iraq is concerned that dam building on the Euphrates River in Turkey and, to a lesser degree, Syria will leave it without enough water to meet its basic needs. The flow into Iraq of the Euphrates River, which gave birth to the ancient Sumerian civilization, has shrunk by half over the last few decades.[73]

Another water flash point involves the way water is divided between Israelis and Palestinians. A U.N. report notes that "nowhere are the problems of water governance as starkly demonstrated as in the Occupied Palestinian Territories." Palestinians experience one of the highest levels of water scarcity in the world. But the flash point is as much over inequity in the distribution of water as it is over scarcity. The Israeli population is roughly double that of the Palestinians, but it gets seven times as much water. As others have noted, peace in the region depends on a more equitable distribution of the region's water. Without this, the peace process itself may dry up.[74]

At the global level, most of the projected population growth of nearly 3 billion by 2050 will come in countries where water tables are already falling. The states most stressed by the scarcity of water tend to be those in arid and semiarid regions, with fast-growing populations and a resistance to family planning. Many of the countries high on the list of failing states are those where populations are outrunning their water supplies, among them Sudan, Iraq, Somalia, Chad, Afghanistan, Pakistan, and Yemen. Unless population can be stabilized in these countries, the continually shrinking supply of water per person will put still more stress on already overstressed governments.[75]

Although spreading water shortages are intimidating, we have the technologies needed to raise water use efficiency, thus buying time to stabilize population size. Prominent among these technologies are those for more water-efficient irrigation, industrial water recycling, and urban water recycling, as discussed in Chapters 9 and 10.

5

Natural Systems Under Stress

In 1938, Walter Lowdermilk, a senior official in the Soil Conservation Service of the U.S. Department of Agriculture (USDA), traveled abroad to look at lands that had been cultivated for thousands of years, seeking to learn how these older civilizations had coped with soil erosion. He found that some had managed their land well, maintaining its fertility over long stretches of history, and were thriving. Others had failed to do so and left only remnants of their illustrious pasts.[1]

In a section of his report entitled "The Hundred Dead Cities," he described a site in northern Syria, near Aleppo, where ancient buildings were still standing in stark isolated relief, but they were on bare rock. During the seventh century, the thriving region had been invaded, initially by a Persian army and later by nomads out of the Arabian Desert. In the process, soil and water conservation practices used for centuries were abandoned. Lowdermilk noted, "Here erosion had done its worst....if the soils had remained, even though the cities were destroyed and the populations dispersed, the area might be re-peopled again and the cities rebuilt, but now that the soils are gone, all is gone."[2]

Now fast-forward to a trip in 2002 by a U.N. team to assess the food situation in Lesotho, a small country of 2 million people embedded within South Africa. Their finding was straightforward: "Agriculture in Lesotho faces a catastrophic future; crop production is declining and could cease altogether over large tracts of the country if steps are not taken to reverse soil erosion, degradation, and the decline in soil fertility." Michael Grunwald reported in the *Washington Post* that nearly half of the children under five in Lesotho are stunted physically. "Many," he wrote, "are too weak to walk to school."[3]

Whether the land is in northern Syria, Lesotho, or elsewhere, the health of the people living on it cannot be separated from the health of the land itself. A large share of the world's 862 million hungry people live on land with soils worn thin by erosion.[4]

Mercilessly expanding human demands are putting stresses on forests, rangelands, and fisheries that they cannot withstand. We are also destroying many of the plant and animal species with which we share the planet. Worldwide, species are now disappearing at 1,000 times the rate at which new species evolve. We have put the extinction clock on fast-forward.[5]

Shrinking Forests: The Many Costs

In early December 2004, Philippine President Gloria Macapagal Arroyo "ordered the military and police to crack down on illegal logging, after flash floods and landslides, triggered by rampant deforestation, killed nearly 340 people," according to news reports. Fifteen years earlier, in 1989, the government of Thailand announced a nationwide ban on tree cutting following severe flooding and the heavy loss of life in landslides. And in August 1998, following several weeks of record flooding in the Yangtze River basin and a staggering $30 billion worth of damage, the Chinese government banned all tree cutting in the upper reaches of the basin. Each of these governments had belatedly learned a costly lesson, namely that services provided by forests, such as flood control, may be far more valuable to society than the lumber in those forests.[6]

At the beginning of the twentieth century, the earth's forested area was estimated at 5 billion hectares. Since then it has shrunk to just under 4 billion hectares, with the remaining forests rather evenly divided between tropical and subtropical forests in developing countries and temperate/boreal forests in industrial countries.[7]

Since 1990, the developing world has lost some 13 million hectares of forest a year. This loss of about 3 percent each decade is an area roughly the size of Greece. Meanwhile, the industrial world is actually gaining an estimated 5.6 million hectares of forestland each year, principally from abandoned cropland returning to forests on its own and from the spread of commercial forestry plantations. Thus, net forest loss worldwide exceeds 7 million hectares per year.[8]

Unfortunately, even these official data from the U.N. Food and Agriculture Organization (FAO) do not reflect the gravity of the situation. For example, tropical forests that are clearcut or burned off rarely recover. They simply become wasteland or at best scrub forest, yet they still may be counted as "forest" in official forestry numbers. Plantations, too, count as forest area, yet they also are a far cry from the old-growth forest they sometimes replace.

The World Resources Institute (WRI) reports that of the forests that do remain standing, "the vast majority are no more than small or highly disturbed pieces of the fully functioning ecosystems they once were." Only 40 percent of the world's remaining forest cover can be classified as frontier forest, which WRI defines as "large, intact, natural forest systems relatively undisturbed and big enough to maintain all of their biodiversity, including viable populations of the wide-ranging species associated with each type."[9]

Pressures on forests continue to mount. Use of firewood, paper, and lumber is expanding. Of the 3.5 billion cubic meters of wood harvested worldwide in 2005, just over half was used for fuel. In developing countries, fuelwood accounts for nearly three fourths of the total.[10]

Deforestation to supply fuelwood is extensive in the Sahelian zone of Africa and the Indian subcontinent. As urban firewood demand surpasses the sustainable yield of nearby forests, the woods slowly retreat from the city in an ever larger circle, a process clearly visible from satellite photographs taken over time. As the circles enlarge, the transport costs of firewood increase, triggering the development of an industry for charcoal, a more concentrated form of energy. March Turnbull writes in *Africa Geographic Online*: "Every large Sahelian town is surrounded by a sterile moonscape. Dakar and Khartoum now reach out further than 500 kilometers for charcoal, sometimes into neighboring countries."[11]

Logging for lumber also takes a heavy toll, as is most evident in Southeast Asia and Africa. In almost all cases, logging is done by foreign corporations more interested in maximizing a one-time harvest than in managing for a sustainable yield in perpetuity. Once a country's forests are gone, companies move on, leaving only devastation behind. Nigeria and the Philippines have both lost their once-thriving tropical hardwood export industries and are now net importers of forest products.[12]

Perhaps the most devastating development affecting the earth's remaining natural forests in this new century is the explosive growth of the wood products industry in China, now supplying the world with furniture, flooring, particle board, and other building materials. In supplying domestic and foreign markets, China has gone on a logging orgy outside its borders, often illegally, to procure logs from Indonesia, Myanmar, Papua New Guinea, and Siberia. And now Chinese logging firms are moving into the Amazon and the Congo Basin.[13]

In a landmark article in April 2007, *Washington Post* reporters Peter Goodman and Peter Finn described how the Chinese went after one of the world's few remaining natural stands of teak across the border in Myanmar. They reported that a Chinese logging boss "handed a rice sack stuffed with $8,000 worth of Chinese currency to two agents with connections in the Burmese borderlands....They used that stash to bribe everyone standing between the teak and China. In came Chinese logging crews. Out went huge logs, over Chinese-built roads."[14]

Forest Trends, a nongovernmental organization consisting of industry and conservation groups, estimates that at the current rate of logging, the natural forests in Indonesia and Myanmar will be gone within a decade or so. Those in Papua New Guinea will last 16 years. Those in the Russian Far East, vast though they are, may not last much more than 20 years.[15]

Forest losses from clearing land for farming and ranching, usually by burning, are concentrated in the Brazilian Amazon, the Congo Basin, and Borneo. After having lost 93 percent of its Atlantic rainforest, Brazil is now destroying the Amazon rainforest. This huge forest, roughly the size of Europe, was largely intact until 1970. Since then, close to 20 percent has been lost.[16]

Africa's Congo Basin, the world's second largest rainforest, spans 10 countries. Like the Amazon rainforest, it is also under assault, primarily from loggers, miners, and farmers. This 190-million-hectare rainforest—home to 400 species of mammals, including the world's largest populations of gorillas, bonobos, chimpanzees, and forest elephants—is shrinking by 1.6 million hectares a year.[17]

The fast-rising demand for palm oil led to an 8-percent annual expansion in the palm plantation area in Malaysian Borneo (Sarawak and Sabah) between 1998 and 2003. In Kalimantan, the Indonesian part of Borneo, growth in oil palm plantings is higher, at over 11 percent. Now that palm oil is emerging as a leading biodiesel fuel, growth in oil palm cultivation will likely climb even faster. The near-limitless demand for biodiesel now threatens the remaining tropical forests in Borneo and elsewhere.[18]

Haiti, a country of 9.6 million people, was once largely covered with forests, but growing firewood demand and land clearing for farming have left forests standing on scarcely 4 percent of its land. First the trees go, then the soil.[19]

Once a tropical paradise, Haiti is a case study of a country caught in an ecological/economic downward spiral from which it has not been able to escape. It is a failed state, a country sustained by international life-support systems of food aid and economic assistance.

The biologically rich rainforest of Madagascar, an island country with 18 million people, is following in Haiti's footsteps. As the trees are cut, either to produce charcoal or to clear land to grow food, the sequence of events is all too familiar. Environmentalists warn that Madagascar could soon become a landscape of scrub growth and sand.[20]

While deforestation accelerates the flow of water back to the ocean, it also can reduce the recycling of rainfall inland. Some 20 years ago two Brazilian scientists, Eneas Salati and Peter Vose, pointed out in *Science* that when rainfall coming from clouds moving in from the Atlantic fell on healthy Amazon rainforest, one fourth of the water ran off and three fourths evaporated into the atmosphere to be carried further inland to provide more rainfall. When land is cleared for grazing or farming, however, the amount that runs off and returns to the sea increases while that which is recycled inland falls alarmingly.[21]

Ecologist Philip Fearnside, who has spent his career studying the Amazon, observes that agriculturally prominent south-central Brazil depends on water that is recycled inland via the Amazon rainforest. As more and more land is cleared for grazing and farming, the forest begins to dry out. At some point, the weakened rainforest becomes vulnerable to fire as lightning strikes. As the Amazon rainforest weakens, it is approaching a tipping point beyond which it cannot be saved.[22]

A similar situation may be developing in Africa, where deforestation and land clearing are proceeding rapidly as firewood use mounts and as logging firms clear large tracts of virgin forests. In Malawi, a country of 14 million people in East Africa, forest cover has shrunk by nearly a quarter since the early 1970s, a loss of up to 1 million hectares. The cutting of trees to produce charcoal and to cure tobacco is leading to a sequence of events paralleling that in Haiti.[23]

As the trees disappear, rainfall runoff increases and the land is deprived of the water from evapotranspiration. Consulting hydrogeologist Jim Anscombe notes: "Driven by energy from the sun, the trees pump water from the water table, through the roots, trunk and leaves, up into the atmosphere through the process of transpiration. Collectively the forest pumps millions of liters of water daily to the atmosphere." Given the local climate conditions, this evapotranspiration translates into summer rainfall, helping to sustain crops. When the forests disappear, this rainfall declines and crop yields follow.[24]

More and more countries are beginning to recognize the risks associated with deforestation. Among the countries that now have total or partial bans on logging in primary forests are China, New Zealand, the Philippines, Sri Lanka, Thailand, and Viet Nam. Unfortunately, all too often a ban in one country simply shifts the deforestation to others or drives illegal logging.[25]

Losing Soil

The thin layer of topsoil that covers the planet's land surface is the foundation of civilization. This soil, typically six inches or so deep, was formed over long stretches of geological time as new soil formation exceeded the natural rate of erosion. As soil accumulated over the eons, it provided a medium in which plants could grow. In turn, plants protect the soil from erosion. Human activity is disrupting this relationship.

Sometime within the last century, soil erosion began to exceed new soil formation over large areas. Now, perhaps a third of all cropland is losing topsoil faster than new soil is forming, reducing the land's inherent productivity. The foundation of civilization is crumbling.[26]

The accelerating soil erosion over the last century can be seen in the dust bowls that form as vegetation is destroyed and wind erosion soars out of control. Among those that stand out are the Dust Bowl in the U.S. Great Plains during the 1930s, the dust bowl in the Soviet Virgin Lands in the 1960s, the huge one that is forming today in northwest China, and the one taking shape in the Sahelian region of Africa. Each of these is associated with a familiar pattern of overgrazing, deforestation, and agricultural expansion onto marginal land, followed by retrenchment as the soil begins to disappear.[27]

Twentieth-century population growth pushed agriculture onto highly vulnerable land in many countries. The overplowing of the U.S. Great Plains during the late nineteenth and early twentieth centuries, for example, led to the 1930s Dust Bowl. This was a tragic era in U.S. history, one that forced hundreds of thousands of farm families to leave the Great Plains. Many migrated to California in search of a new life, a move immortalized in John Steinbeck's novel *The Grapes of Wrath*.[28]

Three decades later, history repeated itself in the Soviet Union. The Virgin Lands Project between 1954 and 1960 centered on plowing an area of grassland for wheat that was larger than the wheatland in Canada and Australia combined. Initially, the result was an impressive expansion in Soviet grain production, but the success was short-lived as a dust bowl developed there as well.[29]

Kazakhstan, at the center of this Virgin Lands Project, saw its grainland area peak at just over 25 million hectares around 1980, then shrink to 15 million hectares today. Even on the remaining land, however, the average wheat yield is scarcely 1 ton per hectare, a far cry from the nearly 7 tons per hectare that farmers get in France, Western Europe's leading wheat producer.[30]

A similar situation exists in Mongolia, where over the last 20

years half the wheatland has been abandoned and wheat yields
have fallen by half, shrinking the harvest by three fourths. Mongolia—a country almost three times the size of France with a
population of 2.6 million—is now forced to import nearly 60
percent of its wheat.[31]

Dust storms originating in the new dust bowls are now faith-
fully recorded in satellite images. On January 9, 2005, the
National Aeronautics and Space Administration (NASA)
released images of a vast dust storm moving westward out of
central Africa. This huge cloud of tan-colored dust stretched
over some 5,300 kilometers (roughly 3,300 miles). NASA noted
that if the storm were relocated to the United States, it would
cover the country and extend into the oceans on both coasts.[32]

Andrew Goudie, Professor of Geography at Oxford University, reports that Saharan dust storms—once rare—are now
commonplace. He estimates they have increased 10-fold during
the last half-century. Among the countries in the region most
affected by topsoil loss from wind erosion are Niger, Chad,
Mauritania, northern Nigeria, and Burkina Faso. In Mauritania, in Africa's far west, the number of dust storms jumped
from 2 a year in the early 1960s to 80 a year today.[33]

The Bodélé Depression in Chad is the source of an estimated 1.3 billion tons of wind-borne soil a year, up 10-fold since
measurements began in 1947. The 2–3 billion tons of fine soil
particles that leave Africa each year in dust storms are slowly
draining the continent of its fertility and biological productivity. In addition, dust storms leaving Africa travel westward
across the Atlantic, depositing so much dust in the Caribbean
that they cloud the water and damage coral reefs.[34]

Water erosion also takes a toll on soils. This can be seen in
the silting of reservoirs and in muddy, silt-laden rivers flowing
into the sea. Pakistan's two large reservoirs, Mangla and
Tarbela, which store Indus River water for the country's
vast irrigation network, are losing roughly 1 percent of their
storage capacity each year as they fill with silt from deforested
watersheds.[35]

Ethiopia, a mountainous country with highly erodible soils
on steeply sloping land, is losing close to 2 billion tons of topsoil a year, washed away by rain. This is one reason Ethiopia
always seems to be on the verge of famine, never able to accu-

mulate enough grain reserves to provide a meaningful measure of food security.[36]

From Grassland to Desert

One tenth of the earth's land surface is cropland, but an area four times this size is rangeland—land that is too dry, too steeply sloping, or not fertile enough to sustain crop production. This area—two fifths of the earth's land surface, most of it semiarid—supports the majority of the world's 3.3 billion cattle, sheep, and goats. These livestock are ruminants, animals with complex digestive systems that enable them to digest roughage, converting it into beef, mutton, and milk.[37]

An estimated 200 million people worldwide make their living as pastoralists tending cattle, sheep, and goats. Many countries in Africa depend heavily on their livestock economies for food and employment. The same is true for large populations in the Middle East, Central Asia, Mongolia, and northwest China. Since most land is held in common in these pastoral societies, controlling overgrazing is difficult.[38]

In other parts of the world, rangelands are owned by individual ranchers. Australia, whose land mass is dominated by rangeland, has a flock of 100 million sheep, five times its human population. Grass-based livestock economies also predominate in Argentina, Brazil, Mexico, and Uruguay. And in the Great Plains of North America, semiarid lands that are not suited to growing wheat are devoted to grazing cattle.[39]

The same ruminants that are uniquely efficient at converting roughage into food also supply leather and wool. The world's leather goods and woolen industries, the livelihood of millions, depend on rangelands for raw materials.

Although public attention often focuses on the role of feedlots in beef production, the share of the world's cattle in feedlots is a tiny fraction of the vast numbers feeding on grass. Even in the United States, which has most of the world's feedlots, the typical steer is in a feedlot for only a matter of months.

Worldwide, almost half of all grasslands are lightly to moderately degraded and 5 percent are severely degraded. The problem is highly visible throughout Africa, the Middle East, Central Asia, and India, where the growth in livestock numbers tracks that in human numbers. In 1950, 238 million Africans relied on 273 million livestock. By 2006, there were nearly 926 million people and 738 million livestock. Demands of the livestock industry now often exceed grassland carrying capacity by half or more.[40]

Iran—with 71 million people—illustrates the pressures facing the Middle East. With 9 million cattle and 80 million sheep and goats—the source of wool for its fabled rug-making industry—Iran's rangelands are deteriorating from overstocking.[41]

China faces similarly difficult challenges. After the economic reforms in 1978 that shifted the responsibility for farming from state-organized production teams to farm families, the government lost control of livestock numbers. As a result, China's cattle, sheep, and goat populations spiraled upward. While the United States, a country with comparable grazing capacity, has 97 million cattle, China has a slightly larger herd of 115 million. But while the United States has only 9 million sheep and goats, China has 366 million. Concentrated in China's western and northern provinces, sheep and goats are destroying the land's protective vegetation. The wind then does the rest, removing the soil and converting productive rangeland into desert.[42]

Fodder needs of livestock in nearly all developing countries now exceed the sustainable yield of rangelands and other forage resources. In India, the demand for fodder greatly outpaces the supply, leaving millions of emaciated, unproductive cattle.[43]

Land degradation from overgrazing is taking a heavy economic toll in lost livestock production. In the early stages of overgrazing, the costs show up in lower land productivity. But as the process continues, it destroys vegetation, leading to erosion and the eventual creation of wasteland and desert. At some point, growth in the livestock population begins to shrink the biologically productive area and thus the earth's capacity to sustain civilization.[44]

Advancing Deserts

Desertification, the process of converting productive land to wasteland through overuse and mismanagement, is unfortunately all too common. Anything that removes protective grass or trees leaves soil vulnerable to wind and water erosion. In the early stages of desertification, the finer particles of soil are removed by the wind, creating the dust storms described earlier.

Once the fine particles are removed, then the coarser particles—the sand—are also carried by the wind in localized sand storms.

Large-scale desertification is concentrated in Africa and Asia—two regions that together contain 5 billion of the world's 6.7 billion people. Populations in countries across the north of Africa are being squeezed by the northward advance of the Sahara.[45]

In the vast east-to-west swath of semiarid Africa between the Sahara Desert and the forested regions to the south lies the Sahel, a region where farming and herding overlap. In countries from Senegal and Mauritania in the west to Sudan, Ethiopia, and Somalia in the east, the explosive demands of growing human and livestock numbers are converting land into desert.[46]

Nigeria, Africa's most populous country, is losing 351,000 hectares of rangeland and cropland to desertification each year. While Nigeria's human population was growing from 34 million in 1950 to 145 million in 2006, a fourfold expansion, its livestock population grew from roughly 6 million to 67 million, an 11-fold increase. With the forage needs of Nigeria's 16 million cattle and 51 million sheep and goats exceeding the sustainable yield of grasslands, the northern part of the country is slowly turning to desert. If Nigeria continues toward its projected 289 million people by 2050, the deterioration will only accelerate.[47]

Iran is also losing its battle with the desert. Mohammad Jarian, who heads Iran's Anti-Desertification Organization, reported in 2002 that sand storms had buried 124 villages in the southeastern province of Sistan-Balochistan, forcing their abandonment. Drifting sands had covered grazing areas, starving livestock and depriving villagers of their livelihood.[48]

Neighboring Afghanistan is faced with a similar situation. The Registan Desert is migrating westward, encroaching on agricultural areas. A U.N. Environment Programme (UNEP) team reports that "up to 100 villages have been submerged by windblown dust and sand." In the country's northwest, sand dunes are moving onto agricultural land in the upper reaches of the Amu Darya basin, their path cleared by the loss of stabilizing vegetation from firewood gathering and overgrazing. The UNEP team observed sand dunes 15 meters high blocking roads, forcing residents to establish new routes.[49]

China's desertification may be the worst in the world. Wang

Tao, one of China's leading desert scholars, reports that from 1950 to 1975 an average of 1,560 square kilometers of land turned to desert each year. Between 1975 and 1987, this climbed to 2,100 square kilometers a year. From then until the century's end, it jumped to 3,600 square kilometers of land going to desert annually.[50]

China is now at war. It is not invading armies that are claiming its territory, but expanding deserts. Old deserts are advancing and new ones are forming like guerrilla forces striking unexpectedly, forcing Beijing to fight on several fronts. Wang Tao reports that over the last half-century, some 24,000 villages in northern and western China have been entirely or partly abandoned as a result of being overrun by drifting sand.[51]

People in China are all too familiar with the dust storms that originate in the northwestern area and western Mongolia, but the rest of the world typically learns about this fast-growing ecological catastrophe from the massive dust storms that travel outside the region. On April 18, 2001, the western United States—from the Arizona border north to Canada—was blanketed with dust. It came from a huge dust storm that originated in northwestern China and Mongolia on April 5. Measuring 1,800 kilometers (1,200 miles) across when it left China, the storm carried millions of tons of topsoil, a resource that will take centuries to replace through natural processes.[52]

Almost exactly one year later, on April 12, 2002, South Korea was engulfed by a huge dust storm from China that left people in Seoul literally gasping for breath. Schools were closed, airline flights were cancelled, and clinics were overrun with patients having difficulty breathing. Retail sales fell. Koreans have come to dread the arrival of what they now call "the fifth season," the dust storms of late winter and early spring.[53]

These two dust storms, among the 10 or so major dust storms that now occur each year in China, offer visual evidence of the ecological catastrophe unfolding in northern and western China. Overgrazing is the principal culprit.[54]

A U.S. Embassy report entitled "Desert Mergers and Acquisitions" describes satellite images showing two deserts in north-central China expanding and merging to form a single, larger desert overlapping Inner Mongolia (Nei Monggol) and Gansu provinces. To the west in Xinjiang Province, two even larger deserts—the Taklimakan and Kumtag—are also heading for a merger. Highways running through the shrinking region between them are regularly inundated by sand dunes.[55]

In Latin America, deserts are expanding in both Brazil and Mexico. In Brazil, where some 58 million hectares of land are affected, economic losses from desertification are estimated at $300 million per year, much of it concentrated in the country's northeast. Mexico, with a much larger share of arid and semi-arid land, is even more vulnerable. The degradation of cropland now prompts some 700,000 Mexicans to leave the land each year in search of jobs in nearby cities or in the United States.[56]

In scores of countries, the overgrazing, overplowing, and overcutting that are driving desertification are intensifying as human and livestock populations continue to grow. Stopping the conversion of productive land to desert may now rest on stopping the growth in human and livestock numbers.

Collapsing Fisheries

After World War II, accelerating population growth and steadily rising incomes drove the demand for seafood upward at a record pace. At the same time, advances in fishing technologies, including huge refrigerated processing ships that enabled trawlers to exploit distant oceans, enabled fishers to respond to the growing world demand.

In response, the oceanic fish catch climbed from 19 million tons in 1950 to its historic high of 93 million tons in 1997. This fivefold growth—more than double that of population during this period—raised the wild seafood supply per person worldwide from 7 kilograms (15.4 pounds) in 1950 to a peak of 17 kilograms in 1988. Since then, it has fallen to 14 kilograms.[57]

As population grows and as modern food marketing systems give more people access to these products, seafood consumption is growing. Indeed, the human appetite for seafood is outgrowing the sustainable yield of oceanic fisheries. Today 75 percent of fisheries are being fished at or beyond their sustainable capacity. As a result, many are in decline and some have collapsed.[58]

While oceanic fisheries face numerous threats, it is overfishing that directly threatens their survival. Oceanic harvests expanded as new technologies evolved, ranging from sonar for

tracking schools of fish to vast driftnets that are collectively
long enough to circle the earth many times over.

A 2003 landmark study by a Canadian-German research
team published in *Nature* concluded that 90 percent of the large
fish in the oceans had disappeared over the last 50 years. Ransom Myers, a fisheries biologist at Canada's Dalhousie University and lead scientist in this study, says: "From giant blue
marlin to mighty bluefin tuna, from tropical groupers to
Antarctic cod, industrial fishing has scoured the global ocean.
There is no blue frontier left."[59]

Myers goes on to say, "Since 1950, with the onset of indus-
trialized fisheries, we have rapidly reduced the resource base to
less than 10 percent—not just in some areas, not just for some
stocks, but for entire communities of these large fish species
from the tropics to the poles."[60]

Fisheries are collapsing throughout the world. The 500-year-
old cod fishery of Canada failed in the early 1990s, putting
some 40,000 fishers and fish processors out of work. Fisheries
off the coast of New England were not far behind. And in
Europe, cod fisheries are in decline, approaching a free fall. Like
the Canadian cod fishery, the European ones may have been
depleted to the point of no return. Countries that fail to meet
nature's deadlines for halting overfishing face fishery decline
and collapse.[61]

Atlantic stocks of the heavily fished bluefin tuna—a large
specimen of which, headed for Tokyo's sushi restaurants, can
bring in $100,000—have been cut by a staggering 94 percent. It
will take years for such long-lived species to recover, even if fishing were to stop altogether. The harvest of the Caspian Sea sturgeon, source of the world's most prized caviar, fell from a record
27,700 tons in 1977 to just 461 tons in 2000. The quota for 2007
was set at 368 tons. Overfishing, much of it illegal, is primarily
responsible for the dramatic drop.[62]

The U.S. Chesapeake Bay, which yielded more than 35 million pounds of oysters per year a half-century ago, now produces scarcely 1 million pounds per year. A deadly combination
of overharvesting, pollutants, oyster disease, and siltation from
soil erosion is responsible.[63]

Even among countries accustomed to working together, such
as those in the European Union (EU), the challenge of negotiat-

ing catch limits at sustainable levels can be difficult. In April 1997, after prolonged negotiations, agreement was reached in Brussels to reduce the fishing capacity of EU fleets by 30 percent for endangered species, such as cod, herring, and sole in the North Sea, and by 20 percent for overfished stocks, such as cod in the Baltic Sea, the bluefin tuna, and swordfish off the Iberian Peninsula. The EU had finally reached agreement on reducing the catch but the cuts were not sufficient to arrest the decline of the region's fisheries.[64]

The catch of North Sea cod, the mainstay of U.K. fisheries, fell from 300,000 tons per year in the mid-1980s to below 50,000 tons in recent years. For 2006, the annual quota was dropped to 23,000 tons, but the fishery continued to decline, leading to an additional 14 percent quota cut in 2007. The history of EU fishery management and the reduction of quotas has been a matter of too little, too late. EU officials are all too aware that Canada's vast Newfoundland cod fishery has not recovered since collapsing in 1992, despite the total ban on fishing imposed then, but even so they have consistently failed to move quickly enough.[65]

When some fisheries collapse, it puts more pressure on those that remain. Local shortages quickly become global shortages. With restrictions on the catch in overfished EU waters, the heavily subsidized EU fishing fleet has turned to the west coast of Africa, buying licenses to fish off the coasts of Cape Verde, Guinea-Bissau, Mauritania, Morocco, and Senegal. They are competing there with fleets from China, Japan, Russia, South Korea, and Taiwan. For impoverished countries like Mauritania and Guinea-Bissau, income from fishing licenses can account for up to half of government revenue.[66]

Unfortunately for the Africans, their fisheries too are collapsing. In Senegal, where local fishers with small boats once could quickly fill their craft with fish, on many days now they cannot catch enough fish to cover even their fuel costs. As one Senegalese tribal elder said, "Poverty came to Senegal with these fishing agreements."[67]

To the north, John Miller, reporting in the *Wall Street Journal* from the Mauritanian port town of Nouadhibou, describes how a 39-year-old fisherman and father of six, Sall Samba, had beached two of the three fishing boats he used to harvest octopus. "You used to be able to fish right in the port," he said, "but now the only thing you can catch here is water."[68]

Overfishing is not the only threat to the world's seafood supply. Some 90 percent of fish residing in the ocean rely on coastal wetlands, mangrove swamps, or rivers as spawning areas. Well over half of the mangrove forests in tropical and subtropical countries have been lost. The disappearance of coastal wetlands in industrial countries is even greater. In Italy, whose coastal wetlands are the nurseries for many Mediterranean fisheries, the loss is a whopping 95 percent.[69]

Damage to coral reefs from higher ocean temperatures and ocean acidification caused by higher atmospheric carbon dioxide levels, as well as damage from pollution and sedimentation, are threatening these breeding grounds for fish in tropical and subtropical waters. Between 2000 and 2004, the worldwide share of destroyed reefs, those that had lost 90 percent of live corals, expanded from 11 percent to 20 percent. The Global Coral Reef Monitoring Network reports that 24 percent of the remaining reefs are at risk of imminent collapse, with another 26 percent facing significant loss in the next few decades, due to mounting human pressures. As the reefs deteriorate, so do the fisheries that depend on them.[70]

A World Resources Institute report on coral reefs in the Caribbean notes that 35 percent of these reefs are threatened by sewage discharge, water-based sediment, and pollution from fertilizer and that 15 percent are threatened by pollution from cruise ship discharges. In economic terms, the Caribbean coral reefs supply goods and services worth at least $3.1 billion per year.[71]

The spectacular coral reefs of the Red Sea, some of the most strikingly beautiful reefs anywhere, are facing extinction due to destructive fishing practices, dredging, sedimentation, and sewage discharge. Anything that reduces sunlight penetration in the sea impairs the growth of corals, leading to die-off.[72]

Pollution is taking a devastating toll, illustrated by the dead zones created by nutrient runoff from fertilizer and from sewage discharge. In the United States, the Mississippi River carries nutrients from the Corn Belt and sewage from cities along its route into the Gulf of Mexico. The nutrient surge creates huge algal blooms that then die and decompose, consuming the free oxygen in the water, leading to the death of fish. This creates a dead zone each summer in the Gulf that can reach the size of New Jersey.[73]

UNEP reported in 2006 that there were more than 200 dead zones in the world's oceans and seas, up from 149 two years earlier. Among the dead zones they counted were ones in the Baltic Sea, the Black Sea, the Gulf of Thailand, Ghana's Fosu Lagoon, and Uruguay's Montevideo Bay. In these oceanic "deserts" there are no fishing trawlers because there are no fish.[74]

Commercial fishing is now largely an economics of today versus tomorrow. Governments are seeking to protect tomorrow's catches by forcing fishers to keep their ships idle; fishing communities are torn between the need for income today versus the future. Ironically, one reason for excess fleet capacity is long-standing government subsidized loans for investing in new boats and fishing gear.[75]

The growing worldwide demand for seafood can no longer be satisfied by expanding the oceanic fish catch. If it is to be satisfied, it will be by expanding fish farming. But once fish are put in ponds or cages they have to be fed, most often corn and soybean meal, putting further pressure on land resources.

Disappearing Plants and Animals

The archeological record shows five great extinctions since life began, each representing an evolutionary setback, a wholesale impoverishment of life on earth. The last of these mass extinctions occurred some 65 million years ago, most likely when an asteroid collided with our planet, spewing vast amounts of dust and debris into the atmosphere. The resultant abrupt cooling obliterated the dinosaurs and at least one fifth of all other extant life forms.[76]

We are now in the early stage of the sixth great extinction. Unlike previous extinction events, which were caused by natural phenomena, this one is of human origin. For the first time in the earth's long history, one species has evolved, if that is the right word, to where it can eradicate much of life.

As various life forms disappear, they diminish the services provided by nature, such as pollination, seed dispersal, insect control, and nutrient cycling. This loss of species is weakening the web of life, and if it continues it could tear huge gaps in its fabric, leading to irreversible changes in the earth's ecosystem.

Species of all kinds are threatened by habitat destruction. One of the leading threats to the earth's biodiversity is the loss of tropical rainforests. As we burn off the Amazon rainforest, we are in effect burning one of the great repositories of genetic information. Our descendants may one day view the wholesale burning of this genetic library much as we view the burning of the library in Alexandria in 48 BC.

Habitat alteration from rising temperatures, chemical pollution, or the introduction of exotic species can also decimate both plant and animal species. As the human population grows, the number of species with which we share the planet shrinks. Yet we cannot separate our fate from that of all life on the earth. If the rich diversity of life that we inherited is continually impoverished, eventually we will be impoverished as well.

The share of birds, mammals, and fish that are vulnerable or in immediate danger of extinction is now measured in double digits: 12 percent of the world's nearly 10,000 bird species; 20 percent of the world's 5,416 mammal species; and 39 percent of the fish species analyzed.[77]

Among mammals, the 296 known species of primates other than humans are most at risk. The World Conservation Union-IUCN reports that 114 of these species are threatened with extinction. Some 95 of the world's primate species live in Brazil, where habitat destruction poses a particular threat. Hunting, too, is a threat, particularly in West and Central Africa, where the deteriorating food situation and newly constructed logging roads are combining to create a lively market for "bushmeat."[78]

The bonobos of West Africa, great apes that are smaller than the chimpanzees of East Africa, may be our closest living relative both genetically and in social behavior. But this connection is not saving them from the bushmeat trade or the destruction of their habitat by loggers. Concentrated in the dense forest of the Democratic Republic of the Congo, a failing state with a prolonged civil conflict, their numbers fell from an estimated 100,000 in 1980 to as few as 10,000 today. In one human generation, 90 percent of the bonobos have disappeared.[79]

Birds, because of their high visibility, are a useful indicator of the diversity of life. Of the 9,817 known bird species, roughly 70 percent are declining in number. Of these, an estimated 1,217 species are in imminent danger of extinction. Habitat loss and degradation affect 91 percent of all threatened bird species. For example, 61 bird species have become locally extinct with the extensive loss of lowland rainforest in Singapore. Some once-abundant species may have already dwindled to the point of no return. The great bustard, once widespread in Pakistan and surrounding countries, is being hunted to extinction. Ten of the world's 17 species of penguins are threatened or endangered, potential victims of global warming. Stanford University biologist Çagan Sekercioglu, who led a study on the status of the world's birds said, "We are changing the world so much that even birds cannot adapt."[80]

Particularly disturbing is the recent precipitous decline in the populations of Britain's most popular songbirds. Within the last 30 years the populations of well-known species such as the willow warbler, the song thrush, and the spotted flycatcher have fallen 50–80 percent; no one seems to know why, although there is speculation that habitat destruction and pesticides may be playing a role. Without knowing the source of the decline, it is difficult to take actions that will arrest the plunge in numbers.[81]

Another decline, which began in late 2006 and had direct economic consequences, is that of the honeybee, the principal pollinator of U.S. fruit and vegetable crops. A survey of U.S. beekeepers, conducted from September 2006 to March 2007 by the Apiary Inspectors of America, found that the bees in nearly one quarter of U.S. bee colonies had simply disappeared as a result of what scientists are calling "colony collapse disorder." Large numbers of colonies have suffered the same fate in Europe, Brazil, and Guatemala.[82]

Scientists are baffled by what the French have labeled "mad bee disease." Bees leaving their hives on pollination forays apparently become disoriented and never return. The principal suspect at this writing is the Israeli acute paralysis virus, which may have originated in Australia. If scientists cannot quickly diagnose this bee malady and devise preventive measures, the world could face an unprecedented disruption of fruit and vegetable production.[83]

The threat to fish may be the greatest of all. The principal causes are overfishing, water pollution, and the excessive extraction of water from rivers and other freshwater ecosystems. An estimated 65 percent of the fish species evaluated by IUCN that once inhabited the lakes and streams of North America are either extinct or in jeopardy. In Europe, some 109 species of freshwater fish out of the 265 that were evaluated are threatened, endangered, or of special concern. One third of the 97 fish species in South Africa need special protection to avoid extinction.[84]

The leatherback turtle, one of the most ancient animals, which can reach a weight of 360 kilograms (800 pounds), also is fast disappearing. Its numbers dropped from 115,000 in 1982 to 34,500 in 1996. At the Playa Grande and Playa Langosta nesting colonies on Costa Rica's west coast, the number of nesting females dropped from 1,504 in 1989 to 62 in 2003, then rose slightly to 174 in 2004. Writing in *Nature*, James Spotila and colleagues warn that "if these turtles are to be saved, immediate action is needed to minimize mortality through fishing and to maximize hatchling production."[85]

One of the fastest-growing threats to the diversity of plant and animal life today is the extraordinary agricultural expansion now under way in Brazil as land is cleared to graze cattle, plant soybeans, and, more recently, produce sugarcane for ethanol. Farmers and ranchers are opening up vast areas in the Amazon basin and in the *cerrado*, a Europe-sized savanna-like region south of the Amazon basin. Although there are mechanisms in place to protect the rich biological diversity of the Amazon, such as the requirement that landowners clear no more than one fifth of their land, the government lacks enforcement capacity.[86]

Like the Amazon, the *cerrado* is biologically rich, home to many large mammals, including the maned wolf, giant armadillo, giant anteater, deer, and several large cats—jaguar, puma, ocelot, and jaguarundi. The *cerrado* contains 607 species of birds, including the rhea, a cousin of the ostrich, which grows up to five feet tall. An estimated 1,000 species of butterflies have been identified. Conservation International reports that the *cerrado* also contains some 10,000 plant species—at least 4,400 of which are endemic, not found anywhere else.[87]

Another worldwide threat to species, and one that is commonly underestimated, is the introduction of non-native species, which can alter local habitats and communities, driving native species to extinction. For example, non-native species may be responsible for 29 percent of the threatened bird species on the IUCN Red List. For plants, alien species are implicated in 5 percent of all the listings.[88]

Efforts to save wildlife traditionally have centered on the creation of parks or wildlife reserves. Unfortunately, this approach may now be less effective, for if we cannot stabilize climate, there is not an ecosystem on earth that we can save. Everything will change.

In the new world we are entering, protecting the diversity of life on earth is no longer simply a matter of setting aside tracts of land, fencing them off, and calling them parks and preserves. Success in this effort depends also on stabilizing both climate and population.

On the plus side, we now have more information on the state of the earth and the life on it than ever before. While knowledge is not a substitute for action, it is a prerequisite for saving the earth's natural systems—and the civilization that they support.

6

Early Signs of Decline

While progress continues on many fronts, disturbing signs of decline are beginning to emerge. In the early years of this new millennium, United Nations demographers stunned the world when they announced that the average life expectancy in 38 AIDS-afflicted countries in sub-Saharan Africa had fallen to only 45 years, 10 years below what it would have been in the absence of AIDS.[1]

For the first time in the modern era, life expectancy, a seminal indicator of development, has dropped for a large segment of humanity. This failure of leadership to curb the spread of the virus in dozens of countries is quite literally reversing the march of progress. Is this breakdown of the political system an anomaly? Or is it an early sign that the complexity of emerging problems is overwhelming weaker national governments?

Troubles are not limited to Africa. In Russia, life expectancy for males has fallen to 59 years, down from some 64 years in 1990. In China, with dangerously high pollution levels, more people are dying from cancer than any other disease. The United States, with a highly productive economy but a troubled society, now has 960,000 farmers and 2 million prison inmates—more than twice as many people in jail as live on the land.[2]

The gap between rich and poor grows ever wider, putting more stress on the international system. Differences in life expectancy are wider than ever, with people in Botswana and Swaziland living on average less than 40 years and those in Japan and Sweden living 80 years or more. One reason for the wide gap in life expectancy is the HIV epidemic; another is hunger. After declining in recent decades, the number of hungry people in the world turned upward in the late 1990s and continues to rise.[3]

The stresses in our early twenty-first century civilization take many forms. Economically we see them in the widening income gap between the world's rich and poor. Socially they take the form of the widening gap in education and health care. Environmentally we have a swelling flow of refugees as productive land turns to desert and as wells go dry. Politically we see the stresses within societies in conflict over basic resources such as cropland, grazing land, and water and, perhaps most fundamentally, in the growing number of failing states.

Our Socially Divided World

The social and economic gap between the world's richest 1 billion people and its poorest 1 billion has no historical precedent. Not only is this gap wide, it is widening. The poorest billion are trapped at subsistence level and the richest billion are becoming wealthier with each passing year. The economic gap can be seen in the contrasts in nutrition, education, disease patterns, family size, and life expectancy.

The U.N. Food and Agriculture Organization reports that 862 million people are undernourished and often hungry. A much larger number, roughly 1.6 billion people, are overnourished and overweight, most of them suffering from excessive caloric intake, exercise deprivation, or a combination of the two. While close to 1 billion people worry whether they will be able to eat, another 1.6 billion worry about eating too much.[4]

Hunger is the most visible face of poverty. Those that are chronically hungry are not getting enough food to achieve full physical and mental development and to maintain adequate levels of physical activity. The majority of the underfed and under-

weight people are concentrated in the Indian subcontinent and
sub-Saharan Africa—regions that contain 1.4 billion and 800
million people, respectively. Twenty-five years ago, the nutritional status of Asia's population giants, India and China, was
similar, but since then China has eliminated most of its hunger,
whereas India has made limited progress. During this last quar-
ter-century, China has accelerated the shift to smaller families.
While gains in food production in India were absorbed largely
by population growth, those in China went mostly to raising
consumption per person.[5]

Malnutrition takes its heaviest toll among the young, who
are most vulnerable during their rapid physical and mental
development. In both India and Bangladesh, almost half of all
children under five are underweight and malnourished. In
Ethiopia, 47 percent of children are undernourished, while in
Nigeria the figure is 29 percent—and these are two of Africa's
most populous countries.[6]

Although it is not surprising that those who are underfed and
underweight are concentrated in developing countries, it is perhaps surprising that most of them live in rural communities. More
often than not, the undernourished are either landless or they live
on plots of land so small that they are effectively landless.[7]

The penalties of being undernourished begin at birth. A
U.N. report estimates that 20 million underweight infants are
born each year to mothers who also are malnourished. The
study indicates that these children suffer lasting effects in the
form of "impaired immune systems, neurological damage, and
retarded physical growth." David Barker of Britain's University
of Southampton observes soberly "that 60 percent of all newborns in India would be in intensive care had they been born in
California."[8]

Disease patterns also reflect the widening gap between the
rich and the poor. The billion poorest suffer mostly from infectious diseases—malaria, tuberculosis, dysentery, measles, respiratory infections, and AIDS. Malnutrition leaves infants and
small children even more vulnerable to such infectious diseases.
Unsafe drinking water takes a heavier toll on those with hunger-
weakened immune systems, resulting in millions of fatalities
each year. In contrast, among the billion at the top of the global economic scale, it is diseases related to aging and lifestyle

excesses, including cardiovascular disease, obesity, smoking, high fat diets, and exercise deprivation, that cause most deaths.[9]

There is also a demographic divide. Close to 1 billion people live in countries where population size is essentially stable. But another billion or so live in countries where population is projected to double or more by 2050.[10]

Education levels, too, reflect the deep divide. In some industrial countries—for example, Canada and Japan—more than half of all young people now graduate from college with either two- or four-year degrees. By contrast, in developing countries 72 million youngsters of elementary school age are not enrolled in school at all. Although five centuries have passed since Gutenberg invented the printing press, some 781 million adults are illiterate. Unable to read, they are also excluded from the use of computers and the Internet. Without adult literacy programs, their prospects of escaping poverty are not good.[11]

The world's illiterates are concentrated in a handful of the more populous countries, most of them in Asia and Africa. Prominent among these are Bangladesh, China, Egypt, Ethiopia, India, Indonesia, Nigeria, and Pakistan, plus Brazil and Mexico in Latin America. From 1990 to 2000, China and Indonesia made large gains in reducing illiteracy. Other countries also making meaningful progress were Brazil, Mexico, and Nigeria. However, in four other populous countries— Bangladesh, Egypt, India, and Pakistan—the number of illiterates increased.[12]

Illiteracy and poverty tend to reinforce each other because illiterate women typically have much larger families than literate women do and because each year of schooling raises earning power by 10–20 percent. In Brazil, for instance, illiterate women have more than six children each on average; literate women have only two.[13]

To be poor often means to be sick. As with illiteracy, ill health and poverty are closely linked. Health is closely related to access to safe water, something that 1.1 billion people lack. Waterborne diseases claim more than 3 million lives each year, mostly as a result of dysentery and cholera, and mostly among children. Infant mortality in affluent societies averages 8 per thousand live births; in the 50 poorest countries it averages 95 per thousand—nearly 12 times as high.[14]

The connection between poverty and disease is strong, but it has been broken for most of humanity by economic development. The challenge now is to break this link for that remaining minority who do not have access to safe water, vaccines, education, and basic health care.

Health Challenge Growing

Health challenges are becoming more numerous as new infectious diseases such as SARS, West Nile virus, and avian flu emerge. In addition, the accumulation of chemical pollutants in the environment is starting to take a toll. While infectious diseases are fairly well understood, the health effects of many environmental pollutants are not yet known.

Among the leading infectious diseases, malaria claims more than 1 million lives each year, 89 percent of them in Africa. The number of people who suffer from it most of their lives is many times greater. Economist Jeffrey Sachs, head of Columbia University's Earth Institute, estimates that reduced worker productivity and other costs associated with malaria are cutting economic growth by a full percentage point in countries with heavily infected populations.[15]

Although diseases such as malaria and cholera exact a heavy toll, there is no recent precedent of a disease affecting as many people as the HIV epidemic does. To find anything similar to such a potentially devastating loss of life, we have to go back to the smallpox decimation of Native American communities in the sixteenth century or to the bubonic plague that took roughly a fourth of Europe's population during the fourteenth century. HIV is an epidemic of epic proportions that, if not checked soon, could take more lives during this century than were claimed by all the wars of the last century.[16]

Since the human immunodeficiency virus was identified in 1981, it has spread worldwide. By the end of 2006, the number of people infected had climbed to 86 million. Of this total, more than 40 million have died thus far. Today 25 million HIV-positive people today live in sub-Saharan Africa, but only 1 million or so are being treated with anti-retroviral drugs.[17]

Infection rates are climbing. In the absence of effective treatment, the areas of sub-Saharan Africa with the highest infection rates face a staggering loss of life. Countries like Botswana and

Zimbabwe could lose more than a fifth of their adult populations within a decade.[18]

The HIV epidemic affects every facet of life and every sector of the economy. Food production per person, already lagging in most countries in sub-Saharan Africa, is now falling fast in some as the number of field workers shrinks. The downward spiral in family welfare typically begins when the first adult falls victim to the illness—a development that is doubly disruptive because for each person who is sick and unable to work, another adult must care for that person.[19]

Education is also affected as the ranks of teachers are decimated by the virus. With students, when one or both parents die, children are forced to stay home simply because there is not enough money to buy books and to pay school fees.

The effects on health care are equally devastating. In many hospitals in eastern and southern Africa, a majority of the beds are now occupied by AIDS victims, leaving less space for those with other illnesses. Already overworked doctors and nurses are often stretched to the breaking point. With health care systems now unable to provide even basic care, the toll of traditional disease is also rising. Life expectancy is dropping not only because of AIDS, but also because of the deterioration in overall health care associated with it.[20]

The epidemic is leaving millions of orphans in its wake. Sub-Saharan Africa is expected to have 18 million "AIDS orphans" by 2010—children who have lost at least one parent to the disease. There is no precedent for millions of street children in Africa. The extended family, once capable of absorbing orphaned children, is now itself being weakened by the loss of adults, leaving children to bury their parents and fend for themselves. For some girls, the only option is what has come to be known as "survival sex." Michael Grunwald writes from Swaziland in the *Washington Post*: "In the countryside, teenage Swazi girls are selling sex—and spreading HIV—for $5 an encounter, exactly what it costs to hire oxen for a day of plowing."[21]

The HIV epidemic in Africa is now a development problem, threatening not only to undermine future progress but also to eliminate past gains. It threatens food security, undermines the educational system, and dries up foreign investment. It is overwhelming governments, leading to more failing states. Stephen

Lewis, when he was the U.N. Special Envoy for HIV/AIDS in Africa, said that the epidemic can be curbed and the infection trends can be reversed, but it will take help from the international community. The failure to fully fund the Global Fund to Fight AIDS, Tuberculosis and Malaria, he said, is "mass murder by complacency."[22]

Writing in the *New York Times*, Alex de Waal, an adviser to the U.N. Economic Commission for Africa and to UNICEF, sums up the effects of the epidemic well: "Just as HIV destroys the body's immune system, the epidemic of HIV and AIDS has disabled the body politic. As a result of HIV, the worst hit African countries have undergone a social breakdown that is now reaching a new level: African societies' capacity to resist famine is fast eroding. Hunger and disease have begun reinforcing each other. As daunting as the prospect is, we will have to fight them together, or we will succeed against neither."[23]

While the HIV epidemic is concentrated in Africa, air and water pollutants are damaging the health of people everywhere. A joint study by the University of California and the Boston Medical Center shows that some 200 human diseases, ranging from cerebral palsy to testicular atrophy, are linked to pollutants. Other diseases that can be caused by pollutants include an astounding 37 forms of cancer, plus heart disease, kidney disease, high blood pressure, diabetes, dermatitis, bronchitis, hyperactivity, deafness, sperm damage, and Alzheimer's and Parkinson's diseases.[24]

Nowhere is pollution damaging human health more than in China, where deaths from cancer have now eclipsed those from heart ailments and cerebrovascular disease. A Ministry of Health survey of 30 cities and 78 counties that was released in 2007 reveals a rising tide of cancer. Populations of some "cancer villages" are being decimated by the disease.[25]

Jiangsu province, located on the coast just north of Shanghai, is both one of China's most prosperous provinces and one of its most cancer-ridden. Although it has only 5 percent of the country's population it has 12 percent of the cancer deaths. One river in the province was laden with 93 different carcinogens, most of them from untreated factory waste.[26]

Pan Yue, vice minister of China's Environmental Protection Administration, believes his country "is dangerously near a crisis point." The reason, he believes, is that Marxism has given way to "an unrestrained pursuit of material gain devoid of morality. Traditional Chinese culture with its emphasis on harmony between human beings and nature," he says, "was thrown aside."[27]

The new reality is that each year China grows richer and sicker. Although there are frequent pronouncements urging steps to reduce pollution, these official statements are largely ignored. There is not yet a real commitment in the Chinese government to control pollution. China's Environmental Protection Administration has fewer than 300 employees, all located in Beijing. The U.S. Environmental Protection Agency (EPA), in contrast, has 17,000 employees, most of whom work in regional offices around the country where they can observe and monitor pollution at the local level.[28]

Yet the United States is also still feeling the effects of pollution. In July 2005 the Environmental Working Group, in collaboration with Commonweal, released an analysis of umbilical cord blood from 10 randomly selected newborns in U.S. hospitals. They found a total of 287 chemicals in these tests. "Of the 287 chemicals we detected...we know that 180 cause cancer in humans or animals, 217 are toxic to the brain and nervous system, and 208 cause birth defects or abnormal development in animal tests." Everyone on the planet shares this "body burden" of toxic chemicals, but infants are at greater risk because they are in the highly vulnerable formative stage of early development.[29]

WHO reports an estimated 3 million deaths worldwide each year from air pollutants—three times the number of traffic fatalities. In the United States, air pollution each year claims 70,000 lives, compared with the country's 45,000 traffic deaths.[30]

A U.K. research team reports a surprising rise in Alzheimer's and Parkinson's diseases, and in motor neuron disease generally, in 10 industrial countries—6 in Europe plus the United States, Japan, Canada, and Australia. In England and Wales, deaths from these brain diseases increased from 3,000 per year in the late 1970s to 10,000 in the late 1990s. Over an 18-year period, death rates from these diseases, mainly Alzheimer's, more than tripled for men and nearly doubled for women. This increase in dementia is likely linked to a rise in the concentration of pesticides, industrial effluents, car exhaust, and other pollutants in the environment. A 2006 study by the Harvard School of Public Health found that long-term low-level exposure to pesticides raised the risk of developing Parkinson's disease by 70 percent.[31]

Scientists are becoming increasingly concerned about the various effects of mercury, a potent neurotoxin, which now permeates the environment in virtually all countries with coal-burning power plants and many of those with gold mines. For example, gold miners release an estimated 290,000 pounds of mercury into the Amazon ecosystem each year, and coal-burning power plants release nearly 100,000 pounds of mercury into the air in the United States. The U.S. EPA reports that "mercury from power plants settles over waterways, polluting rivers and lakes, and contaminating fish."[32]

In 2006, 48 of the 50 states in the United States (all but Alaska and Wyoming) issued a total of 3,080 fish advisories warning against eating fish from local lakes and streams because of their mercury content. EPA research indicates that one out of every six women of childbearing age in the United States has enough mercury in her blood to harm a developing fetus. This means that 630,000 of the 4 million babies born in the country each year may face neurological damage from mercury exposure before birth.[33]

No one knows exactly how many chemicals are manufactured today, but with the advent of synthetic chemicals the number of chemicals in use has climbed to over 100,000. A random blood test of Americans will show measurable amounts of easily 200 chemicals that did not exist a century ago.[34]

Most of these new chemicals have not been tested for toxicity. Those that are known to be toxic are included in a list of nearly 650 chemicals whose discharge by industry into the environment must be reported to the EPA. The Toxics Release Inventory (TRI), now accessible on the Internet, provides information on a community-by-community basis, arming local groups with data needed to evaluate the potential threats to their health and that of the environment. Since the TRI was inaugurated in 1988, reported toxic chemical emissions have declined dramatically.[35]

Throwaway Economy in Trouble

Another distinctly unhealthy trend is the swelling flow of garbage associated with a throwaway economy. Throwaway products were first conceived following World War II as a convenience and as a way of creating jobs and sustaining economic growth. The more goods produced and discarded, the reasoning went, the more jobs there would be.

What sold throwaways was their convenience. For example, rather than washing cloth towels or napkins, consumers welcomed disposable paper versions. Thus we have substituted facial tissues for handkerchiefs, disposable paper towels for hand towels, disposable table napkins for cloth ones, and throwaway beverage containers for refillable ones. Even the shopping bags we use to carry home throwaway products become part of the garbage flow.

The throwaway economy is on a collision course with the earth's geological limits. Aside from running out of landfills near cities, the world is also fast running out of the cheap oil that is used to manufacture and transport throwaway products. Perhaps more fundamentally, there is not enough readily accessible lead, tin, copper, iron ore, or bauxite to sustain the throwaway economy beyond another generation or two. Assuming an annual 2-percent growth in extraction, U.S. Geological Survey data on economically recoverable reserves show the world has 17 years of reserves remaining for lead, 19 years for tin, 25 years for copper, 54 years for iron ore, and 68 years for bauxite.[36]

The cost of hauling garbage from cities is rising as nearby landfills fill up and the price of oil climbs. One of the first major cities to exhaust its locally available landfills was New York. When the Fresh Kills landfill, the local destination for New York's garbage, was permanently closed in March 2001, the city found itself hauling garbage to landfill sites in New Jersey, Pennsylvania, and even Virginia—with some of the sites being 300 miles away.[37]

Given the 12,000 tons of garbage produced each day in New York and assuming a load of 20 tons of garbage for each of the tractor-trailers used for the long-distance hauling, some 600 rigs are needed to move garbage from New York City daily. These tractor-trailers form a convoy nearly nine miles long—impeding traffic, polluting the air, and raising carbon emissions. This daily convoy led Deputy Mayor Joseph J. Lhota, who supervised the Fresh Kills shutdown, to observe that getting rid of the city's trash is now "like a military-style operation on a daily basis."[38]

Fiscally strapped local communities in other states are willing to take New York's garbage—if they are paid enough. Some see it as an economic bonanza. State governments, however, are saddled with increased road maintenance costs, traffic congestion, increased air pollution, potential water pollution from landfill leakage, and complaints from nearby communities.

In 2001 Virginia's Governor Jim Gilmore wrote to Mayor Rudy Giuliani to complain about the use of Virginia for New York City's trash. "I understand the problem New York faces," he noted, "but the home state of Washington, Jefferson and Madison has no intention of becoming New York's dumping ground."[39]

Garbage travails are not limited to New York City. Toronto, Canada's largest city, closed its last remaining landfill on December 31, 2002, and now ships all its 750-thousand-ton-per-year garbage to Wayne County, Michigan. Ironically, the state of New Jersey, a recipient of New York's waste, is now shipping up to 1,000 tons of demolition debris 600 miles each day—also to Wayne County in Michigan.[40]

In Athens, the capital of ancient and modern Greece, the one landfill available reached saturation at the end of 2006. With local governments in Greece unwilling to accept Athens's garbage, the city's daily output of 6,000 tons began accumulating on the streets, creating a garbage crisis. The country is finally beginning to pay attention to what European Union environment commissioner Stavros Dimas, himself a Greek, calls the waste hierarchy, where priority is given first to the prevention of waste and then to its reuse, recycling, and recovery.[41]

One of the more recent garbage crises is unfolding in China, where, like everything else in the country, the amount of garbage generated is growing fast. Xinhua, a Chinese wire service, reports that a survey using an airborne remote sensor detected 7,000 garbage dumps, each larger than 50 square meters in the suburbs of Beijing, Tianjin, Shanghai, and Chongqing. A large share of China's garbage is recycled, burned, or composted, but an even larger share is dumped in landfills (where they are available) or simply heaped up in unoccupied areas.[42]

The challenge is to replace the throwaway economy with a reduce-reuse-recycle economy. Officials should worry less about what to do with garbage and think more about how to avoid producing it in the first place.

Population and Resource Conflicts

As land and water become scarce, competition for these vital resources intensifies within societies, particularly between the wealthy and those who are poor and dispossessed. The shrinkage of life-supporting resources per person that comes with population growth is threatening to drop the living standards of millions of people below the survival level, leading to potentially unmanageable social tensions.[43]

Access to land is a prime source of social tension. Expanding world population has cut the grainland per person in half, from 0.23 hectares in 1950 to 0.10 hectares in 2007. One tenth of a hectare is half of a building lot in an affluent U.S. suburb. This ongoing shrinkage of grainland per person makes it difficult for the world's farmers to feed the 70 million people added to world population each year.[44]

The shrinkage in cropland per person not only threatens livelihoods; in largely subsistence societies, it threatens survival itself. Tensions within communities begin to build as landholdings shrink below that needed for survival.

The Sahelian zone of Africa, with one of the world's fastest-growing populations, is an area of spreading conflict. In troubled Sudan, 2 million people have died and over 4 million have been displaced in the long-standing conflict of more than 20 years between the Muslim north and the Christian south. The more recent conflict in the Darfur region in western Sudan that began in 2003 illustrates the mounting tensions between two Muslim groups—camel herders and subsistence farmers. Government troops are backing Arab militias, who are engaging in the wholesale slaughter of black Sudanese in an effort to drive them off their land, sending them into refugee camps in neighboring Chad. To date, some 200,000 people have been killed in the conflict and another 250,000 have died of hunger and disease in the refugee camps.[45]

The story of Darfur is that of the Sahel, the semiarid region of grassland and dryland farming that stretches across Africa from Senegal in the west to Somalia in the east. In the northern Sahel, grassland is turning to desert, forcing herders southward into the farming areas. Declining rainfall and overgrazing are combining to destroy the grasslands.

Well before the rainfall decline the seeds for the conflict were being sown as Sudan's population climbed from 9 million in 1950 to 39 million in 2007, more than a fourfold rise. Meanwhile, the cattle population increased from fewer than 7 million to 40 million, an increase of nearly sixfold. The number of sheep and goats together increased from fewer than 14 million to 113 million, an eightfold increase. No grasslands can survive such rapid continuous growth in livestock populations.[46]

In Nigeria, where 148 million people are crammed into an area not much larger than Texas, overgrazing and overplowing are converting grassland and cropland into desert, putting farmers and herders in a war for survival. As Somini Sengupta reported in the *New York Times* in June 2004, "in recent years, as the desert has spread, trees have been felled and the populations of both herders and farmers have soared, the competition for land has only intensified."[47]

Unfortunately, the division between herders and farmers is also often the division between Muslims and Christians. The competition for land, amplified by religious differences and combined with a large number of frustrated young men with guns, has created what the *New York Times* described as a "combustible mix" that has "fueled a recent orgy of violence across this fertile central Nigerian state [Plateau]. Churches and mosques were razed. Neighbor turned against neighbor. Reprisal attacks spread until finally, in mid-May [2004], the government imposed emergency rule."[48]

Similar divisions exist between herders and farmers in northern Mali, the *New York Times* noted, where "swords and sticks have been chucked for Kalashnikovs, as desertification and population growth have stiffened the competition between the largely black African farmers and the ethnic Tuareg and Fulani herders. Tempers are raw on both sides. The dispute, after all, is over livelihood and even more, about a way of life."[49]

Rwanda has become a classic case study in how mounting population pressure can translate into political tension, conflict, and social tragedy. James Gasana, who was Rwanda's Minister of Agriculture and Environment in 1990–92, offers some insights. As the chair of a national agricultural commission in 1990, he had warned that without "profound transformations in its agriculture, [Rwanda] will not be capable of feeding adequately its population under the present growth rate." Although the country's demographers projected major future gains in population, Gasana said in 1990 that he did not see how Rwanda would reach 10 million inhabitants without social disorder "unless important progress in agriculture, as well as other sectors of the economy, were achieved."[50]

Gasana's warning of possible social disorder was prophetic. He further described how siblings inherited land from their parents and how, with an average of seven children per family, plots that were already small were fragmented further. Many farmers tried to find new land, moving onto steeply sloping mountains. By 1989, almost half of Rwanda's cultivated land was on slopes of 10 to 35 degrees, land that is universally considered uncultivable.[51]

In 1950, Rwanda's population was 2.4 million. By 1993, it had tripled to 7.5 million, making it the most densely populated country in Africa. As population grew, so did the demand for firewood. By 1991, the demand was more than double the sustainable yield of local forests. As trees disappeared, straw and other crop residues were used for cooking fuel. With less organic matter in the soil, land fertility declined.[52]

As the health of the land deteriorated, so did that of the people dependent on it. Eventually there was simply not enough food to go around. A quiet desperation developed. Like a drought-afflicted countryside, it could be ignited with a single match. That ignition came with the crash of a plane on April 6, 1994, shot down as it approached the capital Kigali, killing President Juvenal Habyarimana. The crash unleashed an organized attack by Hutus, leading to an estimated 800,000 deaths of Tutsis and moderate Hutus in 100 days. In some villages, whole families were slaughtered lest there be survivors to claim the family plot of land.[53]

Many other African countries, largely rural in nature, are on a demographic track similar to Rwanda's. Tanzania's population of 40 million in 2007 is projected to increase to 85 million by 2050. Eritrea, where the average family has six children, is projected to grow from 5 million to 11 million by 2050. In the

Democratic Republic of the Congo, the population is projected to triple, going from 63 million to 187 million.[54]

Africa is not alone. In India, tension between Hindus and Muslims is never far below the surface. As each successive generation further subdivides already small plots, pressure on the land is intense. The pressure on water resources is even greater.

With India's population projected to grow from 1.2 billion in 2007 to 1.7 billion in 2050, a collision between rising human numbers and shrinking water supplies seems inevitable. The risk is that India could face social conflicts that would dwarf those in Rwanda. As Gasana notes, the relationship between population and natural systems is a national security issue, one that can spawn conflicts along geographic, tribal, ethnic, or religious lines.[55]

Disagreements over the allocation of water among countries that share river systems is a common source of international political conflict, especially where populations are outgrowing the flow of the river. Nowhere is this potential conflict more stark than among Egypt, Sudan, and Ethiopia in the Nile River valley. Agriculture in Egypt, where it rarely rains, is wholly dependent on water from the Nile. Egypt now gets the lion's share of the Nile's water, but its current population of 75 million is projected to reach 121 million by 2050, thus greatly expanding the demand for grain and water. Sudan, whose 39 million people also depend heavily on food produced with Nile water, is expected to have 73 million by 2050. And the number of Ethiopians, in the country that controls 85 percent of the river's headwaters, is projected to expand from 83 million to 183 million.[56]

Since there is already little water left in the Nile when it reaches the Mediterranean, if either Sudan or Ethiopia takes more water, then Egypt will get less, making it increasingly difficult to feed an additional 46 million people. Although there is an existing water rights agreement among the three countries, Ethiopia receives only a minuscule share of water. Given its aspirations for a better life, and with the headwaters of the Nile being one of its few natural resources, Ethiopia will undoubtedly want to take more.[57]

To the north, Turkey, Syria, and Iraq share the waters of the Tigris and Euphrates river system. Turkey, controlling the headwaters, is developing a massive project on the Tigris to increase the water used for irrigation and power. Syria and Iraq, which are both projected to nearly double their respective populations of 20 million and 29 million, are concerned because they too will need more water.[58]

In the Aral Sea basin in Central Asia, there is an uneasy arrangement among five countries over the sharing of the two rivers, the Amu Darya and the Syr Darya, that drain into the sea. The demand for water in Kazakhstan, Kyrgyzstan, Tajikistan, Turkmenistan, and Uzbekistan already exceeds the flow of the two rivers by 25 percent. Turkmenistan, which is upstream on the Amu Darya, is planning to develop another half-million hectares of irrigated agriculture. Racked by insurgencies, the region lacks the cooperation needed to manage its scarce water resources. On top of this, Afghanistan, which controls the headwaters of the Amu Darya, plans to use some of the water for its development. Geographer Sarah O'Hara of the University of Nottingham, who studies the region's water problems, says, "We talk about the developing world and the developed world, but this is the deteriorating world."[59]

Environmental Refugees on the Rise

Desert expansion in sub-Saharan Africa, principally in the Sahelian countries, is displacing millions of people—forcing them to either move southward or migrate to North Africa. A 2006 U.N. conference on desertification in Tunisia projected that by 2020 up to 60 million people could migrate from sub-Saharan Africa to North Africa and Europe. This flow of migrants has been under way for many years.[60]

In mid-October 2003, Italian authorities discovered a boat bound for Italy carrying refugees from Africa. After being adrift for more than two weeks and having run out of fuel, food, and water, many of the passengers had died. At first the dead were tossed overboard. But after a point, the remaining survivors lacked the strength to hoist the bodies over the side. The dead and the living shared the boat, resembling what a rescuer described as "a scene from Dante's Inferno."[61]

The refugees were believed to be Somalis who had embarked from Libya, but the survivors would not reveal their country of origin, lest they be sent home. We do not know whether they were political, economic, or environmental refugees. Failed states like Somalia produce all three. We do know that Somalia is an ecological basket case, with overpopulation, overgrazing, and the resulting desertification destroying its pastoral economy.[62]

On April 30, 2006, a man fishing off the coast of Barbados discovered a 20-foot boat adrift with the bodies of 11 young men on board, bodies that were "virtually mummified" by the sun and salty ocean spray. As the end drew near, one passenger left a note tucked between two bodies: "I would like to send my family in Basada [Senegal] a sum of money. Please excuse me and goodbye." The author of the note was apparently one of a group of 52 who had left Senegal on Christmas Eve aboard a boat destined for the Canary Islands, a jumping off point for Europe. They apparently drifted for some 2,000 miles, ending their trip in the Caribbean. This boat was not unique. During the first weekend of September 2006, police intercepted boats from Mauritania, with a record total of nearly 1,200 people on board.[63]

For Central American countries, including Honduras, Guatemala, Nicaragua, and El Salvador, Mexico is often the gateway to the United States. In 2006, Mexican immigration authorities reported some 240,000 detentions and deportations, up 74 percent since 2002.[64]

In the city of Tapachula on the Guatemala-Mexico border, young men in search of jobs wait along the tracks for a slow-moving freight train moving through the city en route to the north. Some make it onto the train. Others do not. The Jesús el Buen Pastor refuge is home to 25 amputees who lost their grip and fell under the train while trying to board. For these young men, says Olga Sánchez Martínez, the director of the refuge, this is the "end of their American dream." A local priest, Flor María Rigoni, calls the migrants attempting to board the trains "the kamikazes of poverty."[65]

Today, bodies washing ashore in Italy, Spain, and Turkey are a daily occurrence, the result of desperate acts by desperate people. And each day Mexicans risk their lives in the Arizona desert trying to reach jobs in the United States. Some 400–600 Mexicans leave rural areas every day, abandoning plots of land too small or too eroded to make a living. They either head for Mexican cities or try to cross illegally into the United States. Many of those who try to cross the Arizona desert perish in its punishing heat; scores of bodies are found along the Arizona border each year.[66]

With the vast majority of the 3 billion people to be added to the world by 2050 coming in countries where water tables are already falling, water refugees are likely to become commonplace. They will be most common in arid and semiarid regions where populations are outgrowing the water supply and sinking into hydrological poverty. Villages in northwestern India are being abandoned as aquifers are depleted and people can no longer find water. Millions of villagers in northern and western China and in parts of Mexico may have to move because of a lack of water.[67]

Advancing deserts are also displacing people, squeezing expanding populations into an ever smaller geographic area. Whereas the U.S. Dust Bowl displaced 3 million people, the advancing desert in China's dust bowl provinces could displace tens of millions.[68]

In Iran, villages abandoned because of spreading deserts or a lack of water already number in the thousands. In the vicinity of Damavand, a small town within an hour's drive of Tehran, 88 villages have been abandoned. And as the desert takes over in Nigeria, farmers and herders are forced to move, squeezed into a shrinking area of productive land. Desertification refugees typically end up in cities, many in squatter settlements. Many migrate abroad.[69]

Another new source of refugees, potentially a huge one, is rising seas. The refugee flows from falling water tables and expanding deserts are already under way. Those from rising seas are just beginning, but the numbers could eventually reach the hundreds of millions, offering yet another reason for stabilizing climate and population.

Mounting Stresses, Failing States

After a half-century of forming new states from former colonies and from the breakup of the Soviet Union, the international community is today focusing on the disintegration of states. Failing states are now an integral part of the international political landscape. As the Fund for Peace and the Carnegie Endowment for International Peace observe, "Failed states have made a remarkable odyssey from the periphery to the very center of global politics."[70]

As noted in Chapter 1, these groups have together identified a list of 60 states, ranking them according to "their vulnerability to violent internal conflict and societal deterioration." This analysis, published in *Foreign Policy*, is based on 12 social, economic, political, and military indicators. It puts Sudan at the top of the list of failed states, followed by Iraq, Somalia, Zimbabwe, and Chad. Three oil-exporting countries are among the top 20 failing states—Sudan, Iraq, and Nigeria. Indonesia and Iran are farther down the list. Pakistan, now ranking number 12 on the list, is the only failing state with a nuclear arsenal.[71]

Three of the dozen indicators used in constructing the *Foreign Policy* scorecard are uneven development, the loss of governmental legitimacy, and demographic pressure. Uneven development typically means that a small segment of the population is accumulating wealth while much of the society may be suffering a decline in living conditions. This unevenness, often associated with political corruption, creates unrest and can lead to civil conflict.[72]

Governments that fail to effectively manage emerging issues and provide basic services are seen as useless. This often causes segments of the population to shift their allegiance to warlords, tribal chieftains, or religious leaders. A loss of political legitimacy is an early sign of state decline.

A third indicator is demographic pressure. In many countries that have experienced rapid population growth for several decades, governments are suffering from demographic fatigue, unable to cope with the steady shrinkage in cropland and fresh water supplies per person or to build schools fast enough for the swelling ranks of children.[73]

Sudan, which heads the 2007 list of failing states, is a classic case of a country caught in the demographic trap, a situation where it has developed far enough economically and socially to reduce mortality, but not far enough to quickly reduce fertility. As a result, women on average have five children, well beyond the two needed for replacement, and the population of 39 million is growing by 2,400 per day. Under this pressure, Sudan— like scores of other countries—is breaking down.[74]

All but two of the 20 countries (Zimbabwe and North

Korea) at the top of the list of failing states are caught in this demographic trap. They probably cannot break out of this trap on their own. They will need outside help or the political situation will simply continue to deteriorate.[75]

Foreign investment drying up and a resultant rise in unemployment are also part of the decline syndrome. An earlier study by Population Action International showed that one of the key indicators of political instability in a society is the number of unemployed young men, a number that is high in countries at the top of the *Foreign Policy* list.[76]

Another characteristic of failing states is a deterioration of the physical infrastructure—roads and power, water, and sewage systems. Care for natural systems is also neglected as people struggle to survive. Forests, grasslands, and croplands deteriorate, creating a downward economic spiral.

Among the most conspicuous indications of state failure is a breakdown in law and order and a related loss of personal security. In Haiti, armed gangs rule the streets. Kidnapping for ransom of local people who are lucky enough to be among the 30 percent of the labor force that is employed is commonplace. In Afghanistan it is the local warlords, not the central government, that control the country outside of Kabul. Somalia, which now exists only on maps, is ruled by tribal leaders, each claiming a piece of what was once a country.[77]

Some of these countries are involved in long-standing civil conflicts. The Democratic Republic of the Congo, occupying a large part of the Congo River basin in the heart of Africa, was the site of civil war from 1998 to 2003 and has since suffered from numerous outbreaks of violence. This ongoing conflict has claimed nearly 4 million lives and driven millions more from their homes. According to the International Rescue Committee, the vast majority of deaths are nonviolent, including those from hunger, respiratory illnesses, diarrhea, and other diseases.[78]

Failing states are of growing international concern because they are a source of terrorists, drugs, weapons, and refugees. Not only was Afghanistan a training ground for terrorists, but it quickly became, under the Allied occupation, the world's leading supplier of heroin. Now Iraq, number two on the 2007 failing states list, is number one on the terrorist training list. Refugees from Rwanda, including thousands of armed soldiers, contributed to the destabilization of the Congo. As *The Econo-mist* noted in December 2004, "like a severely disturbed indi-vidual, a failed state is a danger not just to itself, but to those around it and beyond."[79]

In many countries, the United Nations or other internation-ally organized peacekeeping forces are trying to keep the peace, often unsuccessfully. Among the countries with U.N. peace-keeping forces are the Democratic Republic of the Congo, Liberia, and Sierra Leone. Other countries with multinational peacekeeping forces include Afghanistan, Haiti, and Sudan. All too often these are token forces, not nearly large enough to ensure stability.[80]

Countries like Haiti and Afghanistan are surviving today because they are on international life-support systems. Eco-nomic assistance—including, it is worth noting, food aid—is helping to sustain them. But there is now not enough assistance to overcome the reinforcing trends of deterioration and replace them with state stability and sustained economic progress.[81]

In an age of increasing globalization and economic integra-tion, the functioning of the global system and thus the well-being of individual states depends on a cooperative network of functioning nation states. When governments lose their capaci-ty to govern they can no longer collect taxes, much less pay off international debts. More failing states means more bad debt. Efforts to control international terrorism depend on coopera-tion among functioning nation states, and these efforts weaken as states fail.

Protecting endangered species almost always requires close international cooperation too. In countries such as the Democ-ratic Republic of the Congo, where government agencies have collapsed, hunger is widespread, and chaos reigns, the popula-tion of lowland mountain gorillas has dropped precipitously. This story is being repeated over and over in Africa, where so much of the world's remaining large mammal species are con-centrated.[82]

Or consider the international network that controls the spread of infectious diseases, such as avian flu, SARS, and polio, or of diseases that affect animals, such as mad cow and hoof-and-mouth disease. In 1988 the international community launched an effort to eradicate polio, an effort patterned after the highly successful one that eliminated smallpox. The goal was to get rid of the dreaded disease that used to paralyze an average of 1,000 children each day. By 2003 the disease had been eradicated in all but a few countries, among them Afghanistan, India, Nigeria, and Pakistan.[83]

In 2003, religious leaders in northern Nigeria began to oppose the vaccination program on the grounds that it was a plot to spread AIDS and sterility. As a result, the number of cases of polio in Nigeria increased rapidly, tripling over the next three years. Meanwhile, Nigerian Muslims making their annual pilgrimage to Mecca may have spread the disease, bringing it back to some countries, such as Indonesia, Chad, and Somalia, that were already polio-free. In response, Saudi officials imposed a polio vaccination requirement on all younger visitors from countries with reported cases of polio.[84]

As of late 2007 the disease is still endemic in Afghanistan, Nigeria, India, and Pakistan, with cases still being reported in a total of 10 countries. With infection reoccurring in failing states, the goal of a world that is polio-free, already reached in some 190 countries, could be slipping away. If the international community cannot effectively address the failing state phenomena, the prospect of reaching other goals could also fade.[85]

II

THE RESPONSE—PLAN B

7

Eradicating Poverty, Stabilizing Population

The new century began on an inspiring note when the countries that belong to the United Nations adopted the goal of cutting the number of people living in poverty in half by 2015. And as of 2007 the world looked to be on track to meet this goal. There are two big reasons for this: China and India. China's annual economic growth of nearly 10 percent over the last two decades, along with India's more recent acceleration to 7 percent a year, have together lifted millions out of poverty.[1]

The number of people living in poverty in China dropped from 648 million in 1981 to 218 million in 2001, the greatest reduction in poverty in history. India is also making impressive economic progress. Under the dynamic leadership of Prime Minister Manmohan Singh, who took office in 2004, poverty is being attacked directly by upgrading infrastructure at the village level. Targeted investments are aimed at the poorest of the poor.[2]

If the international community actively reinforces this effort in reform-minded India, hundreds of millions more could be lifted out of poverty. With India now on the move economically, the world can begin to concentrate intensively on the remaining poverty concentrated in sub-Saharan Africa and in scores of smaller countries in Latin America and Central Asia.

Several countries in Southeast Asia are making impressive gains as well, including Thailand, Viet Nam, and Indonesia. Barring any major economic setbacks, these gains in Asia virtually ensure that the U.N. Millennium Development Goal (MDG) for halving poverty by 2015 will be reached. Indeed, in a 2007 assessment of progress in reaching the MDGs, the World Bank reported that all regions of the developing world, with the notable exception of sub-Saharan Africa, were on track to cut the number living in poverty in half by 2015.[3]

Sub-Saharan Africa—with 800 million people—is sliding deeper into poverty. Hunger, illiteracy, and disease are on the march, partly offsetting the gains in China and India. Africa needs special attention. The failing states as a group are also backsliding; an interregional tally of the Bank's fragile states is not encouraging, since extreme poverty in these countries is over 50 percent—higher than in 1990.[4]

In addition to halving the number of people living in poverty by 2015, other MDGs include reducing the ranks of those who are hungry by half, achieving universal primary school education, halving the number of people without access to safe drinking water, and reversing the spread of infectious diseases, especially HIV and malaria. Closely related to these are the goals of reducing maternal mortality by three fourths and under-five child mortality by two thirds.[5]

While goals for cutting poverty in half by 2015 appear to be on schedule, those for halving the number of hungry are not. Indeed, the long-term decline in the number of those who are hungry and malnourished has been reversed. The number of children with a primary school education appears to be increasing substantially, however, largely on the strength of progress in India.[6]

When the United Nations set the MDGs, it unaccountably omitted any population or family planning goals. In response to this, the U.K. All Party Parliamentary Group on Population Development and Reproductive Health chaired by M.P. Christine McCafferty convened hearings of international experts to consider this omission. In a January 2007 report of the findings, M.P. Richard Ottaway concluded that "the MDGs are difficult or impossible to achieve with current levels of population growth in the least developed countries and regions."[7]

Summarizing the report's findings in an article in *Science*, Martha Campbell and colleagues explained the need for "a substantial increase for support in national family planning, particularly for the 2 billion people currently living on less than $2 per day." Although it came belatedly, the United Nations has since approved a new target that calls for universal access to reproductive health care by 2015.[8]

Countries everywhere have little choice but to strive for an average of two children per couple. There is no feasible alternative. Any population that increases or decreases continually over the long term is not sustainable.

In an increasingly integrated world with a growing number of failing states, eradicating poverty and stabilizing population have become national security issues. Slowing population growth helps eradicate poverty and its distressing symptoms, and, conversely, eradicating poverty helps slow population growth. With time running out, the urgency of moving simultaneously on both fronts is clear.

Universal Basic Education

One way of narrowing the gap between rich and poor segments of society is by ensuring universal education. This means making sure that the 72 million children not enrolled in school are able to attend. Children without any formal education are starting life with a severe handicap, one that almost ensures they will remain in abject poverty and that the gap between the poor and the rich will continue to widen. In an increasingly integrated world, this widening gap itself becomes a source of instability. Nobel Prize–winning economist Amartya Sen focuses the point: "Illiteracy and innumeracy are a greater threat to humanity than terrorism."[9]

In the effort to achieve universal primary education, the World Bank has taken the lead with its Education for All plan, where any country with a well-designed plan to achieve universal primary education is eligible for Bank financial support. The three principal requirements are that a country submit a sensible plan to reach universal basic education, commit a meaningful share of its own resources to the plan, and have transparent budgeting and accounting practices. If fully implemented, all children in poor countries would get a primary school education by 2015, helping them to break out of poverty.[10]

Some progress toward this goal has been made. In 2000, some 78 percent of children were completing primary school, while by 2005 this figure reached 83 percent. Gains have been strong but uneven, leaving the World Bank to conclude that only 95 of the 152 developing countries for which data are available will reach the goal of universal primary school education by 2015.[11]

Poverty is largely inherited. The overwhelming majority of those living in poverty today are the children of people who lived in poverty. The key to breaking out of the culture of poverty is education—particularly the education of girls. As female educational levels rise, fertility falls. And mothers with at least five years of school lose fewer infants during childbirth or to early illnesses than their less educated peers do. Economist Gene Sperling concluded in a 2001 study of 72 countries that "the expansion of female secondary education may be the single best lever for achieving substantial reductions in fertility."[12]

Basic education tends to increase agricultural productivity. Agricultural extension services that can use printed materials to disseminate information have an obvious advantage. So too do farmers who can read the instructions on a bag of fertilizer. The ability to read instructions on a pesticide container can be life-saving.

At a time when HIV is spreading, schools provide the institutional means to educate young people about the risks of infection. The time to inform and educate children about the virus and about the lifestyles that foster its spread is when they are young, not when they are already infected. Young people can also be mobilized to conduct educational campaigns among their peers.

One great need in developing countries, particularly those where the ranks of teachers are being decimated by AIDS, is more teacher training. Providing scholarships for promising students from poor families to attend training institutes in exchange for a commitment to teach for, say, five years, could be a highly profitable investment. It would help ensure that the teaching resources are available to reach universal primary education, and it would also foster an upwelling of talent from the poorest segments of society.

Gene Sperling believes that every plan should provide for getting to the hardest-to-reach segments of society, especially poor girls in rural areas. He notes that Ethiopia has pioneered this with Girls Advisory Committees. Representatives of these groups go to the parents who are seeking early marriage for their daughters and encourage them to keep their girls in school. Some countries, Brazil and Bangladesh among them, actually provide small scholarships for girls or stipends to their parents where needed, thus helping those from poor families get a basic education.[13]

As the world becomes ever more integrated economically, its nearly 800 million illiterate adults are severely handicapped. This deficit can best be overcome by launching adult literacy programs, relying heavily on volunteers. The international community could offer seed money to provide educational materials and outside advisors where needed. Bangladesh and Iran, both of which have successful adult literacy programs, can serve as models.[14]

An estimated $10 billion in external funding, beyond what is being spent today, is needed for the world to achieve universal primary education. At a time when education gives children access not only to books but also to personal computers and the Internet, having children who never go to school is no longer acceptable.[15]

Few incentives to get children in school are as effective as a school lunch program, especially in the poorest countries. Since 1946, every American child in public school has had access to a school lunch program, ensuring at least one good meal each day. There is no denying the benefits of this national program.[16]

Children who are ill or hungry miss many days of school. And even when they can attend, they do not learn as well. Jeffrey Sachs of the Earth Institute at Columbia University notes, "Sick children often face a lifetime of diminished productivity because of interruptions in schooling together with cognitive and physical impairment." But when school lunch programs are launched in low-income countries, school enrollment jumps, the children's academic performance goes up, and children spend more years in school.[17]

Girls benefit especially. Drawn to school by the lunch, they stay in school longer, marry later, and have fewer children. This is a win-win-win situation. Launching school lunch programs in the 44 lowest-income countries would cost an estimated $6 billion per year beyond what the United Nations is now spending to reduce hunger.[18]

Greater efforts are also needed to improve nutrition before children even get to school age, so they can benefit from school lunches later. Former Senator George McGovern notes that "a women, infants and children (WIC) program, which offers nutritious food supplements to needy pregnant and nursing mothers," should also be available in the poor countries. Based on 33 years of experience, it is clear that the U.S. WIC program has been enormously successful in improving nutrition, health, and the development of preschool children from low-income families. If this were expanded to reach pregnant women, nursing mothers, and small children in the 44 poorest countries, it would help eradicate hunger among millions of small children at a time when it could make a huge difference.[19]

These efforts, though costly, are not expensive compared with the annual losses in productivity from hunger. McGovern thinks that this initiative can help "dry up the swamplands of hunger and despair that serve as potential recruiting grounds for terrorists." In a world where vast wealth is accumulating among the rich, it makes little sense for children to go to school hungry.[20]

Stabilizing Population

Some 43 countries now have populations that are either essentially stable or declining slowly. In countries with the lowest fertility rates, including Japan, Russia, Germany, and Italy, populations will likely decline somewhat over the next half-century.[21]

A larger group of countries has reduced fertility to the replacement level or just below. They are headed for population stability after large numbers of young people move through their reproductive years. Included in this group are China and the United States. A third group of countries is projected to more than double their populations by 2050, including Ethiopia, the Democratic Republic of the Congo, and Uganda.[22]

U.N. projections show world population growth under three different assumptions about fertility levels. The medium projection, the one most commonly used, has world population reaching 9.2 billion by 2050. The high one reaches 10.8 billion. The low projection, which assumes that the world will quickly move below replacement-level fertility to 1.6 children per couple, has population peaking at just under 8 billion in 2041 and then declining. If the goal is to eradicate poverty, hunger, and illiteracy, we have little choice but to strive for the lower projection.[23]

Slowing world population growth means that all women who want to plan their families should have access to the family planning services they need. Unfortunately, at present 201 million couples cannot obtain the services they need. Former U.S. Agency for International Development official J. Joseph Speidel notes that "if you ask anthropologists who live and work with poor people at the village level...they often say that women live in fear of their next pregnancy. They just do not want to get pregnant." Filling the family planning gap may be the most urgent item on the global agenda. The benefits are enormous and the costs are minimal.[24]

The good news is that countries that want to help couples reduce family size can do so quickly. My colleague Janet Larsen writes that in just one decade Iran dropped its near-record population growth rate to one of the lowest in the developing world. When Ayatollah Khomeini assumed leadership in Iran in 1979, he immediately dismantled the well-established family planning programs and instead advocated large families. At war with Iraq between 1980 and 1988, Khomeini wanted large families to increase the ranks of soldiers for Islam. His goal was an army of 20 million. In response to his pleas, fertility levels climbed, pushing Iran's annual population growth to a peak of 4.2 percent in the early 1980s, a level approaching the biological maximum. As this enormous growth began to burden the economy and the environment, the country's leaders realized that overcrowding, environmental degradation, and unemployment were undermining Iran's future.[25]

In 1989 the government did an about-face and restored its family planning program. In May 1993, a national family planning law was passed. The resources of several government ministries, including education, culture, and health, were mobilized to encourage smaller families. Iran Broadcasting was given responsibility for raising awareness of population issues and of the availability of family planning services. Some 15,000 "health houses" or clinics were established to provide rural populations with health and family planning services.[26]

Religious leaders were directly involved in what amounted to a crusade for smaller families. Iran introduced a full panoply of contraceptive measures, including the option of male sterilization—a first among Muslim countries. All forms of birth control, including contraceptives such as the pill and sterilization, were free of charge. In fact, Iran became a pioneer—the only country to require couples to take a class on modern contraception before receiving a marriage license.[27]

In addition to the direct health care interventions, a broad-based effort was launched to raise female literacy, boosting it from 25 percent in 1970 to more than 70 percent in 2000. Female school enrollment increased from 60 to 90 percent. Television was used to disseminate information on family planning throughout the country, taking advantage of the 70 percent of rural households with TV sets. As a result of this initiative, family size in Iran dropped from seven children to fewer than three. From 1987 to 1994, Iran cut its population growth rate by half. Its overall population growth rate of 1.3 percent in 2006 is only slightly higher than the U.S. growth rate.[28]

While the attention of researchers has focused on the role of formal education in reducing fertility, soap operas on radio and television can even more quickly change people's attitudes about reproductive health, gender equity, family size, and environmental protection. A well-written soap opera can have a profound short-term effect on population growth. It costs relatively little and can proceed even while formal educational systems are being expanded.

The power of this approach was pioneered by Miguel Sabido, a vice president of Televisa, Mexico's national television network, when he did a series of soap opera segments on illiteracy. The day after one of the characters in his soap opera visited a literacy office wanting to learn how to read and write, a quarter-million people showed up at these offices in Mexico City. Eventually 840,000 Mexicans enrolled in literacy courses after watching the series.[29]

Sabido dealt with contraception in a soap opera entitled Acompáñeme, which translates as *Come With Me*. Over the span of a decade this drama series helped reduce Mexico's birth rate by 34 percent.[30]

Other groups outside Mexico quickly picked up this

approach. The U.S.-based Population Media Center (PMC), headed by William Ryerson, has initiated projects in some 15 countries and is planning launches in several others. The PMC's work in Ethiopia over the last several years provides a telling example. Their radio serial dramas broadcast in Amharic and Oromiffa have addressed issues of reproductive health and gender equity, such as HIV/AIDS, family planning, and the education of girls. A survey two years after the broadcasts began in 2002 found that 63 percent of new clients seeking reproductive health care at Ethiopia's 48 service centers reported listening to one of PMC's dramas.[31]

Among married women in the Amhara region who listened to the dramas, there was a 55-percent increase in those who had used family planning methods. Male listeners sought HIV tests at a rate four times that of non-listeners, while female listeners were tested at three times the rate of female non-listeners. The average number of children born per woman dropped from 5.4 to 4.3. And demand for contraceptives increased 157 percent.[32]

The costs of providing reproductive health and family planning services are small compared with their benefits. Joseph Speidel estimates that expanding these services to reach all women in the developing countries would take close to $17 billion in additional funding from both industrial and developing countries.[33]

The United Nations estimates that meeting the needs of the 201 million women who do not have access to effective contraception could each year prevent 52 million unwanted pregnancies, 22 million induced abortions, and 1.4 million infant deaths. Put simply, the costs to society of not filling the family planning gap may be greater than we can afford.[34]

Shifting to smaller families brings generous economic dividends. For Bangladesh, analysts concluded that $62 spent by the government to prevent an unwanted birth saved $615 in expenditures on other social services. Investing in reproductive health and family planning services leaves more fiscal resources per child for education and health care, thus accelerating the escape from poverty. For donor countries, filling the entire $7.9 billion gap needed to ensure that couples everywhere have access to the services they need would yield strong social returns in improved education and health care.[35]

Better Health for All

While heart disease and cancer (largely the diseases of aging), obesity, and smoking dominate health concerns in industrial countries, in developing countries infectious diseases are the overriding health concern. Besides AIDS, the principal diseases of concern are diarrhea, respiratory illnesses, tuberculosis, malaria, and measles. Child mortality is high.

Progress in reaching the MDG of reducing child mortality two thirds by 2015 is lagging badly. As of 2005 only 32 of 147 developing countries are on track to reach this goal. In 23 countries child mortality has either remained unchanged or risen. And only 2 of the World Bank's 35 fragile states are on track to meet this goal by 2015.[36]

Along with the eradication of hunger, ensuring access to a safe and reliable supply of water for the estimated 1.1 billion people who lack it is essential to better health for all. The realistic option in many cities now may be to bypass efforts to build costly water-based sewage removal and treatment systems and to opt instead for water-free waste disposal systems that do not disperse disease pathogens. (See the description of dry compost toilets in Chapter 10.) This switch would simultaneously help alleviate water scarcity, reduce the dissemination of disease agents in water systems, and help close the nutrient cycle—another win-win-win situation.[37]

One of the most impressive health gains has come from a campaign initiated by a little-heralded nongovernmental group in Bangladesh, BRAC, that taught every mother in the country how to prepare oral rehydration solution to treat diarrhea at home by simply adding salt and sugar to water. Founded by Fazle Hasan Abed, BRAC succeeded in dramatically reducing infant and child deaths from diarrhea in a country that was densely populated, poverty-stricken, and poorly educated.[38]

Seeing this great success, UNICEF used BRAC's model for its worldwide diarrheal disease treatment program. This global administration of a remarkably simple oral rehydration technique has been extremely effective—reducing deaths from diarrhea among children from 4.6 million in 1980 to 1.6 million in 2006. Egypt alone used oral rehydration therapy to cut infant deaths from diarrhea by 82 percent from 1982 to 1989. Few investments have saved so many lives at such a low cost.[39]

The war against infectious diseases is being waged on a broad front. Perhaps the leading privately funded life-saving activity in the world today is the childhood immunization program. In an effort to fill the gap in this global program, the Bill and Melinda Gates Foundation invested more than $1.5 billion through 2006 to protect children from infectious diseases like measles.[40]

Additional investment can help the many countries that cannot afford vaccines for childhood diseases and are falling behind in their vaccination programs. Lacking the funds to invest today, these countries pay a far higher price tomorrow. There are not many situations where just a few pennies spent per youngster can make as much difference as vaccination programs can.[41]

One of the international community's finest hours came with the eradication of smallpox, an effort led in the United Nations by the World Health Organization (WHO). This successful elimination of a feared disease, which required a worldwide immunization program, saves not only millions of lives but also hundreds of millions of dollars each year in smallpox vaccination programs and billions of dollars in health care expenditures. This achievement alone may justify the existence of the United Nations.[42]

Similarly, a WHO-led international coalition, including Rotary International, UNICEF, the U.S. Centers for Disease Control and Prevention (CDC), and Ted Turner's UN Foundation, has waged a worldwide campaign to wipe out polio, a disease that has crippled millions of children. Since 1988, Rotary International has contributed an extraordinary $600 million to this effort. Under this coalition-sponsored Global Polio Eradication Initiative, the number of polio cases worldwide dropped from some 350,000 per year in 1988 to fewer than 700 in 2003.[43]

By late 2007, only 10 countries were still reporting polio cases, including Afghanistan, India, Myanmar, Pakistan, and several countries in central Africa and the Horn of Africa. The number of cases reported worldwide dropped from roughly 2,000 in 2006 to 545 during the first nine months of 2007. A reinvigorated program in Nigeria was on the verge of eradicating polio there.[44]

For the coalition, the prospect of total eradication was within its grasp. But once again, hard-line clerics, this time in a remote region of Pakistan, began saying that the vaccination program was a U.S. conspiracy to render people infertile. Health workers have been attacked and driven from parts of Pakistan's North West Frontier Province where the polio virus still exists. Two workers have been killed. A small group of people refusing to cooperate with the initiative could prevent the eradication of this dreaded disease for all time.[45]

One of the more remarkable health success stories is the near eradication of guinea worm disease (dracunculiasis), a campaign led by former U.S. President Jimmy Carter and the Carter Center. These worms, whose larvae are ingested by drinking unfiltered water from lakes and rivers, mature in a person's body, sometimes reaching more than two feet in length, and then exit slowly through the skin in a very painful and debilitating ordeal that can last several weeks.[46]

With no vaccine to prevent infection or drug for treatment, eradication depends on filtering drinking water to prevent larvae ingestion, thus eradicating the worm, which can survive only in a human host. Six years after the CDC launched a global campaign in 1980, the Carter Center took the reins and has since led the effort with additional support from partners like WHO, UNICEF, and the Gates Foundation. The number of people infected by the worm has been reduced from 3.5 million in 1986 to 25,217 cases in 2006—an astounding drop of 99 percent. In the three countries where the worm existed outside Africa—India, Pakistan, and Yemen—eradication is complete. The remaining cases are found in a handful of countries in Africa, mainly in Sudan and Ghana.[47]

Some leading sources of premature death are lifestyle-related, such as smoking. WHO estimates that 5.4 million people died in 2005 of tobacco-related illnesses, more than from any single infectious disease. Today there are some 25 known health threats that are linked to tobacco use, including heart disease, stroke, respiratory illness, many forms of cancer, and male impotence. Cigarette smoke kills more people each year than all other air pollutants combined—more than 5 million versus 3 million.[48]

Impressive progress is being made in reducing cigarette smoking. After a century-long buildup of the tobacco habit, the world is turning away from cigarettes, led by WHO's Tobacco

Free Initiative. This gained further momentum when the Framework Convention on Tobacco Control, the first international accord to deal entirely with a health issue, was adopted unanimously in Geneva in May 2003. Among other things, the treaty calls for raising taxes on cigarettes, limiting smoking in public places, and strong health warnings on cigarette packages. In addition to WHO's initiative, the Bloomberg Global Initiative to Reduce Tobacco Use, funded by New York City Mayor Michael Bloomberg, is working to reduce smoking in lower- and middle-income countries, including China.[49]

Ironically, the country where tobacco originated is now leading the world away from it. In the United States, the average number of cigarettes smoked per person has dropped from its peak of 2,814 in 1976 to 1,225 in 2006—a decline of 56 percent. Worldwide, where the downturn lags that of the United States by roughly a dozen years, usage has dropped from the historical high of 1,027 cigarettes smoked per person in 1988 to 859 in 2004, a fall of 16 percent. Media coverage of the health effects of smoking, mandatory health warnings on cigarette packs, and sharp increases in cigarette sales taxes have all contributed to the steady decline.[50]

Indeed, smoking is on the decline in nearly all the major cigarette-smoking countries, including such strongholds as France, China, and Japan. The number of cigarettes smoked per person has dropped 20 percent in France since peaking in 1991, 5 percent in China since its peak in 1990, and 20 percent in Japan since 1992.[51]

Following approval of the Framework Convention, a number of countries took strong steps in 2004 to reduce smoking. Ireland imposed a nationwide ban on smoking in workplaces, bars, and restaurants; India banned smoking in public places; Norway and New Zealand banned smoking in bars and restaurants; and Scotland banned smoking in public buildings. Bhutan, a small Himalayan country sandwiched between India and China, has prohibited tobacco sales entirely.[52]

A number of countries have since adopted a variety of measures designed to limit smoking and exposure to smoke for nonsmokers. In 2005, smoking was banned in public places in Bangladesh, and Italy banned it in all enclosed public spaces, including bars and restaurants. More recently, England has forbidden it in workplaces and enclosed public spaces, and France is phasing in a similar ban by 2008.[53]

In the United States, which already has stiff restrictions on smoking, the Union Pacific Corporation stopped hiring smokers in seven states as an economy measure to cut health care costs. General Mills imposes a $20-a-month surcharge on health insurance premiums for employees who smoke. Each of these measures helps the market to more accurately reflect the cost of smoking.[54]

More broadly, a 2001 WHO study analyzing the economics of health care in developing countries concluded that providing the most basic health care services, the sort that could be supplied by a village-level clinic, would yield enormous economic benefits for developing countries and for the world as a whole. The authors estimate that providing basic universal health care in developing countries will require donor grants totaling $27 billion in 2007, scaled up to $38 billion in 2015, or an average of $33 billion per year. In addition to basic services, this $33 billion includes funding for the Global Fund to Fight AIDS, Tuberculosis and Malaria and for universal childhood vaccinations.[55]

Curbing the HIV Epidemic

Although progress is being made in curbing the spread of HIV, 4.3 million people were newly infected in 2006. More than 40 million have died from AIDS thus far, two thirds of them in Africa—the epicenter of the disease.[56]

The key to curbing the AIDS epidemic, which has so disrupted economic and social progress in Africa, is education about prevention. We know how the disease is transmitted; it is not a medical mystery. In Africa, where once there was a stigma associated with even mentioning the disease, governments are beginning to design effective prevention education programs. The first goal is to reduce quickly the number of new infections, dropping it below the number of deaths from the disease, thus shrinking the number of those who are capable of infecting others.

Concentrating on the groups in a society that are most likely to spread the disease is particularly effective. In Africa, infected truck drivers who travel far from home for extended periods often engage in commercial sex, spreading HIV from one country to another. Sex workers are also centrally involved in spreading the disease. In India, for example, educating the country's 2 million female sex workers, who have an average of two encounters per day, about HIV risks and the life-saving value of using a condom pays huge dividends.[57]

Another target group is the military. After soldiers become infected, usually from engaging in commercial sex, they return to their home communities and spread the virus further. In Nigeria, where the adult HIV infection rate is 4 percent, former President Olusegun Obasanjo introduced free distribution of condoms to all military personnel. A fourth target group, intravenous drug users who share needles, figures prominently in the spread of the virus in the former Soviet republics.[58]

At the most fundamental level, dealing with the HIV threat requires roughly 13.1 billion condoms a year in the developing world and Eastern Europe. Including those needed for contraception adds another 4.4 billion. But of the 17.5 billion condoms needed, only 1.8 billion are being distributed, leaving a shortfall of 15.7 billion. At only 3.5¢ each, or $550 million, the cost of saved lives by supplying condoms is minuscule.[59]

The condom gap is huge, but the costs of filling it are small. In the excellent study *Condoms Count: Meeting the Need in the Era of HIV/AIDS*, Population Action International notes that "the costs of getting condoms into the hands of users—which involves improving access, logistics and distribution capacity, raising awareness, and promoting use—is many times that of the supplies themselves." If we assume that these costs are six times the price of the condoms themselves, filling this gap would still cost only $3 billion.[60]

Sadly, even though condoms are the only technology available to prevent the sexual spread of HIV, the U.S. government is de-emphasizing their use, insisting that abstinence be given top priority. While encouraging abstinence is desirable, an effective campaign to curb the HIV epidemic cannot function without condoms.[61]

One of the few African countries to successfully lower the HIV infection rate after the epidemic became well established is Uganda. Under the strong personal leadership of President Yoweri Museveni, the share of adults infected dropped substantially during the 1990s and has remained stable since 2000. Senegal, which acted early and decisively to check the spread of the virus and which has an adult infection rate of less than 1 percent, is also a model for other African countries.[62]

The financial resources and medical personnel currently available to treat people who are already HIV-positive are severely limited compared with the need. For example, of the 4.6 million people who exhibited symptoms of AIDS in sub-Saharan Africa in 2006, just over 1 million were receiving the anti-retroviral drug treatment that is widely available in industrial countries. Although the number getting treatment is only one fourth of those in need, it is double the number treated during the preceding year.[63]

There is a growing body of evidence that the prospect of treatment encourages people to get tested for HIV. It also raises awareness and understanding of the disease and how it is transmitted. And if people know they are infected, they may try to avoid infecting others. To the extent that treatment extends life (the average extension in the United States is about 15 years), it is not only the humanitarian thing to do, it also makes economic sense. Once society has invested in the rearing, education, and on-job training of individuals, the value of extending their working lifetime is high.[64]

Treating HIV-infected individuals is relatively costly, but ignoring the need for treatment is a strategic mistake simply because treatment strengthens prevention efforts. Africa is paying a heavy cost for its delayed response to the epidemic. It is a window on the future of other countries, such as India and China, if they do not move quickly to contain the virus that is already well established within their borders.[65]

Reducing Farm Subsidies and Debt

Eradicating poverty involves much more than international aid programs. For many developing countries, the reform of farm subsidies in aid-giving countries and debt relief may be even more important. A successful export-oriented farm sector—taking advantage of low-cost labor and natural endowments of land, water, and climate to boost rural incomes and to earn foreign exchange—often offers a path out of poverty. Sadly, for many developing countries this path is blocked by the self-serving farm subsidies of affluent countries. Overall, industrial-country farm subsidies of $280 billion are roughly 2.5 times the development assistance flows from these governments.[66]

The size of the agricultural budget of the European Union

(EU) is staggering, accounting for over one third of its total annual budget. It also looms large internationally. In 2005 the EU-25 accounted for $134 billion of the $280 billion spent by affluent countries on farm subsidies. The United States spent $43 billion on farm subsidies. These encourage overproduction of farm commodities, which then are sent abroad with another boost from export subsidies. The result is depressed world market prices, particularly for cotton, one of the commodities where developing countries have the most to lose.[67]

Although the European Union accounts for more than half of the $104 billion in development assistance from all countries, much of the economic gain from this assistance in the past was offset by the EU's annual dumping of some 6 million tons of sugar on the world market. This is one farm commodity where developing countries have a strong comparative advantage they should be permitted to capitalize on. Fortunately, in 2005 the EU announced that it would reduce its sugar support price to farmers by 40 percent, thus discouraging the excess production that lowered the world market price. The affluent world can no longer afford farm policies that permanently trap millions in poverty by cutting off their main avenue of escape.[68]

Additional help in raising world sugar prices may come from an unexpected quarter. Rising oil prices appear to be increasing sugar prices as more and more sugarcane-based ethanol refineries are built. In effect, the price of sugar may start to track the price of oil upward, providing an economic boost for those developing-world economies where nearly all the world's cane sugar is produced.[69]

Recent developments may also lift world cotton prices. Production subsidies provided to farmers in the United States have historically enabled them to export cotton at low prices. These subsidies to just 25,000 American cotton farmers exceed U.S. financial aid to all of sub-Saharan Africa's 800 million people. And since the United States is the world's leading cotton exporter, its subsidies depress prices for all cotton exporters.[70]

U.S. cotton subsidies have faced a spirited challenge from four cotton-producing countries in Central Africa: Benin, Burkina Faso, Chad, and Mali. In addition, Brazil successfully challenged U.S. cotton subsidies within the framework of the World Trade Organization (WTO). Using U.S. Department of Agriculture data, Brazil convinced the WTO panel that U.S. cotton subsidies were depressing world prices and harming their cotton producers. In response, the panel ruled in 2004 that the United States had to eliminate the subsidies.[71]

After the 2004 WTO ruling, the United States removed some export-credit guarantees and payments to domestic mills and exporters to buy U.S.-grown cotton. In response, Brazil argued that the U.S. payments to farmers continued to depress world cotton prices. The WTO again ruled in Brazil's favor. Despite this ruling, the Farm Bill passed by the U.S. House of Representatives in the summer of 2007 included cotton subsidies in violation of the WTO rules.[72]

Along with eliminating harmful agricultural subsidies, debt forgiveness is another essential component of the broader effort to eradicate poverty. For example, with sub-Saharan Africa spending four times as much on debt servicing as it spends on health care, debt forgiveness can help boost living standards in this last major bastion of poverty.[73]

In July 2005, heads of the G-8 group of industrial countries, meeting in Gleneagles, Scotland, agreed to the cancellation of the multilateral debt that a number of the poorest countries owed to the World Bank, the International Monetary Fund, and the African Development Bank. This initiative, immediately affecting 18 of the poorest debt-ridden countries (14 in Africa and 4 in Latin America), offered these countries a new lease on life. Up to another 20 of the poorest countries could benefit from this if they can complete the qualification. A combination of public pressure by nongovernmental groups campaigning for debt relief in recent years and strong leadership from the U.K. government were the keys to this poverty reduction breakthrough.[74]

The year after the Gleneagles meeting, Oxfam International reported that the International Monetary Fund had eliminated the debts owed by 19 countries, the first major step toward the debt relief goal set at the G-8 meeting. For Zambia, the $6 billion of debt taken off the books enabled President Levy Mwanawasa to announce that basic health care would be now free. In Oxfam's words, "the privilege of the few became the right of all." In East Africa, Burundi announced it would cancel school fees, permitting 300,000 children from poor families to enroll in school. In Nigeria, debt relief has been used to set up a poverty action fund, some of which will go to training thousands of new teachers.[75]

If the international community continues to forgive debt, it will be a strong step toward eradicating poverty. Yet there is still room for progress. The Gleneagles' commitment eliminates only a minor share of poor-country debt to international lending institutions. In addition to the 19 countries granted relief so far, there are at least 40 more countries with low incomes that desperately need help. The groups that are lobbying for debt relief, such as Oxfam International, believe it is inhumane to force people with incomes of scarcely a dollar per day to use part of that dollar to service debt. They pledge to keep the pressure on until all the debt of these poorest countries is cancelled.[76]

A Poverty Eradication Budget

Many countries that have experienced rapid population growth for several decades are showing signs of demographic fatigue. Countries struggling with the simultaneous challenge of educating growing numbers of children, creating jobs for swelling ranks of young job seekers, and dealing with the environmental effects of population growth are stretched to the limit. When a major new threat arises—such as the HIV epidemic—governments often cannot cope.

Problems routinely managed in industrial societies are becoming full-scale humanitarian crises in developing ones. The rise in deaths in several African countries marks a tragic new development in world demography. In the absence of a concerted effort by national governments and the international community to accelerate the shift to smaller families, events in many countries could spiral out of control, leading to more death and to spreading political instability and economic decline.

There is an alternative to this bleak prospect, and that is to help countries that want to slow their population growth to do so quickly. This brings with it what economists call the demographic bonus. When countries move quickly to smaller families, growth in the number of young dependents—those who need nurturing and educating—declines relative to the number of working adults. In this situation, productivity surges, savings and investment climb, and economic growth accelerates.[77]

Japan, which cut its population growth in half between 1951 and 1958, was one of the first countries to benefit from the demographic bonus. South Korea and Taiwan followed, and more recently China, Thailand, and Viet Nam have benefited from earlier sharp reductions in birth rates. This effect lasts for only a few decades, but it is usually enough to launch a country into the modern era. Indeed, except for a few oil-rich countries, no developing country has successfully modernized without slowing population growth.[78]

The steps needed to eradicate poverty and accelerate the shift to smaller families are clear. They include filling several funding gaps, including those needed to reach universal primary education; to fight infectious diseases, such as AIDS, tuberculosis, and malaria; to provide reproductive health care; and to contain the HIV epidemic. Collectively, the initiatives discussed in this chapter are estimated to cost another $77 billion a year. (See Table 7–1.)[79]

The heaviest investments in this effort center on education and health, which are the cornerstones of both human capital development and population stabilization. Education includes

Table 7–1. *Plan B Budget: Additional Annual Funding Needed to Reach Basic Social Goals*

Goal	Funding
	(billion dollars)
Universal primary education	10
Eradication of adult illiteracy	4
School lunch programs for 44 poorest countries	6
Assistance to preschool children and pregnant women in 44 poorest countries	4
Reproductive health and family planning	17
Universal basic health care	33
Closing the condom gap	3
Total	77

Source: See endnote 79.

both universal primary education and a global campaign to eradicate adult illiteracy. Health care includes the basic interventions to control infectious diseases, beginning with childhood vaccinations.[80]

As Jeffrey Sachs regularly reminds us, for the first time in history we have the technologies and financial resources to eradicate poverty. As noted earlier, the last 15 years have seen some impressive gains. For example, China has not only dramatically reduced the number living in poverty within its borders, but, with its trade and investment initiatives, it is helping poorer countries develop. China is investing substantial sums in Africa—investments often related to helping African countries develop their abundance of mineral and energy resources, something that China needs.[81]

Helping low-income countries break out of the demographic trap is a highly profitable investment for the world's affluent nations, a way of reducing the number of failing states. Industrial-country investments in education, health, and school lunches are in a sense a humanitarian response to the plight of the world's poorest countries. But more fundamentally, they are investments that will shape the world in which our children will live.

8

Restoring the Earth

We are dependent on the earth's natural systems for goods, ranging from building materials to seafood, as well as services, ranging from flood control to crop pollination. If croplands are eroding and harvests are shrinking, if water tables are falling and wells are going dry, if grasslands are turning to desert and livestock are dying, we are in trouble. If civilization's environmental support systems continue to decline, eventually civilization itself will follow.

In Chapter 5 we discussed the deforestation, soil erosion, and devastation of Haiti's countryside. After looking at the desperate situation in Haiti, Craig Cox, Executive Director of the U.S.-based Soil and Water Conservation Society, wrote, "I was reminded recently that the benefits of resource conservation—at the most basic level—are still out of reach for many. Ecological and social collapses have reinforced each other in a downward spiral into poverty, environmental degradation, social injustice, disease, and violence." Unfortunately, the situation Cox describes is what lies ahead for more and more countries if we do not restore the earth's health.[1]

Restoring the earth will take an enormous international

effort, one far larger and more demanding than the often-cited Marshall Plan that helped rebuild war-torn Europe and Japan. And such an initiative must be undertaken at wartime speed lest environmental deterioration translate into economic decline and state failure, just as it did for earlier civilizations that violated nature's thresholds and ignored its deadlines.

Protecting and Restoring Forests

Protecting the earth's nearly 4 billion hectares of remaining forests and replanting those already lost are both essential for restoring the earth's health, an important foundation for the new economy. Reducing rainfall runoff and the associated flooding and soil erosion, recycling rainfall inland, and restoring aquifer recharge depend on simultaneously reducing pressure on forests and on reforestation.[2]

There is a vast unrealized potential in all countries to lessen the demands that are shrinking the earth's forest cover. In industrial nations the greatest opportunity lies in reducing the quantity of wood used to make paper, and in developing countries it depends on reducing fuelwood use.

The rates of paper recycling in the top 10 paper-producing countries range widely, from China and Finland on the low end, recycling 33 and 38 percent of the paper they use, to South Korea and Germany on the high end, at 77 and 66 percent. The United States, the world's largest paper consumer, is far behind South Korea, but it has raised the share of paper recycled from roughly one fourth in the early 1980s to 50 percent in 2005. If every country recycled as much of its paper as South Korea does, the amount of wood pulp used to produce paper worldwide would drop by one third.[3]

The use of paper, perhaps more than any other single product, reflects the throwaway mentality that evolved during the last century. There is an enormous possibility for reducing paper use simply by replacing facial tissues, paper napkins, disposable diapers, and paper shopping bags with reusable cloth alternatives.

The largest single demand on trees—the need for fuel—accounts for just over half of all wood removed from forests. Some international aid agencies, including the U.S. Agency for International Development (AID), are sponsoring fuelwood efficiency projects. One of AID's more promising projects is the distribution of 780,000 highly efficient wood cookstoves in Kenya that not only use far less wood than a traditional stove but also pollute less.[4]

Kenya is also the site of a solar cooker project sponsored by Solar Cookers International. These inexpensive cookers, made from cardboard and aluminum foil and costing $10 each, cook slowly, much like a crockpot. Requiring less than two hours of sunshine to cook a complete meal, they can greatly reduce firewood use at little cost. They can also be used to pasteurize water, thus saving lives.[5]

Over the longer term, developing alternative energy sources is the key to reducing forest pressure in developing countries. Replacing firewood with solar thermal cookers, or even with electric hotplates fed by wind-generated electricity or with some other energy source, will lighten the load on forests.

Despite the high value to society of intact forests, only about 290 million hectares of global forest area are legally protected from logging. An additional 1.4 billion hectares are economically unavailable for harvesting because of geographic inaccessibility or low-value wood. Of the remaining area available for exploitation, 665 million hectares are undisturbed by humans and nearly 900 million hectares are semi-natural and not in plantations.[6]

Forests protected by national decree are often safeguarded not so much to preserve the long-term wood supply capacity as to ensure that they continue to provide invaluable services such as flood control. Countries that provide legal protection for forests often do so after they have suffered the consequences of extensive deforestation. The Philippines, for example, has banned logging in most remaining old-growth and virgin forests largely because the country has become so vulnerable to flooding, erosion, and landslides. The country was once covered by rich stands of tropical hardwood forests, but after years of massive clearcutting, it lost the forest's products as well as its services and became a net importer of forest products.[7]

Although nongovernmental organizations (NGOs) have worked for years to protect forests from clearcutting, sustainable forestry is now seen as another way to protect forests. If only mature trees are felled, and on a selective basis, a forest and its productivity can be maintained in perpetuity. The World Bank has only recently begun to systematically consider sustainable forestry projects. In 1997, the Bank joined forces with the World Wide Fund for Nature to form the Alliance for Forest Conservation and Sustainable Use; by 2005 they had helped designate 55 million hectares of new forest protected areas and certify 22 million hectares of forest. In mid-2005, the Alliance announced a goal of reducing global net deforestation to zero by 2020.[8]

There are several additional forest product certification programs that inform environmentally conscious consumers about the sustainable management of the forest where wood products originate. The most rigorous international program, certified by a group of NGOs, is the Forest Stewardship Council (FSC). Some 88 million hectares of forests in 76 countries are certified by FSC-accredited bodies as responsibly managed. Among the leaders in certified forest area are Canada, with nearly 18 million hectares; Russia, with more than 15 million hectares; Sweden, with 11 million hectares; the United States, with 9 million hectares; and Poland and Brazil, each with close to 5 million hectares.[9]

Forest plantations can reduce pressures on the earth's remaining forests as long as they do not replace old-growth forest. As of 2005, the world had 205 million hectares in forest plantations, an area equal to nearly one third of the 700 million hectares planted in grain. Tree plantations produce mostly wood for paper mills or for wood reconstitution mills. Increasingly, reconstituted wood is substituting for natural wood as the world lumber and construction industries adapt to a shrinking supply of large logs from natural forests.[10]

Production of roundwood (logs) on plantations is estimated at 432 million cubic meters per year, accounting for 12 percent of world wood production. This means that the lion's share, some 88 percent of the world timber harvest, comes from natural forest stands.[11]

Six countries account for 60 percent of tree plantations. China, which has little original forest remaining, is by far the largest, with 54 million hectares of plantations. India and the United States follow, at 17 million hectares each. Russia, Canada, and Sweden are close behind. As tree farming expands, it is shifting geographically to the moist tropics. In contrast to grain yields, which tend to rise with distance from the equator and the longer summer growing days, tree plantation yields rise with proximity to the equator and year-round growing conditions.[12]

In eastern Canada, the average hectare of forest plantation produces 4 cubic meters of wood per year. In the southeastern United States, where U.S. plantations are concentrated, the yield is 10 cubic meters. But in Brazil, newer plantations may be getting close to 40 cubic meters. While corn yields in the United States are nearly triple those in Brazil, timber yields are the reverse, favoring Brazil by nearly 4 to 1. To satisfy a given demand for wood, Brazil requires only one fourth as much land as the United States, which helps explain why growth in pulp capacity is now concentrated in equatorial regions.[13]

Projections of future growth show that plantations can sometimes be profitably established on already deforested, often degraded, land. They can also come at the expense of existing forests. And there is competition with agriculture as well, since land that is suitable for crops is also good for growing trees. Water scarcity is yet another constraint. Fast-growing plantations require abundant moisture.

Nonetheless, the U.N. Food and Agriculture Organization (FAO) projects that as plantation area expands and yields rise, the harvest could more than double during the next three decades. It is entirely conceivable that plantations could one day satisfy most of the world's demand for industrial wood, thus helping to protect the world's remaining forests.[14]

Reed Funk, professor of plant biology at Rutgers University, believes the vast areas of deforested land can be used to grow trillions of trees bred for food (mostly nuts), fuel, and other purposes. Funk sees nuts used to supplement meat as a source of high-quality protein in developing-country diets. He also sees trees grown on this deforested land being converted into ethanol for automotive fuel.[15]

Historically, some highly erodible agricultural land in industrial countries has been reforested by natural regrowth. Such is the case for New England in the United States. Settled early by Europeans, this geographically rugged region was suffering from cropland productivity losses because soils were thin and the land was rocky, sloping, and vulnerable to erosion. As highly productive farmland opened up in the Midwest and the Great

Plains during the nineteenth century, pressures on New England farmland lessened, permitting cropped land to return to forest. New England's forest cover has increased from a low of roughly one third two centuries ago to four fifths today, slowly regaining its original health and diversity.[16]

A somewhat similar situation exists now in parts of the former Soviet Union and in several East European countries. As central planning was replaced by market-based agriculture in the early 1990s, unprofitable marginal land was abandoned. Precise figures are difficult to come by, but millions of hectares of farmland are now returning to forest.[17]

South Korea is in many ways a reforestation model for the rest of the world. When the Korean War ended, half a century ago, the mountainous country was largely deforested. Beginning around 1960, under the dedicated leadership of President Park Chung Hee, the South Korean government launched a national reforestation effort. Relying on the formation of village cooperatives, hundreds of thousands of people were mobilized to dig trenches and to create terraces for supporting trees on barren mountains. Se-Kyung Chong, researcher at the Korea Forest Research Institute, writes, "The result was a seemingly miraculous rebirth of forests from barren land."[18]

Today forests cover 65 percent of the country, an area of roughly 6 million hectares. While driving across South Korea in November 2000, it was gratifying for me to see the luxuriant stands of trees on mountains that a generation ago were bare. We can reforest the earth![19]

In Turkey, a mountainous country largely deforested over the millennia, a leading environmental group, TEMA (Türkiye Erozyona Mücadele, Agaclandirma) has made reforestation its principal activity. Founded by two prominent Turkish businessmen, Hayrettin Karuca and Nihat Gokyigit, TEMA launched in 1998 a 10-billion-acorn campaign to restore tree cover and reduce runoff and soil erosion. During the years since, 850 million oak acorns have been planted. The program is also raising national awareness of the services that forests provide.[20]

On the other side of the world, in Niger, farmers faced with severe drought and desertification in the 1980s began leaving some emerging acacia tree seedlings in their fields as they prepared the land for crops. As these trees matured they slowed wind speeds, thus reducing soil erosion. The acacia, a legume, fixes nitrogen, thus enriching the soil and helping to raise crop yields. During the dry season the leaves and pods provide fodder for livestock. The trees also supply firewood.[21]

This approach of leaving 20–150 seedlings per hectare to mature on some 3 million hectares has revitalized farming communities in Niger. Assuming an average of 40 trees per hectare reach maturity, this comes to 120 million trees. This practice also has been central to reclaiming 250,000 hectares of abandoned land. The key to this success story was the shift in tree ownership from the state to individual farmers, giving them the responsibility for protecting the trees.[22]

Shifting subsidies from building logging roads to planting trees would help protect forest cover worldwide. The World Bank has the administrative capacity to lead an international program that would emulate South Korea's success in blanketing mountains and hills with trees.

In addition, FAO and the bilateral aid agencies can work with individual farmers in national agroforestry programs to integrate trees wherever possible into agricultural operations. Well-chosen, well-placed trees provide shade, serve as windbreaks to check soil erosion, and can fix nitrogen, reducing the need for fertilizer.

Reducing wood use by developing more-efficient wood stoves and alternative cooking fuels, systematically recycling paper, and banning the use of throwaway paper products all lighten pressure on the earth's forests. But a global reforestation effort cannot succeed unless it is accompanied by the stabilization of population. With such an integrated plan, coordinated country by country, the earth's forests can be restored.

Conserving and Rebuilding Soils

In reviewing the literature on soil erosion, references to the "loss of protective vegetation" occur again and again. Over the last half-century, we have removed so much of that protective cover by clearcutting, overgrazing, and overplowing that we are fast losing soil accumulated over long stretches of geological time. Preserving the biological productivity of highly erodible cropland depends on planting it in grass or trees before it becomes wasteland.

The 1930s Dust Bowl that threatened to turn the U.S. Great Plains into a vast desert was a traumatic experience that led to revolutionary changes in American agricultural practices, including the planting of tree shelterbelts (rows of trees planted beside fields to slow wind and thus reduce wind erosion) and strip-cropping, the planting of wheat on alternate strips with fallowed land each year. Strip-cropping permits soil moisture to accumulate on the fallowed strips, while the alternating planted strips reduce wind speed and hence erosion on the idled land.[23]

In 1985, the U.S. Congress, with strong support from the environmental community, created the Conservation Reserve Program (CRP) to reduce soil erosion and control overproduction of basic commodities. By 1990 there were some 14 million hectares (35 million acres) of highly erodible land with permanent vegetative cover under 10-year contracts. Under this program, farmers were paid to plant fragile cropland to grass or trees. The retirement of 14 million hectares under the CRP, together with the use of conservation practices on 37 percent of all cropland, reduced U.S. soil erosion from 3.1 billion tons to 1.9 billion tons during the 15 years between 1982 and 1997. The U.S. approach offers a model for the rest of the world.[24]

Another tool in the soil conservation toolkit—and a relatively new one—is conservation tillage, which includes both no-till and minimum-tillage. Instead of the traditional cultural practices of plowing land, discing or harrowing it to prepare the seedbed, and then using a mechanical cultivator to control weeds in row crops, farmers simply drill seeds directly through crop residues into undisturbed soil, controlling weeds with herbicides. The only soil disturbance is the narrow slit in the soil surface where the seeds are inserted, leaving the remainder of the soil undisturbed, covered by crop residues and thus resistant to both water and wind erosion. In addition to reducing erosion, this practice helps retain water, raises soil carbon content, and reduces energy use.[25]

In the United States, where farmers during the 1990s were required to implement a soil conservation plan on erodible cropland to be eligible for commodity price supports, the no-till area went from 7 million hectares in 1990 to 25 million hectares in 2004. Now widely used in the production of corn and soybeans, no-till has spread rapidly in the western hemisphere, covering 25 million hectares in 2006 in Brazil, 20 million hectares in Argentina, and 13 million in Canada. Australia, with 9 million hectares, rounds out the five leading no-till countries.[26]

Once farmers master the practice of no-till, its use can spread rapidly, particularly if governments provide economic incentives or require farm soil conservation plans for farmers to be eligible for crop subsidies. Recent FAO reports describe the early growth in no-till farming over the last few years in Europe, Africa, and Asia.[27]

Other approaches are being used to halt soil erosion and desert encroachment on cropland. Algeria, trying to halt the northward advance of the Sahara Desert, announced in December 2000 that it was concentrating its orchards and vineyards in the southern part of the country, hoping that these perennial plantings will halt the desertification of its cropland. In July 2005, the Moroccan government, responding to severe drought, announced that it was allocating $778 million to cancel farmers' debts and to convert cereal-planted areas into less vulnerable olive and fruit orchards.[28]

Sub-Saharan Africa faces a similar situation, with the desert moving southward all across the Sahel, from Senegal on the west coast to Djibouti on the east coast. Countries are concerned about the growing displacement of people as grasslands and croplands turn to desert. As a result, the African Union has launched the Green Wall Sahara Initiative. This plan, originally proposed by Olusegun Obasanjo when he was President of Nigeria, calls for the planting of 300 million trees on 3 million hectares of land, in a long band stretching across Africa. Senegal, which is currently losing 50,000 hectares of productive land each year, would anchor the green wall on the western end. Senegal's Environment Minister Modou Fada Diagne says, "Instead of waiting for the desert to come to us, we need to attack it."[29]

China is likewise planting a belt of trees to protect land from the expanding Gobi Desert. This green wall, a modern version of the Great Wall, is projected to reach some 4,480 kilometers (2,800 miles) in length, stretching from outer Beijing through Inner Mongolia. In addition to its Great Green Wall, China is paying farmers in the threatened provinces to plant their cropland in trees. The goal is to plant trees on 10 million hectares of grainland, easily one tenth of China's current grainland area.[30]

In Inner Mongolia (Nei Monggol), efforts to halt the advancing desert and to reclaim the land for productive uses rely on planting desert shrubs to stabilize the sand dunes. And in many situations, sheep and goats have been banned entirely. In Helin County, south of the provincial capital of Hohhot, the planting of desert shrubs on abandoned cropland has now stabilized the soil on the county's first 7,000-hectare reclamation plot. Based on this success, the reclamation effort is being expanded.[31]

The Helin County strategy centers on replacing the large number of sheep and goats with dairy cattle, increasing the number of dairy animals from 30,000 in 2002 to 150,000 by 2007. The cattle are kept within restricted areas, feeding on cornstalks, wheat straw, and the harvest from a drought-tolerant forage crop resembling alfalfa, which is grown on reclaimed land. Local officials estimate that this program will double incomes within the county during this decade.[32]

To relieve pressure on the country's rangelands, Beijing is asking herders to reduce their flocks of sheep and goats by 40 percent. But in communities where wealth is measured in livestock numbers and where most families are living in poverty, such cuts are not easy or, indeed, likely, unless alternative livelihoods are offered to pastoralists along the lines proposed in Helin County.[33]

The only viable way to eliminate overgrazing on the two fifths of the earth's land surface classified as rangelands is to reduce the size of flocks and herds. Not only do the excessive numbers of cattle, and particularly sheep and goats, remove the vegetation, but their hoofs pulverize the protective crust of soil that is formed by rainfall and that naturally checks wind erosion. In some situations, the only viable option is to keep the animals in restricted areas, bringing the forage to them. India, which has successfully adopted this practice for its thriving dairy industry, is the model for other countries.[34]

Protecting the earth's soil also warrants a worldwide ban on the clearcutting of forests in favor of selective harvesting, simply because with each clearcut there are heavy soil losses until the forest regenerates. Thus with each subsequent cutting, productivity declines further. Restoring the earth's tree and grass cover, as well as practicing conservation agriculture, protects soil from erosion, reduces flooding, and sequesters carbon. It is one way we can restore the earth so that it can support the next generation.

Regenerating Fisheries

For decades governments tried to save specific fisheries by restricting the catch of individual species. Sometimes this worked; sometimes it failed and fisheries collapsed. In recent years, support for another approach—the creation of marine reserves or marine parks—has been gaining momentum. These reserves, where fishing is restricted, serve as natural hatcheries, helping to repopulate the surrounding area.

In 2002, at the World Summit on Sustainable Development in Johannesburg, coastal nations pledged to create national networks of marine parks, which together could constitute a global network of such parks. At the World Parks Congress in Durban in 2003, delegates recommended protecting 20–30 percent of each marine habitat from fishing. This would be up from 0.6 percent of the oceans that are currently included in marine reserves of widely varying size. It compares with the nearly 13 percent of the earth's land area that is in parks.[35]

A U.K. team of scientists led by Dr. Andrew Balmford of the Conservation Science Group at Cambridge University analyzed the costs of operating marine reserves on a large scale based on data from 83 relatively small, well-managed reserves. They concluded that managing reserves that covered 30 percent of the world's oceans would cost $12–14 billion a year. This did not take into account the likely additional income from recovering fisheries, which would reduce the actual cost.[36]

At stake in the creation of a global network of marine reserves is the protection and possible increase of an annual oceanic fish catch worth $70–80 billion. Balmford said, "Our study suggests that we could afford to conserve the seas and their resources in perpetuity, and for less than we are now spending on subsidies to exploit them unsustainably."[37]

Coauthor of the U.K. study, Callum Roberts of the University of York, noted: "We have barely even begun the task of creating marine parks. Here in Britain a paltry one-fiftieth of one percent of our seas is encompassed by marine nature reserves and only one-fiftieth of their combined area is closed to fishing." Still the seas are being devastated by unsustainable fishing, pollution, and mineral exploitation. The creation of the global network of marine reserves—"Serengetis of the seas," as some have dubbed them—would create more than 1 million jobs. Roberts went on to say, "If you put areas off limits to fishing, there is no more effective way of allowing things to live longer, grow larger, and produce more offspring."[38]

Jane Lubchenco, former President of the American Association for the Advancement of Science, strongly underlined Roberts' point when releasing a statement signed by 161 leading marine scientists calling for urgent action to create the global network of marine reserves. Drawing on the research on scores of marine parks, she said: "All around the world there are different experiences, but the basic message is the same: marine reserves work, and they work fast. It is no longer a question of whether to set aside fully protected areas in the ocean, but where to establish them."[39]

The signatories noted how quickly sea life improves once the reserves are established. A case study of a snapper fishery off the coast of New England showed that fishers, though they violently opposed the establishment of the reserve, now champion it because they have seen the local population of snapper increase 40-fold. In a study in the Gulf of Maine, all fishing methods that put ground fish at risk were banned within three marine reserves totaling 17,000 square kilometers. Unexpectedly, scallops flourished in this undisturbed environment, and their populations increased by up to 14-fold within five years. This population buildup within the reserves also greatly increased the scallop population outside the reserves. The 161 scientists noted that within a year or two of establishing a marine reserve, population densities increased 91 percent, average fish size went up 31 percent, and species diversity rose 20 percent.[40]

While the creation of marine reserves is clearly the overriding priority in the long-standing effort to protect marine ecosystems, other measures are also required. One is to reduce the nutrient flows from fertilizer runoff and untreated sewage that create the world's 200 or so dead zones.[41]

In the end, governments need to eliminate fishery subsidies. There are now so many fishing trawlers that their catch potential is nearly double any yield the oceans can sustain. Managing a network of marine reserves governing 30 percent of the oceans would cost only $12–14 billion—less than the $22 billion in harmful subsidies that governments dole out today to fishers.[42]

Protecting Plant and Animal Diversity

The two steps essential to protecting the earth's extraordinary biological diversity are the stabilization of both the human population and the earth's climate. If the world's population increases to 9 billion by mid-century as projected, countless more plant and animal species may simply be crowded off the planet. If carbon dioxide levels and temperatures continue to rise, every ecosystem will change.

One reason for our goal of stabilizing population at 8 billion by 2040 is to protect the earth's rich diversity of life. As it becomes more difficult to raise land productivity, continuing population growth will force farmers to clear ever more tropical forests in the Amazon and Congo basins and the outer islands of Indonesia.[43]

Water management at a time of growing water shortages is a key to protecting fresh water and marine species. When rivers are drained dry to satisfy growing human needs for irrigation and for urban water, fish species cannot survive.

Perhaps the best known and most popular way of trying to protect plant and animal species is to create reserves. Millions of square kilometers have been set aside as parks. Indeed, some 13 percent of the earth's land area is now included in parks and nature preserves. With more resources for enforced protection, some of these parks in developing countries that now exist only on paper could become a reality.[44]

Some 20 years ago, Norman Myers and other scientists conceived the idea of biodiversity "hotspots"—areas that were especially rich biologically and thus deserving of special protection. The 34 hotspots identified once covered nearly 16 percent of the earth's land surface but, largely because of habitat destruction, they now cover less than 3 percent. Concentrating preservation efforts in these biologically rich regions is now a common strategy among conservation groups and governments.[45]

In 1973 the United States enacted the Endangered Species Act. This legislation prohibited any activities, such as clearing new land for agriculture and housing developments or draining wetlands, that would threaten an endangered species. There are numerous species in the United States, such as the bald eagle, that might now be extinct had it not been for this legislation. And now this act is seen by some conservationists as a potential leverage point in battling global warming because of the need to protect species particularly threatened by warmer temperatures, including coral and polar bears.[46]

The traditional approach to protecting biological diversity by building a fence around an area and calling it a park or nature preserve is no longer sufficient. If we cannot stabilize human numbers and stabilize the climate, there is not an ecosystem on earth that we can save.

As a species, humans have an enormous influence on the habitability of the planet for the millions of other species with which we share it. This influence brings with it responsibility.

Planting Trees to Sequester Carbon

As of 2007, the shrinking forests in the tropical regions were releasing 2.2 billion tons of carbon per year. Meanwhile, expanding forests in the temperate regions were absorbing 0.7 billion tons of carbon annually. On balance, a net of some 1.5 billion tons of carbon were being released into the atmosphere each year, contributing to global warming.[47]

The tropical deforestation in Asia is driven primarily by the fast-growing demand for timber. In Latin America, by contrast, it is the growing demand for soybeans and beef that is deforesting the Amazon. In Africa, it is mostly the gathering of fuelwood and the clearing of new land for agriculture as existing cropland is degraded and abandoned. Two countries, Indonesia and Brazil, account for more than half of all deforestation. The Democratic Republic of the Congo, also high on the list, is a failing state, making forest management difficult.[48]

The Plan B goals are to end net deforestation worldwide and to sequester carbon through a variety of tree planting initiatives and the adoption of improved agricultural land management practices. Today, because the earth's forests are shrinking, they are a major source of CO_2. The goal is to expand the earth's tree cover, growing more trees to soak up CO_2.

Although banning deforestation may seem farfetched, environmental reasons have pushed three countries—Thailand, the Philippines, and China—to implement complete or partial bans on logging. All three bans were imposed following devastating floods and mudslides resulting from the loss of forest cover. After suffering record losses from several weeks of nonstop flooding in the Yangtze River basin, Beijing noted that when forest policy was viewed not through the eyes of the individual logger but through those of society as a whole, it simply did not make economic sense to continue deforesting. The flood control service of trees standing, they said, was three times as valuable as the timber from trees cut. With this in mind, Beijing then took the unusual step of paying the loggers to become tree planters—to reforest instead of deforest.[49]

Other countries cutting down large areas of trees will also face the environmental effects of deforestation, including flooding. If Brazil's Amazon rainforest continues to shrink, it may also continue to dry out, becoming vulnerable to fire. If the Amazon rainforest disappears, it would be replaced largely by desert and scrub forestland. The capacity of the rainforest to cycle water to the interior, including to the agricultural areas to the south, would be lost. At this point, a fast-unfolding local environmental calamity would become an economic disaster, and because the burning Amazon would release billions of tons of carbon into the atmosphere, it would accelerate global warming.[50]

Just as national concerns about the effects of continuing deforestation eventually eclipsed local interests, now global interests are beginning to eclipse national ones as deforestation has become a major driver of global warming. Deforestation is no longer just a matter of local flooding, but also rising seas worldwide and the many other effects of climate change. Nature has just raised the ante on protecting forests.

Reaching a goal of zero net deforestation will require reducing the pressures to deforest that come from population growth, rising affluence, the construction of ethanol distilleries and biodiesel refineries, and the fast-growing use of paper. Protecting the earth's forests means halting population growth as soon as possible, and, for the earth's affluent residents who are responsible for the growing demand for beef and soybeans that is deforesting the Amazon basin, it means moving down the food chain. A successful deforestation ban may require a ban on the construction of additional biodiesel refineries and ethanol distilleries.

Against this backdrop of growing concern about the forest-climate relationship, a leading Swedish energy firm, Vattenfall, has examined the large-scale potential for foresting wasteland to sequester carbon dioxide. They begin by noting that there are 1.86 billion hectares of degraded land in the world—land that was once forestland, cropland, or grassland—and that half of this, or 930 million hectares, has a decent chance of being profitably reclaimed. Some 840 million hectares of this total are in the tropical regions, where reclamation would mean much higher rates of carbon sequestration. (Every newly planted tree seedling in the tropics removes an average of 50 kilograms of CO_2 from the atmosphere each year during its growth period of 20–50 years, compared with 13 kilograms of CO_2 per year for a tree in the temperate regions.)[51]

Vattenfall estimates that the maximum technical potential of these 930 million hectares is to absorb roughly 21.6 billion tons of CO_2 per year. If, as part of a global climate stabilization strategy, carbon sequestration were valued at $210 per ton of carbon, the company believes that 18 percent of this technical potential could be realized. If so, this would mean planting 171 million hectares of land to trees. This area—larger than that planted to grain in India—would sequester 3.5 billion tons of CO_2 per year, or over 950 million tons of carbon. The total cost of sequestering carbon at $210 per ton would be $200 billion. Spread over a decade, this would mean investing $20 billion a year to give climate stabilization a large and potentially decisive boost. This global forestation plan to remove atmospheric CO_2, most of it put there by industrial countries, would be funded by them. An independent body would be set up to administer, fund, and monitor the vast tree planting initiative.[52]

Aside from the Vattenfall forestation idea, there are already many tree planting initiatives under way that are driven by a range of concerns, from climate change to desert expansion, to soil conservation, to making cities more habitable. These include the worldwide Billion Tree Campaign launched in 2007, urban tree planting initiatives in many cities, the Great Green Wall being planted in China, and the Saharan Green Wall of

Africa, as well as a big push to expand tree plantations within a number of countries.

The Billion Tree Campaign was inspired by Kenyan Nobel laureate Wangari Maathai, who had earlier organized women in Kenya and several nearby countries to plant 30 million trees. The United Nations Environment Programme, which is administering the Billion Tree Campaign, reported as of October 2007 that it had received pledges to plant a total of 1.2 billion trees by year end. Of that total, 431 million already had been planted. Among the leaders are Mexico, which pledged to plant 250 million trees, and Ethiopia, which promised to plant 60 million trees to commemorate its millennium celebration. Senegal signed up for 20 million trees.[53]

Some state and provincial governments have also joined in. In Brazil, the state of Paraná, which launched an effort to plant 90 million trees in 2003 to restore its riparian zones, committed to planting 20 million trees in 2007. Uttar Pradesh, India's most populous state, mobilized 600,000 people to plant 10.5 million trees in a single day in July 2007, planting the trees on farmland, in state forests, and on school grounds. If the goal of 1 billion trees is reached and half of them survive, these trees would sequester 5.6 million tons of carbon per year.[54]

Independent of the Billion Tree Campaign, in September 2007 New Zealand Prime Minister Helen Clarke announced an impressive package of steps to cut carbon emissions, including expanding forested area by 250,000 hectares (617,000 acres) by 2020. This would roughly total some 125 million trees, or 30 for each New Zealander.[55]

Many of the world's cities are planting trees. Tokyo, for example, has been planting trees and shrubs on the rooftops of buildings to help offset the urban heat island effect and cool the city. Washington, D.C., is in the early stages of a campaign to greatly restore its tree canopy.[56]

An analysis of the value of planting trees on the streets and in the parks of five western U.S. cities—from Cheyenne, Wyoming, to Berkeley, California—concluded that for every dollar spent on planting and caring for trees, the benefits to the community exceeded two dollars. A mature tree canopy in a city shades buildings and can reduce air temperatures by 5–10 degrees Fahrenheit, thus reducing the energy needed for air conditioning. In cities with severe winters like Cheyenne, the reduction of winter wind speed by evergreen trees cuts heating costs. Real estate values on tree-lined streets are typically 3–6 percent higher than where there are few or no trees.[57]

Planting trees is just one of many activities that will remove meaningful quantities of carbon from the atmosphere. One activity that involves a good use of wasteland is the planting in Africa and Asia of jatropha, a four-foot perennial shrub that produces seeds that can be used to produce biodiesel. This covers wasteland and sequesters carbon.[58]

A number of agricultural practices can also increase the carbon stored as organic matter in soils. Farming practices that reduce soil erosion and raise cropland productivity usually also lead to higher carbon content in the soil. Among these are shifting from conventional tillage to minimum-till and no-till, the more extensive use of cover crops, the return of all livestock and poultry manure to the land, expansion of irrigated area, a return to more mixed crop-livestock farming, and the forestation of marginal farmlands.

Rattan Lal, a Senior Agronomist with the Carbon Management and Sequestration Center at Ohio State University, has calculated the range of potential carbon sequestration for each of many practices, such as those just cited. For example, expanding the use of cover crops to protect soil during the off-season can store from 68 million to 338 million tons of carbon worldwide each year. Calculating the total carbon sequestration for the practices he cites, using the low end of the range for each, shows a potential for sequestering 400 million tons of carbon each year. Aggregating the numbers from the more optimistic high end of the range for each practice yields a total of 1.2 billion tons of carbon per year. For our carbon budget we are assuming, perhaps conservatively, that 600 million tons of carbon can be sequestered as a result of adopting these carbon-sensitive farming and land management practices.[59]

The Earth Restoration Budget

Although we lack detailed data in some cases, we can roughly estimate how much it will cost to reforest the earth, protect topsoil, restore rangelands and fisheries, stabilize water tables, and protect biological diversity. Where data and information are lacking, we fill in with assumptions. The goal is to have not a set of precise numbers but a set of reasonable estimates for an earth restoration budget. (See Table 8–1.)[60]

Calculating the cost of reforestation is complicated by the range of approaches used. As noted, the big national success story is South Korea, which has reforested its once denuded mountains and hills using locally mobilized labor. Other countries, including China, have tried extensive reforestation, but mostly under more arid conditions and with less success.[61]

In calculating reforestation costs, the focus is on developing countries since forested area is already expanding in the northern hemisphere's industrial countries. Meeting the growing fuelwood demand in developing countries will require an estimated 55 million additional hectares of forested area. Conserving soils and restoring hydrological stability would require roughly another 100 million hectares located in thousands of watersheds in developing countries. Recognizing some overlap between these two, we will reduce the 155 million total to 150 million hectares. Beyond this, an additional 30 million hectares will be needed to produce lumber, paper, and other forest products.[62]

Table 8–1. *Plan B Budget:*
Additional Annual Funding Needed to Restore the Earth

Activity	Funding
	(billion dollars)
Planting trees to reduce flooding and conserve soil	6
Planting trees to sequester carbon	20
Protecting topsoil on cropland	24
Restoring rangelands	9
Restoring fisheries	13
Protecting biological diversity	31
Stabilizing water tables	10
Total	113

Source: See endnote 60.

Only a small share of this tree planting will likely come from plantations. Much of the planting will be on the outskirts of villages, along field boundaries and roads, on small plots of marginal land, and on denuded hillsides. The labor for this will be local; some will be paid labor, some volunteer. Much of it will be rural off-season labor. In China, farmers now planting trees where they once planted grain are compensated with grain from state-held stocks over a five-year period while the trees are becoming established.[63]

If seedlings cost $40 per thousand, as the World Bank estimates, and if the typical planting rate is roughly 2,000 per hectare, then seedlings cost $80 per hectare. Labor costs for planting trees are high, but since much of the labor for planting these trees would consist of locally mobilized volunteers, we are assuming a total of $400 per hectare, including both seedlings and labor. With a total of 150 million hectares to be planted over the next decade, this will come to roughly 15 million hectares per year at $400 each for an annual expenditure of $6 billion.[64]

Planting trees to conserve soil, reduce flooding, and provide firewood sequesters carbon. But because climate stabilization is essential, we tally the cost of planting trees for carbon separately. Doing so along the lines proposed by Vattenfall would reforest or afforest 171 million hectares of wasteland over 10 years. Because it would be a more highly commercialized undertaking focused exclusively on wasteland reclamation and carbon sequestration, it would be more costly. Using the value of sequestered carbon of $210 per ton, it would cost close to $20 billion per year. For comparison, this is less than two months of U.S. military spending in Iraq.[65]

Conserving the earth's topsoil by reducing erosion to the rate of new soil formation or below involves two principal steps. One is to retire the highly erodible land that cannot sustain cultivation—the estimated one tenth of the world's cropland that accounts for perhaps half of all excess erosion. For the United States, that has meant retiring 14 million hectares (nearly 35 million acres). The cost of keeping this land out of production is close to $50 per acre or $125 per hectare. In total, annual payments to farmers to plant this land in grass or trees under 10-year contracts approached $2 billion.[66]

The second initiative consists of adopting conservation practices on the remaining land that is subject to excessive erosion—that is, erosion that exceeds the natural rate of new soil formation. This initiative includes incentives to encourage farmers to adopt conservation practices such as contour farming, strip cropping, and, increasingly, minimum-till or no-till farming. These expenditures in the United States total roughly $1 billion per year.[67]

In expanding these estimates to cover the world, it is assumed that roughly 10 percent of the world's cropland is highly erodible and should be planted to grass or trees before the topsoil is lost and it becomes barren land. In both the United States and China, the two leading food-producing countries, which account for a third of the world grain harvest, the official goal is to retire one tenth of all cropland. In Europe, it likely would be much less than 10 percent, but in Africa and the Andean countries it could be substantially higher than that. For the world as a whole, converting 10 percent of cropland that is highly erodible to grass or trees seems a reasonable goal. Since this costs roughly $2 billion in the United States, which represents one eighth of the world cropland area, the total for the world would be roughly $16 billion annually.[68]

Assuming that the need for erosion control practices for the rest of the world is similar to that in the United States, we again multiply the U.S. expenditure by eight to get a total of $8 billion for the world as a whole. The two components together—$16 billion for retiring highly erodible land and $8 billion for adopting conservation practices—give an annual total for the world of $24 billion.[69]

For cost data on rangeland protection and restoration, we turn to the United Nations Plan of Action to Combat Desertification. This plan, which focuses on the world's dryland regions, containing nearly 90 percent of all rangeland, estimates that it would cost roughly $183 billion over a 20-year restoration period—or $9 billion per year. The key restoration measures include improved rangeland management, financial incentives to eliminate overstocking, and revegetation with appropriate rest periods, when grazing would be banned.[70]

This is a costly undertaking, but every dollar invested in rangeland restoration yields a return of $2.50 in income from the increased productivity of the rangeland ecosystem. From a societal point of view, countries with large pastoral populations, where the rangeland deterioration is concentrated, are invariably among the world's poorest. The alternative to action—ignoring the deterioration—brings a loss not only of land productivity but of livelihood, and ultimately leads to millions of refugees. Though not quantified here, restoring this vulnerable land will also have carbon sequestration benefits.[71]

The restoration of oceanic fisheries centers primarily on the establishment of a worldwide network of marine reserves, which would cover roughly 30 percent of the ocean's surface. For this exercise we use the detailed calculations by the U.K. team cited earlier in the chapter. Their estimated range of expenditures centers on $13 billion per year.[72]

For wildlife protection, the bill is somewhat higher. The World Parks Congress estimates that the annual shortfall in funding needed to manage and to protect existing areas designated as parks comes to roughly $25 billion a year. Additional areas needed, including those encompassing the biologically diverse hotspots not yet included in designated parks, would cost perhaps another $6 billion a year, yielding a total of $31 billion.[73]

For stabilizing water tables, we have only a guess. The key to stabilizing water tables is raising water productivity, and for this we have the experience gained when the world started to systematically raise land productivity beginning a half-century ago. The elements needed in a comparable water model are research to develop more water-efficient irrigation practices and technologies, the dissemination of these research findings to farmers, and economic incentives that encourage farmers to adopt and use these improved irrigation practices and technologies.

The area for raising irrigation water productivity is much smaller than that for land productivity. Indeed, only about one fifth of the world's cropland is irrigated. In disseminating the results of irrigation research, there are actually two options today. One is to work through agricultural extension services, which were created to funnel new information to farmers on a broad range of issues, including irrigation. Another possibility is to work through the water users associations that have been formed in many countries. The advantage of the latter is that they are focused exclusively on water.[74]

Effectively managing underground water supplies requires
knowledge of the amount of water being pumped and aquifer
recharge rates. In most countries this information is simply not
available. Finding out how much is pumped may mean installing
meters on irrigation well pumps, much as has been done in Jordan and Mexico.[75]

In some countries, the capital needed to fund a program to
raise water productivity can come from eliminating subsidies
that now often encourage the wasteful use of irrigation water.
Sometimes these are energy subsidies, as in India; other times
they are subsidies that provide water at prices well below costs,
as in the United States. Removing these subsidies will effectively raise the price of water, thus encouraging its more efficient
use. In terms of additional resources needed worldwide, including research needs and the economic incentives for farmers to
use more water-efficient practices and technologies, we assume
it will take additional expenditures of $10 billion.[76]

Altogether, restoring the earth will require additional expenditures of $113 billion per year. Many will ask, Can the world
afford this? But the only appropriate question is, Can the world
afford to not make these investments?

9

Feeding Eight Billion Well

In April 2005, the World Food Programme and the Chinese government jointly announced that food aid shipments to China would stop at the end of the year. For a country where a generation ago hundreds of millions of people were chronically hungry, this was a landmark achievement. Not only has China ended its dependence on food aid, but almost overnight it has become the world's third largest food aid donor.[1]

The key to China's success was the economic reforms in 1978 that dismantled its system of agricultural collectives, known as production teams, and replaced them with family farms. In each village, the land was allocated among families, giving them long-term leases on their piece of land. The move harnessed the energy and ingenuity of China's rural population, raising the grain harvest by half from 1977 to 1986. With its fast-expanding economy raising incomes, with population growth slowing, and with the grain harvest climbing, China eradicated most of its hunger in less than a decade—in fact, it eradicated more hunger in a shorter period of time than any country in history.[2]

While hunger has been disappearing in China, it has been spreading in sub-Saharan Africa and parts of the Indian subcontinent. As a result, the number of people in developing countries who are hungry has increased from a recent historical low of 800 million in 1996 to 830 million in 2003. In the absence of strong leadership, the record or near-record grain prices in late 2007 will likely raise the number of hungry people even further, with children suffering the most.[3]

One key to the threefold expansion in the world grain harvest since 1950 was the rapid adoption in developing countries of high-yielding wheats and rices originally developed in Japan and hybrid corn from the United States. The spread of these highly productive seeds, combined with a tripling of irrigated area and an 11-fold increase in world fertilizer use, tripled the world grain harvest. Growth in irrigation and fertilizer use essentially removed soil moisture and nutrient constraints on much of the world's cropland.[4]

Now the outlook is changing. Farmers are faced with shrinking supplies of irrigation water, a diminishing response to additional fertilizer use, rising temperatures, the loss of cropland to nonfarm uses, rising fuel costs, and a dwindling backlog of yield-raising technologies.

At the same time, they also face a fast-growing demand for farm products from the annual addition of some 70 million people a year, the desire of some 5 billion people to consume more livestock products, and the millions of motorists turning to crop-based fuels to supplement tightening supplies of gasoline and diesel fuel.[5]

This helps explain why world grain production has fallen short of consumption in seven of the last eight years, dropping world grain stocks to the lowest level since 1974. Farmers and agronomists are now being thoroughly challenged.[6]

Rethinking Land Productivity

The shrinking backlog of unused agricultural technology and the associated loss of momentum in raising cropland productivity is found worldwide. Between 1950 and 1990, world grain yield per hectare climbed by 2.1 percent a year, ensuring rapid growth in the world grain harvest. From 1990 to 2007, however, it rose only 1.2 percent annually. This is partly because the yield response to the additional application of fertilizer is diminishing and partly because irrigation water supplies are limited.[7]

This calls for fresh thinking on how to raise cropland productivity. One way is to breed crops that are more tolerant of drought and cold. U.S. corn breeders have developed corn varieties that are more drought-tolerant, enabling corn production to move westward into Kansas, Nebraska, and South Dakota. Kansas, the leading U.S. wheat-producing state, has used a combination of drought-resistant varieties in some areas and irrigation in others to expand corn planting to where the state now produces more corn than wheat. Similarly, corn production is expanding in more northern states such as North Dakota and Minnesota.[8]

Another way of raising land productivity, where soil moisture permits, is to increase the area of multicropped land that produces more than one crop per year. Indeed, the tripling in the world grain harvest since 1950 is due in part to impressive increases in multiple cropping in Asia. Some of the more common combinations are wheat and corn in northern China, wheat and rice in northern India, and the double or triple cropping of rice in southern China, southern India, and rice-growing countries in Southeast Asia.[9]

The spread in double cropping of winter wheat and corn on the North China Plain helped boost China's grain production to where it rivaled that of the United States. Winter wheat grown there yields close to 4 tons per hectare. Corn averages 5 tons. Together these two crops, grown in rotation, can yield 9 tons per hectare per year. China's double cropped rice yields 8 tons per hectare.[10]

Forty years ago, North India produced only wheat, but with the advent of the earlier maturing high-yielding wheats and rices, wheat could be harvested in time to plant rice. This wheat/rice combination is now widely used throughout the Punjab, Haryana, and parts of Uttar Pradesh. The wheat yield of 3 tons and rice yield of 2 tons combine for 5 tons of grain per hectare, helping to feed India's 1.2 billion people.[11]

In North America and Western Europe, which in the past have restricted cropped area to control surpluses, there is some potential for double cropping that has not been fully exploited. In the United States, the lifting of planting area restrictions in 1996 opened new opportunities for multiple cropping. The most common U.S. double cropping combination is winter wheat with soybeans as a summer crop. Since soybeans fix nitrogen, this reduces the need to apply fertilizer to wheat.[12]

A concerted U.S. effort to both breed earlier maturing varieties and develop cultural practices that would facilitate multiple cropping could substantially boost crop output. If China's farmers can extensively double crop wheat and corn, then U.S. farmers—at a similar latitude and with similar climate patterns—could do the same if agricultural research and farm policy were reoriented to support it.

Western Europe, with its mild winters and high-yielding winter wheat, might also be able to double crop more with a summer grain, such as corn, or with a winter oilseed crop. Elsewhere, Brazil and Argentina have an extended frost-free growing season that supports extensive multicropping, often wheat or corn with soybeans.[13]

In many countries, including the United States, most of those in Western Europe, and Japan, fertilizer use has reached a level where using more has little effect on crop yields. There are still some places, however, such as most of Africa, where additional fertilizer would help boost yields. Unfortunately, sub-Saharan Africa lacks the infrastructure to transport fertilizer economically to the villages where it is needed. As a result of nutrient depletion, grain yields in much of sub-Saharan Africa are stagnating.[14]

One encouraging response to this situation in Africa is the simultaneous planting of grain and leguminous trees. At first the trees grow slowly, permitting the grain crop to mature and be harvested; then the saplings grow quickly to several feet in height, dropping leaves that provide nitrogen and organic matter, both sorely needed in African soils. The wood is then cut and used for fuel. This simple, locally adapted technology, developed by scientists at the International Centre for Research in Agroforestry in Nairobi, has enabled farmers to double their grain yields within a matter of years as soil fertility builds.[15]

Another often overlooked issue is the effect of land tenure on productivity. In China, this issue was addressed in March 2007 when the National People's Congress passed legislation protecting property rights. Farmers who had previously occupied their land under 30-year leases would gain additional protection from land confiscation by local officials who, over a number of years, had seized land from some 40 million farmers, often for development. Secure land ownership encourages farmers to invest in and improve their land. A Rural Development Institute survey in China revealed that farmers with documentation of land rights were twice as likely to make long-term investments in their land, such as adding greenhouses, orchards, or fishponds.[16]

Despite local advances, the overall loss of momentum in expanding food production is unmistakable. It will force us to think more seriously about stabilizing population, moving down the food chain, and using the existing harvest more productively. Achieving an acceptable worldwide balance between food and people may now depend on stabilizing population as soon as possible, reducing the unhealthily high consumption of animal products among the affluent, and restricting the conversion of food crops to automotive fuels.

Raising Water Productivity

With water shortages emerging as a constraint on food production growth, the world needs an effort to raise water productivity similar to the one that nearly tripled land productivity during the last half of the twentieth century. Land productivity is typically measured in tons of grain per hectare or bushels per acre. A comparable indicator for irrigation water is kilograms of grain produced per ton of water. Worldwide, that average is now roughly 1 kilogram of grain per ton of water used.[17]

Since it takes 1,000 tons of water to produce 1 ton of grain, it is not surprising that 70 percent of world water use is devoted to irrigation. Thus, raising irrigation efficiency is central to raising water productivity overall. Using more water-efficient irrigation technologies and shifting to crops that use less water permit the expansion of irrigated area even with a fixed water supply. Eliminating water and energy subsidies that encourage wasteful water use allows water prices to rise to market levels. Higher water prices encourage all water users to use water more efficiently. Institutionally, local rural water users associations that directly involve those using the water in its management have raised water productivity in many countries.[18]

Data on water irrigation efficiency for surface water projects—that is, dams that deliver water to farmers through a network of canals—show that crop usage of irrigation water never reaches 100 percent simply because some irrigation water evaporates, some percolates downward, and some runs off. Water policy analysts Sandra Postel and Amy Vickers found that "surface water irrigation efficiency ranges between 25 and 40 percent in India, Mexico, Pakistan, the Philippines, and Thailand; between 40 and 45 percent in Malaysia and Morocco; and between 50 and 60 percent in Israel, Japan, and Taiwan." Irrigation water efficiency is affected not only by the type and condition of irrigation systems but also by soil type, temperature, and humidity. In hot arid regions, the evaporation of irrigation water is far higher than in cooler humid regions.[19]

In a May 2004 meeting, China's Minister of Water Resources Wang Shucheng outlined for me in some detail the plans to raise China's irrigation efficiency from 43 percent in 2000 to 51 percent in 2010 and then to 55 percent in 2030. The steps he described included raising the price of water, providing incentives for adopting more irrigation-efficient technologies, and developing the local institutions to manage this process. Reaching these goals, he felt, would assure China's future food security.[20]

Raising irrigation water efficiency typically means shifting from the less efficient flood or furrow system to overhead sprinklers or drip irrigation, the gold standard of irrigation efficiency. Switching from flood or furrow to low-pressure sprinkler systems reduces water use by an estimated 30 percent, while switching to drip irrigation typically cuts water use in half.[21]

As an alternative to furrow irrigation, a drip system also raises yields because it provides a steady supply of water with minimal losses to evaporation. Since drip systems are both labor-intensive and water-efficient, they are well suited to countries with a surplus of labor and a shortage of water.[22]

A few small countries—Cyprus, Israel, and Jordan—rely heavily on drip irrigation. Among the big three agricultural producers, this more-efficient technology is used on 1–3 percent of irrigated land in India and China and on roughly 4 percent in the United States.[23]

In recent years, small-scale drip-irrigation systems—virtually a bucket with flexible plastic tubing to distribute the water—have been developed to irrigate small vegetable gardens with roughly 100 plants (covering 25 square meters). Somewhat larger drum systems irrigate 125 square meters. In both cases, the containers are elevated slightly, so that gravity distributes the water. Large-scale drip systems using plastic lines that can be moved easily are also becoming popular. These simple systems can pay for themselves in one year. By simultaneously reducing water costs and raising yields, they can dramatically raise incomes of smallholders.[24]

Sandra Postel estimates that the combination of these drip technologies at various scales has the potential to profitably irrigate 10 million hectares of India's cropland, or nearly one tenth of the total. She sees a similar potential for China, which is now also expanding its drip irrigated area to save scarce water.[25]

In the Punjab, with its extensive double cropping of wheat and rice, fast-falling water tables led the state farmers' commission in 2007 to recommend a delay in transplanting rice from May to late June or early July. This would reduce irrigation water use by roughly one third since transplanting would coincide with the arrival of the monsoon. This reduction in groundwater use would help stabilize the water table, which has fallen from 5 meters below the surface to 30 meters in parts of the state.[26]

Institutional shifts—specifically, moving the responsibility for managing irrigation systems from government agencies to local water users associations—can facilitate the more efficient use of water. In many countries farmers are organizing locally so they can assume this responsibility, and since they have an economic stake in good water management, they tend to do a better job than a distant government agency.[27]

Mexico is a leader in developing water users associations. As of 2002, farmers associations managed more than 80 percent of Mexico's publicly irrigated land. One advantage of this shift for the government is that the cost of maintaining the irrigation system is assumed locally, reducing the drain on the treasury. This means that associations often need to charge more for irrigation water, but for farmers the production gains from managing their water supply themselves more than outweigh this additional outlay.[28]

In Tunisia, where water users associations manage both irrigation and residential water, the number of associations increased from 340 in 1987 to 2,575 in 1999, covering much of the country. Many other countries now have such bodies managing their water resources. Although the early groups were organized to deal with large publicly developed irrigation systems, some recent ones have been formed to manage local groundwater irrigation as well. Their goal is to stabilize the water table to avoid aquifer depletion and the economic disruption that it brings to the community.[29]

Low water productivity is often the result of low water prices. In many countries, subsidies lead to irrationally low water prices, creating the impression that water is abundant when in fact it is scarce. As water becomes scarce, it needs to be priced accordingly. Provincial governments in northern China are raising water prices in small increments to discourage waste. A higher water price affects all water users, encouraging investment in more water-efficient irrigation technologies, industrial processes, and household appliances.[30]

What is needed now is a new mindset, a new way of thinking about water use. For example, shifting to more water-efficient crops wherever possible boosts water productivity. Rice production is being phased out around Beijing because rice is such a thirsty crop. Similarly, Egypt restricts rice production in favor of wheat.[31]

Any measures that raise crop yields on irrigated land also raise the productivity of irrigation water. Similarly, any measures that convert grain into animal protein more efficiently in effect increase water productivity.

For people consuming unhealthy amounts of livestock products, moving down the food chain reduces water use. In the United States, where annual consumption of grain as food and feed averages some 800 kilograms (four fifths of a ton) per person, a modest reduction in the consumption of meat, milk, and eggs could easily cut grain use per person by 100 kilograms. For 300 million Americans, such a reduction would cut grain use by 30 million tons and irrigation water use by 30 billion tons.[32]

Reducing water use to the sustainable yield of aquifers and rivers worldwide involves a wide range of measures not only in agriculture but throughout the economy. The more obvious steps, in addition to more water-efficient irrigation practices and more water-efficient crops, include adopting more water-efficient industrial processes and using more water-efficient household appliances. Recycling urban water supplies is another obvious step to consider in countries facing acute water shortages.

Producing Protein More Efficiently

Another way to raise both land and water productivity is to produce animal protein more efficiently. With some 37 percent (about 740 million tons) of the world grain harvest used to produce animal protein, even a modest gain in efficiency can save a large quantity of grain.[33]

World meat consumption increased from 44 million tons in 1950 to 240 million tons in 2005, more than doubling consumption per person from 17 kilograms to 39 kilograms (86 pounds). Consumption of milk and eggs has also risen. In every society where incomes have risen, meat consumption has too, perhaps reflecting a taste that evolved over 4 million years of hunting and gathering.[34]

As both the oceanic fish catch and the production of beef on rangelands have leveled off, the world has shifted to grain-based production of animal protein to expand output. And as the demand for meat climbs, consumers are shifting from beef and pork to poultry and fish, sources that convert grain into protein most efficiently. Health concerns among industrial-country consumers are reinforcing this shift.

The efficiency with which various animals convert grain into protein varies widely. With cattle in feedlots, it takes roughly 7 kilograms of grain to produce a 1-kilogram gain in live weight. For pork, the figure is over 3 kilograms of grain per kilogram of weight gain, for poultry it is just over 2, and for herbivorous species of farmed fish (such as carp, tilapia, and catfish), it is less than 2. As the market shifts production to the more grain-efficient products, it raises the productivity of both land and water.[35]

Global beef production, most of which comes from rangelands, grew less than 1 percent a year from 1990 to 2006. Growth in the number of cattle feedlots was minimal. Pork production grew by 2.6 percent annually, and poultry by nearly 5 percent. The rapid growth in poultry production, going from 41 million tons in 1990 to 83 million tons in 2006 enabled poultry to eclipse beef in 1995, moving it into second place behind pork. World pork production, half of it now in China, overtook beef production in 1979 and has continued to widen the lead since then.[36]

Fast-growing, highly grain-efficient fish farm output may

also overtake beef production within the next decade or so. In fact, aquaculture has been the fastest-growing source of animal protein since 1990, largely because herbivorous fish convert feed into protein so efficiently. Aquacultural output expanded from 13 million tons in 1990 to 48 million tons in 2005, growing by more than 9 percent a year.[37]

Public attention has focused on aquacultural operations that are environmentally inefficient or disruptive, such as the farming of salmon, a carnivorous species, and shrimp. These operations account for 4.7 million tons of output, less than 10 percent of the global farmed fish total, but they are growing fast. Salmon are inefficient in that they are fed other fish, usually as fishmeal, which comes either from fish processing wastes or from low-value fish caught specifically for this purpose. Shrimp farming often involves the destruction of coastal mangrove forests to create areas for the shrimp.[38]

Worldwide, aquaculture is dominated by herbivorous species—mainly carp in China and India, but also catfish in the United States and tilapia in several countries—and shellfish. This is where the great growth potential for efficient animal protein production lies.

China, the world's leading producer, accounts for an astounding two thirds of global fish farm output. Aquacultural production in China is dominated by finfish (mostly carp), which are produced inland in freshwater ponds, lakes, reservoirs, and rice paddies, and by shellfish (mostly oysters, clams, and mussels), which are produced mostly in coastal regions.[39]

Over time, China has also developed a fish polyculture using four types of carp that feed at different levels of the food chain, in effect emulating natural aquatic ecosystems. Silver carp and bighead carp are filter feeders, eating phytoplankton and zooplankton respectively. The grass carp, as its name implies, feeds largely on vegetation, while the common carp is a bottom feeder, living on detritus. These four species thus form a small ecosystem, with each filling a particular niche. This multispecies system, which converts feed into high-quality protein with remarkable efficiency, allowed China to produce some 14 million tons of carp in 2005.[40]

While poultry production has grown rapidly in China, as in other developing countries, it has been dwarfed by the phenomenal growth of aquaculture. Today aquacultural output in China—at 30 million tons—is double that of poultry, making it the first major country where fish farming has eclipsed poultry farming.[41]

China's aquaculture is often integrated with agriculture, enabling farmers to use agricultural wastes, such as pig or duck manure, to fertilize ponds, thus stimulating the growth of plankton on which the fish feed. Fish polyculture, which commonly boosts pond productivity over that of monocultures by at least half, is widely practiced in both China and India.[42]

With incomes now rising in densely populated Asia, other countries are following China's aquacultural lead. Among them are Thailand and Viet Nam. Viet Nam, for example, devised a plan in 2001 of developing 700,000 hectares of land in the Mekong Delta for aquaculture, which now produces more than 1 million tons of fish and shrimp.[43]

In the United States, catfish, which require less than 2 kilograms of feed per kilogram of live weight, is the leading aquacultural product. U.S. annual catfish production of 600 million pounds (about two pounds per person) is concentrated in the South. Mississippi, with easily 60 percent of U.S. output, is the catfish capital of the world.[44]

When we think of soybeans in our daily diet, it is typically as tofu, veggie burgers, or other meat substitutes. But most of the world's fast-growing soybean harvest is consumed indirectly in the beef, pork, poultry, milk, eggs, and farmed fish that we eat. Although not a visible part of our diets, the incorporation of soybean meal into feed rations has revolutionized the world feed industry, greatly increasing the efficiency with which grain is converted into animal protein.[45]

In 2007, the world's farmers produced 222 million tons of soybeans—1 ton for every 9 tons of grain produced. Of this, some 20 million tons were consumed directly as tofu or meat substitutes. The bulk of the remaining 202 million tons, after some was saved for seed, was crushed in order to extract 37 million tons of soybean oil, separating it from the highly valued, high-protein meal.[46]

The 160 million or so tons of protein-rich soybean meal that remain after the oil is extracted is fed to cattle, pigs, chicken, and fish. Combining soybean meal with grain in roughly one part meal to four parts grain dramatically boosts the efficiency with which grain is converted into animal protein, sometimes nearly doubling it.[47]

The world's three largest meat producers—China, the United States, and Brazil—now all rely heavily on soybean meal as a protein supplement in feed rations.[48]

The use of soybean meal in livestock feed, poultry, and fish both replaces some grain in feed and increases the efficiency with which the remaining grain is converted into livestock products. This helps explain why the share of the world grain harvest used for feed has not increased over the last 20 years even though production of meat, milk, eggs, and farmed fish has climbed. It also explains why world soybean production has increased nearly 14-fold since 1950.[49]

Mounting pressures on land and water resources have led to the evolution of some promising new animal protein production systems that are based on roughage rather than grain, such as milk production in India. Since 1970, India's milk production has increased more than fourfold, jumping from 21 million to 96 million tons. In 1997 India overtook the United States to become the world's leading producer of milk and other dairy products.[50]

The spark for this explosive growth came in 1965 when an enterprising young Indian, Dr. Verghese Kurien, organized the National Dairy Development Board, an umbrella organization of dairy cooperatives. The dairy coop's principal purpose was to market the milk from tiny herds that typically averaged two to three cows each, providing the link between the growing market for dairy products and the millions of village families who had only a small marketable surplus.[51]

Creating the market for milk spurred the fourfold growth in output. In a country where protein shortages stunt the growth of so many children, expanding the milk supply from less than half a cup per person a day 30 years ago to one cup today represents a major advance.[52]

What is so remarkable is that India has built the world's largest dairy industry almost entirely on roughage—wheat straw, rice straw, corn stalks, and grass gathered from the roadside. Even so, the value of the milk produced each year now exceeds that of the rice harvest.[53]

A second new protein production model, one that also relies

on ruminants and roughage, has evolved in four provinces in eastern China—Hebei, Shangdong, Henan, and Anhui—where double cropping of winter wheat and corn is common. Although wheat straw and cornstalks are often used as fuel for cooking, villagers are shifting to other sources of energy for this, which lets them feed the straw and cornstalks to cattle. Supplementing this roughage with small amounts of nitrogen in the form of urea allows the microflora in the complex four-stomach digestive system of cattle to convert roughage into animal protein more efficiently.[54]

These four crop-producing provinces in China, dubbed the Beef Belt by officials, use crop residues to produce much more beef than the vast grazing provinces in the northwest do. The use of crop residues to produce milk in India and beef in China lets farmers reap a second harvest from the original grain crop, thus boosting both land and water productivity.[55]

Although these new protein models have evolved in India and China, both densely populated countries, similar systems can be adopted in other countries as population pressures intensify, as demand for meat and milk increases, and as farmers seek new ways to convert plant products into animal protein.

The world desperately needs more new protein production techniques such as these. Meat consumption is growing twice as fast as population, egg consumption is growing nearly three times as fast, and growth in the demand for fish—both from the oceans and from fish farms—is also outpacing that of population.[56]

While the world has had many years of experience in feeding an additional 70 million people each year, it has no experience with some 5 billion people striving to move up the food chain at the same time. For a sense of what this translates into, consider what has happened in China, where record economic growth has in effect telescoped history, showing how diets change when incomes rise rapidly. As recently as 1978, meat consumption in China consisted mostly of modest amounts of pork. Since then, consumption of meat—pork, beef, poultry, and mutton—has climbed severalfold, pushing China's total meat consumption far above that of the United States.[57]

While diversifying diets has dramatically improved nutrition in China, in most of the developing world nutritional disorders remain. For example, half the women in the developing world

suffer from anemia, the world's most common nutritional deficiency. Diets high in starchy food and low in iron-rich foods,
such as leafy green vegetables, shellfish, nuts, and red meat, lead
to insufficient iron in the diet, which in turn leads to low birth-
weights and high infant and maternal mortality.[58]

Encouragingly, a decade of research by the Canadian-based
Micronutrient Initiative has succeeded in fortifying salt with
iodine and iron together. Just as iodine fortification of salt eliminated iodine deficiency diseases, so, too, can the addition of
iron eliminate iron deficiency diseases. This double-fortified salt
is being introduced initially in India, Kenya, and Nigeria. The
prospect of eliminating iron deficiency disorders at an annual
cost of 20¢ per person is one of the most exciting new options
for improving the human condition in this new century.[59]

Moving Down the Food Chain

One of the questions I am most often asked is, "How many people can the earth support?" I answer with another question: "At
what level of food consumption?" Using round numbers, at the
U.S. level of 800 kilograms of grain per person annually for food
and feed, the 2-billion-ton annual world harvest of grain would
support 2.5 billion people. At the Italian level of consumption of
close to 400 kilograms, the current harvest would support 5 billion people. At the 200 kilograms of grain consumed by the average Indian, it would support a population of 10 billion.[60]

In every society where incomes rise, people move up the food
chain, eating more animal protein as beef, pork, poultry, milk,
eggs, and seafood. The mix of animal products varies with
geography and culture, but the shift to more livestock products
as purchasing power increases appears to be universal.

As consumption of livestock products, poultry, and farmed
fish rises, grain use per person also rises. Of the roughly 800
kilograms of grain consumed per person each year in the United States, about 100 kilograms is eaten directly as bread, pasta,
and breakfast cereals, while the bulk of the grain is consumed
indirectly in the form of livestock and poultry products. By contrast, in India, where people consume just under 200 kilograms
of grain per year, or roughly a pound per day, nearly all grain is
eaten directly to satisfy basic food energy needs. Little is available for conversion into livestock products.[61]

Of the three countries just cited, life expectancy is highest in Italy even though U.S. medical expenditures per person are much higher. People who live very low or very high on the food chain do not live as long as those in an intermediate position. Those consuming a Mediterranean type diet that includes meat, cheese, and seafood, but all in moderation, are healthier and live longer. People living high on the food chain, such as Americans or Canadians, can improve their health by moving down the food chain. For those who live in low-income countries like India, where a starchy staple such as rice can supply 60 percent or more of total caloric intake, eating more protein-rich foods can improve health and raise life expectancy.[62]

In agriculture we often look at how climate affects the food supply but not at how what we eat affects climate. While we understand rather well the link between climate change and the fuel efficiency of the cars we buy, we do not have a comparable understanding of the climate effect of various dietary options. Gidon Eshel and Pamela A. Martin of the University of Chicago have addressed this issue. They begin by noting that the energy used in the food economy to provide the typical American diet and that used for personal transportation are roughly the same. In fact, the range between the more and less carbon-intensive transportation options and dietary options is each about 4 to 1. With cars, the Toyota Prius, a gas-electric hybrid, uses scarcely one fourth as much fuel as a Chevrolet Suburban SUV. Similarly with diets, a plant-based diet requires roughly one fourth as much energy as a diet rich in red meat. Shifting from a diet rich in red meat to a plant-based diet cuts greenhouse gas emissions as much as shifting from a Suburban SUV to a Prius. [63]

The inclusion of soybean meal in feed rations to convert grain into animal protein more efficiently, the shift by consumers to more grain-efficient forms of animal protein, and the movement of consumers down the food chain all can help reduce the demand for land, water, and fertilizer. This reduces carbon emissions and thus helps to stabilize climate as well.

Action on Many Fronts

At this writing in early October 2007, the food prospect does not look particularly promising. Grain prices in recent days have reached historic highs. Wheat has gone over $9 a bushel for the first time in history—more than double the figure a year earlier. International food aid flows are being slashed as rising grain prices collide with fixed budgets.[64]

If we continue with business as usual, the number of hungry people will soar. More and more, those on the lower rungs of the global economic ladder are losing their tenuous grip and are beginning to fall off. Cheap food may now be history.

Historically, the responsibility for food security rested largely with the Ministry of Agriculture. During the last half of the last century, ensuring adequate supplies of grain in the world market at a time of surplus production capacity was a relatively simple matter. Whenever the world grain harvest fell short and prices started to rise, the U.S. Department of Agriculture would return to production the cropland that had been idled under commodity-supply management programs, thus boosting output and stabilizing prices. This era ended in 1996 when the United States discontinued its annual cropland set-aside program.[65]

Now in our overpopulated, climate-changing, water-scarce world, food security is a matter for the entire society and for all government ministries. Since hunger is almost always the result of poverty, eradicating hunger depends on eradicating poverty. And where populations are outrunning their land and water resources, eradicating hunger also depends on stabilizing population. Our Plan B goal is to stabilize world population by 2040 at the 8-billion level. This will not be easy, but the alternative may be a halt in population growth because of rising mortality.

The new reality is that the Ministry of Energy may have a greater influence on future food security than the Ministry of Agriculture. The principal threat to food security today is climate change from the burning of fossil fuels. It is the Ministry of Energy's responsibility to minimize crop-withering heat waves, to prevent the melting of the glaciers that feed Asia's major rivers during the dry season, and to prevent the ice sheet melting that would inundate the river deltas and floodplains that produce much of the Asian rice harvest.

And where water is often a more serious constraint on expanding food production than land, it will be up to the Ministry of Water Resources to do everything possible to raise the efficiency of water use. With water, as with energy, the principal opportunities now are on the demand side in increasing water-use efficiency, not on expanding the supply.

In a world where cropland is scarce and becoming more so, decisions made in the Ministry of Transportation on whether to develop auto-centered systems or more-diversified transport systems that are less land-intensive, including light rail, buses, and bicycles, will directly affect world food security. Transportation policies that diversify transport systems and reduce fossil fuel use will also help stabilize climate.

Decisions made by governments on the production of crop-based automotive fuels are already affecting grain supplies and prices. Given the turmoil in world grain markets in late 2007, it is time for the U.S. government to place a moratorium on the licensing of any more grain-based ethanol distilleries.

And finally, we have a role to play as individuals. Whether we bike or drive to work will affect carbon emissions, climate change, and food security. The size of the car we drive to the supermarket may affect the size of the bill at the supermarket checkout counter. If we are living high on the food chain, we can move down, improving our health while helping to stabilize climate. Food security is something in which we all have a stake—and a responsibility.

10

Designing Cities for People

As I was being driven through Tel Aviv from my hotel to a conference center a few years ago, I could not help but note the overwhelming presence of cars and parking lots. It was obvious that Tel Aviv, expanding from a small settlement a half-century ago to a city of some 3 million today, had evolved during the automobile era. It occurred to me that the ratio of parks to parking lots may be the best single indicator of the livability of a city—an indication of whether the city is designed for people or for cars.[1]

Tel Aviv is not the world's only fast-growing city. Urbanization is the second dominant demographic trend of our time, after population growth itself. In 1900, 150 million people lived in cities. By 2000, it was 2.8 billion people, a 19-fold increase. As of 2008, more than half of us are living in cities—making us, for the first time, an urban species.[2]

In 1900 there were only a handful of cities with a million people. Today 414 cities have at least that many inhabitants. And there are 20 megacities with 10 million or more residents. Tokyo, with 35 million residents, has more people than all of Canada. Mexico City's population of 19 million is nearly equal to that of Australia. New York, São Paulo, Mumbai (formerly Bombay), Delhi, Shanghai, Kolkata (Calcutta), and Jakarta follow close behind.[3]

The world's cities are facing unprecedented problems. In Mexico City, Tehran, Kolkata, Bangkok, Shanghai, and hundreds of other cities, the air is no longer safe to breathe. In some cities, the air is so polluted that breathing is equivalent to smoking two packs of cigarettes per day. Respiratory illnesses are rampant. In the United States, the number of hours commuters spend sitting in traffic-congested streets and highways climbs higher each year, raising frustration levels.[4]

In response to these conditions, we are seeing the emergence of a new urbanism, a planning philosophy that environmentalist Francesca Lyman says "seeks to revive the traditional city planning of an era when cities were designed around human beings instead of automobiles." One of the most remarkable modern urban transformations has occurred in Bogotá, Colombia, where Enrique Peñalosa served as Mayor for three years. When he took office in 1998 he did not ask how life could be improved for the 30 percent who owned cars; he wanted to know what could be done for the 70 percent—the majority—who did not own cars.[5]

Peñalosa realized that a city that has a pleasant environment for children and the elderly would work for everyone. In just a few years, he transformed the quality of urban life with his vision of a city designed for people. Under his leadership, the city banned the parking of cars on sidewalks, created or renovated 1,200 parks, introduced a highly successful bus-based rapid transit system, built hundreds of kilometers of bicycle paths and pedestrian streets, reduced rush hour traffic by 40 percent, planted 100,000 trees, and involved local citizens directly in the improvement of their neighborhoods. In doing this, he created a sense of civic pride among the city's 8 million residents, making the streets of Bogotá in this strife-torn country safer than those in Washington, D.C.[6]

Peñalosa observes that "high quality public pedestrian space in general and parks in particular are evidence of a true democracy at work." He further observes: "Parks and public space are also important to a democratic society because they are the only places where people meet as equals....In a city, parks are as essential to the physical and emotional health of a city as the water supply." He notes this is not obvious from most city budgets, where parks are deemed a luxury. By contrast, "roads, the public space for cars, receive infinitely more resources and less budget cuts than parks, the public space for children. Why," he asks, "are the public spaces for cars deemed more important than the public spaces for children?"[7]

In espousing this new urban philosophy, Peñalosa is not alone. Now government planners everywhere are experimenting, seeking ways to design cities for people not cars. Cars promise mobility, and they provide it in a largely rural setting. But in an urbanizing world there is an inherent conflict between the automobile and the city. After a point, as their numbers multiply, automobiles provide not mobility but immobility.[8]

Some cities in industrial and developing countries alike are dramatically increasing urban mobility by moving away from the car. Jaime Lerner, the former mayor of Curitiba, Brazil, was one of the first to design and adopt an alternative transportation system, one that does not mimic those in the West but that is inexpensive and commuter-friendly. Since 1974 Curitiba's transportation system has been totally restructured. Although 40 percent of the people own cars, these play a minor role in urban transport. Busing, biking, and walking totally dominate, with more than half of all trips in the city by bus. The city's population has tripled since 1974, but its car traffic has declined by a remarkable 30 percent.[9]

The Ecology of Cities

Cities require a concentration of food, water, energy, and materials that nature cannot provide. Collecting these masses of materials and then dispersing them in the form of garbage, sewage, and pollutants in air and water is challenging city managers everywhere.

The evolution of modern cities was tied to advances in transport, initially for ships and trains, but it was the internal combustion engine combined with cheap oil that provided the mobility of people and freight that fueled the phenomenal urban growth of the twentieth century.

Early cities relied on food and water from the surrounding countryside, but today cities often depend on distant sources for basic amenities. Los Angeles, for example, draws much of its water from the Colorado River, some 970 kilometers (600 miles) away. Mexico City's burgeoning population, living at an altitude of 3,000 meters, must now depend on the costly pumping of water from 150 kilometers away and must lift it 1,000 meters or more to augment its inadequate water supplies. Beijing is planning to draw water from the Yangtze River basin some 1,200 kilometers away.[10]

Food comes from even greater distances, as is illustrated by Tokyo. While the city still gets its rice from the highly productive farmers in Japan, with their land carefully protected by government policy, its wheat comes largely from the Great Plains of North America and from Australia. Its corn supply comes largely from the U.S. Midwest. Soybeans come from the U.S. Midwest and the Brazilian *cerrado*.[11]

The very oil used to move resources into and out of cities often comes from distant oil fields. Rising oil prices will affect cities, but they will affect even more the suburbs that many cities have spawned. The growing scarcity of water and the high cost of the energy invested in transporting water over long distances may itself begin to constrain the growth of some cities.

Against this backdrop, Richard Register, author of *Ecocities: Rebuilding Cities in Balance with Nature*, says it is time to fundamentally rethink the design of cities. He agrees with Peñalosa that cities should be designed for people, not for cars. He goes even further, talking about pedestrian cities—communities designed so that people do not need cars because they can walk wherever they need to go or take public transportation.[12]

Register says that a city should be seen as a functioning system not in terms of its parts but in terms of its whole. He also makes a convincing case that cities should be integrated into local ecosystems rather than imposed on them.[13]

He describes with pride an after-the-fact integration into the local ecosystem of San Luis Obispo, a California town of 43,000 north of Los Angeles: "[It] has a beautiful creek restoration project with several streets and through-building passageways lined with shops that connect to the town's main commercial street, and people love it. Before closing a street, turning a small parking lot into a park, restoring the creek and making the main street easily accessible to the 'nature' corridor, that is, the creek, the downtown had a 40 percent vacancy rate in the storefronts, and now it has zero. Of course it's popular. You sit at your restaurant by the creek...where fresh breezes rustle the trees in a world undisturbed by car noise and blasting exhaust."[14]

For Register, the design of the city and its buildings become a part of the local landscape, capitalizing on the local ecology. For example, buildings can be designed to be heated and cooled by nature as much as possible. Urban fresh fruit and vegetable production will expand into vacant lots and onto rooftops as oil prices rise. Cities can largely live on recycled water that is cleaned and used again and again. The "flush and forget" water system will become too costly for many water-short cities in a world after peak oil.[15]

In a world of land, water, and energy scarcity, the cost of each will increase substantially, shifting the terms of trade between the countryside and cities. Ever since the beginning of the Industrial Revolution, the terms of trade have favored cities because they control capital and technology, the scarce resources. But if land and water become the scarcest resources, then people in rural areas who control them may sometimes have the upper hand. With a Plan B economy based on renewable energy, a disproportionate share of that energy, particularly wind and plant-based energy, will come from nearby rural areas.[16]

Redesigning Urban Transport

Urban transport systems based on a combination of rail lines, bus lines, bicycle pathways, and pedestrian walkways offer the best of all possible worlds in providing mobility, low-cost transportation, and a healthy urban environment.

A rail system provides the foundation for a city's transportation system. Rails are geographically fixed, providing a permanent means of transportation that people can count on. Once in place, the nodes on such a system become the obvious places to concentrate office buildings, high-rise apartment buildings, and shops.

Whether the best fit is underground rail, light-rail surface systems, or both depends in part on city size and geography. Megacities regularly turn to underground rail systems to provide mobility. For cities of intermediate size, light rail is often an attractive option.

As noted earlier, some of the most innovative public transportation systems, those that shift huge numbers of people from cars into buses, have been developed in Curitiba and Bogotá. The success of Bogotá's bus rapid transit (BRT) system, TransMilenio, which uses special express lanes to move people quickly through the city, is being replicated not only in six other Colombian cities but elsewhere too: Mexico City, São Paulo, Hanoi, Seoul, Taipei, and Quito. In China, Beijing is one of 20 cities developing BRT systems.[17]

Several cities in Africa are also planning BRT systems. Even industrial-country cities such as Ottawa, Toronto, Minneapolis, Las Vegas, and—much to everyone's delight—Los Angeles have launched or are now considering BRT systems.[18]

Some cities are reducing traffic congestion and air pollution by charging cars to enter the city. Singapore, long a leader in urban transport innovation, has imposed a tax on all roads leading into the city center. Electronic sensors identify each car and then debit the owner's credit card. This system has reduced the number of automobiles in Singapore, providing its residents with both more mobility and cleaner air.[19]

Singapore has been joined by three Norwegian cities—Oslo, Bergen, and Trondheim—as well as London and Stockholm. In London—where the average speed of an automobile a few years ago was comparable to that of a horse-drawn carriage a century ago—a congestion fee was adopted in early 2003. The initial £5 ($10) charge on all motorists driving into the center city between 7 a.m. and 6.30 p.m. immediately reduced the number of vehicles, permitting traffic to flow more freely while cutting pollution and noise.[20]

In the first year after the new tax was introduced, the number of people using buses to travel into the central city climbed by 38 percent, delays dropped by 30 percent, and vehicle speeds on key thoroughfares increased by 21 percent. Since the congestion charge was adopted, the daily flow of cars and minicabs into central London during peak hours has been reduced by 70,000, a drop of 36 percent, while the number of bicycles has increased by 50 percent.[21]

In July 2005, the congestion fee was raised to £8 ($16). With much of the revenue from the congestion fee being used to upgrade and expand the bus system, Londoners are continuing to shift from cars to buses.[22]

In July 2007, Milan announced it would impose a "pollution charge" of $14 on vehicles entering its historic center in daytime hours during the week. Other cites now considering similar measures include New York, São Paulo, San Francisco, and Barcelona.[23]

Paris Mayor Bertrand Delanoë, who was elected in 2001, faced some of Europe's worst traffic congestion and air pollution. He decided traffic would have to be cut 40 percent by 2020. The first step was to invest in better transit in outlying regions to ensure that everyone in the greater Paris area had access to high-quality public transit. The next step was to create express lanes on main thoroughfares for buses and bicycles, thus reducing the number of lanes for cars. As bus speeds increased, more people used this form of transportation.[24]

A third initiative in Paris was the establishment of a city bicycle rental program that by the end of 2007 was to have 20,600 bikes available at 1,450 docking stations throughout the city. Access to the bikes is by credit card, with a choice of daily, weekly, or annual rates ranging from just over $1 per day to $40 per year. Based on the first few months, the bicycles are proving to be immensely popular. Patrick Allin, a 38-year-old Parisian and an enthusiastic user of the bikes, says they are great for conversation: "We are no longer all alone in our cars—we are sharing. It's really changed the atmosphere here; people chat at the stations and even at traffic lights."[25]

In writing about the program in the *New York Times*, Serge Schmemann draws a "lesson for all big cities: this is an idea whose time has come." At this point Mayor Delanoë is well along on his goal of cutting car traffic by 40 percent and carbon emissions by a similar amount.[26]

The United States, which has lagged far behind Europe in developing diversified urban transport systems, is being swept by a "complete streets" movement, an effort to ensure that streets are friendly to pedestrians and bicycles as well as to cars. Many American communities lack sidewalks and bike lanes, making it difficult for pedestrians and cyclists to get around safely, particularly where streets are heavily traveled. In Char-

lotte, North Carolina, transportation planning manager Norm
Steinman says: "We didn't build sidewalks here for 50 years.
Streets designed by traffic engineers in the '60s, '70s, '80s, and
'90s were mostly for autos."[27]

This cars-only model is being challenged by the National
Complete Streets Coalition, a powerful assemblage of citizen
groups including the million-member-strong Natural Resources
Defense Council, AARP (an organization of 38 million older
Americans), and numerous local and national cycling organizations. The "complete streets" movement is the product of a
"perfect storm of issues coming together," says Randy Neufeld,
coordinator of the Chicagoland Bicycle Federation's "Healthy
Streets Campaign." Among these issues are concern over the
obesity epidemic, rising gasoline prices, the urgent need to cut
carbon emissions, air pollution, and the mobility constraints on
aging baby boomers. The elderly who live in urban areas without sidewalks and who no longer drive are effectively impris-
oned in their own homes.[28]

The National Complete Streets Coalition, headed by Barbara McCann, reports that as of July 2007, "complete streets"
policies are in place in 14 states and 52 cities. Two of the country's most populous states, California and Illinois, are expected
to join the group. One reason states have become interested in
passing such legislation is the realization that designing bike
paths, sidewalks, and other such amenities into a project from
the beginning is more efficient and less costly than adding them
later. As McCann notes, it is "cheaper to do it right the first
time." This is why Senator Tom Harkin of Iowa is reportedly
interested in sponsoring a "complete streets" bill in the U.S.
Congress.[29]

Countries that have well-developed urban transit systems
and a mature bicycle infrastructure are much better positioned
to withstand the stresses of a downturn in world oil production
than are countries whose only transport option is the car. With
a full array of walking and biking options, the number of trips
by car can easily be cut by 10–20 percent.[30]

The bicycle, a form of personal transportation, has many
attractions. It alleviates congestion, lowers air pollution,
reduces obesity, increases physical fitness, does not emit
climate-disrupting carbon dioxide, and has a price within reach

for the billions of people who cannot afford an automobile. Bicycles increase mobility while reducing congestion and the area of land paved over. Six bicycles can typically fit into the road space used by one car. For parking, the advantage is even greater, with 20 bicycles occupying the space required to park a car.[31]

The bicycle is not only a flexible means of transportation; it is an ideal way of restoring a balance between caloric intake and expenditure. The opportunity to exercise is valuable in its own right. Regular exercise of the sort provided by cycling to work reduces cardiovascular disease, osteoporosis, and arthritis and it strengthens the immune system.

Few methods of reducing carbon emissions are as effective as substituting a bicycle for a car on short trips. A bicycle is a marvel of engineering efficiency, one where an investment in 22 pounds of metal and rubber boosts the efficiency of individual mobility by a factor of three. On my bike I estimate that I get easily 7 miles per potato. An automobile, which requires at least a ton of material to transport one person, is extraordinarily inefficient by comparison.

The capacity of the bicycle to provide mobility for low-income populations was dramatically demonstrated in China. In 1976, this country produced 6 million bicycles. After the reforms in 1978 that led to an open market economy and rapidly rising incomes, bicycle production started climbing, reaching close to 70 million in 2006. The surge to 500 million bicycle owners in China since 1978 provided the greatest increase in human mobility in history. Bicycles took over rural roads and city streets. Although China's 9 million passenger cars, and the urban congestion they cause, get a lot of attention, it is bicycles that provide personal mobility for hundreds of millions of Chinese.[32]

Many cities are turning to bicycles for various uses. In the United States, nearly 75 percent of police departments serving populations of 50,000 or more now have routine patrols by bicycle. Officers on bikes are more productive in cities partly because they are more mobile and can reach the scene of an accident or crime more quickly and more quietly than officers in cars. They typically make 50 percent more arrests per day than officers in squad cars. Fiscally, the cost of operating a bicycle is trivial compared with that of a police car.[33]

Bicycle messenger services are common in the world's larger cities simply because they deliver small parcels more quickly than cars can and at a lower cost. As e-commerce expands, the need for quick, reliable, urban delivery services is escalating. For Internet marketing firms, quick delivery wins more customers. In New York an estimated 300 bicycle messenger firms compete for $700 million worth of business annually.[34]

The key to realizing the potential of the bicycle is to create a bicycle-friendly transport system. This means providing both bicycle trails and designated street lanes for bicycles. Among the industrial-country leaders in designing bicycle-friendly transport systems are the Dutch, the Danes, and the Germans.[35]

The Netherlands, the unquestioned leader among industrial countries in encouraging bicycle use, has incorporated a vision of the role of bicycles into a Bicycle Master Plan. In addition to creating bike lanes and trails in all its cities, the system also often gives cyclists the advantage over motorists in right-of-way and at traffic lights. Some traffic signals permit cyclists to move out before cars. Roughly 30 percent of all urban trips in the Netherlands are on bicycle. This compares with 1 percent in the United States.[36]

Within the Netherlands, a nongovernmental group called Interface for Cycling Expertise (I-ce) has been formed to share the Dutch experience in designing a modern transport system that prominently features bicycles. It is working with groups in Brazil, Colombia, Ghana, India, Kenya, South Africa, Sri Lanka, Tanzania, and Uganda to facilitate bicycle use. Roelof Wittink, head of I-ce, observes, "If you plan only for cars then drivers will feel like the King of the Road. This reinforces the attitude that the bicycle is backward and used only by the poor. But if you plan for bicycles it changes the public attitude."[37]

Both the Netherlands and Japan have made a concerted effort to integrate bicycles and rail commuter services by providing bicycle parking at rail stations, making it easier for cyclists to commute by train. In Japan, the use of bicycles for commuting to rail transportation has reached the point where some stations have invested in vertical, multi-level parking garages for bicycles, much as is often done for automobiles.[38]

The combination of rail and bicycle, and particularly their integration into a single, overall transport system, makes a city eminently more livable than one that relies almost exclusively on private automobiles. Noise, pollution, congestion, and frustration are all lessened. We and the earth are both healthier.

Reducing Urban Water Use

The one-time use of water to disperse human and industrial wastes is an outmoded practice, made obsolete by new technologies and water shortages. Water enters a city, becomes contaminated with human and industrial wastes, and leaves the city dangerously polluted. Toxic industrial wastes discharged into rivers and lakes or into wells also permeate aquifers, making water—both surface and underground—unsafe for drinking.

The current engineering concept for dealing with human waste is to use vast quantities of water to wash it away, preferably into a sewer system, where it may or may not be treated before being discharged into the local river. The "flush and forget" system takes nutrients originating in the soil and typically dumps them into the nearest body of water. Not only are the nutrients lost from agriculture, but the nutrient overload has contributed to the death of many rivers and to the formation of some 200 dead zones in ocean coastal regions. This outdated system is expensive and water-intensive, it disrupts the nutrient cycle, and it can be a major source of disease and death.[39]

Sunita Narain of the Centre for Science and Environment in India argues convincingly that a water-based disposal system with sewage treatment facilities is neither environmentally nor economically viable for India. She notes that an Indian family of five, producing 250 liters of excrement in a year and using a water flush toilet, contaminates 150,000 liters of water when washing away its wastes.[40]

As currently designed, India's sewer system is actually a pathogen-dispersal system. It takes a small quantity of contaminated material and uses it to make vast quantities of water unfit for human use. With this system, Narain says both "our rivers and our children are dying." India's government, like that of many other developing countries, is hopelessly chasing the goal of universal water-based sewage systems and sewage treatment facilities—unable to close the huge gap between services needed and provided, but unwilling to admit that it is not an economically viable option.[41]

This dispersal of pathogens is a huge public health challenge. Worldwide, poor sanitation and personal hygiene claim the lives of some 2 million children per year, a toll that is one third the 6 million lives claimed by hunger and malnutrition.[42]

Fortunately, there is a low-cost alternative: the composting toilet. This is a simple, waterless, odorless toilet linked to a small compost facility. The dry composting converts human fecal material into a soil-like humus, which is essentially odorless and is scarcely 10 percent of the original volume. Table waste can also be incorporated into the composter. These compost facilities need to be emptied every year or so, depending on design and size. Vendors periodically collect the humus and market it as a soil supplement, thus ensuring that the nutrients and organic matter return to the soil, reducing the need for energy-intensive fertilizer.[43]

This technology sharply reduces residential water use compared with flush toilets, thus cutting water bills and lowering the energy needed to pump and purify water. As a bonus, it also reduces garbage flow if table waste is incorporated, eliminates the sewage water disposal problem, and restores the nutrient cycle. The U.S. Environmental Protection Agency now lists several brands of dry compost toilets approved for use. Pioneered in Sweden, these toilets work well under the widely varying conditions in which they are now used, including Swedish apartment buildings, U.S. private residences, and Chinese villages.[44]

Interest in ecological sanitation, or ecosan, as it is commonly referred to, is spiraling upward as water shortages intensify. Since 2005, international ecosan conferences have been held in several countries, including India, South Africa, Syria, Mexico, and China. The movement, led by the Swedish International Development Agency, can now point to projects in at least a dozen countries. Although ecosan is not yet mainstream, it is fast becoming so.[45]

The first large community to be built with dry compost toilets in every residence is on the outskirts of Dongsheng in Nei Monggol (Inner Mongolia). Designed to house 7,000 people, the town is scheduled for completion by the end of 2007. In this system, urine, which contains 80 percent of the nutrients leaving the human body, is diverted into a designated container. It is then collected and recycled directly onto the land as a fertilizer supplement. Both human solid waste and kitchen waste are composted into a rich humus, sanitized, and used as an organic fertilizer. For many of the 2.6 billion people who lack sanitation facilities, composting toilets may be the answer.[46]

China has emerged as the world leader in this field, with some 100,000 urine-diverting, dry compost toilets now in use. Among the other countries with these toilets in the demonstration stage or beyond are India, Uganda, South Africa, Mexico, Bolivia, and seven countries in West Africa. Once a toilet is separated from the water use system, recycling household water becomes a much simpler process.[47]

For cities, the most effective single step to raise water productivity is to adopt a comprehensive water treatment/recycling system, reusing the same water continuously. With this system, only a small percentage of water is lost to evaporation each time it cycles through. Given the technologies that are available today, it is quite possible to recycle urban water supplies comprehensively, largely removing cities as a claimant on scarce water resources.

Some cities faced with shrinking water supplies and rising water costs are beginning to recycle their water. Singapore, for example, which buys water from Malaysia at a high price, is beginning to recycle water, reducing the amount it imports. For some cities, water recycling may become a condition of their survival.[48]

Individual industries facing water shortages are moving away from the use of water to disperse industrial waste. Some companies segregate effluent streams, treating each individually with the appropriate chemicals and membrane filtration, preparing the water for reuse. Peter Gleick, lead author of the biannual report *The World's Water*, writes: "Indeed, some industries, such as paper and pulp, industrial laundries, and metal finishing, are beginning to develop 'closed-loop' systems where all the wastewater is reused internally, with only small amounts of fresh water needed to make up for water incorporated into the product or lost in evaporation." Industries are moving faster than cities, but the technologies they are developing can also be used in urban water recycling.[49]

At the household level, water can also be saved by using more water-efficient showerheads, flush toilets, dishwashers, and clothes washers. Some countries are adopting water efficiency standards and labeling for appliances, much as has been done for energy efficiency. When water costs rise, as they inevitably will, investments in composting toilets and more water-efficient household appliances will become increasingly attractive to individual homeowners.

Two household appliances—toilets and showers—together account for over half of indoor water use. Whereas traditional flush toilets used 6 gallons (or 22.7 liters) per flush, the legal U.S. maximum for new toilets is 1.6 gallons (6 liters). New toilets with a dual-flush two-button technology use only 1 gallon for a liquid waste flush and 1.6 gallons for a solid waste flush. Shifting from a showerhead flowing at 5 gallons per minute to a 2.5 gallons-per-minute model cuts water use in half. With washing machines, a horizontal axis design developed in Europe uses 40 percent less water than the traditional top-loading U.S. models.[50]

The existing water-based waste disposal economy is not viable. There are too many households, factories, and feedlots to simply try and wash waste away on our crowded planet. To do so is ecologically mindless and outdated—an approach that belongs to a time when there were far fewer people and far less economic activity.

Farming in the City

While attending a conference on the outskirts of Stockholm in the fall of 1974, I walked past a community garden near a highrise apartment building. It was an idyllic Indian summer afternoon, with many people tending gardens a short walk from their residences. More than 30 years later I can still recall the setting because of the aura of contentment surrounding those working in their gardens. They were absorbed in producing not only vegetables, but in some cases flowers as well. I remember thinking, "This is the mark of a civilized society."

In June 2005, the U.N. Food and Agriculture Organization (FAO) reported that urban and peri-urban farms—those within or immediately adjacent to a city—supply food to some 700 million urban residents worldwide. These are mostly small plots—vacant lots, yards, even rooftops.[51]

Within and near the city of Dar es Salaam, the capital of

Tanzania, there are some 650 hectares of land producing vegetables. This land supplies not only the city's fresh produce but
a livelihood for 4,000 farmers who intensively farm their small
plots year-round. On the far side of the continent, an FAO project has urban residents in Dakar, Senegal, producing up to 30
kilograms (66 pounds) of tomatoes per square meter each year
with continuous cropping in rooftop gardens.[52]

In Hanoi, Viet Nam, 80 percent of the fresh vegetables come
from farms in or immediately adjacent to the city. Farms in the
city or its shadow also produce 50 percent of the pork and the
poultry consumed in the city. Half of the city's freshwater fish
are produced by enterprising urban fish farmers. Forty percent
of the egg supply is produced within the city or nearby. Urban
farmers ingeniously recycle human and animal waste to nourish
plants and to fertilize fish ponds.[53]

Fish farmers near Kolkata in India manage wastewater fish
ponds that cover nearly 4,000 hectares and produce 18,000 tons
of fish each year. Bacteria in the ponds break down the organic
waste in the city's sewage. This, in turn, supports the rapid
growth of algae that feed the local strains of herbivorous fish.
This system provides the city with a steady supply of fresh fish
that are consistently of better quality than any others entering
the Kolkata market.[54]

The magazine *Urban Agriculture* describes how Shanghai
has in effect created a nutrient recycling zone around the city.
The municipal government manages 300,000 hectares of farmland to recycle the city's night soil. Half of Shanghai's pork and
poultry, 60 percent of its vegetables, and 90 percent of its milk
and eggs come from the city and the immediately surrounding
region.[55]

In Caracas, Venezuela, a government-sponsored, FAO-assist-
ed project has created 8,000 microgardens of one square meter
each in the city's barrios, many of them within a few steps of
family kitchens. As soon as one crop is mature, it is harvested
and immediately replaced with new seedlings. Each square
meter, continuously cropped, can produce 330 heads of lettuce,
18 kilograms of tomatoes, or 16 kilograms of cabbage per year.
Venezuela's goal is to have 100,000 microgardens in the country's urban areas and 1,000 hectares of urban compost-based
gardens nationwide.[56]

There is a long tradition of community gardens in European cities. As a visitor flies into Paris, numerous community gardens can be seen on the outskirts of the city. The Community Food Security Coalition reports that 14 percent of London's 8 million residents produce some of their own food. For Vancouver, Canada's largest West Coast city, the comparable figure is an impressive 44 percent.[57]

In the U.S. city of Philadelphia, community gardeners were asked why they gardened. Some 20 percent did it for recreational reasons, 19 percent said it improved their mental health, and 17 percent their physical health. Another 14 percent did it because they wanted the higher-quality fresh produce that a garden could provide. Others said it was mostly cost and convenience.[58]

In some countries, such as the United States, there is a huge unrealized potential for urban gardening. A survey indicated that Chicago has 70,000 vacant lots, and Philadelphia, 31,000. Nationwide, vacant lots in cities would total in the hundreds of thousands. The *Urban Agriculture* report summarizes why urban gardening is so desirable. It has "a regenerative effect...when vacant lots are transformed from eyesores—weedy, trash-ridden dangerous gathering places—into bountiful, beautiful, and safe gardens that feed people's bodies and souls."[59]

Closely related to the growth in urban gardening is that of local farmers' markets, where farmers near a city produce fresh fruits and vegetables, meat, milk, eggs, and cheese for direct marketing to consumers in urban markets. A hunger for high-quality fresh produce and a desire to support local farmers has increased the number of U.S. farmers' markets from 1,755 in 1994 to nearly 5,000 in late 2007. This movement toward consuming more locally produced food is now spilling over into restaurants that offer locally produced foods on their menus and into the small but growing number of supermarkets that sell local produce. Both restaurants and supermarkets are able to contract directly with local farmers to supply them with fixed amounts of seasonal products.[60]

Given the near inevitable rise in future oil prices, the economic benefits of expanding both urban agriculture and the use of locally produced food will become more obvious. Aside from supplying more fresh produce, it will help millions discover the social benefits and the psychological well-being that urban gardening and locally produced food can bring.

Upgrading Squatter Settlements

Between 2000 and 2050, world population is projected to grow by 3 billion, but little of this growth is projected for industrial countries or for the rural developing world. Nearly all of it will take place in cities in developing countries, with much of this urban growth taking place in squatter settlements.[61]

Squatter settlements—whether they are *favelas* in Brazil, *barriadas* in Peru, or *gecekondu* in Turkey—typically consist of an urban residential area inhabited by very poor people who do not own any land. They simply "squat" on vacant land, either private or public.[62]

Life in these settlements is characterized by grossly inadequate housing and a lack of access to urban services. As Hari Srinivas, coordinator of the Global Development Research Center, writes, these rural-urban migrants undertake the "drastic option of illegally occupying a vacant piece of land to build a rudimentary shelter" simply because it is their only option. They are often treated if not with apathy then with antipathy by government agencies, who view them as invaders and trouble. Some see squatter settlements as a social "evil," something that needs to be eradicated.[63]

One of the best ways to make rural/urban migration manageable is to improve conditions in the countryside. This means not only providing basic social services, such as health care and education for children, as outlined in Chapter 7, but also encouraging industrial investment in small towns throughout the country rather than just in prime cities, such as Mexico City or Bangkok. Such policies will slow the flow into cities to a more orderly pace.

The evolution of cities in developing countries is often shaped by the unplanned nature of squatter settlements. Letting squatters settle wherever they can—on steep slopes, on river floodplains, or in other high-risk areas—makes it difficult to provide basic services such as transport, water, and sanitation. Curitiba, on the cutting edge of the new urbanism, has designated tracts of land for squatter settlements. By setting aside these planned tracts, the process can at least be structured in a way that is consistent with the development plan of the city.[64]

Among the simplest services that can be provided in a squatter settlement are taps that provide safe running water and community composting toilets located at intervals throughout the area. This combination can go a long way toward controlling disease in overcrowded settlements. Regular bus service enables workers living in the settlements to travel to their place of work. If the Curitiba approach is widely followed, parks and other commons areas can be incorporated into the community from the beginning.

Some political elites simply want to bulldoze squatter settlements out of existence, but this treats the symptoms of urban poverty, not the cause. People who lose what little they have been able to invest in housing are not richer as a result of the demolition, but poorer, as is the city itself. The preferred option by far is in situ upgrading of housing. The key to this is providing security of tenure and small loans to squatters, enabling them to make incremental improvements over time.[65]

Upgrading squatter settlements depends on local governments that respond to them rather than ignore them. Progress in eradicating poverty and creating stable, progressive communities depends on establishing constructive links with governments. Government-supported micro-credit lending facilities can help not only establish a link between the city government and the squatter communities but also offer hope to the residents.[66]

Although political leaders might hope that these settlements will one day be abandoned, the reality is that they will continue expanding. The challenge is to integrate them into urban life in a humane way that provides hope through the potential for upgrading. The alternative is mounting resentment, social friction, and violence.

Cities for People

As the new century begins, it is becoming evident to urban dwellers, whether in industrial or developing countries, that there is an inherent conflict between the automobile and the city. Urban air pollution from automobiles is emerging as a leading health issue in hundreds of cities. Worsening congestion also takes a direct economic toll in rising costs in time and gasoline.

Another cost in cities that are devoted to cars is a psychological one, a deprivation of contact with the natural world—an "asphalt complex." There is a growing body of evidence that there is an innate human need for contact with nature. Ecologists and psychologists have both been aware of this for some time. Ecologists, led by Harvard University biologist E. O. Wilson, have formulated the "biophilia hypothesis," which argues that those who are deprived of contact with nature suffer psychologically and that this deprivation leads to a measurable decline in well-being.[67]

Meanwhile, psychologists have coined their own term—ecopsychology—in which they make the same argument. Theodore Roszak, a leader in this field, cites a study of varying rates of patient recovery in a hospital in Pennsylvania. Those whose rooms overlooked gardens with grass, trees, flowers, and birds recovered from illnesses more quickly than those who were in rooms overlooking the parking lot.[68]

Throughout the modern era, budget allocations for transportation in most countries—and in the United States, in particular—have been heavily biased toward the construction and maintenance of highways and streets. Creating more livable cities and the mobility that people desire depends on shifting resources from roads and highways to urban transit and bicycle support facilities.

The exciting news is that there are signs of change, daily indications of an interest in redesigning cities for people, not for cars. That U.S. public transit ridership nationwide has risen by 2.4 percent a year since 1996 indicates that people are gradually abandoning their cars for buses, subways, and light rail. Higher gasoline prices are encouraging commuters to take the bus or subway or get on their bicycles.[69]

Mayors and city planners the world over are beginning to rethink the role of the car in urban transport systems. A group of eminent scientists in China challenged Beijing's decision to promote an automobile-centered transport system. They noted a simple fact: China does not have enough land to accommodate the automobile and to feed its people. This is also true for India and dozens of other densely populated developing countries.[70]

Some cities plan transport systems that provide mobility, clean air, and exercise—a sharp contrast to those that offer only more congestion, unhealthy air, and little opportunity for exercise. When 95 percent of a city's workers depend on cars for commuting, as in Atlanta, Georgia, the city is in trouble. By contrast, in Amsterdam only 40 percent of workers commute by car; 35 percent bike or walk, while 25 percent use public transit. Copenhagen's commuting patterns are almost identical to Amsterdam's. In Paris, fewer than half of commuters rely on cars, and even this is falling as Mayor Delanoë restructures the transport system. Even though these European cities are older, often with narrow streets, they have far less congestion than Atlanta.[71]

If developing-country transportation planners continue to concentrate fiscal resources in support of the automobile, they will end up with a system built for the small fraction of their people who own cars. There are many ways to restructure the transportation system so that it satisfies the needs of all people, not just the affluent, so that it provides mobility, not immobility, and so that it improves health rather than damaging it. One way is to eliminate the subsidies, often indirect, that many employers provide for parking. In his book *The High Cost of Free Parking*, Donald Shoup estimates that off-street parking subsidies in the United States are worth at least $127 billion a year, obviously encouraging people to drive.[72]

In 1992, California mandated that employers match parking subsidies with cash that can be used by the recipient either to pay public transport fares or to buy a bicycle. In firms where data were collected, this shift in policy reduced automobile use by some 17 percent. At the national level, a provision was incorporated into the 1998 Transportation Equity Act for the 21st Century to change the tax code so that those who used public transit or vanpools would enjoy the same tax-exempt subsidies as those who received free parking. What societies should be striving for is not parking subsidies, but parking fees—fees that reflect the costs of traffic congestion and the deteriorating quality of life as cities are taken over by cars and parking lots.[73]

Scores of cities are declaring car-free areas, among them Stockholm, Vienna, Prague, and Rome. Paris enjoys a total ban on cars along stretches of the Seine River on Sundays and holi-

days and is looking to make much of the central city traffic-free
starting in 2012.[74]

In addition to ensuring that subways are functional and
affordable, the idea of making them attractive, even cultural
centers, is gaining support. In Moscow, with works of art in the
stations, the subway system is justifiably referred to as Russia's
crown jewel. In Washington, D.C., Union Station, which links
the city's subway system with intercity rail lines, is an architectural delight. Since its restoration was completed in 1988, it has
become a social gathering place, with shops, conference rooms,
and a rich array of restaurants.

One of the more innovative steps to encourage the use of
public transportation comes from State College, a small town of
40,000 residents in central Pennsylvania that is home to Penn
State University. To reduce traffic congestion on campus and to
address the lack of sufficient parking, Penn State in 1999 offered
$1 million annually to the bus-based local transit system in
exchange for unlimited free rides for its students, faculty, and
staff. As a result, bus ridership in State College jumped by 240
percent in one year, requiring the transit company to invest
heavily in new buses to accommodate the additional passengers.
This university initiative created a far more pleasant, attractive
campus—an asset in recruiting both students and faculty.[75]

As the new century advances, the world is reconsidering the
urban role of automobiles in one of the most fundamental
shifts in transportation thinking in a century. The challenge is to
redesign communities, making public transportation the centerpiece of urban transport and making streets pedestrian and
bicycle friendly. This also means replacing parking lots with
parks, playgrounds, and playing fields. We can design an urban
lifestyle that systematically restores health by incorporating
exercise into daily routines while reducing carbon emissions and
air pollution.

11

Raising Energy Efficiency

As noted in Chapter 3, the Himalayan glaciers that feed the major rivers in Asia during the dry season are melting, and some of them could disappear entirely in a matter of decades, shrinking the region's grain harvest. We also noted that if the Greenland and West Antarctic ice sheets melt, sea level will rise 12 meters (39 feet).

The ice melting effects of climate change alone could increase the number of failing states to a point where civilization would begin to unravel. We are faced with civilization-threatening climate change and a need to massively reduce carbon emissions—and to do it quickly. We do not need to wait for future temperature rises to see that we are in trouble. The melting just described warrants a crash program to cut carbon emissions.

One of the goals of Plan B is to reestablish a balance between carbon emissions and nature's capacity to sequester carbon by cutting net carbon dioxide (CO_2) emissions 80 percent by 2020. This will halt the rise in atmospheric CO_2, stabilizing it below 400 parts per million (ppm), up only modestly from the 384 ppm in 2007. It will also help keep future temperature rise to a minimum. Such a basic economy restructuring in time to avoid catastrophic climate disruption will be challenging, but how can we face the next generation if we do not try?[1]

Our plan to cut net CO_2 emissions 80 percent by 2020 includes stopping deforestation and an even more ambitious effort to cut fossil fuel use. The latter has two major components—raising energy efficiency to offset all projected demand growth, as discussed in this chapter, and developing the earth's rich array of renewable energy resources in order to close down all coal- and oil-fired power plants, as discussed in the next chapter.

In laying out Plan B, we exclude the oft-discussed option of CO_2 sequestration at coal-fired power plants. Given the costs and the lack of investor interest in the technology, there is reason to doubt that carbon sequestration will be economically viable on a meaningful scale by 2020.

And similarly, we do not count on a buildup in nuclear power. Our assumption is that new openings of nuclear power plants worldwide will simply offset the closing of aging plants, with no overall growth in capacity. If we use full-cost pricing—requiring utilities to absorb the costs of disposing of nuclear waste, of decommissioning the plant when it is worn out, and of insuring the reactors against possible accidents and terrorist attacks—building nuclear plants in a competitive electricity market is simply not economical.

Beyond the economic costs are the political questions. If we say that expanding nuclear power is an important part of our energy future, do we mean for all countries or only for some countries? If the latter, who makes the A-list and the B-list of countries? And who enforces the listings?

For reference, world electricity generation totaled 18.5 trillion kilowatt-hours in 2006. Of this, two thirds came from fossil fuels (40 percent from coal, 6 percent from oil, and 20 percent from natural gas), 15 percent from nuclear, 16 percent from hydropower, and 2 percent or so from other renewables. (The average U.S. home uses roughly 10,000 kilowatt-hours of electricity per year, so 1 billion kilowatt-hours is enough to supply 100,000 U.S. homes).[2]

Since coal supplies 40 percent of the world's electricity but accounts for over 70 percent of the electrical sector's CO_2 emissions, the first priority is to reduce demand enough to avoid constructing any new coal-fired power plants. In the next chapter we focus on phasing out coal-fired power plants. This may appear to be a novel idea, particularly to energy planners in countries such as China and India, but it is not, for example, in Europe. Germany has cut coal use 37 percent since 1990 through efficiency gains and by substituting wind-generated electricity for that from coal. The United Kingdom has cut coal use 43 percent, largely by replacing it with North Sea natural gas.[3]

In early 2007, some 150 new coal-fired power plants were planned in the United States. Then public opposition began to mount. California, which imports 20 percent of its electricity, prohibited the signing of any new contracts to import electricity produced with coal. Several other states, including Florida, Texas, Minnesota, Washington, and Kansas, followed, refusing licenses for coal-fired power plants or otherwise preventing their construction.[4]

Coal's future took a telling blow in July 2007 when Citigroup downgraded coal company stocks across the board and recommended that clients switch to other energy stocks. In August, coal took another hit when U.S. Senate Majority Leader Harry Reid of Nevada, who had been opposing three coal-fired power plants planned for his own state, announced that he was extending his opposition to building coal-fired power plants anywhere in the world. Investment analysts and political leaders are now beginning to see what has been obvious for some time to scientists such as NASA's James Hansen, who says that it makes no sense to build coal-fired power plants when we will have to bulldoze them in a few years.[5]

Banning the Bulb

Perhaps the quickest, easiest, and most profitable way to reduce electricity use worldwide—thus cutting carbon emissions—is simply to change light bulbs. Replacing the inefficient incandescent light bulbs that are still widely used today with new compact fluorescents (CFLs) can reduce electricity use by three fourths. The energy saved by replacing a 100-watt incandescent bulb with an equivalent CFL over its lifetime is sufficient to drive a Toyota Prius hybrid car from New York to San Francisco.[6]

Over its lifetime, each standard (13 watt) CFL will reduce electricity bills by roughly $30. And though a CFL may cost twice as much as an incandescent, it lasts 10 times as long. Since it uses less energy, it also means fewer CO_2 emissions. Each one reduces energy use by the equivalent of 200 pounds of coal over its lifetime. Less coal burning means reduced air pollution, making lighting efficiency an obviously attractive option for fast-growing economies plagued with polluted air, such as China and India.[7]

The world may be moving toward a political tipping point away from inefficient light bulbs. In February 2007 Australia announced it would phase out the sale of incandescent light bulbs by 2010, replacing them with CFLs. Canada soon followed, saying it would phase out incandescents sales by 2012.[8]

In mid-March, a U.S. coalition of environmental groups joined with Philips Lighting to launch an initiative to shift to more-efficient bulbs in all of the country's estimated 4 billion light sockets by 2016.[9]

By mid-2007, some 15 states either had passed or were considering legislation to restrict or ban the sale of incandescent light bulbs. The proposed legislation in New York, for example, would phase out incandescents by 2012, four years ahead of the coalition's deadline. And with a dozen or so others restricting or proposing to restrict use in one way or another, pressure is building to pass legislation making this shift nationwide.[10]

The European Union (EU), with 27 member countries, announced in March 2007 that it plans to cut carbon emissions 20 percent by 2020, with part of the cut coming from replacing incandescent bulbs with CFLs. In the United Kingdom, the civic group Ban the Bulb has been vigorously pushing for a ban on incandescents since early 2006. Further east, the Moscow city government is urging its residents to switch to compact fluorescents.[11]

Brazil, hit by a nationwide electricity shortage in 2000–02, responded with an ambitious program to replace incandescents with CFLs. As a result, an estimated half of its light sockets now contain these efficient bulbs. In 2007, China—working with the Global Environment Facility—announced a plan to replace all its incandescents with more efficient lighting within a decade.[12]

Greenpeace is urging the government of India to ban incandescents in order to cut carbon emissions. Since roughly 640 million of the 650 million bulbs sold each year in this fast-growing economy are the old inefficient incandescents, the potential for cutting carbon emissions, reducing air pollution, lowering the frequency of blackouts, and saving consumers money is huge.[13]

At the industry level, Philips, the world's largest lighting manufacturer, is going to stop marketing incandescents in Europe by 2016. And the European Lamp Companies Federation (the bulb manufacturers' trade association) is supporting a rise in EU lighting efficiency standards that would lead to a phaseout of incandescent bulbs.[14]

Retailers are joining the switch too. Wal-Mart, the world's largest retailer, announced a marketing campaign in November 2006 to boost its sales of compact fluorescents to 100 million by the end of 2007, more than doubling its annual sales of such bulbs. And Currys, Britain's largest electrical retail chain, announced in 2007 that it would discontinue selling incandescent light bulbs.[15]

For office buildings, commercial outlets, and factories, where linear (tubular) fluorescents are widely used, the key to cutting electricity use is shifting to the most advanced models, which are even more efficient than CFLs. Since linear fluorescents are long-lasting, many of those now in use rely on an earlier, less energy-efficient technology.[16]

An even newer lighting technology—light-emitting diodes or LEDs—uses only one fifth as much electricity as the old-fashioned incandescent bulbs. Already, New York City has replaced traditional bulbs with LEDs in many of its traffic lights, cutting its annual bill for maintenance and electricity by $6 million. LED costs are still high, however, discouraging widespread consumer use.[17]

In addition to switching bulbs themselves, huge energy savings can be gained just by turning lights off when not in use. There are numerous technologies for reducing electricity used for lighting, including motion sensors that turn lights off when spaces are unoccupied, such as in washrooms, hallways, and stairwells. In cities, dimmers can be used to reduce street light intensity, and timers can turn off outside lights that illuminate monuments or other landmarks when people are asleep. Dimmers can also be used to take advantage of day lighting to reduce the intensity of interior lighting.

Shifting to CFLs in homes, to the most advanced linear fluorescents in office buildings, commercial outlets, and factories,
and to LEDs in traffic lights would cut the world share of electricity used for lighting from 19 percent to 7 percent. This would
save enough electricity to avoid building 705 coal-fired power
plants. By way of comparison, today there are 2,370 coal-fired
plants in the world.[18]

In a world facing new evidence almost daily of global warming and its consequences, a quick and decisive victory is needed
in the battle to cut carbon emissions and stabilize climate. A
rapid shift to the most energy-efficient lighting technologies
would provide just such a victory—generating momentum for
even greater advances in climate stabilization.

Energy-Efficient Appliances

Although many people know that CFLs use only one fourth as
much electricity as incandescent light bulbs, considerably fewer
know that a similar range of efficiencies exists for many household appliances, such as refrigerators.[19]

The U.S. Energy Policy Act of 2005 included a rise in efficiency standards that will reduce electricity demand enough to
avoid building 29 coal-fired power plants. Other provisions in
the act—such as tax incentives that encourage the adoption of
energy-efficient technologies, a shift to more combined heat and
power generation, and the adoption of real-time pricing of electricity (a measure that will discourage optional electricity use
during peak demand periods)—would cut electricity demand
enough to avoid building an additional 37 coal-fired power
plants. Appliance efficiency standards and other measures in
the bill will also reduce natural gas consumption substantially.
Altogether, these measures will reduce consumer electricity and
gas bills in 2020 by over $20 billion.[20]

Taking into account recent technological advances, the
American Council for an Energy-Efficient Economy (ACEEE)
proposed in March 2006 to raise the bar further for 15 appliances. Included in this group were residential furnaces, pool
heaters, and DVD players. If these new standards were adopted
in 2008, the ACEEE calculates that they would reduce 2020 electricity demand by 52 billion kilowatt-hours, which would be
enough to avoid another 16 coal-fired power plants. The reduc-

tion in CO_2 emissions in 2020 from adoption of these standards would be equal to taking 8 million cars off the road. Better still, for every $1 invested in more-efficient appliances, consumers will save over $4 on their electricity and gas bills.[21]

With appliance efficiency, the big challenge now is China. In 1980 its appliance manufacturers produced only 50,000 refrigerators, virtually all for domestic use. In 2004 they produced 30 million refrigerators, 73 million color TVs, and 24 million clothes washers, many of which were for export.[22]

Market penetration of these modern appliances in urban China today is similar to that in industrial countries. For every 100 urban households there are 133 color TV sets, 96 washing machines, and 70 room air conditioners. In rural areas there are 75 color TVs and 40 washing machines for every 100 households. This phenomenal growth in household appliance use in China, along with the extraordinary growth of industry, raised China's electricity use sevenfold from 1980 to 2004. Although China had established standards for most appliances by 2005, the standards are not strictly enforced.[23]

The other major concentration of appliances is in the European Union, home to 490 million people. Greenpeace notes that even though Europeans on average use roughly half as much electricity as Americans or Canadians, they still have a large potential for reducing their usage. A refrigerator in Europe uses roughly half as much electricity as one in the United States, for example, but the most efficient refrigerators on the market today use only one fourth as much electricity as the average refrigerator in Europe—a huge opportunity for improvement.[24]

But this is not the end of the efficiency trail. There is still a wide gap between the most efficient appliances on the market and the efficiency standards just proposed. And advancing technology keeps raising the efficiency potential.

Among industrial countries, Japan's Top Runner Program is the most dynamic system for upgrading appliance efficiency standards. In this system, the most efficient appliances today set the standard for those sold tomorrow. With this program Japan planned to raise efficiency standards between the late 1990s and the end of 2007 for individual appliances by anywhere from 15 to 83 percent, depending on the appliance. This is an ongoing process that continually exploits advances in efficiency technologies.[25]

In an analysis of potential energy savings by 2030 by type of appliance, the Organisation for Economic Co-operation and Development (OECD) put the potential savings from reducing electricity for standby use—that consumed when the appliance is not being used—at the top of the list. As of 2007, the estimated share of electricity used by appliances in standby mode worldwide is up to 10 percent of total electricity consumption. At the individual household level in OECD countries, standby power ranged from a low of perhaps 30 watts to a high of over 100 watts in both U.S. and New Zealand households. Since this power is used around the clock, even though the wattage is relatively low, the cumulative use of electricity is substantial.[26]

Some governments are capping the amount of standby power used by TV sets, computers, microwaves, DVD players, and so on at 1 watt per appliance. South Korea, for example, is mandating a 1-watt limit on standby levels for many appliances by 2010. Australia is doing the same for nearly all appliances by 2012.[27]

A U.S. study estimates that roughly 5 percent of U.S. residential electricity use is consumed by appliances in standby mode. If this figure dropped to 1 percent, which could be done easily, it would reduce electricity use enough to avoid building 17 coal-fired power plants. If China were to lower its standby losses accordingly, it could avoid building an even larger number of power plants.[28]

Climate change is a global phenomenon requiring a global response. The time has come to set worldwide efficiency standards for all household appliances that are determined by the most efficient models on the market today, like Japan's Top Runner Program. The standards would be raised every few years to take advantage of the latest technological gains in efficiency.

The principal reason that consumers do not buy the most energy-efficient appliances is because the improved design and insulation increase the upfront costs. If, however, societies adopt a carbon tax reflecting the health care costs of breathing polluted air and the costs of climate change, the more efficient appliances would be economically much more attractive.

Although we lack sufficient data to make a detailed calculation of the electricity that can be saved by adopting the more advanced appliance efficiency standards, we are confident that a worldwide set of appliance efficiency standards keyed to the most efficient models on the market would lead to energy savings in the appliance sector approaching or exceeding the 12 percent of world electricity savings from more efficient lighting. This being the case, gains in lighting and appliance efficiencies alone would enable us to avoid building 1,410 coal-fired power plants—more than the 1,382 new coal-fired power plants projected by the International Energy Agency (IEA) to be built by 2020.[29]

More-Efficient Buildings

The building sector is responsible for a large share of world electricity consumption, raw materials use, and waste generation. In the United States, buildings—commercial and residential—account for 70 percent of electricity use and over 38 percent of CO_2 emissions. Worldwide, building construction accounts for 40 percent of materials use.[30]

Because buildings last for 50–100 years or longer, it is often assumed that increasing energy efficiency in the building sector is a long-term process. But that is not the case. An energy retrofit of an older inefficient building can cut energy use by 20–50 percent. The next step, shifting entirely to carbon-free electricity, either generated onsite or purchased, to heat, cool, and light the building completes the job. Presto! A zero-carbon building.[31]

The building construction and real estate industries are recognizing the value of green buildings. An Australian firm, Davis Langdon, notes there is a growing sense of "the looming obsolescence of non-green buildings," one that is driving a wave of reform in both construction and real estate. Further, Davis Langdon says, "going green is future-proofing your asset."[32]

In the United States, the private U.S. Green Building Council (USGBC)—well known for its certification and rating program called Leadership in Energy and Environmental Design (LEED)—heads the field. This voluntary certification program sets standards so high that it has eclipsed the U.S. government Energy Star certification program for buildings. LEED has four certification levels—Certified, Silver, Gold, and Platinum. A LEED-certified building must meet minimal standards in environmental quality, materials use, energy efficiency, and water efficiency. LEED-certified buildings are attractive to buyers because they have lower operating costs, higher lease rates, and happier, healthier occupants than traditional buildings do.[33]

The LEED certification standards for construction of new buildings were issued in 2000. Any builder who wants a building certified must request certification and pay for it. In 2004 the USGBC also began certifying the interiors of commercial buildings and tenant improvements of existing buildings. It was planning to begin issuing certification standards for home builders by the end of 2007.[34]

Looking at the LEED certification criteria and examples of LEED buildings provides an insight into the many ways buildings can become more energy-efficient. The certification process for new buildings begins with site selection, then moves on to energy efficiency, water efficiency, materials used, and indoor environmental quality. In site selection, certification points are awarded for locating the building close to public transport, such as light rail or buses. Beyond this, a higher certification depends on provision of bicycle racks and shower facilities for employees. To be certified, new buildings must maximize the exposure to daylight, with minimum daylight illumination for 75 percent of the occupied space.[35]

With energy, exceeding the high level of efficiency required for basic certification earns additional points. Further points are awarded for the use of renewable energy, including rooftop solar cells to generate electricity, rooftop solar water and space heaters, and the purchase of green power.[36]

Both membership in the USGBC and the number of building proposals being submitted for certification are growing fast. As of August 2007 the Council had 10,688 member organizations, including corporations, government agencies, environmental groups, and other nonprofits. Membership has grown 10-fold since 2000.[37]

Thus far LEED has certified 748 new buildings in the United States, with some 5,200 under construction that have applied for certification. Commercial building space that has been certified or registered for certification approval totals 2 billion square feet of floor space, or some 46,000 acres (think 46,000 football fields).[38]

The Chesapeake Bay Foundation's office building for its 100 staff members near Annapolis, Maryland, was the first to earn a LEED platinum rating. Among its features are a ground source heat pump for heating and cooling, a rooftop solar heater for hot water, and sleekly designed composting toilets that produce a rich humus used to fertilize the landscape surrounding the building. Toyota's North American office in Torrance, California, which houses 2,000 employees, was one of the first large office buildings to earn a LEED gold rating. It is distinguished by a large solar-electric generating facility that provides much of its electricity. The combination of waterless urinals and rainwater recycling enable it to operate with 94 percent less water than a conventionally designed building of the same size. Less water means less energy.[39]

The 54-story Bank of America tower in New York, scheduled to open in early 2008, will be the first large building to earn a platinum rating. It will have its own co-generation power plant and will collect rainwater, reuse waste water, and use recycled materials in construction. The complex of new buildings at the World Trade Center site is being designed to achieve gold certification.[40]

A 60-story office building with a gold rating being built in Chicago will use river water to cool the building in summer, and the rooftop will be covered with plants to reduce runoff and heat loss. Energy-conserving measures will save the owner $800,000 a year in energy bills. The principal tenant, Kirkland and Ellis LLP, a Chicago-based law firm, insisted that the building be gold-certified and that this be incorporated into the lease.[41]

The state of California commissioned Capital E, a green building consulting firm, to analyze the economics of 33 LEED-certified buildings in the state. The study concluded that certification raised construction costs by $4 per square foot, but because operating costs as well as employee absenteeism and turnover were lower and productivity was higher than in non-certified buildings, the standard- and silver-certified buildings earned a profit over the first 20 years of $49 per square foot, and the gold- and platinum-certified buildings earned $67 per square foot.[42]

In 2001 a global version of the USGBC, the World Green Building Council, was formed. It initially consisted of Green Building Councils from six other countries. All told, as of August 2007 there were LEED certification projects in progress in some 41 countries, including Brazil, Canada, India, and Mexico.[43]

Also at the international level, the Clinton Foundation announced in May 2007 its Energy Efficiency Building Retrofit Program, a project of the Clinton Climate Initiative. This program, in cooperation with C40, a large-cities climate leadership group, brings together five of the world's largest banks and four of the leading energy service companies to work with an initial group of 16 cities to retrofit buildings, reducing their energy use by 20–50 percent. Among these cities are some of the world's largest, including Bangkok, Berlin, Karachi, London, Mexico City, Mumbai, New York, Rome, and Tokyo. Each of the banks—ABN AMRO, Citi, Deutsche Bank, JP Morgan Chase, and UBS—is committed to investing up to $1 billion in this effort, enough to easily double the current worldwide level of energy saving retrofits.[44]

The world's four largest energy service companies—Honeywell, Johnson Controls, Siemens, and Trane—will do the actual retrofitting. And, most important, they agreed to provide "performance guarantees," thus ensuring that all the retrofits will be profitable. Cutting energy use and carbon emissions can be highly profitable. At the launch of this program, former President Bill Clinton pointed out that banks and energy service companies would make money, building owners would save money, and carbon emissions would fall.[45]

On the architectural front, a climate-conscious architect from New Mexico, Edward Mazria, has launched the 2030 Challenge. Its principal goal is for the nation's architects to be designing buildings in 2030 that use no fossil fuels. Mazria observes that the buildings sector is the leading source of climate emissions, easily eclipsing transportation. Therefore, he says, "it's the architects who hold the key to turning down the global thermostat." To reach his goal, Mazria has organized a coalition consisting of several organizations, including the American Institute of Architects, the USGBC, and the U.S. Conference of Mayors.[46]

Mazria recognizes the need for faculty retraining in the country's 124 architectural schools to "transform architecture from its mindless and passive reliance on fossil fuels to an architecture intimately linked to the natural world in which we live." It is the responsibility of architects, Mazria believes, "to engage the environment in a way that significantly reduces or elimi-nates the need for fossil fuels." Today's architectural concepts and construction technologies enable architects to easily design new buildings with half the energy requirements of today's buildings. Among the design technologies are natural day-light-ing, rooftop solar-electric cells, natural ventilation, glazed win-dows, reduced water use, more-efficient lighting technologies, and motion sensors for lighting.[47]

Restructuring the Transport System

Aside from the overriding need to stabilize atmospheric CO_2 lev-els, there are several other compelling reasons for countries every-where to restructure their transport systems, including the need to prepare for falling oil production, to alleviate traffic conges-tion, and to reduce air pollution. The U.S. car-centered trans-portation model, with three cars for every four people, that much of the world aspires to will not likely be viable over the long term even for the United States, much less for everywhere else.[48]

The shape of future transportation systems centers around the changing role of the automobile. This in turn is being influ-enced by the transition from a predominantly rural global soci-ety to a largely urban one. By 2020 close to 55 percent of us will be living in cities, where the role of cars is diminishing. In Europe, where this process is well along, car sales in almost every country have peaked and are falling.[49]

With world oil output close to peaking, there will not be enough economically recoverable oil to support a world fleet expansion along U.S. lines or, indeed, to sustain the U.S. fleet. Oil shocks are now a major security risk. The United States, where 88 percent of the 133 million working people travels to work by car, is dangerously vulnerable.[50]

Mounting concern about climate change and the desire to restrict carbon emissions is beginning to permeate transporta-tion policymaking at the urban, provincial, and national level. In addition to a daily $16 toll on cars entering central London, Mayor Ken Livingston proposed in 2007 a $50-per-day charge on sport utility vehicles entering the city because of their high CO_2 emissions. This staggering proposed tax enjoys the sup-port of Londoners by a three to one margin. New York is also considering a tax on cars entering the city.[51]

The mayors of both New York and San Francisco have announced that all taxis in their cities will be hybrids by 2012, a move designed to reduce CO_2 emissions, fuel use, and local air pollution. The New York goal is to replace the 13,000 existing taxis that get roughly 14 miles per gallon with cars that will get 30–50 miles per gallon.[52]

Beyond the desire to stabilize climate, drivers almost everywhere are facing gridlock and worsening congestion that are raising both frustration and the cost of doing business. In the United States, the average commuting time for workers has increased steadily since the early 1980s. The automobile promised mobility, but after a point its growing numbers in an increasingly urbanized world offer only the opposite: immobility.[53]

While the future of transportation in cities lies with a mix of light rail, buses, bicycles, cars, and walking, the future of intercity travel over distances of 500 miles or less belongs to high-speed trains. Japan, with its high-speed bullet trains, has pioneered this mode of travel. Operating at speeds up to 190 miles per hour, Japan's bullet trains carry almost a million passengers a day. On some of the heavily used intercity high-speed rail lines, trains depart every three minutes.[54]

Beginning in 1964 with the 322-mile line from Tokyo to Osaka, Japan's high-speed rail network now stretches for 1,360 miles, linking nearly all its major cities.

One of the most heavily traveled links is the original line between Tokyo and Osaka, where the bullet trains carry 117,000 passengers a day. The transit time of two hours and 30 minutes between the two cities compares with a driving time of eight hours. High-speed trains save time as well as energy.[55]

Although Japan's bullet trains have carried billions of passengers over 40 years at high speeds, there has not been a single casualty. Late arrivals average 6 seconds. If we were selecting seven wonders of the modern world, Japan's high-speed rail system surely would be among them.[56]

While the first European high-speed line, from Paris to Lyon, did not begin operation until 1981, Europe has made enormous strides since then. As of early 2007 there were 3,034 miles (4,883 kilometers) of high-speed rail operating in Europe, with 1,711 more miles to be added by 2010. The goal is to have a Europe-wide high-speed rail system integrating the new eastern countries, including Poland, the Czech Republic, and Hungary, into a continental network by 2020.[57]

Once high-speed links between cities begin operating, they dramatically raise the number of people traveling by train between cities. For example, when the Paris-to-Brussels link, a distance of 194 miles that is covered by train in 85 minutes, opened, the share of those traveling between the two cities by train rose from 24 percent to 50 percent. The car share dropped from 61 percent to 43 percent, and CO_2-intensive plane travel virtually disappeared.[58]

Carbon dioxide emissions per passenger mile on Europe's high-speed trains are one third those of its cars and only one fourth those of its planes. In the Plan B economy, CO_2 emissions from trains will essentially be zero, since they will be powered by green electricity. In addition to being comfortable and convenient, these rail links reduce air pollution, congestion, noise, and accidents. They also free travelers from the frustrations of traffic congestion and long airport security check lines.

Existing international links, such as the Paris-Brussels link, are being joined by links between Paris and Stuttgart, Frankfurt and Paris, and a new link from the Channel Tunnel to London that cuts the London-Paris travel time to scarcely two hours and 20 minutes. On the newer lines, trains are operating at up to 200 miles per hour. As *The Economist* notes, "Europe is in the grip of a high speed rail revolution."[59]

There is a huge gap in high-speed rail between Japan and Europe on one hand and the rest of the world on the other. The United States has a "high-speed" Acela Express that links Washington, New York, and Boston, but unfortunately neither its speed nor its reliability come close to the trains in Japan and Europe.[60]

China is beginning to develop high-speed trains linking some of its major cities. The one introduced in 2007 from Beijing to Shanghai reduced travel time from 12 to 10 hours. China now has 3,750 miles of track that can handle train speeds up to 125 miles per hour. The plan is to double the mileage of high-speed track by 2020.[61]

In the United States, the need both to cut carbon emissions and to prepare for shrinking oil supplies calls for a shift in investment from roads and highways to railways. In 1956 U.S. President Dwight Eisenhower launched the interstate highway system, justifying it on national security grounds. Today the threat of climate change and the insecurity of oil supplies both argue for the construction of a high-speed electrified rail system, for both passenger and freight traffic. The relatively small amount of additional electricity needed could come from renewable sources, mainly wind farms.[62]

The passenger rail system would be modeled after those of Japan and Europe. A high-speed transcontinental line that averaged 170 miles per hour would mean traveling coast-to-coast in 15 hours, even with stops in major cities along the way. There is a parallel need to develop an electrified national rail freight network that would greatly reduce the need for long-haul trucks.

Any meaningful global effort to cut transport CO_2 emissions begins with the United States, which consumes more gasoline than the next 20 countries combined, including Japan, China, Russia, Germany, and Brazil. The United States—with 238 million vehicles out of the global 860 million, or roughly 28 percent of the world total—not only has the largest automobile fleet but is near the top in miles driven per car and near the bottom in fuel efficiency.[63]

Three initiatives are needed in the United States. One is a meaningful gasoline tax. Phasing in a gasoline tax of 40¢ per gallon per year for the next 12 years (for a total rise of $4.80 a gallon) and offsetting it with a reduction in income taxes would raise the U.S. gasoline tax to the $4–5 per gallon prevailing today in Europe and Japan. Combined with the rising price of gas itself, such a tax should be more than enough to encourage a shift to more fuel-efficient cars.

The second measure is raising the fuel-efficiency standard from the 22 miles per gallon of cars sold in 2006 to 45 miles per gallon by 2020. This would help move the U.S. automobile industry in a fuel-efficient direction. Third, reaching our CO_2 reduction goal depends on a heavy shift of transportation funds from highway construction to urban transit and intercity rail construction.[64]

A New Materials Economy

The production, processing, and disposal of material in our modern throwaway economy wastes not only material but energy as well. In nature, one-way linear flows do not survive long.

Nor, by extension, can they survive long in the expanding global economy. The throwaway economy that has been evolving over the last half-century is an aberration, now itself headed for the junk heap of history.

The potential for sharply reducing materials use was pioneered in Germany, initially by Friedrich Schmidt-Bleek in the early 1990s and then by Ernst von Weizsäcker, an environmental leader in the German Bundestag. They argued that modern industrial economies could function very effectively using only one fourth the virgin raw material prevailing at the time. A few years later, Schmidt-Bleek, who founded the Factor Ten Institute in France, showed that raising resource productivity even more—by a factor of 10—was well within the reach of existing technology and management, given the right policy incentives.[65]

In 2002, American architect William McDonough and German chemist Michael Braungart coauthored *Cradle to Cradle: Remaking the Way We Make Things*. They concluded that waste and pollution are to be avoided entirely. "Pollution," said McDonough, "is a symbol of design failure."[66]

Industry, including the production of plastics, fertilizers, steel, cement, and paper, accounts for more than 30 percent of world energy consumption. The petrochemical industry, which produces products such as plastics, fertilizers, and detergents, is the biggest consumer of energy in the manufacturing sector, accounting for about a third of worldwide industrial energy use. Since a large part of industry fossil fuel use is for feedstock, to manufacture plastics and other materials, increased recycling can reduce feedstock needs. Worldwide, increasing recycling rates and moving to the most efficient manufacturing systems in use today could reduce energy use in the petrochemical industry by 32 percent.[67]

The global steel industry, producing over 1.2 billion tons in 2006, is the second largest consumer of energy in the manufacturing sector, accounting for 19 percent of industrial energy use. Energy efficiency measures, such as adopting the most efficient blast furnace systems in use today and the complete recovery of used steel, could reduce energy use in the steel industry by 23 percent.[68]

Reducing materials use means recycling steel, the use of which dwarfs that of all other metals combined. Steel use is

dominated by three industries—automobile, household appliances, and construction. In the United States, virtually all cars
are recycled. They are simply too valuable to be left to rust in
out-of-the-way junkyards. The U.S. recycling rate for household
appliances is estimated at 90 percent. For steel cans it is 60 percent, and for construction steel it is 97 percent for steel beams
and girders, but only 65 percent for reinforcement steel. Still, the
steel discarded each year is enough to meet the needs of the U.S.
automobile industry.[69]

Steel recycling started climbing more than a generation ago
with the advent of the electric arc furnace, a technology that
produces steel from scrap using only one fourth the energy it
would take to produce it from virgin ore. Electric arc furnaces
using scrap now account for half or more of steel production in
more than 20 countries. A few countries, including Venezuela
and Saudi Arabia, use electric arc furnaces for all of their steel
production. While the present shortage of scrap limits the ability to switch entirely to electric arc furnaces, more scrap will be
available in 2020 when developing economies begin retiring
aging infrastructure. If three fourths of steel production were to
switch to electric arc furnaces using scrap, energy use in the steel
industry could be cut by almost 40 percent.[70]

The cement industry, turning out 2.3 billion tons in 2006, is
another major player in industrial energy consumption,
accounting for 7 percent of industrial energy use. China, at
close to half of world production, manufactures more cement
than the next top 20 countries combined, yet it does so with
extraordinary inefficiency. If China used the same technologies
as Japan, it could reduce its energy consumption for cement
production by 45 percent. Worldwide, if all cement producers
used the most efficient dry kiln process in use today, energy use
in the cement industry could drop 42 percent.[71]

Restructuring the transportation system also has a huge
potential for reducing materials use. For example, improving
urban transit means that one 12-ton bus can replace 60 cars
weighing 1.5 tons each, or a total of 90 tons, reducing material
use by 87 percent. Every time someone decides to replace a car
with a bike, material use is reduced by 99 percent.[72]

The big challenge in cities everywhere is to recycle the many
components of garbage, since recycling uses only a fraction of

the energy of producing the same items from virgin raw materials. Virtually all paper products can now be recycled, including cereal boxes, junk mail, and paper bags in addition to newspapers and magazines. So too can glass, most plastics, aluminum, and other materials from buildings being torn down. Advanced industrial economies with stable populations, such as those in Europe and Japan, can rely primarily on the stock of materials already in the economy rather than using virgin raw materials. Metals such as steel and aluminum can be used and reused indefinitely.[73]

One of the most effective ways to encourage recycling is to adopt a landfill tax. For a recent example, the state of New Hampshire adopted a "pay-as-you-throw" program that encourages municipalities to charge residents for each bag of garbage. This has dramatically reduced the flow of materials to landfills. In the town of Lyme, with nearly 2,000 people, adoption of a landfill tax raised the share of garbage recycled from 13 percent in 2005 to 52 percent in 2006.[74]

The quantity of recycled material in Lyme, which jumped from 89 tons in 2005 to 334 tons in 2006, included corrugated cardboard, which sells for $90 a ton; mixed paper, $45 a ton; and aluminum, $1,500 per ton. This program simultaneously reduces the town's landfill fees while generating a cash flow from the sale of recycled material.[75]

San José, California, already diverting 62 percent of its municipal waste from landfills for reuse and recycling, is now focusing on the large flow of trash from construction and demolition sites. This material is trucked to one of two dozen specialist recycling firms in the city. For example, at Premier Recycle up to 300 tons of building debris is delivered each day. It is skillfully separated into recyclable piles of concrete, scrap metal, wood, and plastics. Some materials the company sells, some it gives away, and some it pays someone to take.[76]

Before the program began, only about 100,000 tons per year of the city's mixed construction and demolition materials were reused or recycled. Now it is nearly 500,000 tons. The scrap metal that is salvaged goes to recycling plants, wood can be converted into mulch or wood chips for fueling power plants, and concrete can be recycled to build road banks. By deconstructing a building instead of simply demolishing it, most of the material in it can be reused or recycled, thus dramatically reducing energy use and carbon emissions. San José is becoming a model for cities everywhere.[77]

Germany and, more recently, Japan are requiring that products such as automobiles, household appliances, and office equipment be designed for easy disassembly and recycling. In May 1998, the Japanese Diet enacted a tough appliance recycling law, one that prohibits discarding household appliances, such as washing machines, TV sets, or air conditioners. With consumers bearing the cost of disassembling appliances in the form of a disposal fee to recycling firms, which can come to $60 for a refrigerator or $35 for a washing machine, the pressure to design appliances so they can be more easily and cheaply disassembled is strong.[78]

Closely related to this concept is that of remanufacturing. Within the heavy industry sector, Caterpillar has emerged as a leader. At a plant in Corinth, Mississippi, it recycles some 17 truckloads of diesel engines a day. These engines, retrieved from Caterpillar's clients, are disassembled by hand by workers who do not throw away a single component, not even a bolt or screw. Once the engine is disassembled, it is then reassembled with all worn parts repaired. The resulting engine is as good as new. Caterpillar's remanufacturing division is racking up $1 billion a year in sales and growing at 15 percent annually, contributing impressively to the company's bottom line.[79]

Another emerging industry is airliner recycling. Daniel Michaels writes in the *Wall Street Journal* that Boeing and Airbus, which have been building jetliners in competition for nearly 40 years, are now vying to see who can dismantle them most efficiently. The first step is to strip the plane of its marketable components, such as engines, landing gear, galley ovens, and hundreds of other items. For a jumbo jet, these key components can collectively sell for up to $4 million. Then comes the final dismantling and recycling of aluminum, copper, plastic, and other materials. The next time around the aluminum may show up in cars, bicycles, or another jetliner.[80]

The goal is to recycle 90 percent of the plane, and perhaps one day 95 percent or more. With more than 3,000 airliners already put out to pasture and many more to come, this retired fleet has become the equivalent of an aluminum mine.[81]

With computers becoming obsolete every few years as technology advances, the need to be able to quickly disassemble and recycle them is a paramount challenge in building an eco-economy. In Europe, information technology (IT) firms are going into the reuse of computer components big-time. Because European law requires that manufacturers pay for the collection, disassembly and recycling of toxic materials in IT equipment, manufacturers have begun to focus on how to disassemble everything from computers to cell phones. Nokia, for example, has designed a cell phone that will virtually disassemble itself.[82]

On the clothing front, Patagonia, an outdoor gear retailer, has launched a garment recycling program beginning with its polyester fiber garments. Working with Teijin, a Japanese firm, Patagonia is now recycling not only the polyester garments it sells but also those that are sold by its competitors. Patagonia estimates that a garment made from recycled polyester, which is indistinguishable from the initial polyester made from petroleum, uses less than one fourth as much energy. With this success behind it, Patagonia is beginning to work on nylon garments and plans also to recycle cotton and wool clothing.[83]

In addition to measures that encourage the recycling of materials, there are those that encourage the reuse of products such as beverage containers. Finland, for example, has banned the use of one-way soft drink containers. Canada's Prince Edward Island has adopted a similar ban on all nonrefillable beverage containers. The result in both cases is a sharply reduced flow of garbage to landfills.[84]

A refillable glass bottle used over and over requires about 10 percent as much energy per use as an aluminum can that is recycled. Cleaning, sterilizing, and re-labeling a used bottle requires little energy compared with recycling cans made from aluminum, which has a melting point of 660 degrees Celsius (1,220 degrees Fahrenheit). Banning nonrefillables is a quintuple win option—cutting material use, carbon emissions, air pollution, water pollution, and garbage flow to landfills. There are also substantial transport fuel savings, since the refillable containers are simply back-hauled by delivery trucks to the original bottling plants or breweries for refilling.[85]

Another increasingly attractive option for cutting CO_2 emissions is to discourage energy-intensive but, to use a World War

II term, nonessential industries. The gold and bottled water industries are prime examples. The annual production of 2,500 tons of gold requires the processing of 500 million tons of ore, more than one third the amount of virgin ore used to produce steel each year. One ton of steel requires the processing of two tons of ore. For one ton of gold, in stark contrast, the figure is 200,000 tons of ore. Processing 500 million tons of ore consumes a huge amount of energy—and emits as much CO_2 as 5.5 million cars.[86]

From a climate point of view, it is very difficult to justify bottling water, often tap water to begin with, hauling it long distance and selling it for outlandish prices. Although clever marketing has convinced many consumers that bottled water is safer and healthier than what they can get from their faucets, a detailed study by the World Wide Fund for Nature could not find any support for this claim. It notes that in the United States and Europe there are more standards regulating the quality of tap water than of bottled water. For people in developing countries where water is unsafe, it is far cheaper to boil or filter water than to buy it in bottles.[87]

Charles S. Fishman writes in *Fast Company* magazine that "when a whole industry grows up around supplying us with something we don't need...it's worth asking how that happened, and what the impact is." In effect, the industry's advertising is designed to undermine public confidence in the safety and quality of municipal water supplies. In the words of Gina Solomon, a Natural Resources Defense Council senior scientist, "Bottled water is largely a market based on anxiety."[88]

Manufacturing the nearly 28 billion plastic bottles used to package water in the United States alone requires 17 million barrels of oil. Including the energy for hauling 1 billion bottles of water every two weeks from bottling plants to supermarkets or convenience stores for sale, sometimes covering hundreds of kilometers, and the energy needed for refrigeration, the U.S. bottled water industry consumes roughly 50 million barrels of oil per year.[89]

The good news is that people are beginning to see how climate-disruptive this industry is. Mayors of U.S. cities are realizing that they are spending millions of taxpayer dollars to buy bottled water for their employees—water that costs 1,000 times as much as the tap water that is already available in city buildings. San Francisco mayor Gavin Newsom has banned the use of city funds to purchase bottled water and the use of bottled water in city buildings, on city property, and at any events sponsored by the city. Other cities following a similar strategy include Los Angeles, Salt Lake City, and St. Louis. New York City has launched a $5 million ad campaign to promote its tap water and thus to rid the city of bottled water and the fleets of delivery trucks that tie up traffic.[90]

In summary, there is a vast worldwide potential for cutting carbon emissions by reducing materials use. This begins with the major metals—steel, aluminum, and copper—where recycling requires only a fraction of the energy needed to produce these metals from virgin ore. It continues with the design of cars, household appliances, and other products so they are easily disassembled into their component parts for reuse or recycling.

Household garbage, as noted, can be sorted and extensively recycled or composted. With deconstruction, nearly all building materials can be reused or recycled. Switching to refillable beverage containers can lead to a 90-percent reduction in material use and carbon emissions in the beverage industry. The remanufacturing of products, as Caterpillar is doing with diesel engines, helps reduce CO_2 emissions. Phasing out energy-intensive, nonessential industries such as the gold and bottled water industries will also move the world closer to the time when atmospheric concentrations of CO_2 are once again stable.

The Energy Savings Potential

The goal for this chapter was to identify measures that will offset the 30 percent growth in energy demand projected by IEA between 2006 and 2020. We are confident that the measures proposed will more than offset the projected growth in energy use. Shifting to more energy-efficient lighting alone lowers world electricity use by 12 percent.[91]

With appliances, the key to raising energy efficiency is to establish international efficiency standards for appliances that reflect the most efficient models on the market today, regularly raising this level as technologies advance. Given the potential for raising appliance efficiency, the energy saved by 2020 should at least match the savings in the lighting sector.

With transportation, the short-term keys to reducing gasoline use involve shifting to highly fuel-efficient cars, restructuring urban transport systems, and building intercity rapid rail systems modeled after those in use in Japan and Europe. This shift in focus from car-dominated transport systems to more diversified systems is evident in the actions of hundreds of mayors who struggle with traffic congestion and air pollution every day. They are devising ingenious ways of restricting not only the use of cars but the very need for them. Neither the nature of the city nor the future role of the car will be the same, as nearly all public initiatives are diminishing the car's urban presence.

Within the industrial sector, there is a hefty potential for reducing energy use. In the petrochemical industry, moving to the most efficient production technologies now available and recycling more plastic can cut energy use by 32 percent. With steel, gains in manufacturing efficiency can cut energy use by 23 percent. Even larger gains are within reach for cement, where simply shifting to the most efficient dry kiln technologies can reduce energy use by 42 percent.[92]

With buildings—even older buildings, where retrofitting can reduce energy use by 20–50 percent—there is a profitable potential for saving energy. As we have noted, such a reduction in energy use combined with the use of green electricity to heat, cool, and light the building means that it may be easier to create carbon-neutral buildings than we may have thought.

One easy way to achieve these gains is through the imposition of a carbon tax that would help reflect the full cost of burning fossil fuels. We recommend increasing the carbon tax by $20 per ton each year over the next 12 years, for a total of $240. High though this may seem, it does not come close to covering the indirect costs of burning fossil fuels.

In seeking to raise energy efficiency, as described in this chapter there have been some pleasant surprises at the potential for doing so. We now turn to developing the earth's renewable sources of energy, where there are equally exciting possibilities.

12

Turning to Renewable Energy

Just as the nineteenth century belonged to coal and the twentieth century to oil, the twenty-first century will belong to the sun, the wind, and energy from within the earth. In Europe, the addition of electrical generating capacity from renewable energy sources in 2006 exceeded that from conventional sources, making it the first continent to enter the new energy era. Meanwhile, in the United States electrical generating capacity from wind increased 27 percent in 2006, while that from coal decreased slightly.[1]

We can see the Plan B energy economy emerging in many areas. In Texas, the state government is coordinating a vast expansion of wind power that could yield 23,000 megawatts of new generating capacity, an amount equal to 23 coal-fired power plants. In China, some 160 million people now get their hot water from rooftop solar water heaters. In Iceland, almost 90 percent of homes are heated with geothermal energy. In Europe, 60 million people rely on wind farms for their electricity. And in the Philippines, 19 million people get their electricity from geothermal power plants.[2]

In the last chapter, we described how to offset the projected increases in energy use to 2020 with gains in efficiency. This chapter addresses the challenge of harnessing renewable energy on a scale that will help reduce worldwide carbon dioxide (CO_2) emissions by 80 percent. The first priority is to replace all coal- and oil-fired electricity generation with renewable sources.

The Plan B goals for developing renewable sources of energy by 2020 that are laid out in this chapter are based not on what is conventionally believed to be politically feasible, but on what we think is needed to prevent irreversible climate change. This is not Plan A, business as usual. This is Plan B—a wartime mobilization, an all-out response proportionate to the threat that global warming presents to our future.

Can we expand renewable energy use fast enough? We think so. Recent trends in the use of mobile phones and personal computers give a sense of how quickly new technologies can spread. Once cumulative mobile phone sales reached 1 million units in 1986, the stage was set for explosive growth, and the number of cell phone subscribers doubled in each of the next three years. Over the next 12 years the number of people owning a mobile phone more than doubled every two years. By 2001 there were 995 million cell phones—a 1,000-fold increase in just 15 years. As of 2007, there were more than 2 billion cell phone subscribers worldwide.[3]

Sales of personal computers followed a similar trajectory. In 1983 roughly a million were sold, but by 2003 the figure was an estimated 160 million—a 160-fold jump in 20 years. We are now seeing similar growth figures for renewable energy technologies. Sales of solar cells are doubling every two years, and the annual growth in wind generating capacity is not far behind. Just as the information and communications economies have changed beyond recognition over the past two decades, so too will the energy economy over the next decade.[4]

There is one outstanding difference. Whereas the restructuring of the information and communications sectors was shaped by advancing technology and market forces, the restructuring of the energy economy will be driven also by the realization that the fate of our global civilization may depend not only on doing so, but doing so at wartime speed.

Harnessing the Wind

A worldwide survey of wind energy by the Stanford team of Cristina Archer and Mark Jacobson concluded that harnessing one fifth of the earth's available wind energy would provide seven times as much electricity as the world currently uses. For example, China—with vast wind-swept plains in the north and west, countless mountain ridges, and a long coastline, all rich with wind—has enough readily harnessable wind energy to easily double its current electrical generating capacity.[5]

In 1991 the U.S. Department of Energy (DOE) released a national wind resource inventory, noting that three wind-rich states—North Dakota, Kansas, and Texas—had enough harnessable wind energy to satisfy national electricity needs. Advances in wind turbine design since then allow turbines to operate at lower wind speeds and to convert wind into electricity more efficiently. And because they are now 100 meters tall, instead of less than 40 meters, they harvest a far larger, stronger, and more reliable wind regime, generating 20 times as much electricity as the turbines installed in the early 1980s when modern wind power development began. With these new turbine technologies, the three states singled out by DOE could satisfy not only national electricity needs but national energy needs.[6]

In addition, a 2005 DOE assessment of offshore wind energy concluded that U.S. offshore wind out to a distance of 50 miles alone is sufficient to meet 70 percent of national electricity needs. Europe is already tapping its offshore wind. A 2004 assessment by the Garrad Hassan wind energy consulting group concluded that if governments aggressively develop their vast offshore resources, wind could supply all of Europe's residential electricity by 2020.[7]

From 2000 to 2007, world wind generating capacity increased from 18,000 megawatts to an estimated 92,000 megawatts. In early 2008 it will pass the 100,000-megawatt milestone. Since 2000, capacity has been growing at 25 percent annually, doubling every three years.[8]

The world leader in total capacity is Germany, followed by the United States, Spain, India, and Denmark. Measured by share of national electricity supplied by wind, Denmark is the leader, at 20 percent. Three north German states now get more than 30 percent of their electricity from wind. For Germany as a whole, it is 7 percent—and climbing.[9]

Denmark is now looking to push the wind share of its electricity to 50 percent, with most of the additional power coming from offshore. In contemplating the prospect of wind becoming the leading source of electricity, Danish planners have turned energy policy upside down. They are looking at using wind as the mainstay of their electrical generating system and fossil-fuel-generated power to fill in when the wind ebbs.[10]

For many years now, the top five countries—with roughly 70 percent of world wind generating capacity—have dominated growth in the industry, but this is now changing as the industry goes global, with 70 countries now harnessing their wind resources. Among the emerging wind powers are China, France, and Canada, each of which doubled its wind electric generation in 2006.[11]

One of the early concerns with wind energy was the risk it posed to birds, but this can be overcome by conducting studies and careful siting to avoid risky areas for birds. The most recent research indicates that bird fatalities from wind farms are minuscule compared with deaths from flying into skyscrapers, colliding with cars, or being captured by cats.[12]

Other critics are concerned about the visual effect. When some people see a wind farm they see a blight on the landscape. Others see a civilization-saving source of energy. Although there are NIMBY problems ("not in my backyard"), the PIMBY response ("put it in my backyard") is much more pervasive. Within U.S. communities, for instance, among ranchers in Colorado or dairy farmers in upstate New York, the competition for wind farms is intense. This is not surprising, since a large, advanced design wind turbine can generate $300,000 worth of electricity in a year. Farmers, with no investment on their part, typically receive $3,000–10,000 a year in royalties for each wind turbine erected on their land.[13]

One of wind's attractions is that it requires so little land compared with other sources of renewable energy. For example, a corn farmer in northern Iowa can put a wind turbine on a quarter-acre of land that can produce $300,000 worth of electricity per year. This same quarter-acre would produce 40 bushels of corn that in turn could produce 120 gallons of ethanol worth $300. Since the turbines occupy less than 1 percent of the land in a wind farm, this technology lets farmers harvest both energy and crops from the same land. Thousands of ranchers in the wind-rich Great Plains will soon be earning more from wind royalties than from cattle sales.[14]

At the moment, growth in wind electricity generation is primarily constrained by wind turbine manufacturing capacity. But the important question is how much of the world's energy needs can wind power meet. To gain perspective, we look at what governments are planning, the size of wind farms under construction and proposed, and the transmission lines that are being planned.[15]

The official U.S. goal of one day getting 20 percent of its electricity from wind means developing at least 300,000 megawatts of wind generating capacity. Since 1 megawatt of wind generating capacity can supply electricity to 300 U.S. homes, wind development on this scale would satisfy the needs of 90 million households. In France, a newcomer to wind energy, the government target is 14,000 megawatts of wind by 2010. Spain, which already has nearly 12,000 megawatts of capacity, is shooting for 20,000 megawatts by 2010.[16]

At the local level, Texas, the state that long led the country in oil production, has taken the lead in wind generation as well. Governor Rick Perry assembled a number of wind farm developers and transmission line builders to link wind-rich west Texas and the Texas panhandle to the state's population centers. This package could lead to the development of 23,000 megawatts of wind generating capacity, enough to satisfy the residential electricity needs of 7 million homes.[17]

In California, the electric utility Southern California Edison is planning a 4,500-megawatt wind project in the southern end of the state. In east central South Dakota, Clipper Windpower has purchased wind rights on enough land to develop 3,000 megawatts of generating capacity. At the national level, wind farm proposals in late 2007 exceeded an estimated 100,000 megawatts, nearly 10 times existing capacity.[18]

In Canada, Katabatic Power and Deutsche Bank are planning a 3,000-megawatt wind farm in British Columbia, which would produce enough electricity to supply some 900,000 homes. The United Kingdom has a 1,000-megawatt offshore wind farm, the London Array, under construction in the Severn Estuary and a 1,500-megawatt wind farm, the Atlantic Array,

off the coast of Devon, in the planning stage. Germany is planning several offshore wind farms of a similar size. And China
has several 1,000-megawatt wind farms on the drawing board.[19]

Another clue to the scale of future wind farm development
can be seen in transmission lines under construction and being
planned. Legislatures in Texas, Colorado, New Mexico, California, and Minnesota in the United States combined their support for huge wind farm complexes with the construction of
transmission lines to ensure that the two move forward together, avoiding the chicken-and-egg problem.[20]

A number of interstate transmission lines are also being built
and discussed. In the north central United States, wind farms in
eastern North Dakota and South Dakota are being linked to
load centers in Minnesota and Wisconsin. A group of operators
is proposing a transmission line that would link the vast wind
resources of Kansas and Oklahoma with the southeastern United States, carrying electricity from proposed wind farms with
13,000 megawatts of generating capacity. Another group in the
upper Midwest is looking at transmission lines that will link the
wind resource riches of the Dakotas with the densely populated
East Coast. In the West, the governors of California, Nevada,
Utah, and Wyoming have agreed to build a "Frontier Line" that
would link the low-cost wind resources of Wyoming with Salt
Lake City, Las Vegas, and power-hungry California.[21]

In Europe, Airtricity, an Irish development firm with wind
farms in several countries, and ABB, a leader in building energy
infrastructure, have proposed an offshore super-grid for Europe
stretching from the Baltic Sea to the North Sea and southward
to the coast of Spain. This grid would not only aid in realizing
Europe's huge offshore wind potential, it would link national
grids with each other, thus facilitating more-efficient electricity
use throughout the continent. To begin, the companies propose
a 10,000-megawatt wind farm project in the North Sea between
Germany, the United Kingdom, and the Netherlands that would
supply 6 million homes with electricity.[22]

Wind is the centerpiece of the Plan B energy economy. It is
abundant, low cost, and widely distributed; it scales up easily
and can be developed quickly. Oil wells go dry and coal seams
run out, but the earth's wind resources cannot be depleted.

Plan B involves a crash program to develop 3 million

megawatts of wind generating capacity by 2020. This will require a near doubling of capacity every two years, up from the doubling every three years for the last decade. It will mean 1 megawatt for every 2,500 of the world's projected 2020 population of 7.5 billion people. Denmark—with 1 megawatt for every 1,700 people—is already well beyond this goal. Spain will likely exceed this per capita goal before 2010 and Germany shortly thereafter.[23]

This climate-stabilizing initiative would require the installation of 1.5 million 2-megawatt wind turbines. Manufacturing such a huge number of wind turbines over the next 12 years sounds intimidating until the initiative is compared with the 65 million cars the world produces each year. At $3 million per installed turbine, this would involve investing $4.5 trillion over the next dozen years, or $375 billion per year. This compares with world oil and gas capital expenditures that are projected to reach $1 trillion per year by 2016.[24]

Wind turbines can be mass-produced on assembly lines. Indeed, the idled capacity in the U.S. automobile industry is sufficient to produce the wind turbines to reach the Plan B global goal.[25]

Not only do the idle plants exist, but there are skilled workers in these communities eager to return to work. The state of Michigan, for example, in the heart of the wind-rich Great Lakes region, has more than its share of idled auto assembly plants. The Spanish firm Gamesa, a leading wind turbine manufacturer, recently set up operations in an abandoned U.S. Steel plant in Pennsylvania.[26]

Wind-Powered Plug-in Hybrid Cars

In Chapter 10 we discussed measures that cities are using to reduce the need for cars. But even with fewer cars, the world desperately needs a new automotive energy economy, a new source of fuel. Fortunately, the foundation for this has been laid with two new technologies: the gas-electric hybrid cars pioneered by Toyota and advanced-design wind turbines.

The Toyota Prius—a fast-selling mid-size hybrid car—gets an impressive 46 miles per gallon in combined city/highway driving, compared with 20 miles per gallon for the average new U.S. passenger vehicle. The United States could easily cut its gasoline use in half simply by converting the U.S. automobile fleet to highly efficient hybrid cars. No change in the number of vehicles. No change in the miles driven. Just doing it with the most efficient propulsion technology on the market.[27]

Now that hybrid cars are well established, it is a relatively small step to manufacturing plug-in hybrids that run largely on electricity. By putting a larger battery in a gas-electric hybrid to increase its storage of electricity and adding a plug-in capacity so the battery can be recharged from the power grid, drivers can do their commuting, grocery shopping, and other short-distance travel almost entirely with electricity, saving gasoline for the occasional long trip. Even more exciting, recharging batteries with off-peak wind-generated electricity would cost the equivalent of less than $1 per gallon of gasoline. This modification of hybrids to run largely on electricity could reduce remaining gasoline use an additional 60 percent, for a total reduction of 80 percent.[28]

But this is not all. Amory Lovins—an energy efficiency pioneer—notes that substituting advanced polymer composites for steel in auto bodies can "roughly double the efficiency of a normal-weight hybrid without materially raising its total manufacturing cost." Thus, building gas-electric hybrids using the new advanced polymer composites, which are being introduced by Boeing in its new 787 Dreamliner jumbo jet, can cut the remaining 20 percent of fuel use by another half, for a total reduction of 90 percent.[29]

The plug-in electric hybrid/wind power transportation model does not require a costly new infrastructure, since the network of gasoline service stations and the electricity grid are already in place. A 2006 study by the U.S. government's Pacific Northwest National Laboratory estimated that 84 percent of the electricity used by a national fleet of plug-in cars, pickup trucks, and SUVs could be satisfied with the existing electrical infrastructure since the recharging would take place largely at night, when there is an excess of generating capacity.[30]

The variability of wind energy is of concern to many commentators, but it can be largely offset by integrating local and regional grids into a strong national grid, something that is needed anyhow to raise load-management efficiency. Since no two wind farms have identical wind flows, each wind farm added to a large grid reduces variability. With many wind farms on a large grid, variability largely disappears.[31]

Another major source of stability will come from the shift to plug-in hybrids, since the vehicle batteries become a storage system for wind energy. With a smart grid, motorists could profitably sell electricity back to the grid when needed during peak demand. In effect, the shift to plug-in hybrids, with their electricity storage capacity and backup tank of gasoline, buffers the variability of wind energy, enabling it to become the centerpiece of the Plan B energy economy.[32]

The shift to fuel-efficient plug-in hybrid cars combined with the construction of thousands of wind farms across the United States will rejuvenate farm and ranch communities and dramatically shrink the U.S. balance-of-trade deficit. Even more important, it could cut automobile CO_2 emissions by some 90 percent, making the United States a model for other countries.[33]

The fast-growing support for plug-in hybrids has coalesced into a national grassroots initiative called Plug-In Partners. As of late 2007, Plug-In Partners had 617 members, including 169 electrical utilities, 168 corporations, 71 city governments, and 67 environmental groups. A number of the Plug-In Partners have announced advanced orders for plug-in cars and delivery vans, including the government of New York State, Southern California Edison, and Pacific Gas and Electric. These so called soft orders, now totaling more than 11,000 vehicles, will go to the first company that makes it to the market with a plug-in hybrid.[34]

Among the companies planning to manufacture these vehicles are Nissan, Toyota, General Motors (GM, with its Chevrolet Volt), and Ford Motor Company (with the Airstream). Chrysler's Dodge Sprinter plug-in hybrid vans are already being tested by various firms, including Pacific Gas and Electric. The first companies to market plug-in hybrids may find it difficult to keep up with the demand.[35]

The Chevrolet Volt, which will be on the market in 2010, will have a 40-mile range on electricity only. Beyond this distance, a small gasoline engine will generate electricity to recharge the battery. For the 78 percent of Americans who live 20 miles or less from their work site, it will be possible to commute without using any gasoline. For those with longer commutes, plugging in at the worksite is also an option. Based on an analysis of U.S. driving patterns, GM estimates that the Volt will get 150 miles per gallon, since the gas-powered recharger engine would come into play only occasionally. It is this prospect of triple-digit gasoline mileage that is selling consumers on plug-in hybrids.[36]

Solar Cells and Collectors

Several technologies are now used to harness the sun's energy, including both solar thermal collectors and solar photovoltaic cells. Solar thermal collectors, widely used to heat water, are now also used for space heating. Collectors, which concentrate sunlight to boil water and produce steam-generated electricity, and assemblages of solar electric cells are both used on a commercial power plant scale, with individual plants capable of supplying thousands of homes with electricity.

Perhaps the most exciting recent development in the world solar economy is the installation of some 40 million rooftop solar water heaters in China. With 2,000 Chinese companies manufacturing rooftop solar water heaters, this relatively simple low-cost technology is not only widely used in cities, it has also leapfrogged into villages that do not yet have electricity. For as little as $200, villagers can have a rooftop solar collector installed and take their first hot shower. This technology is sweeping China like wildfire, already approaching market saturation in some communities. Even more exciting, Beijing plans to more than double the current 124 million square meters of rooftop solar collectors for heating water to 300 million by 2020.[37]

The energy harnessed by these installations in China is equal to the electricity generated by 54 coal-fired power plants. Other developing countries such as India and Brazil may also soon see millions of households turning to this inexpensive water heating technology. This leapfrogging into rural areas without an electricity grid is similar to the way cell phones bypassed the traditional fixed-line grid, providing services to millions of people who would still be on waiting lists if they had relied on traditional phone lines. The great attraction of rooftop solar water heaters is that once the initial installment cost is paid, the hot water is essentially free.[38]

In Europe, where energy costs are relatively high, rooftop solar water heaters are also spreading fast. In Austria, Europe's leader, 15 percent of all households now rely on them for hot water. And, as in China, in some Austrian villages nearly all homes have rooftop collectors. Germany is also forging ahead. Janet Sawin of Worldwatch Institute notes that some 2 million Germans are now living in homes where water and space are both heated by rooftop solar systems.[39]

Inspired by the rapid adoption of rooftop water and space heaters in Europe in recent years, the European Solar Thermal Industry Federation (ESTIF) has established an ambitious goal of 500 million square meters, or one square meter of rooftop collector for every European by 2020, a goal that exceeds the 0.74 square meters per person today in Israel, the world leader. Most installations are projected to be Solar-Combi systems that are engineered to heat both water and space.[40]

In 2007, Europe's solar collectors were concentrated in Germany, Austria, and Greece, with France and Spain also beginning to mobilize. Spain's initiative was boosted by a March 2006 mandate requiring installation of collectors on all new or renovated buildings. ESTIF estimates that the European Union has a long-term potential of developing 1,200 thermal gigawatts of solar water and space heating, which means that the sun could meet most of Europe's low-temperature heating needs.[41]

The U.S. rooftop solar water heating industry has thus far concentrated on a niche market—selling and marketing 10 million square meters of water heaters for swimming pools between 1995 and 2005. Given this base, however, the industry is poised to mass-market residential solar water and space heating systems.[42]

We now have the data to make some global projections. With China setting a goal of 300 million square meters of solar water heating capacity by 2020, and ESTIF's goal of 500 million square meters by 2020, a U.S. installation of 200 million square meters by 2020 is certainly within reach given the recently adopted tax incentives. Japan, which now has 11 million square meters of rooftop solar collectors heating water but which imports almost all its fossil fuels, could easily reach 80 million square meters by 2020. If China, the United States, Japan, and the European Union achieve their goals, they will have a combined total of 1,080 million square meters of water and space heating capacity by 2020. This would come to 0.45 square meters per person for the 2.4 billion people in these countries, still well below Israel's figure today.[43]

If the developing world's 5 billion people in 2020 have 0.1 square meter of rooftop water heating capacity per person by 2020, roughly the same as in China or Turkey today, this would add 500 million square meters to the world total, pushing it over 1.5 billion square meters. If we assume that each meter provides 0.7 thermal kilowatts of power, then we are looking at a world solar thermal capacity by 2020 of 1,100 thermal gigawatts, the equivalent of 690 coal-fired power plants.[44]

The huge projected expansion in solar water and space heating in industrial countries could close some existing coal-fired power plants and reduce natural gas use, as solar water heaters replace electric and gas water heaters. In countries such as China and India, however, solar water heaters will simply reduce the need for new coal-fired power plants.

One reason for the explosive growth of solar water and space heaters in Europe and China is the economic appeal. On average, in industrial countries these systems pay for themselves from electricity savings in fewer than 10 years.[45]

With the cost of rooftop heating systems declining, other countries will likely join Israel and Spain in mandating that all new buildings incorporate rooftop water and space heaters. No longer a passing fad, these rooftop appliances are fast becoming a mainstream source of energy as fossil fuel prices rise.[46]

While the direct use of sunlight to heat water has dominated the harnessing of solar energy to date, the world's fastest-growing energy source is the solar cells that convert sunlight into electricity. Installations worldwide now total 8,600 megawatts. Although solar cells are still only a minor source of electricity, their use is growing by over 40 percent annually, doubling every two years. In 2006, Germany installed 1,150 megawatts of solar cell–generating capacity, making it the first country to install over 1 gigawatt (1,000 megawatts) in a year.[47]

Until recently, the production of solar cells was concentrated in Japan, Germany, and the United States, but several energetic new players have recently entered the industry, featuring companies in China, Taiwan, the Philippines, South Korea, and the United Arab Emirates. China overtook the United States in solar cell production in 2006. Taiwan may do so in 2007. Today there are scores of firms competing in the world market, driving investments in both research and manufacturing.[48]

For the nearly 1.6 billion people living in communities not yet connected to an electrical grid, it is now often cheaper to install solar cells rooftop-by-rooftop than to build a central power plant and a grid to reach potential consumers. For Andean villagers, for example, who have depended on tallow-based candles for their lighting, the monthly payment for a solar cell installation over 30 months is less than the monthly outlay for candles.[49]

Villagers in India who are not yet connected to a grid and who depend on kerosene lamps face a similar cost calculation. Installing a home solar electric system in India, including batteries, costs roughly $400. Such systems will power two, three, or four small appliances or lights and are widely used in homes and shops in lieu of polluting and increasingly costly kerosene lamps. In one year a kerosene lamp burns nearly 20 gallons of kerosene, which at $3 a gallon means $60 per lamp. A solar cell lighting system that replaced only two lamps would pay for itself within four years.[50]

The estimated 1.5 billion kerosene lamps in use today provide only 0.5 percent of all residential lighting but account for 29 percent of residential lighting's CO_2 emissions. They use the equivalent of 1.3 million barrels of oil per day, which is equal to roughly half the oil production of Kuwait. Replacing these lamps with solar cell installations would cut world oil use by 1.5 percent and reduce annual carbon emissions by 52 million tons.[51]

For industrial countries, Michael Rogol and his PHOTON consulting company estimate that by 2010 fully integrated companies that encompass all phases of solar cell manufacturing will be installing systems that produce electricity for 12¢ a kilowatt-hour in sun-drenched Spain and 18¢ a kilowatt-hour in southern Germany. Although solar cell costs will be dropping below those of conventional electricity in many locations, this will not automatically translate into a wholesale conversion to solar cells. But as one energy CEO observes, the "big bang" is under way.[52]

With sales of solar cells now doubling every two years and likely to continue doing so at least until 2020, the estimated sales for 2008 of over 5,000 megawatts will climb to 320,000 megawatts in 2020. By this time the cumulative installed capacity would exceed 1 million megawatts (1,000 gigawatts). Although this projection may seem ambitious, it may in fact turn out to be conservative. For one thing, if most of the nearly 1.6 billion people who lack electricity today get it by 2020, it will likely be because they have installed solar home systems.[53]

When a villager buys a solar cell system, that person is in effect buying a 25-year supply of electricity. Since there is no fuel cost and very little maintenance, it is the upfront outlay that counts, and that typically requires financing. Recognizing this, the World Bank and the U.N. Environment Programme have stepped in with programs to help local lenders set up credit systems to finance this cheap source of electricity. An initial World Bank loan has helped 50,000 home owners in Bangladesh obtain solar cell systems. A second, much larger round of funding will enable 200,000 more families to do the same.[54]

Investors are also turning to large-scale solar cell power plants. A 20-megawatt facility under construction in South Korea, scheduled for completion in late 2008, is the largest in the world. It will soon be eclipsed, however, by a 40-megawatt facility being built near Leipzig, Germany, that is scheduled to start supplying electricity by 2009. In Spain, BP Solar contracted to build some 278 small generating facilities with a combined capacity of 25 megawatts. At its headquarters in Mountain View, California, Google—one of the many companies investing in solar electric cells—has installed a 1.6-megawatt array of solar cells to convert sunlight into electricity.[55]

More and more countries, states, and provinces are setting solar cell installation goals. Japan, for example, is planning 4,800 megawatts of solar cell–generating capacity by 2010, a goal it will likely exceed. The state of California has set a goal of 3,000 megawatts by 2017. On the U.S. East Coast, Maryland is aiming for 1,500 megawatts of solar installations by 2022. And in China, Shanghai is shooting for 100,000 rooftop solar cell installations, though for a city with 6 million rooftops this is only a beginning. Altogether, the global Plan B economy is projected to have 1,190 gigawatts of solar cell capacity by 2020.[56]

Another promising way to harness solar energy uses sunlight to heat water and produce steam to generate electricity. This solar thermal technology—often referred to as concentrated solar power—simply uses reflectors with automated tracking systems to concentrate sunlight on a closed vessel containing water or some other liquid, raising the temperature as high as 750 degrees Fahrenheit to produce steam. California installed 354 megawatts of solar thermal–generating capacity nearly 20 years ago, but with cheap fossil-fuel-fired electricity, investments in solar thermal power dried up. With fossil fuel prices and concern about climate change both climbing, there is now a resurgence of interest. A 64-megawatt solar thermal power plant completed in 2007 in Nevada, a similar one under construction in Spain, and a 300-megawatt facility proposed in Florida represent the new wave of these facilities.[57]

Prominent among the regions with the solar intensity needed to profitably operate solar thermal power plants are the U.S. Southwest, North Africa, Mediterranean Europe, the Middle East, Central Asia, and the desert regions of Pakistan, northwestern India, and northern and western China.[58]

The dream of using the Sahara Desert's vast solar resources to supply electricity to Europe may soon become a reality. In June 2007 Algeria announced plans to build 6,000 megawatts of solar thermal generating capacity for export by cable to Europe. In July 2007 construction began on a 150-megawatt natural gas/solar hybrid plant, where the gas takes over entirely at night when there is no sunlight. This plant is located at Hassi R'mel, 260 miles south of Algiers, the capital.[59]

Painfully aware that its oil and gas exports will not last forever, the Algerian government has created a company, New Energy Algeria, to manage the development and export of its solar energy. Its managing director, Tewfik Hasni, says "our potential in thermal solar power is four times the world's energy consumption." Construction of undersea cables linking the solar thermal–generating plants in the Sahara to Europe is planned for 2010–12.[60]

The great attraction of solar thermal generation in sunny climates is that it peaks during the day when air conditioning needs and personal power demands are also peaking. An American Solar Energy Society (ASES) study concluded that the sun-rich southwestern United States—after excluding its less promising areas—has a potential solar power generating capacity of 7,000 gigawatts of electricity, roughly seven times current U.S. generating capacity from all sources. Assuming that the 30 percent tax credit for investment in solar generating facilities continues and that the price of carbon climbs to $35 per ton, the ASES study concluded that 80 gigawatts of this generating potential could be developed by 2030.[61]

Greenpeace and ESTIF have outlined a worldwide plan to develop 600,000 megawatts of solar thermal power plant capacity by 2040. We suggest a more immediate goal of 200,000 megawatts by 2020, a goal that may well be exceeded as climate change concerns escalate.[62]

Energy from the Earth

It is widely known within the energy community that there is enough solar energy reaching the earth each hour to power the world economy for one year, but few people know that the heat in the upper six miles of the earth's crust contains 50,000 times as much energy as found in all the world's oil and gas reserves combined. Despite this abundance, only 9,300 megawatts of geothermal generating capacity have been harnessed worldwide.[63]

Partly because of the dominance of the oil, gas, and coal industries, which have been providing cheap fuel by omitting the indirect costs of fossil fuel burning, relatively little has been invested in developing the earth's geothermal heat resources. Over the last decade, geothermal energy has been growing at scarcely 3 percent a year. Half the world's generating capacity is concentrated in the United States and the Philippines. Four other countries—Mexico, Indonesia, Italy, and Japan—account for most of the remainder. Altogether some 24 countries now convert geothermal energy into electricity. The Philippines, with geothermally generated power supplying 25 percent of its electricity, and El Salvador, at 22 percent, are the leaders.[64]

Beyond this, an estimated 100,000 thermal megawatts of geothermal energy, roughly 10 times the amount converted to electricity, is used directly—without conversion into electricity—to heat homes and greenhouses and as process heat in industry. This includes, for example, the energy used in hot baths in Japan and to heat homes in Iceland and greenhouses in Russia.[65]

An interdisciplinary team of 13 scientists and engineers assembled by the Massachusetts Institute of Technology (MIT) in 2006 assessed U.S. geothermal electrical-generating potential. Drawing on the latest technologies, including those used by oil and gas companies in drilling and in enhanced oil recovery, the team estimated that enhanced geothermal systems could be used to develop 100,000 megawatts of electrical generating capacity in the United States by 2050, a capacity equal to 250 coal-fired power plants. To fully realize this potential, the MIT team estimated that the government would have to invest up to $1 billion in geothermal research and development in the years immediately ahead, roughly the cost of one large coal-fired power plant.[66]

Even without this research commitment, some 61 U.S. geothermal projects were under construction or in development in early 2007. If the United States can develop 100,000 megawatts of geothermal generating capacity, how much could other countries, many of them far more richly endowed, develop with the same technologies? A decade-old estimate for Japan indicated that country could develop 69,000 megawatts of generating capacity. With enhanced geothermal systems, this might easily double to 140,000 megawatts.[67]

Indonesia, with 500 volcanoes, 128 of which are still active, undoubtedly has a far greater potential. It could get all its electricity from cheap, easily tapped geothermal energy. With its oil production falling, Indonesia is fortunate to be so richly endowed with an energy source that can last forever.[68]

The potential of geothermal energy to provide electricity, to heat homes, and to supply process heat for industry is vast. Among the countries rich in geothermal energy are those bordering the Pacific in the so-called ring of fire, including Chile, Peru, Colombia, Mexico, the United States, Canada, Russia, China, Japan, the Philippines, Indonesia, and Australia. Other geothermally rich countries include those along the Great Rift Valley of Africa, such as Kenya and Ethiopia, and those around the Eastern Mediterranean.[69]

In the direct use of geothermal heat, Iceland and France are among the leaders. Iceland's use of geothermal energy to heat almost 90 percent of its houses has largely eliminated the use of coal for home heating. Geothermal energy accounts for more

than one third of Iceland's total energy use. Following the two
oil price hikes in the 1970s, some 70 geothermal heating facilities were constructed in France, providing both heat and hot
water for an estimated 200,000 residences. In the United States,
individual homes are supplied directly with geothermal heat in
Reno, Nevada, and in Klamath Falls, Oregon. Other countries
that have extensive geothermally based district-heating systems
include China, Japan, and Turkey.[70]

Geothermal heat is ideal for greenhouses in northern countries. Russia, Hungary, Iceland, and the United States are among
the many countries that use it to produce fresh vegetables in the
winter. With rising oil prices boosting fresh produce transport
costs, this practice will likely become far more common in the
years ahead.[71]

Among the 16 countries using geothermal energy for aquaculture are China, Israel, and the United States. In California,
for example, 15 fish farms annually produce some 10 million
pounds (4.5 million kilograms) of tilapia, striped bass, and catfish using warm water from underground.[72]

The number of countries turning to geothermal energy for
both electricity and heat is rising fast. So, too, is the range of
uses. Romania, for instance, uses geothermal energy for district
heating, for greenhouses, and to supply hot water for homes
and factories.[73]

Hot underground water is widely used for both bathing and
swimming. Japan has 2,800 spas, 5,500 public bathhouses, and
15,600 hotels and inns that use geothermal hot water. Iceland
uses geothermal energy to heat some 100 public swimming
pools, most of them year-round open-air pools. Hungary heats
1,200 swimming pools with geothermal energy.[74]

If the four most populous countries located on the Pacific
"ring of fire"—the United States, Japan, China, and Indonesia,
with nearly 2 billion people—were to seriously invest in developing their geothermal resources, they could easily make geothermal energy one of the world's leading sources of electricity.
With a potential in the United States and Japan alone of 240,000
megawatts of geothermal power generation, it is easy to envis-
age a world with 200,000 megawatts of geothermally generated
electricity by 2020.[75]

Plant-Based Sources of Energy

As oil and natural gas reserves are being depleted, the world's attention is turning to plant-based energy sources. These include forest industry byproducts, sugar industry byproducts, urban waste, livestock waste, energy crops, crop residues, and urban tree and yard wastes—all of which can be used for electrical generation, heating, or the production of automotive fuels.

In the forest products industry, including both sawmills and paper mills, waste has long been used to generate electricity. U.S. companies burn forest wastes both to produce process heat for their own use and to generate electricity for sale to local utilities. The bulk of the nearly 10,000 megawatts in U.S. plant-based electrical generation comes from burning forest waste.[76]

Wood waste is also widely used in urban areas for combined heat and power production, with the heat typically used in district heating systems. In Sweden, nearly half of all residential and commercial buildings are served with district heating systems. As recently as 1980, imported oil supplied over 90 percent of the heat for these systems, but by 2005 it had been largely replaced by wood chips, urban waste, and lignite.[77]

In the United States, St. Paul, Minnesota—a city of nearly 300,000 people—began to develop district heating more than 20 years ago. It built a combined heat and power plant using tree waste from the city's parks, industrial wood waste, and wood from other sources. The combined heat and power plant, using 250,000 tons or more of waste wood per year, now supplies district heating to some 80 percent of the downtown area, or more than 1 square mile of residential and commercial floor space. This shift to wood waste largely replaced coal, thus simultaneously cutting carbon emissions by 76,000 tons per year, disposing of waste wood, and providing a sustainable source of heat and electricity.[78]

The sugar industry recently has begun to burn cane waste to cogenerate heat and power. This received a big boost in Brazil, when companies with cane-based ethanol distilleries realized that burning bagasse, the fibrous material left after the sugar syrup is extracted, could simultaneously produce heat for fermentation and generate electricity that they could sell to the local utility. This system, now well established in the Brazilian ethanol industry, is spreading to sugar mills in other countries that produce the remaining 80 percent of the world sugar harvest.[79]

Within cities, once recyclable materials are removed, garbage can also be burned to produce heat and power. In Europe, waste-to-energy plants supply 20 million consumers with heat. Germany, with 65 plants, and France are the European leaders. In the United States, some 89 waste-to-energy plants convert 20 million tons of waste into power for 6 million consumers.[80]

With U.S. livestock and poultry production now concentrated in large facilities, the use of animal waste in anaerobic digesters to produce methane (natural gas) is catching on fast. AES Corporation, one of the world's largest electrical power companies, is creating a business of capturing methane from animal waste. Using biodigesters, AES contracts with farmers to process their animal waste, producing methane and a nutrient-rich solid waste that farmers return to the fields as fertilizer. The methane collected in these generators can be burned to supply heat and generate power.[81]

Corporations and utilities are also tapping the methane produced in landfills as organic materials in buried garbage decompose, to produce industrial process heat or to generate electricity in combined heat and power plants. Interface—the world's largest manufacturer of industrial carpet—near Atlanta, Georgia, convinced the city to invest $3 million in capturing methane from the municipal landfill and build a nine-mile pipeline to an Interface factory. The natural gas in this pipeline, priced 30 percent below the world market price, meets 20 percent of the factory's needs. The landfill is projected to supply methane for 40 years, earning the city $35 million on its original $3 million investment. For Interface, operating costs are reduced and it gains an offset of its greenhouse gas emissions, thus enabling the factory to become climate-neutral.[82]

Crops can also be used to produce automotive fuels, including both ethanol and biodiesel. In 2007 the world produced 13.1 billion gallons of fuel ethanol and 2.3 billion gallons of biodiesel. Half of the ethanol came from the United States, a third came from Brazil, and the remainder came from a dozen other countries, led by China and Canada. Almost one fourth of the biodiesel was produced in Germany; the other major producers were the United States, France, and Italy.[83]

The United States, which surged ahead of Brazil in ethanol production in 2005, relies heavily on corn as a feedstock. With U.S. ethanol production projected to nearly double between 2007 and the end of 2008, U.S. output will jump to 13 billion gallons. This may already be exceeding the amount of U.S. grain that can be diverted to fuel without driving world food prices to an unacceptably high level. And expanding cane-based ethanol in Brazil means putting more pressure on the remaining Amazonian rainforest. Shifting to plug-in hybrids powered with wind or solar generated electricity would avoid that.[84]

As of mid-2007, growth in investment in ethanol and biodiesel was losing momentum as feedstock prices rose for both ethanol distilleries and biodiesel refineries and as soaring grain prices sounded alarm bells for food consumers everywhere. In Europe, with high goals for biodiesel use and low potential for expanding oilseed production, biodiesel refiners are turning to palm oil from Malaysia and Indonesia, where the clearing of rainforests for palm plantations is raising worldwide concern.[85]

Work is now under way to develop efficient technologies to convert cellulosic materials such as switchgrass, woodchips, wheat straw, and corn stalks into ethanol. Switchgrass and hybrid poplars would produce relatively high ethanol yields on marginal lands, but it likely will be another decade before cellulosic ethanol can compete with corn-based ethanol.[86]

An analysis by the American Solar Energy Society indicates that burning cellulosic crops to directly generate electricity is much more efficient than converting them to ethanol. The question is how much could plant materials contribute to the world's energy supply. ASES estimates that the United States could generate 110 gigawatts of electricity from burning crops such as switchgrass and fast growing trees, roughly 10 times the current level. This projected growth assumes that the anticipated expansion in cellulosic crop production would be used primarily for electricity generation rather than ethanol production. We anticipate that the worldwide use of plant materials to generate electricity could contribute 200 gigawatts to generating capacity by 2020.[87]

River, Tidal, and Wave Power

Roughly 16 percent of the world's electricity comes from
hydropower, most of it from large dams. Some countries such as
Brazil and the Democratic Republic of the Congo get most of
their electricity from river power. Large dam building flourished
during the third quarter of the last century, but then slowed as
the remaining good sites for dam building dwindled and as
opposition built because of the displacement of people and
inundation of productive land.[88]

Small-scale projects continue to be built. In 2006 small dams
with a combined 6,000 megawatts of generating capacity were
built in rural areas of China. For many rural communities these
are the only source of electricity. Though China leads, many
other countries also are building small-scale structures, as the
economics of generation increasingly favor renewable sources
over fossil fuels. There is also a growing interest in in-stream
turbines that do not need a dam and are thus less environmentally intrusive.[89]

The first large tidal generating facility—La Rance barrage,
with a generating capacity of 240 megawatts—was built 40
years ago in France and is still operating today. Within the last
few years interest in tidal power has spread rapidly. South Korea,
for example, is building a 254-megawatt project on its west
coast. When completed in 2009, this facility will provide enough
electricity for the half-million people living in the nearby city of
Ansan. At another site 30 miles to the north, engineers are planning an 812-megawatt tidal facility near Inchon.[90]

Not far away, China is planning a 300-megawatt tidal facility at the mouth of the Yalu River near North Korea. Far to the
south, New Zealand is planning a 200-megawatt project in the
Kaipara Harbour on the country's north coast.[91]

Gigantic projects are under consideration in several countries, including India, Britain, and Russia. India is planning to
build a 39-mile barrage across the Gulf of Khambhat on the
country's northwest coast with a 7,400-megawatt generating
capacity. In the United Kingdom, several political leaders are
pushing for an 8,600-megawatt tidal facility in the Severn Estuary on the county's southwest coast. Russian planners are also
talking in terms of 10,000-megawatt tidal power plants. One
such facility is to be built in the Sea of Okhotsk on the east

coast, and another is proposed for the White Sea in northwestern Russia, near Finland.[92]

In the United States, the focus is on smaller tidal facilities. The Federal Energy Regulatory Commission has issued preliminary permits for projects in Puget Sound, San Francisco Bay, and New York's East River. The San Francisco Bay project by Oceana Energy Company will have 40 or more megawatts of generating capacity. In addition to these proposals, 38 applications are pending from states on both coasts.[93]

Wave power, though it is a few years behind tidal power, is now attracting the attention of both engineers and investors. In the United States, the northern Californian utility PG&E has filed a plan to develop two 40-megawatt wave farms off the state's north coast. Oil giant Chevron filed for a permit to develop up to 60 megawatts of wave generating capacity nearby.[94]

The South West of England Regional Development Agency invited bids by firms to test their technologies in the Wave Hub Project off the coast of Cornwall. The authority will provide cable connections to the U.K. grid from the offshore facilities for up to 20 megawatts of power. Ireland has the most ambitious wave power development goal: 500 megawatts of wave generating capacity by 2020, enough to supply 7 percent of its electricity.[95]

We project that the 850 gigawatts (850,000 megawatts) of hydroelectric power in operation worldwide in 2006 will expand to 1,350 gigawatts by 2020. According to China's official projections, 270 gigawatts will be added there, mostly from large dams in the country's southwest. The remaining 230 gigawatts in our projected growth by 2020 would come from a scattering of large dams still being built in countries like Brazil and Turkey, a large number of small hydro facilities, a fast-growing number of tidal projects (some of them in the multi-gigawatt range), and numerous smaller wave power projects. If the interest in tidal and wave power continues to escalate, the additional capacity from hydro, tidal, and wave by 2020 could easily exceed the 500 gigawatts needed to reach the Plan B goal.[96]

The World Energy Economy of 2020

Backing out fossil fuels begins with the electricity sector, where the development of 5,153 gigawatts of new renewable generating capacity by 2020, over half of it from wind, would be more than enough to replace all the coal and oil and 70 percent of the natural gas now used to generate electricity. (See Table 12–1.) The addition of 1,530 gigawatts of thermal capacity by 2020 will reduce the use of both oil and gas for heating buildings and water. Roughly two thirds of this growth will come from rooftop solar water and space heaters.[97]

In looking at the broad shifts from 2006 to the Plan B energy economy of 2020, fossil fuel–generated electricity drops by 90 percent. This is more than offset by the fivefold growth in renewably generated electricity. In the transportation sector, energy use from fossil fuels drops by some 70 percent. This comes from shifting not just to hybrids that run partly on electricity but to highly efficient plug-in hybrids that run largely on electricity from renewable sources. And it also comes from shifting to electric trains, which are much more efficient than diesel-powered trains.[98]

Closely related to this overall energy restructuring are several indirect energy savings. For example, when coal is phased out as a power source the vast amount of energy used to extract the coal, bring it to the surface, and transport it—typically hundreds of miles by rail to power plants—is no longer needed. Some 42 percent of U.S. freight is coal transported by diesel-powered locomotives.[99]

The new energy economy will be based much less on energy from combustion and more on the direct harnessing of energy from wind, the sun, and the earth itself. In the new economy, for example, cars will be running largely on wind energy.

Electricity will be much more prominent in the new energy economy. In 2020 it will be the principal source of energy for cars, largely replacing gasoline. For trains it will replace diesel fuel. In the new economy, many buildings will be all-electric—heated, cooled, and illuminated entirely with carbon-free renewable electricity.

Just as renewable energy technologies are advancing, so too are those that will lead to a smart grid, one that uses smart meters, to constantly monitor not only electricity flows but specific uses at the household level. It gives consumers a choice, for example, between running a dishwasher during peak demand and paying 9¢ per kilowatt-hour for electricity and running it at 3 a.m. using 5¢ electricity. Giving consumers options like this can

Table 12–1. *World Energy from Renewables in 2006*
and Plan B Goals for 2020

Source	2006	Goal for 2020
Electricity Generating Capacity	(electrical gigawatts)	
Wind	74	3,000
Rooftop solar electric systems	9	1,090
Solar electric power plants	0	100
Solar thermal power plants	0	200
Geothermal	9	200
Biomass	45	200
Hydropower	850	1,350
Total	987	6,140
Thermal Energy Capacity	(thermal gigawatts)	
Solar rooftop water and space heaters	100	1,100
Geothermal	100	500
Biomass	220	350
Total	420	1,950

Source: See endnote 97.

shrink their electricity bills and benefit utilities by reducing the generating capacity that utilities will need.[100]

Whereas fossil fuels helped globalize the energy economy, shifting to renewable sources will localize it. We anticipate that the energy transition will be driven largely by mounting concerns about climate change, by climbing oil prices, and by the restructuring of taxes to incorporate the indirect costs of burning fossil fuels. It is encouraging to know that we now have the technologies to build a new energy economy, one that is not climate-disruptive, that does not pollute the air, and that can last as long as the sun itself. The question is no longer whether we can develop a climate-stabilizing energy economy, but whether we can develop it before climate change spins out of control.

III

AN EXCITING NEW OPTION

13

The Great Mobilization

There are many things we do not know about the future. But one thing we do know is that business as usual will not continue for much longer. Massive change is inevitable. Will the change come because we move quickly to restructure the economy or because we fail to act and civilization begins to unravel?

Saving civilization will take a massive mobilization, and at wartime speed. The closest analogy is the belated U.S. mobilization during World War II. But unlike that chapter in history, in which one country totally restructured its economy, the Plan B mobilization requires decisive action on a global scale.

On the climate front, official attention has now shifted to negotiating a post-Kyoto protocol to reduce carbon emissions. But that will take years. We need to act now. There is simply not time for years of negotiations and then more years for ratification of another international agreement.

It is time for individual countries to take initiatives on their own. Prime Minister Helen Clarke of New Zealand is leading the way. In late 2007 she announced that New Zealand will boost the renewable share of its electricity from 70 percent, mostly hydro and geothermal, to 90 percent by 2025. The country plans to cut per capita carbon emissions from transport in half by 2040. Beyond this, New Zealand plans to expand its forested area by some 250,000 hectares by 2020, ultimately sequestering roughly 1 million tons of carbon per year. Additional initiatives will be announced in coming months. The challenge, Clarke says, is "to dare to aspire to be carbon neutral."[1]

We know from our analysis of global warming, from the accelerating deterioration of the economy's ecological supports, and from our projections of future resource use in China that the western economic model—the fossil-fuel-based, automobile-centered, throwaway economy—will not last much longer. We need to build a new economy, one that will be powered by renewable sources of energy, that will have a diversified transport system, and that will reuse and recycle everything.

We can describe this new economy in some detail. The question is how to get from here to there before time runs out. Can we reach the political tipping points that will enable us to cut carbon emissions before we reach the ecological tipping points where the melting of the Himalayan glaciers becomes irreversible? Will we be able to halt the deforestation of the Amazon before it dries out, becomes vulnerable to fire, and turns into wasteland?

What if, for example, three years from now scientists announced that we have waited too long to cut carbon emissions and that the melting of the Greenland ice sheet is irreversible? How would the realization that we are responsible for a coming 7-meter (23-foot) rise in sea level and hundred of millions of refugees from rising seas affect us? How would it affect our sense of self, our sense of who we are?[2]

It could trigger a fracturing of society along generational lines like the more familiar fracturing of societies along racial, religious, and ethnic lines. How will we respond to our children when they ask, "How could you do this to us? How could you leave us facing such chaos?" These are questions we need to be thinking about now—because if we fail to act quickly enough, these are precisely the questions we will be asked.

As we have seen, a corporate accounting system that left costs off the books drove Enron, one of the largest U.S. corporations, into bankruptcy. Unfortunately, our global economic accounting system that also leaves costs off the books has potentially far more serious consequences.

The key to building a global economy that can sustain economic progress is the creation of an honest market, one that tells the ecological truth. To create an honest market, we need to restructure the tax system by reducing taxes on work and raising them on various environmentally destructive activities to incorporate indirect costs into the market price.

If we can get the market to tell the truth, then we can avoid being blindsided by a faulty accounting system that leads to bankruptcy. As Øystein Dahle, former Vice President of Exxon for Norway and the North Sea, has observed: "Socialism collapsed because it did not allow the market to tell the economic truth. Capitalism may collapse because it does not allow the market to tell the ecological truth."[3]

Shifting Taxes and Subsidies

The need for tax shifting—lowering income taxes while raising levies on environmentally destructive activities—has been widely endorsed by economists. For example, a tax on coal that incorporated the increased health care costs associated with mining it and breathing polluted air, the costs of damage from acid rain, and the costs of climate disruption would encourage investment in clean renewable sources of energy such as wind or solar.[4]

A market that is permitted to ignore the indirect costs in pricing goods and services is irrational, wasteful, and, in the end, self-destructive. It is precisely what Nicholas Stern was referring to when he described the failure to incorporate the costs of climate change in the prices of fossil fuels as "a market failure on the greatest scale the world has ever seen."[5]

The first step in creating an honest market is to calculate indirect costs. Perhaps the best model for this is a U.S. government study on the costs to society of smoking cigarettes that was undertaken by the Centers for Disease Control and Prevention (CDC). In 2006 the CDC calculated the cost to society of smoking cigarettes, including both the cost of treating smoking-related illnesses and the lost worker productivity from these illnesses, at $10.47 per pack.[6]

This calculation provides a framework for raising taxes on cigarettes. In Chicago, smokers now pay $3.66 per pack in state and local cigarette taxes. New York City is not far behind at $3 per pack. At the state level, New Jersey—which has boosted the tax in four of the last five years to a total of $2.58—has the highest tax. Since a 10-percent price rise typically reduces smoking by 4 percent, the health benefits of tax increases are substantial.[7]

Tax restructuring can also be used to create an honest pricing system for ecological services. For example, forest ecologists can estimate the values of services that trees provide, such as flood control and carbon sequestration. Once these are determined, they can be incorporated into the price of trees as a stumpage tax. Anyone wishing to cut a tree would have to pay a tax equal to the value of the services provided by that tree. The market for lumber would then be based on ecologically honest prices, prices that would reduce tree cutting and encourage wood reuse and paper recycling.

The most efficient means of restructuring the energy economy to stabilize atmospheric CO_2 levels is a carbon tax. Paid by the primary producers—the oil or coal companies—it would permeate the entire fossil fuel energy economy. The tax on coal would be almost double that on natural gas simply because coal has a much higher carbon content. As noted in Chapter 11, we propose a worldwide carbon tax of $240 per ton to be phased in at the rate of $20 per year between 2008 and 2020. Once a schedule for phasing in the carbon tax and reducing the tax on income is in place, the new prices can be used by all economic decisionmakers to make more intelligent decisions.[8]

For a gasoline tax, the most detailed analysis available of indirect costs is found in *The Real Price of Gasoline* by the International Center for Technology Assessment. The many indirect costs to society—including climate change, oil industry tax breaks, oil supply protection, oil industry subsidies, and treatment of auto exhaust-related respiratory illnesses—total around $12 per gallon ($3.17 per liter), slightly more than the cost to society of smoking a pack of cigarettes. If this external or social cost is added to the roughly $3 per gallon average price of gas in the United States in early 2007, gas would cost $15 a gallon. These are real costs. Someone bears them. If not us, our children. Now that these costs have been calculated, they can be used to set tax rates on gasoline, just as the CDC analysis is being used to raise taxes on cigarettes.[9]

Gasoline's indirect costs of $12 per gallon provide a reference point for raising taxes to where the price reflects the environmental truth. Gasoline taxes in Italy, France, Germany, and the United Kingdom averaging $4.40 per gallon are almost halfway there. The average U.S. gas tax of 47¢ per gallon, scarcely one tenth that in Europe, helps explain why more gasoline is used in the United States than in the next 20 countries combined.[10]

Phasing in a gasoline tax of 40¢ per gallon per year for the next 12 years, for a total rise of $4.80 a gallon, and offsetting it with a reduction in income taxes would raise the U.S. gas tax to the $4–5 per gallon prevailing today in Europe and Japan. This will still fall short of the $12 of indirect costs currently associated with burning a gallon of gasoline, but combined with the rising price of gasoline itself it should be enough to encourage people to use improved public transport and motorists to buy the plug-in hybrid cars scheduled to enter the market in 2010.

These carbon and gasoline taxes may seem high, but there is at least one dramatic precedent. In November 1998 the U.S. tobacco industry agreed to reimburse state governments $251 billion for the Medicare costs of treating smoking-related illnesses—nearly $1,000 for every person in the United States. This landmark agreement was, in effect, a retroactive tax on cigarettes smoked in the past, one designed to cover indirect costs. To pay this enormous bill, companies raised cigarette prices, bringing them closer to their true costs and further discouraging smoking.[11]

A carbon tax of $240 per ton of carbon by 2020 may seem steep, but it is not. If gasoline taxes in Europe, which were designed to generate revenue and to discourage excessive dependence on imported oil, were thought of as a carbon tax, the $4.40 per gallon would translate into a carbon tax of $1,815 per ton. This is a staggering number, one that goes far beyond any carbon emission tax or cap-and-trade carbon-price proposals to date. It suggests that the official discussions of carbon prices in the range of $15 to $50 a ton are clearly on the modest end of the possible range of prices. The high gasoline taxes in Europe have contributed to an oil-efficient economy and to far greater investment in high-quality public transportation over the decades, making it less vulnerable to supply disruptions.[12]

Tax shifting is not new in Europe. A four-year plan adopted in Germany in 1999 systematically shifted taxes from labor to energy. By 2003, this plan had reduced annual CO_2 emissions by 20 million tons and helped to create approximately 250,000 additional jobs. It had also accelerated growth in the renewable energy sector, creating some 64,000 jobs by 2006 in the wind industry alone, a number that is projected to rise to 103,000 by 2010.[13]

Between 2001 and 2006, Sweden shifted an estimated $2 billion of taxes from income to environmentally destructive activities. Much of this shift of $500 or so per household was levied on road transport, including hikes in vehicle and fuel taxes. Electricity is also picking up part of the shift. Environmental tax shifting is becoming commonplace in Europe, where France, Italy, Norway, Spain, and the United Kingdom are also using this policy instrument. In Europe and the United States, polls indicate that at least 70 percent of voters support environmental tax reform once it is explained to them.[14]

Environmental taxes are now being used for several purposes. As noted earlier, landfill taxes adopted by either national or local governments are becoming more common. A number of cities are now taxing cars that enter the city. Others are simply imposing a tax on automobile ownership. In Denmark, the tax on the purchase of a new car exceeds the price of the car itself. A new car that sells for $25,000 costs the buyer more than $50,000. Other governments are moving in this direction. *New York Times* reporter Howard French writes that Shanghai, which is being suffocated by automobiles, "has raised the fees for car registrations every year since 2000, doubling over that time to about $4,600 per vehicle—more than twice the city's per capita income."[15]

Some 2,500 economists, including eight Nobel Prize winners in economics, have endorsed the concept of tax shifts. Harvard economics professor N. Gregory Mankiw wrote in *Fortune* magazine: "Cutting income taxes while increasing gasoline taxes would lead to more rapid economic growth, less traffic congestion, safer roads, and reduced risk of global warming—all without jeopardizing long-term fiscal solvency. This may be the closest thing to a free lunch that economics has to offer."[16]

Cap-and-trade systems using tradable permits are sometimes

an alternative to environmental tax restructuring. The principal difference between them is that with permits, governments set the amount of a given activity that is allowed, such as the harvest from a fishery, and let the market set the price of the permits as they are auctioned off. With environmental taxes, in contrast, the price of the environmentally destructive activity is incorporated in the tax rate, and the market determines the amount of the activity that will occur at that price. Both economic instruments can be used to discourage environmentally irresponsible behavior.

The use of cap-and-trade systems with marketable permits has been effective at the national level, ranging from restricting the catch in an Australian fishery to reducing sulfur emissions in the United States. For example, the government of Australia, concerned about lobster overharvesting, estimated the sustainable yield of lobsters and then issued catch permits totaling that amount. Fishers could then bid for these permits. In effect, the government decided how many lobsters could be taken each year and let the market decide what the permits were worth. Since the permit trading system was adopted in 1986, the fishery has stabilized and appears to be operating on a sustainable basis.[17]

Although tradable permits are popular in the business community, permits are administratively more complicated and not as well understood as taxes. Edwin Clark, former senior economist with the White House Council on Environmental Quality, observes that tradable permits "require establishing complex regulatory frameworks, defining the permits, establishing the rules for trades, and preventing people from acting without permits." In contrast to restructuring taxes, something with which there is wide familiarity, tradable permits are a concept not widely understood by the public, making it more difficult to generate broad public support.[18]

Each year the world's taxpayers provide an estimated $700 billion of subsidies for environmentally destructive activities, such as fossil fuel burning, overpumping aquifers, clearcutting forests, and overfishing. An Earth Council study, *Subsidizing Unsustainable Development*, observes that "there is something unbelievable about the world spending hundreds of billions of dollars annually to subsidize its own destruction."[19]

Iran provides a classic example of extreme subsidies when it prices oil for internal use at one tenth the world price, strongly encouraging car ownership and gas consumption. If its $37-billion annual subsidy were phased out, the World Bank reports that Iran's carbon emissions would drop by a staggering 49 percent. This move would also strengthen the economy by freeing up public revenues for investment in the country's economic development. Iran is not alone. The Bank reports that removing energy subsidies would reduce carbon emissions in India by 14 percent, in Indonesia by 11 percent, in Russia by 17 percent, and in Venezuela by 26 percent. Carbon emissions could be cut in scores of countries by simply eliminating fossil fuel subsidies.[20]

Some countries are already doing this. Belgium, France, and Japan have phased out all subsidies for coal. Germany reduced its coal subsidy from $2.8 billion in 1989 to $1.4 billion in 2002, meanwhile lowering its coal use by 38 percent. It plans to phase out this support entirely by 2018. As oil prices have climbed, a number of countries have greatly reduced or eliminated subsidies that held fuel prices well below world market prices because of the heavy fiscal cost. Among these are China, Indonesia, and Nigeria.[21]

A study by the U.K. Green Party, *Aviation's Economic Downside*, describes the extent of subsidies to the U.K. airline industry. The giveaway begins with $18 billion in tax breaks, including a total exemption from the federal tax. External or indirect costs that are not paid, such as treating illness from breathing the air polluted by planes, the costs of climate change, and so forth, add nearly $7.5 billion to the tab. The subsidy in the United Kingdom totals $426 per resident. This is also an inherently regressive tax policy simply because a part of the U.K. population cannot afford to fly, yet they help subsidize this high-cost travel for their more affluent compatriots.[22]

While some leading industrial countries have been reducing subsidies to fossil fuels—notably coal, the most climate-disrupting of all fuels—the United States has increased its support for the fossil fuel and nuclear industries. Douglas Koplow, founder of Earth Track, calculated in a 2006 study that annual U.S. federal energy subsidies have a total value to the industry of $74 billion. Of this, the oil and gas industry gets $39 billion, coal $8 billion, and nuclear $9 billion. At a time when there is a need to conserve oil resources, U.S. taxpayers are subsidizing their depletion.[23]

Just as there is a need for tax shifting, there is also a need for subsidy shifting. A world facing the prospect of economically disruptive climate change, for example, can no longer justify subsidies to expand the burning of coal and oil. Shifting these subsidies to the development of climate-benign energy sources such as wind, solar, biomass, and geothermal power will help stabilize the earth's climate. Shifting subsidies from road construction to rail construction could increase mobility in many situations while reducing carbon emissions. And shifting the $22 billion in annual fishing industry subsidies, which encourage destructive overfishing, to the creation of marine parks to regenerate fisheries would be a giant step in restoring oceanic fisheries.[24]

In a troubled world economy, where many governments are facing fiscal deficits, these proposed tax and subsidy shifts can help balance the books, create additional jobs, and save the economy's eco-supports. Tax and subsidy shifting promise energy efficiency, cuts in carbon emissions, and reductions in environmental destruction—a win-win-win situation.

Summing Up Climate Stabilization Measures

Earlier we outlined the need to cut net carbon dioxide emissions 80 percent by 2020 to minimize the future rise in temperature. Here we summarize the Plan B measures for doing so, including both reducing fossil fuel use and increasing biological sequestration.

Replacing fossil fuels with renewable sources of energy for generating electricity and heat will reduce carbon emissions in 2020 by more than 3.1 billion tons. (See Table 13–1.) The biggest single cut in carbon emissions comes from phasing out the use of coal to generate electricity, a step that will also sharply reduce the 3 million deaths from air pollution each year. Other cuts come from entirely backing out all the oil used to generate electricity and 70 percent of the natural gas.[25]

In the transport sector, the greatly reduced use of oil will eliminate close to 1.2 billion tons of carbon emissions. This reduction relies heavily on the shift to plug-in hybrid cars that will run on carbon-free sources of electricity such as wind. The remainder comes largely from shifting long-haul freight from trucks to trains, electrifying freight and passenger trains, and

Table 13–1. *Plan B Carbon Dioxide Emissions Reductions and Sequestration in 2020*

Action	Amount
	(million tons carbon)
Energy Restructuring	
Replacing fossil fuels with renewables for electricity and heat	3,140
Restructuring the transport system	1,190
Reducing coal and oil use in industry	100
Biological Carbon Sequestration	
Ending net deforestation	1,500
Planting trees to sequester carbon	950
Managing soils to sequester carbon	600
Total Carbon Dioxide Reductions in 2020	7,480
Carbon Dioxide Emissions in 2006	9,180
Percent Reduction from 2006 Baseline	81.5

Source: See endnote 25.

using green electricity to power them.[26]

At present, net deforestation of the earth is responsible for an estimated 1.5 billion tons of carbon emissions per year. The Plan B goal is to bring deforestation to a halt by 2020, thus totally eliminating this source of carbon emissions. The idea of banning logging may seem novel, but in fact a number of countries already have total or partial bans.[27]

We're not content with just halting deforestation. We want to increase the number of trees on the earth in order to sequester carbon. The forestation of wastelands will fix more than 950 million tons of carbon each year. This does not include the similarly ambitious planting of trees to control flooding, reduce rainfall runoff to recharge aquifers, and protect soils from erosion.[28]

The other initiative to sequester carbon biologically is achieved through land use management. This includes expanding the area of minimum- or no-till cropland, planting more cover crops during the off-season, and using more perennials instead of annuals in cropping patterns. The latter would mean, for example, using less corn and more switchgrass to produce fuel ethanol. These practices can fix an estimated 600 million tons of carbon per year.[29]

Together, replacing fossil fuels in electricity generation with renewable sources of energy, switching to plug-in hybrid cars, going to all-electric railways, banning deforestation, and sequestering carbon by planting trees and improving soil management will drop carbon dioxide emissions in 2020 more than 80 percent below today's levels. This reduction will stabilize atmospheric CO_2 concentrations below 400 parts per million, limiting the future rise in temperature.[30]

Although we devoted a chapter to increasing energy efficiency—doing what we do with less energy—there is also a huge potential for cutting carbon emissions through conservation by not doing some of the things we do, or doing them differently. For example, in the summer of 2006 Prime Minister Junichiro Koizumi of Japan announced that in order to save energy, Japanese men would be encouraged to not wear jackets and ties in the office. This meant thermostats could be raised, thus reducing electricity use for air conditioning while maintaining the same comfort level.[31]

Our tabulated carbon cuts do not include lifestyle changes like this, which can make a huge difference. Urban planner Richard Register recounts meeting a bicycle activist friend wearing a T-shirt that said, "I just lost 3,500 pounds. Ask me how." When asked, he said he had sold his car. Replacing a 3,500-pound car with a 22-pound bicycle obviously reduces energy use dramatically, but it also reduces materials use by 99 percent, indirectly saving still more energy.[32]

Dietary changes can also make a difference. We learned in Chapter 9 that the energy differences between a diet rich in red meat and a plant-based diet is roughly the same as the energy-use difference between driving a Chevrolet Suburban sports utility vehicle and a Toyota Prius gas-electric hybrid. The bottom line is that those of us with diets rich in livestock products can do both ourselves and civilization a favor by moving down the food chain.[33]

For countries everywhere, particularly developing ones, the economic good news is that the Plan B energy economy is much more labor-intensive than the fossil-fuel-based economy it is replacing. For example, in Germany, a leader in the energy transition, renewable energy industries already employ more workers than the long-standing fossil fuel and nuclear industries do. In a world where expanding employment is a universal goal, this is welcome news indeed.[34]

The restructuring of the energy economy outlined here will not only dramatically drop CO_2 emissions, helping to stabilize climate, but it will also eliminate much of the air pollution that we know today. The idea of a pollution-free environment is difficult for us even to imagine, simply because none of us has ever known an energy economy that was not highly polluting. Working in coal mines will be history. Black lung disease will eventually disappear. So too will "code red" alerts warning of health threats from extreme air pollution.

And, finally, in contrast to investments in oil fields and coal mines, where depletion and abandonment are inevitable, the new energy sources are inexhaustible. While wind turbines, solar cells, and solar-thermal panels will all need repair and occasional replacement, the initial investment can last forever. This well will not go dry.

A Response to Failing States

If the number of failing states continues to increase, at some point this trend will translate into a failing civilization. These declining states threaten the political stability of the international system. Somehow we must turn the tide of state decline. One thing seems clear: business as usual will not do it.

Failing states, a relatively new phenomenon, require a new response. Historically, as noted in Chapter 1, the principal threat to international stability and the security of individual countries has been the concentration of power in one country. Today the threat to security comes from the loss of power and the descent of nation-states into anarchy and chaos. These failing states become terrorist training grounds (as in Iraq and Afghanistan), drug producers (Afghanistan and Myanmar), and weapons traders (Somalia and Nigeria).

The goals discussed earlier of stabilizing population, eradicating poverty, and restoring the earth are indispensable, but we also need a focused effort to deal specifically with states that are failing or at risk of doing so. The United Kingdom and Norway have recognized that failing states need special attention and have each set up interagency funds to provide a response mechanism. They are the first to devise a specific institutional response.[35]

At present, U.S. efforts to deal with weak and failing states are fragmented. Several U.S. government departments are involved, including State, Treasury, and Agriculture, to name a few. And within the State Department, several different offices are concerned with this issue. This lack of focus was recognized by the Hart-Rudman U.S. Commission on National Security in the Twenty-first Century: "Responsibility today for crisis prevention and response is dispersed in multiple AID [U.S. Agency for International Development] and State bureaus, and among State's Under Secretaries and the AID Administrator. In practice, therefore, no one is in charge."[36]

What is needed now is a new cabinet-level agency— a Department of Global Security—that would fashion a coherent policy toward each weak and failing state. This recommendation, initially set forth in a report of the Commission on Weak States and U.S. National Security, recognizes that the threats to security are now coming less from military power and more from the trends that undermine states, such as rapid population growth, poverty, deteriorating environmental support systems, and spreading water shortages. The new agency would incorporate AID (now part of the State Department) and all the various foreign assistance programs that are now in other government departments, thereby assuming responsibility for U.S. development assistance across the board. The State Department would provide diplomatic support for this new agency, helping in the overall effort to reverse the process of state failure.[37]

The new Department of Global Security (DGS) would be funded by shifting fiscal resources from the Department of Defense. In effect, the DGS budget would be the new defense budget. It would focus on the central sources of state failure by helping to stabilize population, restore environmental support systems, eradicate poverty, provide universal primary school education, and strengthen the rule of law through bolstering police forces and court systems.

The DGS would deal with the production and international trafficking in drugs. It would make such issues as debt relief and market access an integral part of U.S. policy. The DGS would provide a focus for the United States to help lead what it can be hoped will be a growing international effort to reduce the number of failing states. This agency would also encourage private investment in failing states by providing loan guarantees to spur development.

The United States might also benefit from the creation of a U.S. youth service corps, which would provide for one year of compulsory public service for its young people. Young people could serve at home or abroad, depending on their interests and on national needs. At home, they could teach in inner-city schools, work on environmental clean-up programs, plant trees, and help restore and maintain the infrastructure in national parks, much as the Civilian Conservation Corps did in the 1930s. In developing countries, they could contribute in many ways, including teaching and helping to organize family planning, tree planting, and micro-lending programs. This program would involve young people in helping the world while developing a sense of civic pride and social responsibility.[38]

At a more senior level, the United States has a fast-growing reservoir of retired people who are highly skilled in such fields as management, accounting, law, education, and medicine and who are eager to be of use. Their talents could be mobilized through a voluntary senior service corps. The enormous reservoir of management skills in this age group could be tapped to provide the skills so lacking in failing-state governments.

There are already, of course, a number of volunteer organizations that rely on the talents, energy, and enthusiasm of both U.S. young people and seniors, such as the Peace Corps, Teach for America, and the Senior Corps. But conditions now require a much more ambitious, systematic effort to tap this talent pool.

The world has quietly entered a new era, one where there is no national security without global security. We need to recognize this and to restructure and refocus our efforts to respond to this new reality.

A Wartime Mobilization

As we contemplate mobilizing to save civilization, we see both similarities and contrasts with the mobilization for World War II. In this earlier case, there was an economic restructuring, but it was temporary. Mobilizing to save civilization, in contrast, requires an enduring economic restructuring.

Still, the U.S. entry into World War II offers an inspiring case study in rapid mobilization. Initially, the United States resisted involvement in the war and responded only after it was directly attacked at Pearl Harbor on December 7, 1941. But respond it did. After an all-out commitment, the U.S. engagement helped turn the tide of war, leading the Allied Forces to victory within three-and-a-half years.[39]

In his State of the Union address on January 6, 1942, one month after the bombing of Pearl Harbor, President Roosevelt announced the country's arms production goals. The United States, he said, was planning to produce 45,000 tanks, 60,000 planes, 20,000 anti-aircraft guns, and 6 million tons of merchant shipping. He added, "Let no man say it cannot be done."[40]

No one had ever seen such huge arms production numbers. But Roosevelt and his colleagues realized that the world's largest concentration of industrial power at that time was in the U.S. automobile industry. Even during the Depression, the United States was producing 3 million or more cars a year. After his State of the Union address, Roosevelt met with automobile industry leaders and told them that the country would rely heavily on them to reach these arms production goals. Initially they wanted to continue making cars and simply add on the production of armaments. What they did not yet know was that the sale of new cars would soon be banned. From early 1942 through the end of 1944, nearly three years, there were essentially no cars produced in the United States.[41]

In addition to a ban on the production and sale of cars for private use, residential and highway construction was halted, and driving for pleasure was banned. Strategic goods—including tires, gasoline, fuel oil, and sugar—were rationed beginning in 1942. Cutting back on private consumption of these goods freed up material resources that were vital to the war effort.[42]

The year 1942 witnessed the greatest expansion of industrial output in the nation's history—all for military use. Wartime aircraft needs were enormous. They included not only fighters, bombers, and reconnaissance planes, but also the troop and cargo transports needed to fight a war on distant fronts. From the beginning of 1942 through 1944, the United States far exceeded the initial goal of 60,000 planes, turning out a staggering 229,600 aircraft, a fleet so vast it is hard even today to visualize it. Equally impressive, by the end of the war more than 5,000 ships were added to the 1,000 or so that made up the American Merchant Fleet in 1939.[43]

In her book *No Ordinary Time*, Doris Kearns Goodwin describes how various firms converted. A sparkplug factory was among the first to switch to the production of machine guns. Soon a manufacturer of stoves was producing lifeboats. A merry-go-round factory was making gun mounts; a toy company was turning out compasses; a corset manufacturer was producing grenade belts; and a pinball machine plant began to make armor-piercing shells.[44]

In retrospect, the speed of this conversion from a peacetime to a wartime economy is stunning. The harnessing of U.S. industrial power tipped the scales decisively toward the Allied Forces, reversing the tide of war. Germany and Japan, already fully extended, could not counter this effort. Winston Churchill often quoted his foreign secretary, Sir Edward Grey: "The United States is like a giant boiler. Once the fire is lighted under it, there is no limit to the power it can generate."[45]

This mobilization of resources within a matter of months demonstrates that a country and, indeed, the world can restructure the economy quickly if convinced of the need to do so. Many people—although not yet the majority—are already convinced of the need for a wholesale economic restructuring. The purpose of this book is to convince more people of this need, helping to tip the balance toward the forces of change and hope.

Mobilizing to Save Civilization

Mobilizing to save civilization means restructuring the economy, restoring its natural support systems, eradicating poverty, stabilizing population and climate, and, above all, restoring hope. We have the technologies, economic instruments, and financial resources to do this. The United States, the wealthiest society that has ever existed, has the resources to lead this effort. Jeffrey Sachs of Columbia University's Earth Institute sums it up well: "The tragic irony of this moment is that the rich countries are so rich and the poor so poor that a few added tenths of one percent of GNP from the rich ones ramped up over the coming decades could do what was never before possible in human history: ensure that the basic needs of health and education are met for all impoverished children in this world. How many more tragedies will we suffer in this country before we wake up to our capacity to help make the world a safer and more prosperous place not only through military might, but through the gift of life itself?"[46]

It is not possible to put a precise price tag on the changes needed to move our twenty-first century civilization off the decline-and-collapse path and onto a path that will sustain economic progress. But we can at least provide some rough estimates of the scale of effort needed.

As noted in Chapter 7, the additional external funding needed to achieve universal primary education in developing countries that require help, for instance, is conservatively estimated at $10 billion per year. (See Table 13–2.) Funding for an adult literacy program based largely on volunteers will take an estimated additional $4 billion annually. Providing for the most basic health care in developing countries is estimated at $33 billion by the World Health Organization. The additional funding needed to provide reproductive health care and family planning services to all women in developing countries amounts to $17 billion a year.[47]

Closing the condom gap by providing the additional 9.5 billion condoms needed to control the spread of HIV in the developing world and Eastern Europe requires $3 billion—$550 million for condoms and $2.75 billion for AIDS prevention education and condom distribution. The cost of extending school lunch programs to the 44 poorest countries is $6 billion. An estimated $4 billion per year would cover the cost of assistance to preschool children and pregnant women in these countries. Altogether, the cost of reaching basic social goals comes to $77 billion a year.[48]

As noted in Chapter 8, a poverty eradication effort that is not accompanied by an earth restoration effort is doomed to

Table 13–2. *Plan B Budget: Additional Annual Expenditures Needed to Meet Social Goals and to Restore the Earth*

Goal	Funding
	(billion dollars)
Basic Social Goals	
Universal primary education	10
Eradication of adult illiteracy	4
School lunch programs for 44 poorest countries	6
Assistance to preschool children and pregnant women in 44 poorest countries	4
Reproductive health and family planning	17
Universal basic health care	33
Closing the condom gap	3
Total	77
Earth Restoration Goals	
Planting trees to reduce flooding and conserve soil	6
Planting trees to sequester carbon	20
Protecting topsoil on cropland	24
Restoring rangelands	9
Restoring fisheries	13
Protecting biological diversity	31
Stabilizing water tables	10
Total	113
Grand Total	190

Source: See endnote 47.

fail. Protecting topsoil, reforesting the earth, restoring oceanic fisheries, and other needed measures will cost an estimated $113 billion in additional expenditures per year. The most costly activities, protecting biological diversity at $31 billion and conserving soil on cropland at $24 billion, account for almost half of the earth restoration annual outlay.[49]

Combining social goals and earth restoration components into a Plan B budget yields an additional annual expenditure of

$190 billion, roughly one third of the current U.S. military budget or one sixth of the global military budget. (See Table 13–3.) In a sense this is the new defense budget, the one that addresses the most serious threats to our security.[50]

Unfortunately, the United States continues to focus on building an ever-stronger military, largely ignoring the threats posed by continuing environmental deterioration, poverty, and population growth. Its defense budget for 2006, including $118 billion for the military operations in Iraq and Afghanistan, brought the U.S. military expenditure to $560 billion. Other North Atlantic Treaty Organization members spend a combined $328 billion a year on the military. Russia spends about $35 billion, and China, $50 billion. U.S. military spending is now roughly equal to that of all other countries combined.[51]

As of late 2007, direct U.S. appropriations for the Iraq war, which has lasted longer than World War II, total some $450 billion. Economists Joseph Stiglitz and Linda Bilmes calculate that if all the costs are included, such as the lifetime of care required for returning troops who are brain-injured or psychologically shattered, the war will cost in the end some $2 trillion. Yet the Iraq war may prove to be one of history's most costly mistakes not so much because of fiscal outlay but because it has diverted the world's attention from climate change and the other threats to civilization itself.[52]

It is decision time. Like earlier civilizations that got into environmental trouble, we can decide to stay with business as usual and watch our modern economy decline and eventually collapse, or we can consciously move onto a new path, one that will sustain economic progress. In this situation, no action is a de facto decision to stay on the decline-and-collapse path.

No one can argue today that we do not have the resources to eradicate poverty, stabilize population, and protect the earth's natural resource base. We can get rid of hunger, illiteracy, disease, and poverty, and we can restore the earth's soils, forests, and fisheries. Shifting one sixth of the world military budget to the Plan B budget would be more than adequate to move the world onto a path that would sustain progress. We can build a global community where the basic needs of all the earth's people are satisfied—a world that will allow us to think of ourselves as civilized.

This economic restructuring depends on tax restructuring, on getting the market to be ecologically honest. The benchmark of political leadership will be whether leaders succeed in restructuring the tax system. Restructuring the tax system, not additional appropriations, is the key to restructuring the energy economy.

It is easy to spend hundreds of billions in response to terrorist threats, but the reality is that the resources needed to disrupt a modern economy are small, and a U.S. Department of Homeland Security, however heavily funded, provides only minimal protection from suicidal terrorists. The challenge is not to provide a high-tech military response to terrorism but to build a global society that is environmentally sustainable and equitable—one that restores hope for everyone. Such an effort would do more to combat terrorism than any increase in military expenditures or than any new weapons systems, however advanced.

Table 13–3. *Military Budgets by Country and for the World in 2006 and Plan B Budget*

Country	Budget
	(billion dollars)
United States	560
United Kingdom	59
France	53
China	50
Japan	44
Germany	37
Russia	35
Italy	30
Saudi Arabia	29
India	24
All other	314
World Military Expenditure	1,235
Plan B Budget	190

Source: See endnote 50.

Just as the forces of decline can reinforce each other, so can the forces of progress. Fortunately, the steps to reverse destructive trends or to initiate constructive new trends are often mutually reinforcing, win-win solutions. For example, efficiency gains that lower oil dependence also reduce carbon emissions and air pollution. Steps to eradicate poverty help stabilize population. Reforestation fixes carbon, increases aquifer recharge, and reduces soil erosion. Once we get enough trends headed in the right direction, they will reinforce each other.

The world needs a major success story in reducing carbon emissions and dependence on oil to bolster hope in the future. If the United States, for instance, were to launch a crash program to shift to plug-in hybrid cars while simultaneously investing in thousands of wind farms, Americans could do most of their short-distance driving with wind energy, dramatically reducing pressure on the world's oil supplies.[53]

With many U.S. automobile assembly lines idled, it would be a relatively simple matter to retool some of them to produce wind turbines, enabling the country to quickly harness its vast wind energy potential. This would be a rather modest initiative compared with the restructuring during World War II, but it would help the world to see that restructuring an economy is entirely doable and that it can be done quickly, profitably, and in a way that enhances national security both by reducing dependence on vulnerable oil supplies and by avoiding disruptive climate change.

What You and I Can Do

One of the questions I am frequently asked when I am speaking in various countries is, given the environmental problems that the world is facing, can we make it? That is, can we avoid economic decline and the collapse of civilization? My answer is always the same: it depends on you and me, on what you and I do to reverse these trends. It means becoming politically active. Saving our civilization is not a spectator sport.

We have moved into this new world so fast that we have not yet fully grasped the meaning of what is happening. Traditionally, concern for our children has translated into getting them the best health care and education possible. But if we do not act quickly to reverse the earth's environmental deterioration, eradicate poverty, and stabilize population, their world will decline economically and disintegrate politically.

The two overriding policy challenges are to restructure taxes and reorder fiscal priorities. Saving civilization means restructuring taxes to get the market to tell the ecological truth. And it means reordering fiscal priorities to get the resources needed for Plan B. Write or e-mail your elected representative about the need for tax restructuring to create an honest market. Remind him or her that corporations that left costs off the books appeared to prosper in the short run, only to collapse in the long run.

Or better yet, gather some like-minded friends together to meet with your elected representatives to discuss why we need to raise environmental taxes and reduce income taxes. Before the meeting, draft a brief statement of your collective concerns and the policy initiatives needed. Feel free to download the information on tax restructuring in this chapter from our Web site to use in these efforts.

Let your political representatives know that a world spending more than $1 trillion a year for military purposes is simply out of sync with reality when the future of civilization is in question. Ask them if $190 billion a year is an unreasonable expenditure to save civilization. Ask them if diverting one sixth of the global military budget to saving civilization is too costly. Introduce them to Plan B. Remind them of how we mobilized in World War II.[54]

Make a case for the inclusion of poverty eradication, family planning, reforestation, and renewable energy development in international assistance programs. Urge an increase in these appropriations and a cut in military appropriations, pointing out that advanced weapons systems are useless in dealing with the new threats to our security. Someone needs to speak on behalf of our children and grandchildren, because it is their world that is at stake.

In short, we need to persuade our elected representatives and leaders to support the changes outlined in Plan B. We need to lobby them for these changes as though our future and that of our children depended on it—because it does.

Educate yourself on environmental issues. If you found this book useful, share it with others. It can be downloaded free of charge from the Earth Policy Institute Web site. If you want to know what happened to earlier civilizations that also found themselves in environmental trouble, read *Collapse* by Jared Diamond or *A Short History of Progress* by Ronald Wright.[55]

If you like to write, try your hand at an op-ed piece for your local newspaper on the need to raise taxes on environmentally destructive activities and offset this with a lowering of income taxes. Try a letter to the editor. Put together your own personal listserv to help you communicate useful information to friends, colleagues, and local opinion leaders.

The scale and urgency of the challenge we face has no precedent, but what we need to do can be done. It is doable. Sit down and map out your own personal plan and timetable for what you want to do to move the world off a path headed toward economic decline and onto one of sustainable economic progress. Set your own goals. Identify people in your community you can work with to achieve these goals. Pick an issue that is meaningful to you, such as restructuring the tax system, banning inefficient light bulbs, phasing out coal-fired power plants, or working for "complete streets" that are pedestrian- and bicycle-friendly in your community. What could be more exciting and rewarding?

The choice is ours—yours and mine. We can stay with business as usual and preside over an economy that continues to destroy its natural support systems until it destroys itself, or we can adopt Plan B and be the generation that changes direction, moving the world onto a path of sustained progress. The choice will be made by our generation, but it will affect life on earth for all generations to come.

Notes

Chapter 1. Entering a New World

1. David Adam, "Ice-Free Arctic Could be Here in 23 Years," *Guardian* (London), 5 September 2007.

2. Ibid.

3. Paul Brown, "Melting Ice Cap Triggering Earthquakes," *Guardian* (London), 8 September 2007.

4. Ibid.

5. Ibid.

6. Alister Doyle, "Sea Rise Seen Outpacing Forecasts Due to Antarctica," *Reuters*, 23 August 2007.

7. Emily Wax, "A Sacred River Endangered By Global Warming," *Washington Post*, 17 June 2007.

8. Clifford Coonan, "China's Water Supply Could be Cut Off as Tibet's Glaciers Melt," *The Independent* (London), 31 May 2007; "Glacier Study Reveals Chilling Prediction," *China Daily*, 23 September 2004.

9. U.N. Environment Programme (UNEP), *Global Outlook for Ice and Snow* (Nairobi: 2007), p.103; J. Hansen et al., "Climate Change and Trace Gases," *Philosophical Transactions of the Royal Society A*, vol. 365 (15 July 2007), pp. 1949–50.

10. Gordon McGranahan et al., "The Rising Tide: Assessing the Risks of Climate Change and Human Settlements in Low Elevation Coastal Zones," *Environment and Urbanization*, vol. 18, no. 1 (April 2007),

pp. 17–37; U.N. Population Division, *World Population Prospects: The 2006 Revision Population Databasae,* at esa.un.org/unpp, updated 2007.

11. Lester R. Brown, *Outgrowing the Earth* (New York: W. W. Norton and Company, 2004), pp.101–02; U.N. Population Division, op. cit. note 10.

12. Fund for Peace and Carnegie Endowment for International Peace, "The Failed States Index," *Foreign Policy*, July/August 2005, July/August 2006, and July/August 2007.

13. Nicholas Stern, *The Stern Review on the Economics of Climate Change* (London: HM Treasury, 2006).

14. Agnus Maddison, "World Population, GDP, and Per Capita GDP, 1-2003 AD," at www.ggdc.net/maddison, viewed 8 August 2007; U.N. Population Division, op. cit. note 10.

15. Costs of burning coal from DSS Management Consultants Inc. and RWDI Air Inc., *Cost-Benefit Analysis: Replacing Ontario's Coal-Fired Electricity Generation* (Ontario, Canada: April 2005), p. v.

16. U.S. Department of Energy (DOE), Energy Information Administration, "Weekly Retail Gasoline and Diesel Prices," at tonto.eia.doe .gov/dnav/pet/pet_pri_gnd_dcus_nus_w.htm, viewed 8 August 2007.

17. International Center for Technology Assessment (ICTA), *The Real Cost of Gasoline: An Analysis of the Hidden External Costs Consumers Pay to Fuel Their Automobiles* (Washington, DC: 1998); ICTA, *Gasoline Cost Externalities Associated with Global Climate Change: An Update to CTA's Real Price of Gasoline Report* (Washington, DC: September 2004); ICTA, *Gasoline Cost Externalities: Security and Protection Services: An Update to CTA's Real Price of Gasoline Report* (Washington, DC: January 2005); Terry Tamminen, *Lives Per Gallon: The True Cost of Our Oil Addiction* (Washington, DC: Island Press, 2006), p. 60; adjusted to 2007 prices with Bureau of Economic Analysis, "Table 3–Price Indices for Gross Domestic Product and Gross Domestic Purchases," *GDP and Other Major Series, 1929–2007* (Washington, DC: August 2007); DOE, op. cit. note 16.

18. Munich Re, *Topics Annual Review: Natural Catastrophes 2001* (Munich, Germany: 2002), pp. 16–17; value of China's wheat and rice harvests from USDA, *Production, Supply and Distribution*, electronic database at www.fas.usda.gov/psdonline, updated 12 July 2007, using prices from International Monetary Fund (IMF), *International Financial Statistics*, electronic database, at ifs.apdi.net/imf.

19. "Forestry Cuts Down on Logging," *China Daily*, 26 May 1998; Erik Eckholm, "China Admits Ecological Sins Played Role in Flood Disaster," *New York Times*, 26 August 1998.

20. Eric Pfanner, "Failure Brings Call for Tougher Standards: Accounting for Enron: Global Ripple Effects," *International Herald Tribune*, 17 January 2002; share price data from www.marketocracy.com, viewed 9 August 2007.

21. World Business Academy, "Interface's Ray Anderson: Mid-Course Correction," *Global Reconstruction*, vol. 19, issue 5 (2 June 2005); Ray Anderson, "A Call for Systemic Change," speech at the National Conference on Science, Policy, & the Environment: Education for a Secure and Sustainable Future, Washington, DC, 31 January 2003.

22. Jared Diamond, *Collapse: How Societies Choose to Fail or Succeed* (New York: Penguin Group, 2005).

23. Sandra Postel, *Pillar of Sand* (New York: W. W. Norton & Company, 1999), pp. 13–21.

24. Ibid.

25. Ibid.

26. Robert McC. Adams quoted in Joseph Tainter, *The Collapse of Complex Societies* (Cambridge, U.K.: Cambridge University Press, 1988), p. 1.

27. "Maya," *Encyclopedia Britannica*, online encyclopedia, viewed 13 September 2007.

28. Guy Gugliotta, "The Maya: Glory and Ruin," *National Geographic*, August 2007.

29. Maddison, op. cit. note 14; IMF, *World Economic Outlook Database 2007*, electronic database, at www.imf.org/external/pubs, updated April 2007.

30. Mathis Wackernagel et al., "Tracking the Ecological Overshoot of the Human Economy," *Proceedings of the National Academy of Sciences*, vol. 99, no. 14 (9 July 2002), pp. 9,266–71; Global Footprint Network, WWF, and Zoological Society of London, *Living Planet Report 2006* (Oakland, CA: Global Footprint Network, 2006), p. 14.

31. Brown, op. cit. note 11, pp.101–02; Peter H. Gleick et al., *The World's Water 2004–2005* (Washington, DC: Island Press, 2004), p. 88; U.N. Population Division, op. cit. note 10.

32. Millennium Ecosystem Assessment (MA), *Ecosystems and Human Well-Being: Synthesis* (Washington, DC: Island Press, 2005); MA, *Ecosystems and Human Well-Being: Policy Responses* (Washington, DC: Island Press, 2005), p. 180.

33. Geoffrey Lean, "A Disaster to Take Everyone's Breath Away," *Independent* (London), 24 July 2006; Daniel Nepstad, "Climate Change and the Forest," *Tomorrow's Amazonia: Using and Abusing the World's Last Great Forests* (Washington, DC: The American Prospect, September 2007).

34. Lean, op. cit. note 33.

35. Ibid.; Nepstad, op. cit. note 33.

36. U.N. Food and Agriculture Organization (FAO), *ForesSTAT*, electronic database, at faostat.fao.org, updated 22 December 2006; Patrick B. Durst et al., *Forests Out of Bounds: Impacts and Effectiveness of*

Logging Bans in Natural Forests in Asia-Pacific (Bangkok: FAO, Asia-Pacific Forestry Commission, 2001); Eckholm, op. cit. note 19; Andy White et al., *China and the Global Market for Forest Products: Transforming Trade to Benefit Forests and Livelihood* (Washington, DC: Forest Trends, March 2006), p. 12.

37. FAO, *The State of World Fisheries and Aquaculture 2004* (Rome: 2004), pp. 24, 30–32; Ted Williams, "The Last Bluefin Hunt," in Valerie Harms et al., *The National Audubon Society Almanac of the Environment* (New York: Grosset/Putnam, 1994), p. 18; Konstantin Volkov, "The Caviar Game Rules," Reuters-IUCN Environmental Media Award winner, 2001; Camillo Catarci, *World Markets and Industry of Selected Commercially-Exploited Aquatic Species* (Rome: FAO, 2004).

38. The New Road Map Foundation, "All-Consuming Passion: Waking up from the American Dream," factsheet, *EcoFuture*, updated 17 January 2002.

39. USDA, op. cit. note 18; International Iron and Steel Institute, *Steel Statistical Yearbook 2006* (Brussels: 2006), pp. 77–79.

40. IMF, op. cit. note 29; U.N. Population Division, op. cit. note 10.

41. U.N. Population Division, op. cit. note 10; FAO, op. cit. note 36.

42. Ward's Automotive Group, *World Motor Vehicle Data 2006* (Southfield, MI: Ward's Automotive Group, 2006); area for paving calculated using 0.02 hectare per car from Lester R. Brown, "Paving the Planet: Cars and Crops Competing for Land," *Issue Alert* (Washington, DC: Earth Policy Institute, 14 February 2001); USDA, op. cit. note 18.

43. BP, *Statistical Review of World Energy 2007* (London: 2007); U.N. Population Division, op. cit. note 10; International Energy Agency (IEA), Oil Market Report (Paris: July 2007).

44. U.N. Population Division, op. cit. note 10.

45. Carlotta Gall, "Opium Harvest at Record Levels in Afghanistan," *New York Times*, 3 September 2006; Ania Lichtarowica, "Conquering Polio's Last Frontier," *BBC News*, 2 August 2007.

46. Fund for Peace and Carnegie Endowment, July/August 2005, op. cit. note 12.

47. World Bank, *Global Monitoring Report 2007: Millennium Development Goals* (Washington, DC: 2007) p. 5; Department for International Development, *Why We Need to Work More Effectively in Fragile States* (London: January 2005), pp. 27–28.

48. Fund for Peace and Carnegie Endowment, July/August 2005, 2006, and 2007, op. cit. note 12.

49. Fund for Peace and Carnegie Endowment, July/August 2005, op. cit. note 12.

50. Fund for Peace and Carnegie Endowment, July/August 2005, 2006, and 2007, op. cit. note 12.

51. Table 1–1 from Ibid.

52. U.N. Population Division, op. cit. note 10; Fund for Peace and Carnegie Endowment, July/August 2007, op. cit. note 12.

53. U.N. Population Division, op. cit. note 10; Fund for Peace and Carnegie Endowment, July/August 2007, op. cit. note 12; Richard Cincotta and Elizabeth Leahy, "Population Age Structure and Its Relation to Civil Conflict: A Graphic Metric," *Woodrow Wilson International Center for Scholars Environmental Change and Security Program Report*, vol. 12 (2006–07), pp. 55–58.

54. Lydia Polgreen, "In Congo, Hunger and Disease Erode Democracy," *New York Times*, 23 June 2006; Richard Brennan and Anna Husarska, "Inside Congo, An Unspeakable Toll," *Washington Post*, 16 July 2006; Lydia Polgreen, "Hundreds Killed Near Chad's Border With Sudan," *New York Times*, 14 November 2006.

55. Postel, op. cit. note 23, pp. 13–21; Gugliotta, op. cit. note 28.

56. UNAIDS, "HIV and AIDS Estimates and Data, 2003 and 2005," *2006 Report on the Global Aids Epidemic* (Geneva: May 2006).

57. U.N. Population Division, op. cit. note 10.

58. Colin J. Campbell, "Short Written Submission to the National Petroleum Council," e-mail to Frances Moore, Earth Policy Institute, 14 August 2007, p. 5; "Iceland Launches Energy Revolution," *BBC News*, 24 December 2001; John Vidal, "Sweden Plans to be World's First Oil-Free Economy," *The Guardian* (London), 8 February 2006.

59. USDA, op. cit. note 18; Chicago Board of Trade, "Market Commentaries," for wheat and corn, at www.cbot.com, viewed various dates September 2007; historical commodity prices from futures.tradingcharts.com, viewed 3 October 2007.

60. Ethanol requirement in 2008 from Renewable Fuels Association, "Ethanol Biorefinery Locations," at www.ethanolrfa.org, updated 28 September 2007; 2008 grain harvest from Interagency Agricultural Projections Committee, *Agricultural Projections to 2016* (Washington, DC: USDA, February 2007); 2006 corn used for ethanol from USDA Economic Research Service, *Feed Grains Database*, at www.ers.usda. gov/Data/FeedGrains, updated 28 September 2007; 2006 grain harvest from USDA, op. cit. note 18.

61. John B. Rae, *The American Automobile Industry* (Boston: Thwayne Publishers, 1984), pp. 87–97.

62. James Brooke, "Japan Squeezes to Get the Most of Costly Fuel," *New York Times*, 4 June 2005; hybrid mileage based on new EPA estimates at www.fueleconomy.gov, viewed 23 August 2007; fleet average from Robert M. Heavenrich, *Light Duty Automotive Technology and Fuel Economy Trends: 1975 Through 2006* (Washington, DC: EPA Office of Transportation and Air Quality, July 2006), updated using EPA Office of Transportation and Air Quality, "EPA Issues New Test Method for Fuel Economy Window Stickers," regulatory announce-

ment (Washington, DC: EPA, December 2006).

63. Share of wind power generation in Denmark calculated using BP, op.
cit. note 43, and Global Wind Energy Council, *Global Wind 2006
Report* (Brussels: 2007), p. 4, with capacity factor from National
Renewable Energy Laboratory, *Power Technologies Energy Data Book*
(Oak Ridge, TN: DOE, August 2006); Flemming Hansen, "Denmark
to Increase Wind Power to 50% by 2025, Mostly Offshore," *Renewable Energy Access*, 5 December 2006; Global Wind Energy Council,
"Global Wind Energy Markets Continue to Boom-2006 Another
Record Year," press release (Brussels: 2 February 2007), with European
per person consumption from European Wind Energy Association,
"Wind Power on Course to Become Major European Energy Source by
the End of the Decade," press release (Brussels: 22 November 2004);
China water heaters calculated from Renewable Energy Policy Network for the 21st Century, *Renewables Global Status Report, 2006
Update* (Washington, DC: Worldwatch Institute, 2006), p. 21, and
from Bingham Kennedy, Jr., *Dissecting China's 2000 Census* (Washington, DC: Population Reference Bureau, June 2001); Iceland
National Energy Authority and Ministries of Industry and Commerce, *Geothermal Development and Research in Iceland* (Reykjavik,
Iceland: April 2006), p. 16.

64. FAO, *FAOSTAT*, electronic database, at faostat.fao.org, updated 30
June 2007.

65. FAO, *FISHSTAT Plus*, electronic database, at www.fao.org, updated
March 2007.

66. Se-Kyung Chong, "Anmyeon-do Recreation Forest: A Millennium of
Management," in Patrick B. Durst et al., *In Search of Excellence:
Exemplary Forest Management in Asia and the Pacific*, Asia-Pacific
Forestry Commission (Bangkok: FAO Regional Office for Asia and the
Pacific, 2005), pp. 251–59.

67. Daniel Hellerstein, "USDA Land Retirement Programs," in USDA,
Agricultural Resources and Environmental Indicators 2006 (Washington, DC: July 2006); USDA, Economic Research Service, *Agri-Environmental Policy at the Crossroads: Guideposts on a Changing
Landscape*, Agricultural Economic Report No. 794 (Washington, DC:
January 2001); USDA, op. cit. note 18.

68. City of Amsterdam, "Bike Capital of Europe," at www.iamsterdam.
com/visiting_exploring, viewed 23 August 2007; Molly O'Meara,
Reinventing Cities for People and the Planet, Worldwatch Paper 147
(Washington, DC: Worldwatch Institute, June 1999), p. 47; population
from U.N. Population Division, *World Urbanization Prospects: The
2005 Revision Population Database*, electronic database, at
esa.un.org/unup, updated 2006; Serge Schmemann, "I Love Paris on a
Bus, a Bike, a Train and in Anything but a Car," *New York Times*, 26
July 2007; Randy Kennedy, "The Day The Traffic Disappeared," *New
York Times Magazine*, 20 April 2003, pp. 42–45.

69. CalCars, "All About Plug-In Hybrids," at www.calcars.org, viewed 22

August 2007.

70. Tim Johnston, "Australia Is Seeking Nationwide Shift to Energy-Saving Light Bulbs," *New York Times*, 21 February 2007; Rob Gillies, "Canada Announces Greenhouse Gas Targets," *Associated Press*, 25 April 2007; Matthew L. Wald, "A U.S. Alliance to Update the Light Bulb," *New York Times*, 14 March 2007; Ian Johnston, "Two Years to Change EU Light Bulbs," *Scotsman* (U.K.), 10 March 2007; Deborah Zabarenko, "China to Switch to Energy-Efficient Lightbulbs," *Reuters*, 3 October 2007; energy savings from lighting efficiency calculated by Earth Policy Institute using IEA, *Light's Labour's Lost: Policies for Energy-Efficient Lighting* (Paris: February 2006), and IEA, *World Energy Outlook 2006* (Paris: 2006).

Chapter 2. Deteriorating Oil and Food Security

1. Oil production data from International Energy Agency (IEA), *Oil Market Report* (Paris: August 2001), includes oil, natural gas liquids, and processing gains; historical data from U.S. Department of Defense, Twentieth Century Petroleum Statistics (Washington, DC: 1945), cited in Christopher Flavin and Seth Dunn, "Reinventing the Energy System," in Lester R. Brown, Christopher Flavin, and Hilary French, *State of the World 1999* (New York: W. W. Norton & Company, 1999), p. 25; coal from Seth Dunn, "Coal Use Continues Rebound," in Lester R. Brown et al., *Vital Signs 1998* (New York: W. W. Norton & Company, 1998), pp. 52–53.

2. U.N. Population Division, *World Urbanization Prospects: The 2005 Revision* (New York: 2006), p. 1; U.N. Population Division, *World Population Prospects: The 2006 Revision Population Database*, at esa.un.org/unpp, updated 2007; grain production in 1900 is author's estimate based on historic trends.

3. IEA, *Oil Market Report* (Paris: October 2007); Colin J. Campbell, "Short Written Submission to the National Petroleum Council," e-mail to Frances Moore, Earth Policy Institute, 14 August 2007.

4. Michael T. Klare, "Entering the Tough Oil Era," *TomDispatch.com*, 16 August 2007; Campbell, op. cit. note 3.

5. Historic data from International Monetary Fund, International Financial Statistics, on-line database, at ifs.apdi.net, updated July 2007; recent wheat prices from Chicago Board of Trade, "Market Commentaries," at www.cbot.com, viewed various dates in September and October 2007.

6. Gary Schnitkey, Darrel Good, and Paul Ellinger, "Crude Oil Price Variability and Its Impact on Break—Even Corn Prices," *Farm Business Management*, 30 May 2007; 2006 grain used for ethanol from U.S. Department of Agriculture (USDA), Economic Research Service (ERS), *Feed Grains Database*, at www.ers.usda.gov, updated 28 September 2007; 2006 grain harvest from USDA, *Production, Supply and Distribution*, electronic database at www.fas.usda.gov/psdonline,

updated 12 September 2007; 2008 ethanol requirement from Renewable Fuels Association, "Ethanol Biorefinery Locations," at www.ethanolrfa.org, updated 28 September 2007; 2008 grain harvest from Interagency Agricultural Projections Committee, *Agricultural Projections to 2016* (Washington, DC: USDA, February 2007).

7. U.S. Department of Energy (DOE), Energy Information Administration (EIA), "Select Crude Oil Spot Prices," at www.eia.doe.gov/emeu/international/crude1.html, updated 20 October 2007; John Vidal, "The End of Oil Is Closer Than You Think," *Guardian* (London), 21 April 2005; Alfred J. Cavallo, "Oil: Caveat Empty," *Bulletin of the Atomic Scientists*, vol. 61, no. 3 (May/June 2005), pp. 16–18.

8. Vidal, op. cit. note 7; M. King Hubbert, "Nuclear Energy and the Fossil Fuels," paper presented at the spring meeting of the Southern District Division of Production, American Petroleum Institute, March 1956.

9. DOE, EIA, "Table 4.1: World Crude Oil Production, 1970–2006, Selected Countries," at www.eia.doe.gov/emeu/international/oil production.html, viewed 14 September 2007.

10. Production figures are for crude oil, including lease condensate, from DOE, op. cit. note 9; Vidal, op. cit. note 7; DOE, EIA, "Petroleum (Oil) Production," *International Petroleum Monthly*, at www.eia.doe.gov/ipm/supply.html, updated 12 July 2007.

11. DOE, op. cit. note 9; Klare, op. cit.note 4; Paula Dittrick, "CGES: OPEC Pushing Limits of Oil Production Capacity," *Oil and Gas Journal*, 20 October 2004.

12. Neil Chatterjee, "'Peak Oil' Gathering Sees $100 Crude This Decade," *Reuters*, 26 April 2005; Adam Porter, "Expert Says Saudi Oil May Have Peaked," *Al Jazeera*, 20 February 2005; James D. Hamilton, "Running Dry?" *The Atlantic*, October 2007; IEA, op. cit. note 3.

13. DOE, op. cit. note 9; Vidal, op. cit. note 7; Walter Youngquist, geologist, letter to author, 12 September 2007.

14. Michael T. Klare, "The Energy Crunch to Come," *TomDispatch.com*, 22 March 2005; Jad Mouawad, "Big Oil's Burden of Too Much Cash," *New York Times*, 12 February 2005; Mark Williams, "The End of Oil?" *Technology Review*, February 2005; Vidal, op. cit. note 7.

15. Peter Maass, "The Breaking Point," *New York Times Magazine*, 21 August 2005.

16. James Picerno, "If We Really Have the Oil," *Bloomberg Wealth Manager*, September 2002, p. 45; Klare, op. cit. note 14; Kenneth S. Deffeyes, *Beyond Oil: The View from Hubbert's Peak* (New York: Hill and Wang, 2005); Richard C. Duncan and Walter Youngquist, "Encircling the Peak of World Oil Production," *Natural Resource Research*, vol. 12, no. 4 (December 2003), p. 222; A. M. Samsan Bakhtiari, "World Oil Production Capacity Model Suggests Output Peak by 2006–07," *Oil and Gas Journal*, 26 April 2004, pp. 18–20.

17. IEA, op. cit. note 3; IEA, *Oil Market Report* (Paris: May 2007).

18. Fredrik Robelius, *Giant Oil Fields—The Highway to Oil* (Uppsala, Sweden: Uppsala University Press, 9 March 2007).

19. IEA, op. cit. note 3; IEA, *Oil Market Report* (Paris: July 1993); U.N. Population Division, *World Population Prospects*, op. cit. note 2; IEA, *World Energy Outlook 2006* (Paris: 2006), pp. 85, 492.

20. Robert Collier, "Canadian Oil Sands: Vast Reserves Second to Saudi Arabia Will Keep America Moving, But at a Steep Environmental Cost," *San Francisco Chronicle*, 22 May 2005; Vidal, op. cit. note 7; Walter Youngquist, "Survey of Energy Resources: Oil Shale," *Energy Bulletin*, 24 April 2005.

21. Gargi Chakrabarty, "Shale's New Hope," *Rocky Mountain News*, 18 October 2004; Walter Youngquist, "Alternative Energy Sources," in Lee C. Gerhard, Patrick Leahy, and Victor Yannacone, eds., *Sustainability of Energy and Water through the 21st Century*, Proceedings of the Arbor Day Farm Conference, 8–11 October 2000 (Lawrence, KS: Kansas Geological Survey, 2002), p. 65; Cavallo, op. cit. note 7.

22. Collier, op. cit. note 20; Alberta Energy and Utilities Board, *Alberta Energy Resource Industries Monthly Statistics*, at www.eub.ca, viewed 8 August 2007; BP, *BP Statistical Review of World Energy* (London: June 2007).

23. "Exxon Says N. America Gas Production Has Peaked," *Reuters*, 21 June 2005; Collier, op. cit. note 20; Richard Heinberg, "The End of the Oil Age," *Earth Island Journal*, vol. 18, no. 3 (Fall 2003).

24. Youngquist, op. cit. note 20; Youngquist, op. cit. note 21, p. 64; Vidal, op. cit. note 7; WWF-Canada, "Oil Sands Pushing Canada Further from Kyoto, WWF and UK Think-Tank Warn," press release (Toronto: 6 June 2007).

25. Danielle Murray, "Oil and Food: A Rising Security Challenge," *Eco-Economy Update* (Washington, DC: Earth Policy Institute, 9 May 2005); "Energy Use in Agriculture," in USDA, *U.S. Agriculture and Forestry Greenhouse Gas Inventory: 1990–2001*, Technical Bulletin No. 1907 (Washington, DC: Global Change Program Office, Office of the Chief Economist, 2004), p. 94.

26. James Duffield, USDA, e-mail to Danielle Murray, Earth Policy Institute, 31 March 2005; James Duffield, USDA, e-mail to Frances Moore, Earth Policy Institute, 17 August 2007; USDA, *Production, Supply and Distribution*, op. cit. note 6.

27. Conservation Technology Information Center, "Conservation Tillage and Other Tillage Types in the United States—1990–2004," in *2004 National Crop Residue Management Survey* (West Lafayette, IN: Purdue University, 2004); Duffield, e-mail to Murray, op. cit. note 26; tractor use and horse stocks from U.N. Food and Agriculture Organization (FAO), *FAOSTAT Statistics Database*, at apps.fao.org, updated 4 April 2005.

28. Fertilizer energy use data from Duffield, e-mail to Murray, op. cit. note 26; USDA, *Production, Supply and Distribution*, op. cit. note 6.

29. DOE, EIA, *Annual Energy Outlook 2003* (Washington, DC: 2004); "Table 20: Energy Expenses for On-Farm Pumping of Irrigation Water by Water Source and Type of Energy: 2003 and 1998," in USDA, National Agricultural Statistics Service, *2003 Farm & Ranch Irrigation Survey, Census of Agriculture* (Washington, DC: 2004); Fred Pearce, "Asian Farmers Sucking the Continent Dry," *New Scientist.com*, 28 August 2004.

30. Murray, op. cit. note 25; DOE, EIA, "Total Primary Energy Consumption, All Countries, 1980–2004," at www.eia.doe.gov/emeu /international/energyconsumption.html, viewed 2 August 2007.

31. Murray, op. cit. note 25; M. Heller and G. Keoleian, *Life-Cycle Based Sustainability Indicators for Assessment of the U.S. Food System* (Ann Arbor, MI: Center for Sustainable Systems, University of Michigan, 2000), p. 42.

32. U.S. Department of Transportation (DOT), Bureau of Transportation Statistics (BTS), *Freight Shipments in America* (Washington, DC: 2004), pp. 9–10; Andy Jones, *Eating Oil—Food in a Changing Climate* (London: Sustain and Elm Farm Research Centre, 2001), p. 2 of summary.

33. "Shipment Characteristics by Three-Digit Commodity and Mode of Transportation: 2002," in BTS and U.S. Census Bureau, *2002 Commodity Flow Survey* (Washington, DC: December 2004); Jones, op. cit. note 32; James Howard Kunstler, author of *Geography of Nowhere,* in *The End of Suburbia: Oil Depletion and the Collapse of The American Dream*, documentary film (Toronto, ON: The Electric Wallpaper Co., 2004).

34. Heller and Keoleian, op. cit. note 31, p. 42; food energy content and packaging content calculated by Danielle Murray, Earth Policy Institute, using USDA nutritional information and packaging energy costs from David Pimentel and Marcia Pimentel, *Food, Energy and Society* (Boulder, CO: University Press of Colorado, 1996).

35. Center for American Progress, *Resources for Global Growth: Agriculture, Energy and Trade in the 21st Century* (Washington, DC: 2005); USDA, ERS, "Price Spreads from Farm to Consumer," at www.ers.usda.gov/Data, updated 22 June 2007.

36. Murray, op. cit. note 25, pp. 1, 3; Duffield, e-mail to Murray, op. cit. note 26; John Miranowski, "Energy Demand and Capacity to Adjust in U.S. Agricultural Production," presentation at Agricultural Outlook Forum 2005, Arlington, VA, 24 February 2005, p.11.

37. 1950–59 data from Worldwatch Institute, *Signposts 2001*, CD-Rom (Washington, DC: 2001); 1960–2006 data from USDA, *Production, Supply and Distribution*, op. cit. note 6.

38. 1950–59 grain data from Worldwatch Institute, op. cit. note 37; 1960–2006 data from USDA, *Production, Supply and Distribution*, op. cit. note 6.

39. Worldwatch Institute, *Signposts 2002*, CD-Rom (Washington, DC: 2002); USDA, *Production, Supply and Distribution*, op. cit. note 6.

40. Lester R. Brown, *Outgrowing the Earth* (New York: W. W. Norton & Company, 2004), pp. 60–69.

41. USDA, *Production, Supply and Distribution*, op. cit. note 6; U. N. Population Division, *World Population Prospects*, op. cit. note 2; FAO, *FAOSTAT Food Security*, electronic database, at www.fao.org/faostat, updated 30 June 2006.

42. USDA, *Production, Supply and Distribution*, op. cit. note 6; Brown, op. cit. note 40, p. 50.

43. USDA, *Production, Supply and Distribution*, op. cit. note 6; Kelly Day Rubenstein et al., *Crop Genetic Resources: An Economic Appraisal* (Washington, DC: USDA Economic Research Service, May 2005), p. 19.

44. USDA, *Production, Supply and Distribution*, op. cit. note 6; U.N. Population Division, *World Population Prospects*, op. cit. note 2.

45. USDA, *Production, Supply and Distribution*, op. cit. note 6; U.N. Population Division, *World Population Prospects*, op. cit. note 2; Michael Ma, "Northern Cities Sinking as Water Table Falls," *South China Morning Post*, 11 August 2001; share of China's grain harvest from the North China Plain based on Hong Yang and Alexander Zehnder, "China's Regional Water Scarcity and Implications for Grain Supply and Trade," *Environment and Planning A*, vol. 33 (2001), and on USDA, *Production, Supply and Distribution*, op. cit. note 6.

46. Shaobing Peng et al., "Rice Yields Decline with Higher Night Temperature from Global Warming," *Proceedings of the National Academy of Sciences*, 6 July 2004, pp. 9971–75; Intergovernmental Panel on Climate Change, *Summary for Policymakers* in *Climate Change 2007: Impacts, Adaptation, and Vulnerability* (New York: Cambridge University Press, 2007), pp. 15–16.

47. F.O. Licht, "Too Much Too Soon? World Ethanol Production to Break Another Record in 2005," *World Ethanol and Biofuels Report*, vol. 3, no. 20 (21 June 2005), pp. 429–35; DOE, World Crude Oil Prices, and U.S. All Grades All Formulations Retail Gasoline Prices, at tonto.eia.doe.gov, viewed 31 July 2007; Renewable Fuels Association, op. cit. note 6.

48. F.O. Licht, "World Ethanol Production 2007 to Hit New Record," *World Ethanol and Biofuels Report*, vol. 5, no. 17 (8 May 2007); corn used for ethanol in 2007 marketing year, from September 2007 to August 2008, from USDA, ERS, op. cit. note 6; corn ethanol conversion is author's estimate, based on Keith Collins, chief economist, USDA, statement before the U.S. Senate Committee on Environment and Public Works, 6 September 2006, p. 8; energy content of ethanol relative to gasoline from Oak Ridge National Laboratory (ORNL), "Bioenergy Conversion Factors," at bioenergy.ornl.gov/papers/ misc/energy_ conv.html, viewed 3 August 2007; U.S. gasoline con-

sumption in 2007 from "Table 2: Energy Consumption by Sector and Source," in DOE, EIA, *Annual Energy Outlook 2007* (Washington, DC: February 2007); USDA, *Production, Supply and Distribution*, op. cit. note 6.

49. Sergio Barros, *Brazil-Sugar-Annual Report-2006, GAIN Report BR6002* (Washington, DC: USDA, Foreign Agricultural Service, April 2006); CEPEA, Indicadores de Preços—Açúcar Cristal, at www.cepea.esalq.usp.br/acucar, viewed 31 July 2007.

50. F.O. Licht, op. cit. note 48; "Stung by Bad Experience, Dutch Propose Tough Criteria for Importing Sustainable Biofuels," *International Herald Tribune*, 26 April 2007; "EU Ministers Agree Biofuel Target," *BBC News*, 15 February 2007.

51. F.O. Licht, op. cit. note 48; corn ethanol conversion author's estimate based on Collins, op. cit. note 48; F.O. Licht, "E-5 Mandate to be Introduced by May," *World Ethanol and Biofuels Report*, vol. 4, no. 15 (7 April 2006), p. 355; Eric Unmacht, "Faced with Soaring Oil Prices, Indonesia Turns to Biodiesel," *Christian Science Monitor*, 5 July 2006; Naveen Thukral, "Malaysia Approves 52 Biodiesel Plants So Far," *Reuters*, 16 August 2006.

52. USDA, *Production, Supply and Distribution*, op. cit. note 6.

53. Ibid.; USDA, *Crop Production 2006 Summary* (Washington, DC: 2007).

54. Robert Wisner, e-mail to Janet Larsen, Earth Policy Institute, 2 January 2007, data updated 29 December 2006 in preparation for Iowa State University Crop Advantage seminar, Cedar Rapids and Burlington, IA, 4–5 January 2007; historical corn production data for Iowa at USDA, National Agricultural Statistics Service, "Quick Stats," *Agricultural Statistics Database*, at www.nass.usda.gov, viewed 27 December 2006.

55. Madelene Pearson and Danielle Rossingh, "Wheat Price Rises to Record $9 a Bushel on Global Crop Concerns," *Bloomberg*, 12 September 2007; wheat, soybeans, and corn from Chicago Board of Trade, op. cit. note 5; historical commodity prices from futures.tradingcharts.com, viewed 3 October 2007.

56. Ronald Buchanan, "Mexico Protest Prompts Food Price Assurance," *Financial Times*, 1 February 2007; Carolyn Said, "Nothing Flat about Tortilla Prices: Some in Mexico Cost 60 Percent More, Leading to a Serious Struggle for Low-Income People," *San Francisco Chronicle*, 13 January 2007; "Italy Urged to go on Pasta Strike," *BBC News*, 13 September 2007; Karen Atwood, "Rising Price of Wheat Signals End of Low-Cost Food, Warns Premier Chief," *The Independent* (London), 5 September 2007.

57. Lester R. Brown, "Distillery Demand for Grain to Fuel Cars Vastly Understated: World May be Facing Highest Grain Prices in History," *Eco-Economy Update* (Washington, DC: Earth Policy Institute, 4 January 2007); corn ethanol conversion is author's estimate, based on

Collins, op. cit. note 48; energy content of ethanol relative to gasoline from ORNL, op. cit. note 48; U.S. gasoline consumption in 2007 from DOE, op. cit. note 48; USDA, *Production, Supply and Distribution*, op. cit. note 6.

58. Ward's Communications, *Ward's World Motor Vehicle Data 2006* (Southfield, MI: 2006), p. 240; income calculations from World Bank, "GNI Per Capita 2006, Atlas Method and PPP," *World Development Indicators*, at siteresources.worldbank.org, updated 1 July 2007, and from U.N. Population Division, *World Population Prospects*, op. cit. note 2.

59. Corn used for ethanol in 2007 from USDA, *Feed Grains Database*, op. cit. note 6; corn ethanol conversion author's estimate based on Collins, op. cit. note 48; energy content of ethanol relative to gasoline from ORNL, op. cit. note 48; U.S. gasoline consumption in 2007 from DOE, op. cit. note 48.

60. California Cars Initiative (CalCars), "All About Plug-In Hybrids (PHEVs)," at www.calcars.org/vehicles.html, viewed 27 December 2006.

61. Patrick Barta, "Jatropha Plant Gains Steam in Global Race for Biofuels," *Wall Street Journal*, 24 August 2007.

62. Ibid.

63. Ibid.; Ben Macintyre, "Poison Plant Could Help to Cure the Planet," *The Times* (London), 28 July 2007.

64. Barta, op. cit. note 61; Rebecca Renner, "Green Gold in a Shrub: Entrepreneurs Target the Jatropha Plant as the Next Big Biofuel," *Scientific American*, June 2007.

65. IEA, op. cit. note 3; 2030 from DOE, EIA, *International Energy Outlook 2007* (Washington, DC: May 2007), p. 29, and from IEA, *World Energy Outlook 2006*, op. cit. note 19, p. 86; Thomas Wheeler, "It's the End of the World as We Know It," *Baltimore Chronicle*, 3 August 2004.

66. "Table 1–12: U.S. Sales or Deliveries of New Aircraft, Vehicles, Vessels, and Other Conveyances," in BTS, *National Transportation Statistics 2005* (Washington, DC: DOT, 2005).

67. Darrin Qualman, "'Peak Oil': The Short, Medium, and Long-Term," *Union Farmer Monthly*, vol. 56, no. 4 (August 2005).

68. Oliver Prichard, "SUV Drivers Reconsider," *Philadelphia Inquirer*, 1 June 2005; Danny Hakim and Jonathan Fuerbringer, "Fitch Cuts G.M. to Junk, Citing Poor S.U.V. Sales," *New York Times*, 24 May 2005; Fitch Corporate Ratings, at fitchratings.com, viewed 8 August 2007.

69. U.N. Human Settlements Programme, *The State of the World's Cities 2004/2005* (London: Earthscan, 2004), pp. 24–25; U.N. Population Division, *Urban Agglomerations 2005*, wall chart (New York: March 2006).

70. U.S. Census Bureau, "American Spend More Than 100 Hours Commuting to Work Each Year, Census Bureau Reports," press release (Washington, DC: 30 March 2005).

71. Wheeler, op. cit. note 65.

72. Micheline Maynard, "Surging Fuel Prices Catch Most Airlines Unprepared, Adding to the Industry's Gloom," *New York Times*, 26 April 2005; "Revealed: The Real Cost of Air Travel," *The Independent* (London), 29 May 2005; DOT and FAA, *FAA Aerospace Forecasts—Fiscal Years 2006–2017* (Washington, DC: 2006), p. 63.

73. "Table 1–4: Public Road and Street Mileage in the United States by Type of Surface," in BTS, *National Transportation Statistics 2007* (Washington, DC: DOT, 2007).

74. Gerhard Metschies, "Pain at the Pump," *Foreign Policy*, July–August 2007.

75. Edith M. Lederer, "U.N.: Hunger Kills 18,000 Kids Each Day," *Associated Press*, 17 February 2007; Iraq Coalition Casualty Count, icasualties.org/oif, updated 31 July 2007.

76. Loganaden Naiken, "Keynote Paper: FAO Methodology for Estimating the Prevalence of Undernourishment," at www.fao.org/docrep/005/y4249e/y4249e06.htm, viewed 1 August 2007; FAO, op. cit. note 41.

77. C. Ford Runge and Benjamin Senauer, "How Biofuels Could Starve the Poor," *Foreign Affairs*, May/June 2007.

78. Missy Ryan, "Commodity Boom Eats into Aid for World's Hungry," *Reuters*, 5 September 2007.

79. FAO, Crop Prospects and Food Situation, no. 3, May 2007; Fund for Peace and Carnegie Endowment for International Peace, "The Failed States Index 2007," *Foreign Policy*, July/August 2007; U.N. Population Division, *World Population Prospects*, op. cit. note 2.

80. Lederer, op. cit. note 75.

Chapter 3. Rising Temperatures and Rising Seas

1. U.N. Environment Programme (UNEP), *Global Outlook for Ice and Snow* (Nairobi: 2007).

2. Ibid.

3. U.S. Department of Agriculture (USDA), *Production, Supply and Distribution*, electronic database, at www.fas.usda.gov/psdonline, updated 11 June 2007; Janet Larsen, "Record Heat Wave in Europe Takes 35,000 Lives," *Eco-Economy Update* (Washington, DC: Earth Policy Institute, 9 October 2003); USDA, National Agricultural Statistics Service, "Crop Production," news release (Washington, DC: 12 August 2005).

4. Janet Larsen, "Setting the Record Straight: More than 52,000 Europeans Died from Heat in Summer 2003," *Eco-Economy Update*

(Washington, DC: Earth Policy Institute, 26 July 2006); National Commission on Terrorist Attacks Upon the United States, *The 9/11 Commission Report* (Washington, DC: U.S. Government Printing Office, 2004).

5. "Awful Weather We're Having," *The Economist*, 2 October 2004; Richard Milne, "Hurricanes Cost Munich Re Reinsurance," *Financial Times*, 6 November 2004.

6. J. Hansen, NASA's Goddard Institute for Space Studies (GISS), "Global Temperature Anomalies in 0.1 C," at data.giss.nasa.gov/gistemp/tabledata/GLB.Ts.txt, updated June 2007; climate monitoring stations from Reto A. Ruedy, GISS, e-mail to Janet Larsen, Earth Policy Institute, 14 May 2003.

7. Temperature change calculated from Hansen, op. cit. note 6; crops from USDA, op. cit. note 3; USDA, *Grain: World Markets and Trade* (Washington, DC: various months).

8. Carbon dioxide data from Pieter Tans, "Trends in Atmospheric Carbon Dioxide–Mauna Loa," NOAA/ESRL, at www.cmdl.noaa.gov, viewed 16 October 2007, with historical estimate in data from Seth Dunn, "Carbon Emissions Dip," in Worldwatch Institute, *Vital Signs 1999* (New York: W. W. Norton & Company, 1999), pp. 60–61; fossil fuel emissions calculated from International Energy Agency, *World Energy Outlook 2006* (Paris: 2006), p. 493; deforestation emissions from Vattenfall, *Global Mapping of Greenhouse Gas Abatement Opportunities up to 2030: Forestry Sector Deep-Dive* (Stockholm: June 2007), p. 27.

9. Intergovernmental Panel on Climate Change (IPCC), *Summary for Policymakers*, in *Climate Change 2007: The Physical Science Basis. Contribution of Working Group I to the Fourth Assessment Report of the Intergovernmental Panel on Climate Change* (Cambridge and New York: Cambridge University Press, 2007), p. 13; IPCC, "Intergovernmental Panel on Climate Change and Its Assessment Reports," fact sheet, at www.ipcc.ch/press, viewed 27 July 2007.

10. IPCC, *Summary for Policymakers*, op. cit. note 9, p. 15.

11. National Center for Atmospheric Research and UCAR Office of Programs, "Drought's Growing Reach: NCAR Study Points to Global Warming as Key Factor," press release (Boulder, CO: 10 January 2005); Aiguo Dai, Kevin E. Trenberth, and Taotao Qian, "A Global Dataset of Palmer Drought Severity Index for 1870–2002: Relationship with Soil Moisture and Effects of Surface Warming," *Journal of Hydrometeorology*, vol. 5 (December 2004), pp. 1117–30.

12. Donald McKenzie et al., "Climatic Change, Wildfire, and Conservation," *Conservation Biology*, vol. 18, no. 4 (August 2004), pp. 890–902.

13. Camille Parmesan and Hector Galbraith, *Observed Impacts of Global Climate Change in the U.S.* (Arlington, VA: Pew Center on Global Climate Change, 2004); DeNeen L. Brown, "Signs of Thaw in a Desert of Snow," *Washington Post*, 28 May 2002; IPCC, *Summary for Policymakers*, op. cit. note 9, p. 13.

14. Patty Glick, *Fish Out of Water: A Guide to Global Warming and Pacific Northwest Rivers* (Seattle: National Wildlife Federation, March 2005); Elizabeth Gillespie, "Global Warming May Be Making Rivers Too Hot: Cold-Water Fish Will Struggle, Report Says," *Seattle Post-Intelligencer*, 24 March 2005.

15. Douglas B. Inkley et al., *Global Climate Change and Wildlife in North America* (Bethesda, MD: The Wildlife Society, December 2004); J. R. Pegg, "Global Warming Disrupting North American Wildlife," *Environment News Service*, 16 December 2004.

16. John E. Sheehy, International Rice Research Institute, e-mail to Janet Larsen, Earth Policy Institute, 1 October 2002; Pedro Sanchez, "The Climate Change–Soil Fertility–Food Security Nexus," speech, Sustainable Food Security for All by 2020, Bonn, Germany, 4–6 September 2002; USDA, op. cit. note 3.

17. Mohan K. Wali et al., "Assessing Terrestrial Ecosystem Sustainability," *Nature & Resources*, October–December 1999, pp. 21–33.

18. Sheehy, op. cit. note 16; Sanchez, op. cit. note 16.

19. Shaobing Peng et al., "Rice Yields Decline with Higher Night Temperature from Global Warming," *Proceedings of the National Academy of Sciences*, 6 July 2004, pp. 9971–75; *Proceedings of the National Academy of Sciences*, "Warmer Evening Temperatures Lower Rice Yields," press release (Washington, DC: 29 June 2004).

20. K. S. Kavi Kumar and Jyoti Parikh, "Socio-Economic Impacts of Climate Change on Indian Agriculture," *International Review for Environmental Strategies*, vol. 2, no. 2 (2001), pp. 277–93; U.N. Population Division, *World Population Prospects: The 2006 Revision Population Database,* at esa.un.org/unpp, updated 2007.

21. UNEP, op. cit. note 1, p. 131.

22. Emily Wax, "A Sacred River Endangered by Global Warming," *Washington Post*, 17 June 2007; UNEP, op. cit. note 1, p. 131.

23. Clifford Coonan, "China's Water Supply Could be Cut Off as Tibet's Glaciers Melt," *The Independent* (London), 31 May 2007; UNEP, op. cit. note 1, p. 131; rice irrigation from "Yangtze River–Agriculture," *Encyclopedia Britannica*, online encyclopedia, viewed 25 July 2007.

24. Jonathan Watts, "Highest Icefields Will Not Last 100 Years, Study Finds: China's Glacier Research Warns of Deserts and Floods Due to Warming," *Guardian* (London), 24 September 2004; "Glacier Study Reveals Chilling Prediction," *China Daily*, 23 September 2004.

25. UNEP, op. cit. note 1, p. 131.

26. Lonnie G. Thompson, "Disappearing Glaciers Evidence of a Rapidly Changing Earth," American Association for the Advancement of Science Annual Meeting, San Francisco, February 2001; "The Peak of Mt Kilimanjaro As It Has Not Been Seen for 11,000 Years," *Guardian* (London), 14 March 2005; Bancy Wangui, "Crisis Looms as Rivers

Around Mt. Kenya Dry Up," *East Africa Standard*, 1 July 2007.

27. Eric Hansen, "Hot Peaks," *OnEarth*, fall 2002, p. 8.

28. Leslie Josephus, "Global Warming Threatens Double-Trouble for Peru: Shrinking Glaciers and a Water Shortage," *Associated Press*, 12 February 2007; *Citation World Atlas* (Union, NJ: Hammond World Atlas Corporation, 2004).

29. Josephus, op. cit. note 28; U.N. Population Division, op. cit. note 20.

30. James Painter, "Peru's Alarming Water Truth," *BBC News*, 12 March 2007; U.N. Population Division, *Urban Agglomerations 2005 Wall Chart*, at www.un.org/esa/population, viewed 28 September 2007.

31. Michael Kiparsky and Peter Gleick, *Climate Change and California Water Resources: A Survey and Summary of the Literature* (Oakland, CA: Pacific Institute, 2003); Timothy Cavagnaro et al., *Climate Change: Challenges and Solutions for California Agricultural Landscapes* (Sacramento, CA: California Climate Change Center, 2006).

32. John Krist, "Water Issues Will Dominate California's Agenda This Year," *Environmental News Network*, 21 February 2003.

33. Michael J. Scott et al., "Climate Change and Adaptation in Irrigated Agriculture—A Case Study of the Yakima River," in UCOWR/NIWR Conference, *Water Allocation: Economics and the Environment* (Carbondale, IL: Universities Council on Water Resources, 2004); Pacific Northwest National Laboratory, "Global Warming to Squeeze Western Mountains Dry by 2050," press release (Richland, WA: 16 February 2004).

34. UNEP, op. cit. note 1, p. 131; Mehrdad Khalili, "The Climate of Iran: North, South, Kavir (Desert), Mountains," *San'ate Hamlo Naql*, March 1997, pp. 48–53.

35. UNEP, op. cit. note 1, p. 103; IPCC, *Summary for Policymakers*, op. cit. note 9, p. 13; Paul Brown, "Melting Ice Cap Triggering Earthquakes," *Guardian* (London), 8 September 2007.

36. Arctic Climate Impact Assessment (ACIA), *Impacts of a Warming Arctic* (Cambridge, U.K.: Cambridge University Press, 2004); ACIA Web site, at www.acia.uaf.edu, updated 13 July 2005; "Rapid Arctic Warming Brings Sea Level Rise, Extinctions," *Environment News Service*, 8 November 2004; UNEP, op. cit. note 1, p. 103.

37. J. R. Pegg, "The Earth is Melting, Arctic Native Leader Warns," *Environment News Service*, 16 September 2004.

38. ACIA, op. cit. note 36; Steven Armstrup et al., "Recent Observations of Intraspecific Predation and Cannibalism among Polar Bears in the Southern Beaufort Sea," *Polar Biology*, vol. 29, no. 11 (October 2006), pp. 997–1002.

39. Julienne Stroeve et al., "Arctic Sea Ice Decline: Faster than Forecast," *Geophysical Research Letters*, vol. 34 (May 2007); National Snow and Ice Data Center (NSIDC), "Arctic Sea Ice Shatters all Previous Record

Lows," press release (Boulder, CO: 1 October 2007); Stroeve quoted in "Arctic Ice Retreating 30 Years Ahead of Projections," *Environment News Service*, 30 April 2007.

40. Marc Kaufman, "Decline in Winter Arctic Ice Linked to Greenhouse Gases," *Washington Post*, 14 September 2006; Joséfino C. Comiso, "Abrupt Decline in the Arctic Winter Sea Ice Cover," *Geophysical Research Letters*, vol. 33, 30 September 2006.

41. David Adam, "Meltdown Fear as Arctic Ice Cover Falls to Record Winter Low," *Guardian* (London), 15 May 2006.

42. NSIDC, "Processes: Thermodynamics: Albedo," at nsidc.org/seaice/processes/albedo.html, viewed 26 July 2007.

43. UNEP, op. cit. note 1.

44. H. Jay Zwally et al., "Surface Melt-Induced Acceleration of Greenland Ice-Sheet Flow," *Science*, vol. 297 (12 July 2002), pp. 218–22.

45. J. L. Chen, C. R. Wilson, and B. D. Tapley, "Satellite Gravity Measurements Confirm Accelerated Melting of Greenland Ice Sheet," *Science*, vol. 313 (29 September 2006), pp. 1958–60; Isabella Velicogna and John Wahr, "Acceleration of Greenland Ice Mass Loss in Spring 2004," *Nature*, vol. 443 (21 September 2006), pp. 329–31; S. B. Luthke et al., "Recent Greenland Ice Mass Loss from Drainage System from Satellite Gravity Observations," *Science*, vol. 314 (24 November 2006), pp. 1286-89; "Gravity Measurements Confirm Greenland's Glaciers Precipitous Meltdown," *Scientific American*, 19 October 2006.

46. U.S. Department of Energy, Energy Information Administration, "Antarctica: Fact Sheet," at www.eia.doe.gov, September 2000.

47. University of Colorado at Boulder, "NASA, CU-Boulder Study Shows Vast Regions of West Antarctica Melted in Recent Past," press release (Boulder: 15 May 2007).

48. "Breakaway Bergs Disrupt Antarctic Ecosystem," *Environment News Service*, 9 May 2002; "Giant Antarctic Ice Shelves Shatter and Break Away," *Environment News Service*, 19 March 2002.

49. NSIDC, "Antarctic Ice Shelf Collapses," at nsidc.org/iceshelves/larsenb2002, 19 March 2002; "Breakaway Bergs Disrupt Antarctic Ecosystem," op. cit. note 48; "Giant Antarctic Ice Shelves Shatter and Break Away," op. cit. note 48.

50. "Giant Antarctic Ice Shelves Shatter and Break Away," op. cit. note 48; Vaughan quoted in Andrew Revkin, "Large Ice Shelf in Antarctica Disintegrates at Great Speed," *New York Times*, 20 March 2002.

51. Michael Byrnes, "New Antarctic Iceberg Split No Threat," *Reuters*, 20 May 2002.

52. Gordon McGranahan et al., "The Rising Tide: Assessing the Risks of Climate Change and Human Settlements in Low Elevation Coastal Zones," *Environment and Urbanization*, vol. 18, no. 1 (April 2007), pp. 17–37.

53. Ibid.

54. Ibid.; U.N. Population Division, op. cit. note 20.

55. International Institute for Environment and Development, "Climate Change: Study Maps Those at Greatest Risk from Cyclones and Rising Seas," press release (London: 28 March 2007); Catherine Brahic, "Coastal Living–A Growing Global Threat," *New Scientist.com*, 28 March 2007; UNEP, op. cit. note 1.

56. Thomas R. Knutson and Robert E. Tuleya, "Impact of CO_2-Induced Warming on Simulated Hurricane Intensity and Precipitation: Sensitivity to the Choice of Climate Model and Convective Parameterization," *Journal of Climate*, vol. 17, no. 18 (15 September 2004), pp. 3477–95.

57. Lester R. Brown, "Global Warming Forcing U.S. Coastal Population to Move Inland," *Eco-Economy Update* (Washington DC: Earth Policy Institute, 16 August 2006); water and power from Connie Kline, "New Orleans Looks Like Katrina Hit Yesterday; U.S. Needs to Step Up," *Ventura County Star*, 6 August 2006; garbage collection from Susan Saulny, "Despite a City's Hopes, an Uneven Repopulation," *New York Times*, 30 July 2006; telecommunications from Gary Rivlin, "Patchy Recovery in New Orleans," *New York Times*, 5 April 2006; sewer system from "Katrina Recovery Deemed a Mixed Bag," *Associated Press*, 15 August 2006.

58. Peter Grier, "The Great Katrina Migration," *Christian Science Monitor*, 12 September 2005; Louisiana Recovery Authority, *Migration Patterns: Estimates of Parish Level Migrations Due to Hurricanes Katrina and Rita* (Baton Rouge, LA: August 2007), pp. 7–9.

59. National Weather Service National Hurricane Center, *NHC Archive of Hurricane Seasons*, at www.nhc.noaa.gov, updated June 2007; Kevin E. Trenberth, "Warmer Oceans, Stronger Hurricanes," *Scientific American*, July 2007; Joseph Treaster, "High Winds, Then Premiums," *New York Times*, 26 September 2006.

60. Janet N. Abramovitz, "Averting Unnatural Disasters," in Lester R. Brown et al., *State of the World 2001* (New York: W. W. Norton & Company, 2001) pp. 123–42.

61. Storm death toll from National Climatic Data Center, National Oceanic & Atmospheric Administration, "Mitch: The Deadliest Atlantic Hurricane Since 1780," at www.ncdc.noaa.gov, updated 1 July 2004; Flores quoted in Arturo Chavez et al., "After the Hurricane: Forest Sector Reconstruction in Honduras," *Forest Products Journal*, November/December 2001, pp. 18–24; gross domestic product from International Monetary Fund (IMF), *World Economic Outlook Database*, at www.imf.org, updated April 2003.

62. Michael Smith, "Bad Weather, Climate Change Cost World Record $90 Billion," *Bloomberg*, 15 December 2004; "Insurers See Hurricane Costs as High as $23 Billion," *Reuters*, 4 October 2004.

63. "Awful Weather We're Having," op. cit. note 5; Munich Re, *Topics*

Geo Annual Review: Natural Catastrophes 2006 (Munich: 2007), p. 47.

64. "Disaster and Its Shadow," *The Economist*, 14 September 2002, p. 71; "Moody's Downgrades Munich Re's Ratings to 'Aa1,'" *Insurance Journal*, 20 September 2002; Moody's Investor Service, "Issuer Research" for Munich Re, Hanover Re, and Swiss Re, at www.moodys.com, viewed 26 July 2007.

65. Tim Hirsch, "Climate Change Hits Bottom Line," *BBC News*, 15 December 2004.

66. Munich Re, "Natural Disasters: Billion-$ Insurance Losses," in Louis Perroy, "Impacts of Climate Change on Financial Institutions' Medium to Long Term Assets and Liabilities," presented to the Staple Inn Actuarial Society, 14 June 2005; Munich Re, *Topics Geo Significant Natural Catastrophes in 2004, 2005, and 2006* (Munich: 2005, 2006, and 2007.

67. Munich Re, *Topics Annual Review: Natural Catastrophes 2001* (Munich: 2002), pp. 16-17; value of China's wheat and rice harvests from USDA, op. cit. note 3, using prices from IMF, *International Financial Statistics*, electronic database, at ifs.apdi.net/imf, updated June 2007.

68. Munich Re, "Natural Disasters," op. cit. note 66; Munich Re, *Significant Natural Catastrophes in 2005 and 2006*, op. cit. note 66.

69. Andrew Dlugolecki, "Climate Change and the Financial Services Industry," speech delivered at the opening of the UNEP Financial Services Roundtable, Frankfurt, Germany, 16 November 2000; "Climate Change Could Bankrupt Us by 2065," *Environment News Service*, 24 November 2000.

70. Sir Nicholas Stern, *The Stern Review on the Economics of Climate Change* (London: HM Treasury, 2006), pp vi–ix.

71. S. Pacala and R. Socolow, "Stabilization Wedges: Solving the Climate Problem for the Next 50 Years with Current Technologies," *Science*, vol. 305 (13 August 2004), pp. 968–72.

72. Ibid.

73. "Earth's Climate Approaches Dangerous Tipping Point," *Environment News Service*, 1 June 2007; James Hansen et al., "Climate Change and Trace Gases," *Philosophical Transactions of the Royal Society A*, vol. 365 (2007), pp. 1925–54.

74. Wax, op. cit. note 22; Coonan, op. cit. note 23; Watts, op. cit. note 24; "Glacier Study Reveals Chilling Prediction," op. cit. note 24.

75. World Bank, *World Development Report 1999/2000* (New York: Oxford University Press, September 1999).

76. Brown, op. cit. note 35.

77. Ibid.

78. Adam, op. cit. note 41.

79. IPCC, *Summary for Policymakers*, op. cit. note 9, p. 33; Sergey A. Zimov et al., "Permafrost and the Global Carbon Budget," *Science*, vol. 312, no. 3780 (16 June 2006), pp. 1612–13.

80. Figure of 400 ppm calculated using fossil fuel emissions from G. Marland et al., "Global, Regional, and National CO_2 Emissions," in *Trends: A Compendium of Data on Global Change* (Oak Ridge, TN: Carbon Dioxide Information and Analysis Center, Oak Ridge National Laboratory, 2007), and land use change emissions from R. A. Houghton and J. L. Hackler, "Carbon Flux to the Atmosphere from Land-Use Changes," in *Trends: A Compendium of Data on Global Change* (Oak Ridge, TN: Carbon Dioxide Information and Analysis Center, Oak Ridge National Laboratory, 2002), with decay curve cited in J. Hansen et al., "Dangerous Human-Made Interference with Climate: A GISS ModelE Study," *Atmospheric Chemistry and Physics*, vol. 7 (2007), pp. 2287–312.

Chapter 4. Emerging Water Shortages

1. U.N. Environment Programme (UNEP), *Africa's Lakes: Atlas of Our Changing Environment* (Nairobi: 2006); M. T. Coe and J. A. Foley, "Human and Natural Impacts on the Water Resources of the Lake Chad Basin," *Journal of Geophysical Research (Atmospheres)*, vol. 106, no. D4 (2001), pp. 3349–56; population information from U.N. Population Division, *World Population Prospects: The 2006 Revision Population Database*, at csa.un.org/unpp, updated 2007.

2. Water use tripling from I. A. Shiklomanov, "Assessment of Water Resources and Water Availability in the World," *Report for the Comprehensive Assessment of the Freshwater Resources of the World* (St. Petersburg, Russia: State Hydrological Institute, 1998), cited in Peter H. Gleick, *The World's Water 2000–2001* (Washington, DC: Island Press, 2000), p. 52; grain production from U.S. Department of Agriculture (USDA), *Production, Supply and Distribution*, electronic database, at www.fas.usda.gov/psd/psdonline, updated 11 June 2007.

3. Emily Wax, "A Sacred River Endangered by Global Warming," *Washington Post*, 17 June 2007; Clifford Coonan, "China's Water Supply Could be Cut Off as Tibet's Glaciers Melt," *The Independent* (London), 31 May 2007.

4. Jacob W. Kijne, *Unlocking the Water Potential of Agriculture* (Rome: U.N. Food and Agriculture Organization (FAO), 2003), p. 26; water use from Shiklomanov, op. cit. note 2, p. 53.

5. Michael Ma, "Northern Cities Sinking as Water Table Falls," *South China Morning Post*, 11 August 2001; share of China's grain harvest from the North China Plain based on Hong Yang and Alexander Zehnder, "China's Regional Water Scarcity and Implications for Grain Supply and Trade," *Environment and Planning A*, vol. 33 (2001), and on USDA, op. cit. note 2.

6. Ma, op. cit. note 5.

7. World Bank, *China: Agenda for Water Sector Strategy for North China* (Washington, DC: April 2001), pp. vii, xi.

8. John Wade, Adam Branson, and Xiang Qing, *China Grain and Feed Annual Report 2002* (Beijing: USDA, 21 February 2002).

9. Wheat production from USDA, op. cit. note 2.

10. World Bank, op. cit. note 7, p. viii; calculations based on 1,000 tons of water to produce 1 ton of grain in FAO, *Yield Response to Water* (Rome: 1979).

11. Number of farmers and well investment from Peter H. Gleick et al., *The World's Water 2006–2007* (Washington, DC: Island Press, 2006), p. 148; number of wells and rate of aquifer depletion from Fred Pearce, "Asian Farmers Sucking the Continent Dry," *New Scientist.com*, 28 August 2004.

12. Pearce, op. cit. note 11; Tamil Nadu population from 2001 census, "Tamil Nadu at a Glance: Area and Population," at www.tn.gov.in.

13. Pearce, op. cit. note 11.

14. Grain production and imports from USDA, op. cit. note 2; John Briscoe, *India's Water Economy: Bracing for a Turbulent Future* (New Delhi: World Bank, 2005); population data from U.N. Population Division, op. cit. note 1.

15. Energy used for groundwater pumping from Tingju Zhu et al., "Energy Price and Groundwater Extraction for Agriculture: Exploring the Energy-Water-Food Nexus at the Global and Basin Level," presented at Linkages Between Energy and Water Management for Agriculture in Developing Countries, Hyderabad, India, January 2007; coal from U.S. Department of Energy, Energy Information Administration, *Country Analysis Briefs: India* and *Country Analysis Briefs: China* (Washington, DC: updated January 2007 and August 2006).

16. USDA, *Agricultural Resources and Environmental Indicators 2000* (Washington, DC: February 2000), Chapter 2.1, p. 6; irrigated share calculated from FAO, *ResourceSTAT*, electronic database, at faostat.fao.org/site/405/default.aspx, updated 30 June 2007; harvest from USDA, op. cit. note 2; Sandra Postel, *Pillar of Sand* (New York: W. W. Norton & Company, 1999), p. 77.

17. USDA, "Table 10: Irrigation 2002 and 1997," *2002 Census of Agriculture*, vol. 1 (Washington, DC: June 2004), pp. 319–26.

18. U.N. Population Division, op. cit. note 1; fall in water table from "Pakistan: Focus on Water Crisis," *U.N. Integrated Regional Information Networks News*, 17 May 2002.

19. "Pakistan: Focus on Water Crisis," op. cit. note 18; Garstang quoted in "Water Crisis Threatens Pakistan: Experts," *Agence France-Presse*, 26 January 2001.

20. Sardar Riaz A. Khan, "Declining Land Resource Base," *Dawn* (Pak-

istan), 27 September 2004.

21. USDA, op. cit. note 2.

22. U.N. Population Division, op. cit. note 1; overpumping from Chenaran Agricultural Center, Ministry of Agriculture, according to Hamid Taravati, publisher, Iran, e-mail to author, 25 June 2002.

23. U.N. Population Division, op. cit. note 1; Craig S. Smith, "Saudis Worry as They Waste Their Scarce Water," *New York Times*, 26 January 2003; grain production from USDA, op. cit. note 2.

24. Smith, op. cit. note 23.

25. Ibid.

26. U.N. Population Division, op. cit. note 1; Yemen's water situation from Christopher Ward, "Yemen's Water Crisis," based on a lecture to the British Yemeni Society in September 2000, July 2001; Christopher Ward, *The Political Economy of Irrigation Water Pricing in Yemen* (Sana'a, Yemen: World Bank, November 1998).

27. Marcus Moench, "Groundwater: Potential and Constraints," in Ruth S. Meinzen-Dick and Mark W. Rosegrant, eds., *Overcoming Water Scarcity and Quality Constraints* (Washington, DC: International Food Policy Research Institute, October 2001).

28. U.N. Population Division, op. cit. note 1; Yemen's water situation from Ward, *Political Economy of Irrigation Water Pricing*, op. cit. note 26; grain production and imports from USDA, op. cit. note 2, updated 13 September 2005; Fund for Peace and Carnegie Endowment for International Peace, "The Failed States Index 2007," *Foreign Policy*, July/August 2007, p. 57.

29. Deborah Camiel, "Israel, Palestinian Water Resources Down the Drain," *Reuters*, 12 July 2000.

30. U.N. Population Division, op. cit. note 1; Tushaar Shah et al., *The Global Groundwater Situation: Overview of Opportunities and Challenges* (Colombo, Sri Lanka: International Water Management Institute, 2000); Karin Kemper, "Groundwater Management in Mexico: Legal and Institutional Issues," in Salman M. A. Salman, ed., *Groundwater: Legal and Policy Perspectives*, Proceedings of a World Bank Seminar (Washington, DC: World Bank, 1999), p. 117; U.N. Development Programme (UNDP), *Human Development Report 2006* (Gordonsville, VA: Palgrave Macmillan, 2006), p. 146.

31. Colorado, Ganges, Indus, and Nile rivers from Postel, op. cit. note 16, pp. 59, 71–73, 94, 261–62; Yellow River from Lester R. Brown and Brian Halweil, "China's Water Shortages Could Shake World Food Security," *World Watch*, July/August 1998, p. 11.

32. Water use tripling from Shiklomanov, op. cit. note 2, p. 52.

33. Sandra Postel, *Last Oasis* (New York: W. W. Norton & Company, 1997), pp. 38–39; World Commission on Dams, *Dams and Development: A New Framework for Decision-Making* (London: Island Press, 2000), p. 8.

34. Postel, op. cit. note 16, pp. 261–62; Jim Carrier, "The Colorado: A River Drained Dry," *National Geographic*, June 1991, pp. 4–32.

35. UNEP, *Afghanistan: Post-Conflict Environmental Assessment* (Geneva: 2003), p. 60.

36. Brown and Halweil, op. cit. note 31.

37. Postel, op. cit. note 16, pp. 71, 146.

38. Ibid., pp. 56–58; U.N. Population Division, op. cit. note 1; Fund for Peace and Carnegie Endowment, op. cit. note 28. p. 57.

39. Moench, op. cit. note 27; U.N. Population Division, op. cit. note 1.

40. Curtis J. Richardson et al., "The Restoration Potential of the Mesopotamian Marshes of Iraq," *Science*, vol. 307 (25 February 2005), pp. 1307–10.

41. Janet Larsen, "Disappearing Lakes, Shrinking Seas," *Eco-Economy Update* (Washington, DC: Earth Policy Institute, 7 April 2005).

42. Megan Goldin, "Israel's Shrinking Sea of Galilee Needs Miracle," *Reuters*, 14 August 2001; Jordan River diminishing from Annette Young, "Middle East Conflict Killing the Holy Water," *The Scotsman*, 12 September 2004.

43. Caroline Hawley, "Dead Sea 'to Disappear by 2050,'" *BBC*, 3 August 2001; Gidon Bromberg, "Water and Peace," *World Watch*, July/August 2004, pp. 24–30.

44. Quirin Schiermeier, "Ecologists Plot to Turn the Tide for Shrinking Lake," *Nature*, vol. 412 (23 August 2001), p. 756.

45. "Sea to Disappear within 15 Years," *News 24*, 22 July 2003; Caroline Williams, "Long Time No Sea," *New Scientist*, 4 January 2003, pp. 34–37.

46. Fred Pearce, "Poisoned Waters," *New Scientist*, 21 October 1995, pp. 29–33; Williams, op. cit. note 45.

47. Larsen, op. cit. note 41; NASA, Earth Observatory, "Aral Sea," at earthobservatory.nasa.gov/Newsroom/NewImages/images.php3?img_id=16277, viewed 25 January 2005; Alex Kirby, "Kazakhs 'to Save North Aral Sea,'" *BBC*, 29 October 2003.

48. Li Heng, "20 Natural Lakes Disappear Each Year in China," *People's Daily*, 21 October 2002; "Glaciers Receding, Wetlands Shrinking in River Fountainhead Area," *China Daily*, 7 January 2004.

49. Jim Carlton, "Shrinking Lake in Mexico Threatens Future of Region," *Wall Street Journal*, 3 September 2003; U. N. Population Division, *World Urbanization Prospects: 2005 Revision*, electronic database, at esa.un.org/unup, updated October 2006.

50. Water to make steel from Postel, op. cit. note 33; 1,000 tons of water for 1 ton of grain from FAO, op. cit. note 10; price of steel from International Monetary Fund, *International Financial Statistics*, at ifs.apdi.net, July 2007; wheat prices from Chicago Board of

Trade, "Market Commentaries," various dates, at www.cbot.com.

51. Noel Gollehon and William Quinby, "Irrigation in the American West: Area, Water and Economic Activity," *Water Resources Development*, vol. 16, no. 2 (2000), pp. 187–95; Postel, op. cit. note 33, p. 137.

52. R. Srinivasan, "The Politics of Water," *Info Change Agenda*, issue 3 (October 2005); U. N. Population Division, op. cit. note 49.

53. Srinivasan, op. cit. note 52; Pearce, op. cit. note 11.

54. "China Politics: Growing Tensions Over Scarce Water," *The Economist*, 21 June 2004.

55. Shah et al., op. cit. note 30.

56. Gollehon and Quinby, op. cit. note 51; *The Water Strategist*, various issues, at www.waterstrategist.com; Jedidiah Brewer et al., "Water Markets in the West: Prices, Trading and Contractual Forms," *Arizona Legal Studies Discussion Paper No. 07-07* (8 February 2007).

57. Arkansas River basin from Joey Bunch, "Water Projects Forecast to Fall Short of Needs: Study Predicts 10% Deficit in State," *Denver Post*, 22 July 2004.

58. Dean Murphy, "Pact in West Will Send Farms' Water to Cities," *New York Times*, 17 October 2003; Tim Molloy, "California Water District Approves Plan to Pay Farmers for Irrigation Water," *Associated Press*, 13 May 2004.

59. U.N. Population Division, op. cit. note 1.

60. FAO, op. cit. note 10.

61. Grain from USDA, op. cit. note 2.

62. Grain from USDA, Foreign Agricultural Service, *Grain: World Markets and Trade* (Washington, DC: various years).

63. UN. Population Division, op. cit. note 1; grain from USDA, op. cit. note 2.

64. Nile River flow from Postel, op. cit. note 16, p. 77; grain imports from USDA, op. cit. note 2; calculation based on 1,000 tons of water for 1 ton of grain from FAO, op. cit. note 10.

65. U.N. Population Division, op. cit. note 1; grain from USDA, op. cit. note 2.

66. David Seckler, David Molden, and Randolph Barker, "Water Scarcity in the Twenty-First Century," Water Brief 1 (Colombo, Sri Lanka: International Water Management Institute, 1999), p. 2.

67. USDA, op. cit. note 2; FAO, op. cit. note 16.

68. UNDP, op. cit. note 30, p. 135.

69. FAO, *AQUASTAT*, electronic database, at www.fao.org/nr/aquastat, updated 11 February 2003.

70. Country averages from ibid.; World Resources Institute, *Annual*

Renewable Water Supply per Person by River Basin, 1995, at earth
trends.wri.org/maps_spatial, updated 2000.

71. "World Conflict Chronology," table in Gleick et al., op. cit. note 11,
     pp. 192–213; UNDP, op. cit. note 30, pp. 177–78; "At Least 14 Killed as
     Kenyan Tribes Clash over Scarce Water Supplies," *Associated Press,*
     25 January 2005; "Pakistanis Clash Over Water, 12 Hurt," *Reuters,*
     20 June 2006.

72. Naser I. Faruqui, "Responding to the Water Crisis in Pakistan," *Water
     Resources Development,* vol. 20, no. 2 (June 2004), pp. 177-92.

73. Pete Harrison, "Iraq Calls for Water Treaty to Avert Crisis," *Reuters,*
     23 August 2007.

74. UNDP, op. cit. note 30, p. 216.

75. Population projection from U.N. Population Division, op. cit. note 1.

Chapter 5. Natural Systems Under Stress

1. Walter C. Lowdermilk, *Conquest of the Land Through 7,000 Years,*
    USDA Bulletin No. 99 (Washington, DC: U.S. Department of Agricul-
    ture (USDA), Natural Resources Conservation Service, 1939).

2. Ibid., p. 10.

3. U.N. Food and Agriculture Organization (FAO), "FAO/WFP Crop and
    Food Assessment Mission to Lesotho Special Report," at
    www.fao.org, viewed 29 May 2002; Michael Grunwald, "Bizarre
    Weather Ravages Africans' Crops," *Washington Post,* 7 January 2003.

4. FAO, *Number of Undernourished Persons,* at www.fao.org/faostat/
    foodsecurity, updated 30 June 2006.

5. Species Survival Commission, *2000 IUCN Red List of Threatened
    Species* (Gland, Switzerland, and Cambridge, U.K.: World Conserva-
    tion Union–IUCN, 2000), p. 1.

6. Teresa Cerojano, "Decades of Illegal Logging Blamed for High Death
    Toll in Philippine Storm," *Associated Press,* 1 December, 2004; Thai-
    land from Patrick B. Durst et al., *Forests Out of Bounds: Impacts and
    Effectiveness of Logging Bans in Natural Forests in Asia-Pacific*
    (Bangkok: FAO, Asia-Pacific Forestry Commission, 2001); Munich Re,
    "Munich Re's Review of Natural Catastrophes in 1998," press release
    (Munich: 19 December 1998); Harry Doran, "Human Activities Aid
    Force of Nature: Massive Destruction Has Worsened the Floods
    Which Have Struck Throughout History, But Lessons Are Being
    Learned," *South China Morning Post,* 24 July 2003.

7. World forested area from FAO, *Global Forest Resources Assessment
    2005* (Rome: 2006), p. 16.

8. Ibid., pp. xii–xvi.

9. Forest Frontiers Initiative, *The Last Frontier Forests: Ecosystems and
    Economies on the Edge* (Washington, DC: World Resources Institute

(WRI), 1997).

10. FAO, *ForesSTAT*, electronic database, at faostat.fao.org, updated 22 December 2006.

11. Alain Marcoux, "Population and Deforestation," in *Population and the Environment* (Rome: FAO, 2000); March Turnbull, "Life in the Extreme," *Africa Geographic Online*, 4 April 2005.

12. Nigel Sizer and Dominiek Plouvier, *Increased Investment and Trade by Transnational Logging Companies in Africa, the Caribbean, and the Pacific* (Belgium: World Wide Fund for Nature (WWF) and WRI Forest Frontiers Initiative, 2000), pp. 21–35; Lester R. Brown, "Nature's Limits," in Lester R. Brown et al., *State of the World 1995* (New York: W. W. Norton & Company, 1995), p. 9.

13. Peter S. Goodman and Peter Finn, "Corruption Stains Timber Trade," *Washington Post*, 1 April 2007; Evan Osnos, "China Feeds U.S. Demand for Wood as Forests Suffer," *Chicago Tribune*, 18 December 2006.

14. Goodman and Finn, op. cit. note 13.

15. Andy White et al., *China and the Global Market for Forest Products* (Washington, DC: Forest Trends, 2006).

16. Atlantic forest loss from World Land Trust, "REGUA Project, Brazil," at www.worldlandtrust.org/projects/brazil.htm, viewed 6 September 2007; remaining Amazon calculated from WWF, "Amazon Deforestation," at www.panda.org/about_wwf/where_we_work/ latin_america _and_caribbean, viewed 6 September 2007, and from Raymond Col- itt, "Amazon Deforestation Drops Sharply: Brazilian Gov't," *Reuters*, 10 August 2007.

17. Christian Tsoumou, "Britain Gives US$98 Mln to Protect Congo-Forests," *Reuters*, 29 March 2007.

18. Mario Rautner, Martin Hardiono, and Raymond J. Alfred, *Borneo: Treasure Island at Risk* (Frankfurt: WWF Germany, June 2005), p. 7.

19. U.N. Population Division, *World Population Prospects: The 2006 Revision Population Database,* at esa.un.org/unpp, updated 2007; FAO, op. cit. note 7, p. 193.

20. U.N. Population Division, op. cit. note 19; "Madagascar's Rainforest Faces Destruction," *Guardian* (London), 29 June 2003.

21. Eneas Salati and Peter B. Vose, "Amazon Basin: A System in Equilib- rium," *Science*, vol. 225 (13 July 1984), pp. 129–38.

22. Philip Fearnside quoted in Barbara J. Fraser, "Putting a Price on the Forest," *LatinamericaPress.org*, 10 November 2002; Philip M. Fearn- side, "The Main Resources of Amazonia," paper for presentation at the Latin American Studies Association XX International Congress, Guadalajara, Mexico, 17–19 April 1997; Geoffrey Lean, "Dying For- est: One Year to Save the Amazon," *The Independent*, 23 July 2006; Geoffrey Lean, "A Disaster to Take Everyone's Breath Away," *The*

Independent, 24 July 2006.

23. U.N. Population Division, op. cit. note 19; Malawi Ministry of Mines, Natural Resources, and the Environment, *State of the Environment Report for Malawi 2002* (Lilongwe, Malawi: 2004); FAO, op. cit. note 7, p. 196.

24. Anscombe quoted in Charles Mkoka, "Unchecked Deforestation Endangers Malawi Ecosystems," *Environment News Service*, 16 November 2004.

25. Patrick B. Durst et al., *Forests Out of Bounds: Impacts and Effectiveness of Logging Bans in Natural Forests in Asia-Pacific* (Bangkok: FAO, Asia-Pacific Forestry Commission, 2001); Zhu Chunquan, Rodney Taylor, and Feng Guoqiang, *China's Wood Market, Trade and Environment* (Monmouth Junction, NJ, and Beijing: Science Press USA Inc. and WWF International, 2004).

26. One third is author's estimate.

27. Yang Youlin, Victor Squires, and Lu Qi, eds., *Global Alarm: Dust and Sandstorms from the World's Drylands* (Bangkok: Secretariat of the U.N. Convention to Combat Desertification, 2002), pp. 15–28.

28. John Steinbeck, *The Grapes of Wrath* (New York: Viking Penguin, Inc., 1939).

29. FAO, *The State of Food and Agriculture 1995* (Rome: 1995), p. 175.

30. Ibid.; USDA,*Production, Supply and Distribution*, electronic database, at www.fas.usda.gov/psdonline, updated 12 July 2007; yield from FAO, *ProdSTAT*, electronic database, at faostat.fao.org, updated 30 June 2007.

31. U.N. Environment Programme (UNEP), *Mongolia: State of the Environment 2002* (Pathumthani, Thailand: Regional Resource Centre for Asia and the Pacific, 2001), pp. 3–7; USDA, op. cit. note 30; U.N. Population Division, op. cit. note 19.

32. National Aeronautics and Space Administration (NASA) Earth Observatory, "Dust Storm off Western Sahara Coast," at earth observatory.nasa.gov, viewed 9 January 2005.

33. Paul Brown, "4x4s Replace the Desert Camel and Whip Up a Worldwide Dust Storm," *Guardian* (London), 20 August 2004.

34. Ibid.

35. Asif Farrukh, *Pakistan Grain and Feed Annual Report 2002* (Islamabad, Pakistan: USDA Foreign Agricultural Service, 2003).

36. UNEP, *Africa Environment Outlook: Past, Present, and Future Perspectives* (Nairobi: 2002), at www.unep.org/dewa/Africa.

37. Land area estimate from Stanley Wood, Kate Sebastian, and Sara J. Scherr, *Pilot Analysis of Global Ecosystems: Agroecosystems* (Washington, DC: International Food Policy Research Institute and WRI, 2000), p. 3; livestock counts from FAO, op. cit. note 30.

38. Number of pastoralists from FAO, *The State of Food Insecurity in the World 2003* (Rome 2003), p.15; FAO, op. cit. note 30.

39. FAO, op. cit. note 30; U.N. Population Division, op. cit. note 19.

40. Robin P. White, Siobhan Murray, and Mark Rohweder, *Pilot Analysis of Global Ecosystems: Grassland Ecosystems* (Washington, DC: WRI, 2000); FAO, op. cit. note 30; U.N. Population Fund (UNFPA), *State of World Population 2006* (New York: 2006), p. 98; Southern African Development Coordination Conference, *SADCC Agriculture: Toward 2000* (Rome: FAO, 1984).

41. U.N. Population Division, op. cit. note 19; FAO, op. cit. note 30.

42. FAO, op. cit. note 30.

43. B. S. Sathe, "Dairy/Milk Production," in *Livestock Investment Opportunities in India*, FAO Web site, at www.fao.org/DOCREP/ARTICLE/AGRIPPA/657_en00.htm, viewed 9 September 2005.

44. H. Dregne et al., "A New Assessment of the World Status of Desertification," *Desertification Control Bulletin*, no. 20, 1991.

45. U.N. Population Division, op. cit. note 19.

46. "Case Studies of Sand-Dust Storms in Africa and Australia," in Yang Youlin, Victor Squires, and Lu Qi, eds., *Global Alarm: Dust and Sandstorms from the World's Drylands* (Bangkok: Secretariat of the U.N. Convention to Combat Desertification, 2002), pp. 123–66.

47. Government of Nigeria, *Combating Desertification and Mitigating the Effects of Drought in Nigeria*, Revised National Report on the Implementation of the United Nations Convention to Combat Desertification (Nigeria: April 2002); U.N. Population Division, op. cit. note 19; livestock from FAO, op. cit. note 30.

48. Iranian News Agency, "Official Warns of Impending Desertification Catastrophe in Southeast Iran," *BBC International Reports*, 29 September 2002.

49. UNEP, *Afghanistan: Post-Conflict Environmental Assessment* (Geneva: 2003), p. 52.

50. Wang Tao et al., "A Study on Spatial-temporal Changes of Sandy Desertified Land During Last 5 Decades in North China," *Acta Geographica Sinica*, vol. 59 (2004), pp. 203–12.

51. Wang Tao, Cold and Arid Regions Environmental and Engineering Research Institute (CAREERI), Chinese Academy of Sciences, e-mail to author, 4 April 2004; Wang Tao, "The Process and Its Control of Sandy Desertification in Northern China," CAREERI, Chinese Academy of Sciences, seminar on desertification, held in Lanzhou, China, May 2002.

52. Ann Schrader, "Latest Import From China: Haze," *Denver Post*, 18 April 2001; Brown, op. cit. note 33.

53. Howard W. French, "China's Growing Deserts Are Suffocating

Korea," *New York Times*, 14 April 2002.

54. For number of dust storms in China, see Table 1–1 in Lester R. Brown, Janet Larsen, and Bernie Fischlowitz Roberts, *The Earth Policy Reader* (New York: W. W. Norton & Company, 2002), p. 13.

55. U.S. Embassy, "Desert Mergers and Acquisitions," *Beijing Environment, Science, and Technology Update* (Beijing: 19 July 2002), p. 2.

56. See Table 5–2 in Lester Brown, *Outgrowing the Earth* (New York: W. W. Norton & Company, 2005), pp. 86–87.

57. FAO, *FishStat Plus*, electronic database, at www.fao.org, updated March 2007.

58. FAO, *The State of World Fisheries and Aquaculture 2006* (Rome: 2007), p. 29.

59. Ransom A. Myers and Boris Worm, "Rapid Worldwide Depletion of Predatory Fish Communities," *Nature*, vol. 432 (15 May 2003), pp. 280–83; Charles Crosby, "'Blue Frontier' is Decimated," *Dalhousie News*, 11 June 2003.

60. Myers and Worm, op. cit. note 59; Crosby, op. cit. note 59.

61. Myers and Worm, op. cit. note 59.

62. Stephen Leahy, "Atlantic Bluefin Going Way of Northern Cod," *Interpress Service News Agency*, 24 August 2007; Ted Williams, "The Last Bluefin Hunt," in Valerie Harms et al., *The National Audubon Society Almanac of the Environment* (New York: Grosset/Putnam, 1994), p. 185; Callum Roberts, *The Unnatural History of the Sea* (Washington, DC: Island Press, 2007), p. 280; Konstantin Volkov, "The Caviar Game Rules," Reuters-IUCN Environmental Media Award winner, 2001; 2007 quota from UNEP, "2006 Ban on Caviar Lifted," press release (Geneva: 2 January 2007).

63. Harvests from National Marine Fisheries Service, National Oceanic and Atmospheric Administration, *Annual Commercial Landing Statistics*, electronic database, at www.st.nmfs.noaa.gov/st1/commercial/landings/annual_landings.html, updated 12 February 2007.

64. Caroline Southey, "EU Puts New Curbs on Fishing," *Financial Times*, 16 April 1997.

65. Alex Kirby, "UK Cod Fishing 'Could be Halted'," *BBC News*, 6 November 2000; ; Norway Ministry of Fisheries and Coastal Affairs, "Norway and EU Agree Fish Quotas for 2006," press release (Oslo, Norway: 2 December 2005); European Commission, "Council Decision on 2007 Fish Quotas Confirms Gradual Approach to Sustainable Fisheries," press release (Brussels: 21 December 2006); European Commission, "Outcome of the Fisheries Council of 16-20 December 2002," at ec.europa.eu/fisheries/press_corner, updated 23 December 2002; Indrani Lutchman et al., *Indicators of Environmental Integration: Final Report* (London: Institute for European Environmental Policy, June 2006).

66. Diadie Ba, "Senegal, EU Prepare for Fisheries Deal Tussle," *Reuters*, 28 May 2001; Charles Clover, *The End of the Line: How Overfishing is Changing the World and What We Eat* (London: Ebury Press, 2004), ppd. 37–46.

67. Clover, op. cit. note 66, p. 38.

68. John W. Miller, "Global Fishing Trade Depletes African Waters," *Wall Street Journal*, 23 July 2007.

69. Lauretta Burke et al., *Pilot Analysis of Global Ecosystems: Coastal Ecosystems* (Washington, DC: WRI, 2001), pp. 19, 51; coastal wetland loss in Italy from Lester R. Brown and Hal Kane, *Full House* (New York: W. W. Norton & Company, 1994).

70. Clive Wilkinson, ed., *Status of Coral Reefs of the World: 2004* (Townsville, Australia: Global Coral Reef Monitoring Network, 2004), p. 9.

71. Lauretta Burke and Jonathan Maidens, *Reefs at Risk in the Caribbean* (Washington, DC: WRI, 2004), pp. 12–14, 27–31.

72. Mohammed Kotb et al., "Status of Coral Reefs in the Red Sea and Gulf of Aden in 2004," in Wilkinson, op. cit. note 70, pp. 137–39.

73. UNEP and Global Programme of Action for the Protection of the Marine Environment from Land-Based Activities, *The State of the Marine Environment: Trends and Processes* (The Hague: 2006); Nancy Rabalais and Gene Turner, "Dead Zone Size Near Top End," press release (Cocodrie, LA: Louisiana Universities Marine Consortium, 28 July 2007).

74. UNEP, "Further Rise in Number of Marine 'Dead Zones'," press release (Beijing and Nairobi: 19 October 2006); UNEP, *GEO Yearbook 2003* (Nairobi: 2004), p. 58.

75. Organisation for Economic Co-operation and Development, *OECD Environmental Outlook* (Paris: 2001), pp. 109–20.

76. David Quammen, "Planet of Weeds," *Harper's Magazine*, October 1998.

77. Species Survival Commission, *2007 IUCN Red List of Threatened Species*, at www.iucnredlist.org, updated 12 September 2007.

78. Ibid.; TRAFFIC, *Food for Thought: The Utilization of Wild Meat in Eastern and Southern Africa* (Cambridge, U.K.: 2000).

79. Danna Harman, "Bonobos' Threat: Hungry Humans," *Christian Science Monitor*, 7 June 2001; "Video: New Bonobo Ape Population Discovered," *National Geographic News*, 6 March 2007.

80. Species Survival Commission, op. cit. note 77; "Great Indian Bustard Facing Extinction," *India Abroad Daily*, 12 February 2001; Çagan Sekercioglu, Gretchen C. Daily, and Paul R. Ehrlich, "Ecosystem Consequences of Bird Declines," *Proceedings of the National Academy of Sciences*, vol. 101, no. 52 (28 December 2004).

81. Michael McCarthy, "Mystery of the Silent Woodlands: Scientists Are Baffled as Bird Numbers Plummet," *Independent* (London), 25 February 2005; British Trust for Ornithology, "Tough Time for Woodland Birds," press release (Thetford, Norfolk, U.K.: 25 February 2005); J. A. Thomas et al., "Comparative Losses of British Butterflies, Birds, and Plants and the Global Extinction Crisis," *Science*, vol. 303 (19 March 2004), pp. 1879–81.

82. Dennis Van Engelsdorp et al., "An Estimate of Managed Colony Losses in the Winter of 2006–2007: A Report Commissioned by the Apiary Inspectors of America," *American Bee Journal* (July 2007), pp. 599–603; Alexei Barrionuevo, "Bees Vanish, and Scientists Race for Reasons," *New York Times*, 24 April 2007.

83. Joel Garreau, "Honey, I'm Gone," *Washington Post*, 1 June 2007; Erik Stokstad, "Puzzling Decline of U.S. Bees Linked to Virus from Australia," *Science*, vol. 317, issue 5843 (7 September 2007), pp. 1304–05.

84. Species Survival Commission, *2004 IUCN Red List of Threatened Species* (Gland, Switzerland, and Cambridge, U.K.: IUCN, 2004), p. 89; Species Survival Commission, op. cit. note 77.

85. James R. Spotila et al., "Pacific Leatherback Turtles Face Extinction," *Nature*, vol. 405 (1 June 2000), pp. 529–30; "Leatherback Turtles Threatened," *Washington Post*, 5 June 2000; Pilar Santidrián Tomillo et al., "Reassessment of the Leatherback Turtle (*Dermochelys coriacea*) Nesting Population at Parque Nacional Marino Las Baulas, Costa Rica: Effects of Conservation Efforts," *Chelonian Conservation and Biology*, vol. 6, no. 1 (2007), pp. 54–62.

86. David Kaimowitz et al., *Hamburger Connection Fuels Amazon Destruction* (Jakarta, Indonesia: Center for International Forestry Research, 2004).

87. Conservation International, "The Brazilian Cerrado," at www.bio diversityhotspots.org, viewed 19 July 2007; Center for Applied Biodiversity Science, "Hotspots Revisited: Cerrado," at www.biodiversity science.org/publications/hotspots/Cerrado.html, viewed 19 July 2007; butterfly diversity from Helena C. Morais et al., "Caterpillar Seasonality in a Central Brazilian Cerrado," *Revista de Biología Tropical*, vol. 47, no. 4 (1999), pp. 1025–33.

88. Species Survival Commission, op. cit. note 77.

Chapter 6. Early Signs of Decline

1. U.N. Population Division, *World Population Prospects: The 2002 Revision—Volume III: Analytical Report* (New York: 2004), pp. 136–58, 169.

2. Cancer in China from World Health Organization (WHO), "Death by Causes, Sex and Mortality Stratum in WHO Regions, Estimates for 2002," *World Health Report 2004* (Geneva: May 2004); U.N. Population Division, *World Population Prospects: The 2006 Revision Popula-*

tion Database, electronic database, at esa.un.org/unpp, updated 2007; "Number of Inmates in State or Federal Prisons and Local Jails by Gender, Race, Hispanic Origin, and Age, June 30, 2006," Bureau of Justice Statistics, U.S. Department of Justice, at www.ojp.gov/bjs/prisons.htm, updated 18 July 2007; U.S. Environmental Protection Agency (EPA), "Ag 101: Agricultural Demographics," fact sheet, at www.epa.gov/oecaagct, viewed 3 September 2007.

3. Life expectancy from WHO, *World Health Statistics 2007* (Geneva: 2007), pp. 22–31; hunger from U.N. Food and Agriculture Organization (FAO), *Number of Undernourished Persons*, at www.fao.org/faostat/foodsecurity, updated 30 June 2006.

4. FAO, op. cit. note 3; WHO, "Obesity and Overweight," fact sheet (Geneva: September 2006).

5. FAO, *The State of Food Insecurity in the World 2006* (Rome: 2006), pp. 8, 32, 33; FAO, *The State of Food Insecurity in the World 2002* (Rome: 2002); U.N. Population Division, op. cit. note 2.

6. FAO, *The State of Food Insecurity in the World 2005* (Rome: 2005), p. 33.

7. FAO, *The State of Food Insecurity in the World 2004* (Rome: 2004).

8. Gary Gardner and Brian Halweil, "Nourishing the Underfed and Overfed," in Lester R. Brown et al., *State of the World 2000* (New York: W. W. Norton & Company, 2000), pp. 70–73.

9. WHO and UNICEF, *Global Water Supply and Sanitation Assessment 2000 Report* (New York: 2000), pp. v, 2; WHO, op. cit. note 2.

10. Stable populations compiled from Population Reference Bureau, *Datafinder*, electronic database, at www.prb.org/DataFind/datafinder7.htm, updated 2007; doubling projections from U.N. Population Division, op. cit. note 2.

11. "Population That Has Attained Tertiary Education (2003)," in Organisation for Economic Co-operation and Development (OECD), *Education at a Glance 2005* (Paris: 2005); children not enrolled from United Nations, *Millennium Development Goals Report 2007* (New York: 2007), p. 11; adult illiteracy from UNESCO, *EFA Global Monitoring Report 2007: Strong Foundations* (Paris: 2006), p. 2.

12. Hilaire A. Mputu, *Literacy and Non-Formal Education in the E-9 Countries* (Paris: UNESCO, 2001), pp. 5–13; UNESCO Institute for Statistics, "National Illiteracy Rates Youths (15–24) and Adults (15+)," at www.uis.unesco.org, updated 19 June 2007.

13. Gene B. Sperling, "Toward Universal Education," Foreign Affairs, September/October 2001, pp. 7–13.

14. Access to safe water from World Bank, *Global Monitoring Report 2007: Millennium Development Goals* (Washington, DC: 2007), p. 13; Peter H. Gleick, *Dirty Water: Estimated Deaths from Water-Related Disease 2000–2020* (Oakland, CA: Pacific Institute, 2002); U.N. Population Division, op. cit. note 2.

15. Deaths calculated from U.N. Population Division, *World Population Prospects: The 2004 Revision* (New York: 2005), and from WHO/UNICEF, *World Malaria Report 2005* (Geneva: 2005); Sachs from Center for International Development at Harvard University and London School of Hygiene and Tropical Medicine, "Executive Summary for Economics of Malaria," at www.rbm.who.int, viewed 3 August 2005.

16. More deaths from AIDS than wars from Lawrence K. Altman, "U.N. Forecasts Big Increase in AIDS Death Toll," *New York Times*, 3 July 2002.

17. Total deaths and historical estimates calculated using UNAIDS statistics in Worldwatch Institute, *Signposts 2004*, CD-Rom (Washington, DC: 2004) and in UNAIDS, *AIDS Epidemic Update* (Geneva: various years); sub-Saharan Africa from UNAIDS, *2006 AIDS Epidemic Update* (Geneva: December 2006), p. 10.

18. UNAIDS, *2006 Report on the Global AIDS Epidemic* (Geneva: May 2006), pp. 2–6, 320, 488.

19. UNAIDS, *2004 Report on the Global AIDS Epidemic* (Geneva: 2004), pp. 39–66; FAO, "The Impact of HIV/AIDS on Food Security," 27th Session of the Committee on World Food Security, Rome, 28 May–1 June 2001.

20. UNAIDS, op. cit. note 18, p. 95.

21. UNAIDS, UNICEF, and U.S. Agency for International Development, *Children on the Brink 2004: A Joint Report on New Orphan Estimates and a Framework for Action* (Washington, DC: 2004), p. 29; Michael Grunwald, "Sowing Harvests of Hunger in Africa," *Washington Post*, 17 November 2002.

22. Stephen Lewis, press briefing, New York, 8 January 2003; Edith M. Lederer, "Lack of Funding for HIV/AIDS is Mass Murder by Complacency, Says U.N. Envoy," *Associated Press*, 9 January 2003.

23. Alex de Waal, "What AIDS Means in a Famine," *New York Times*, 19 November 2002.

24. Sarah Janssen, Gina Solomon, and Ted Schettler, *Chemical Contaminants and Human Disease: A Summary of Evidence* (Boston: Alliance for a Healthy Tomorrow, 2004); Geoffrey Lean, "US Study Links More than 200 Diseases to Pollution," *Independent News* (London), 14 November 2004.

25. Jonathan Watts, "Beijing Blames Pollutants for Rise in Killer Cancers," *Guardian* (London), 22 May 2007.

26. Ibid.

27. Pan Yue, "View: China's Green Debt," *Daily Times* (Pakistan), 1 December 2006.

28. Kent Ewing, "Behind the Hysteria About China's Tainted Goods," *Asia Times*, 18 July 2007; EPA, "About EPA," at www.epa.gov, viewed

25 July 2007.

29. Jane Houlihan et al., *Body Burden: The Pollution in Newborns* (Washington, DC: Environmental Working Group, 2005).

30. Bernie Fischlowitz-Roberts, "Air Pollution Fatalities Now Exceed Traffic Fatalities by 3 to 1," *Eco-Economy Update* (Washington, DC: Earth Policy Institute, September 2002), citing WHO, "Air Pollution," *Fact Sheet 187* (Geneva: revised September 2000); traffic accident deaths from WHO, "Estimated Total Deaths, by WHO Member State, 2002," table downloaded from WHO Web site, "Burden of Disease Statistics," www.who.int/healthinfo; U.S. deaths from Joel Schwartz, quoted in Harvard School of Public Health, "Air Pollution Deadlier Than Previously Thought," press release (Cambridge, MA: 2 March 2000).

31. C. Pritchard, D. Baldwin, and A. Mayers, "Changing Patterns of Adult (45–74 years) Neurological Deaths in the Major Western World Countries 1979–1987," *Public Health*, vol. 118, issue 4 (June 2004), pp. 268–83; Juliette Jowit, "Pollutants Cause Huge Rise in Brain Diseases: Scientists Alarmed as Number of Cases Triples in 20 Years," *The Observer* (London), 15 August 2004; A. Ascherio et al., "Pesticide Exposure and Risk for Parkinson's Disease," *Annals of Neurology*, vol. 60, issue 2 (August 2006), pp. 197–203.

32. Global Environment Facility, U.N. Development Programme (UNDP), and United Nations Industrial Development Organization, "Removal of Barriers to the Introduction of Cleaner Artisanal Gold Mining and Extraction Technologies," *UNDP Global Mercury Project Inception Document GLO/01/G34* (Washington, DC: April 2002), p. 8; Ilan Levin and Eric Schaeffer, *Dirty Kilowatts: America's Most Polluting Power Plants* (Washington, DC: Environmental Integrity Project, July 2007), p. 2; EPA, "EPA Decides Mercury Emissions from Power Plants Must Be Reduced," press release (Washington, DC: 15 December 2000).

33. EPA, Office of Science and Technology, "National Listing of Fish Advisories: 2005–06 National Listing," fact sheet (Washington, DC: July 2007); Kathryn Mahaffey, EPA, Methylmercury: Epidemiology Update, presentation at The National Forum on Contaminants in Fish, San Diego, CA, January 2004, at www.epa.gov/waterscience.

34. Anne Platt McGinn, *Why Poison Ourselves? A Precautionary Approach to Synthetic Chemicals*, Worldwatch Paper 153 (Washington, DC: Worldwatch Institute, 2000), p. 7; 200 chemicals in body from Pete Myers, plenary discussion on Emerging Environmental Issues, at USAID Environmental Officers Training Workshop, "Meeting the Environmental Challenges of the 21st Century," Airlie Center, Warrenton, VA, 26 July 1999.

35. EPA, "Toxics Release Inventory (TRI) Program," fact sheet, at www.epa.gov/tri, updated 9 June 2006; EPA, "EPA Issues New Toxics Report, Improves Means of Reporting," press release (Washington,

DC: 11 April 2001).

36. Calculated from U.S. Geological Survey, *Mineral Commodity Summaries 2007* (Washington, DC: U.S. Government Printing Office, 2007).

37. Eric Lipton, "The Long and Winding Road Now Followed by New York City's Trash," *New York Times*, 24 March 2001.

38. Lester R. Brown, "New York: Garbage Capital of the World," *Eco-Economy Update* (Washington, DC: Earth Policy Institute, April 2002); calculations by author, updated with The City of New York Department of Sanitation, "DSNY-Fact Sheet," updated 27 October 2003; Kirk Johnson, "To City's Burden, Add 11,000 Tons of Daily Trash," *New York Times*, 24 March 2001; Lhota quoted in Lipton, op. cit. note 37.

39. Gilmore quoted in Lipton, op. cit. note 37.

40. Joel Kurth, "N.J. Piles Demolition Trash on Michigan," *Detroit News*, 28 December 2004; City of Toronto, Canada, Solid Waste Management Division, "Facts about Toronto's Trash," Fact Sheet, at www.toronto.ca/garbage/facts.htm, updated 10 August 2006; Lipton, op. cit. note 37.

41. Niki Kitsantonis, "Athens Is in the Grip of a Garbage Crisis," *International Herald Tribune*, 28 January 2007.

42. "Fast Urbanization Dumps Garbage in Chinese Cities," *Xinhua News Agency*, 18 August 2006.

43. Günther Baechler, "Why Environmental Transformation Causes Violence: A Synthesis," *Environmental Change and Security Project Report*, Issue 4 (spring 1998), pp. 24–44.

44. U.S. Department of Agriculture (USDA), *Production, Supply, and Distribution Country Reports* (Washington, DC: October 1990); 2007 grainland area from USDA, *Production, Supply and Distribution*, electronic database, at www.fas.usda.gov/psdonline, updated 10 August 2007; U.N. Population Division, op. cit. note 2.

45. "Time for Action on Sudan" (editorial), *New York Times*, 18 June 2004; "A First Step to Save Darfur" (editorial), *New York Times*, 3 August 2007; Coalition for International Justice, "Estimates from Retrospective Mortality Surveys in Darfur and Chad Displacement Camps, Circa February 2003–April 2005," at www.cij.org, April 2005; "Sudan," in U.S. Central Intelligence Agency, *The World Fact Book*, at www.cia.gov/library/publications, updated 6 September 2007.

46. U.N. Population Division, op. cit. note 2; livestock from FAO, *Prod-STAT*, electronic database, at faostat.fao.org, updated 30 June 2007.

47. Somini Sengupta, "Where the Land is a Tinderbox, the Killing Is a Frenzy," *New York Times*, 16 June 2004; U.N. Population Division, op. cit. note 2; Government of Nigeria, *Combating Desertification and Mitigating the Effects of Drought in Nigeria*, National Report on the Implementation of the United Nations Convention to Combat

Desertification (Nigeria: November 1999).

48. Sengupta, op. cit. note 47.

49. Ibid.

50. James Gasana, "Remember Rwanda?" *World Watch,* September/October 2002, pp. 24–32.

51. Ibid.

52. U.S. Census Bureau, Population Division, International Programs Center, *International Database,* at www.census.gov/ipc/www/idbacc.html, updated 26 April 2005; Gasana, op. cit. note 50.

53. Gasana, op. cit. note 50; Emily Wax, "At the Heart of Rwanda's Horror: General's History Offers Clues to the Roots of Genocide," *Washington Post,* 21 September 2002.

54. U.N. Population Division, op. cit. note 2.

55. Ibid.; Gasana, op. cit. note 50

56. U.N. Population Division, op. cit. note 2; Sandra Postel, *Pillar of Sand* (New York: W. W. Norton & Company, 1999), pp. 141–49.

57. U.N. Population Division, op. cit. note 2, p. 43; Postel, op. cit. note 56, pp. 141–49.

58. Postel, op. cit. note 56, pp. 141–49; U.N. Population Division, op. cit. note 2.

59. O'Hara quoted in Michael Wines, "Grand Soviet Scheme for Sharing Water in Central Asia is Foundering," *New York Times,* 9 December 2002.

60. "Scientists Meeting in Tunis Called for Priority Activities to Curb Desertification," *UN News Service,* 21 June 2006.

61. Alan Cowell, "Migrants Found off Italy Boat Piled With Dead," *International Herald Tribune,* 21 October 2003.

62. Ibid.

63. Miranda Leitsinger, "African Migrants Die an Ocean Away," *Washington Post,* 2 June 2006; Mai Roman, "A New Record For Africans Risking Boat Route to Europe," *Washington Post,* 4 September 2006.

64. Ginger Thompson, "Mexico Worries About Its Own Southern Border," *New York Times,* 18 June 2006.

65. "Mexico's Immigration Problem: The Kamikazes of Poverty," *The Economist,* 31 January 2004.

66. Frank Bruni, "Off Sicily, Tide of Bodies Roils Immigrant Debate," *New York Times,* 23 September 2002; Flora Botsford, "Spain Recovers Drowned Migrants," *BBC News,* 25 April 2002; "Boat Sinks Off Coast of Turkey: One Survivor and 7 Bodies Found," *Agence France-Presse,* 22 December 2003; Mary Jordan and Kevin Sullivan, "Trade Brings Riches, But Not to Mexico's Poor," *Washington Post,* 22 March

2003; Robert McLeman and Barry Smit, "Climate Change, Migration and Security," *Commentary No. 86* (Ottawa: Canadian Security Intelligence Service, 2 March 2004); Arizona desert deaths from "Humane Approach to Border," *Denver Post*, 24 April 2003.

67. Abandoned villages in India from Tushaar Shah et al., *The Global Groundwater Situation: Overview of Opportunities and Challenges* (Colombo, Sri Lanka: International Water Management Institute, 2000); U.N. Population Division, op. cit. note 2, p. 42.

68. Wang Tao, *Cold and Arid Regions Environmental and Engineering Research Institute* (CAREERI), Chinese Academy of Sciences, e-mail to author, 4 April 2004; Wang Tao, "The Process and Its Control of Sandy Desertification in Northern China," CAREERI, Chinese Academy of Sciences, seminar on desertification, held in Lanzhou, China, May 2002.

69. Iranian News Agency, "Official Warns of Impending Desertification Catastrophe in Southeast Iran," *BBC International Reports*, 29 September 2002; Government of Nigeria, op. cit. note 47, p. 6.

70. Fund for Peace and Carnegie Endowment for International Peace, "The Failed States Index," *Foreign Policy*, July/August 2005, pp. 56–65.

71. Fund for Peace and Carnegie Endowment for International Peace, "The Failed States Index," *Foreign Policy*, July/August 2007, pp. 54–63.

72. Fund for Peace and Carnegie Endowment, op. cit. note 70.

73. Fund for Peace and Carnegie Endowment, op. cit. note 71.

74. Ibid.; U.N. Population Division, op. cit. note 2.

75. U.N. Population Division, op. cit. note 2.

76. Richard Cincotta, Robert Engelman, and Daniele Anastasion, *The Security Demographic: Population and Civil Conflict After the Cold War* (Washington, DC: Population Action International, 2003).

77. Ginger Thompson, "A New Scourge Afflicts Haiti: Kidnappings," *New York Times*, 6 July 2005; Madeleine K. Albright and Robin Cook, "The World Needs to Step It Up in Afghanistan," *International Herald Tribune*, 5 October 2004; Desmond Butler, "5-Year Hunt Fails to Net Qaeda Suspect in Africa," *New York Times*, 14 June 2003.

78. Abraham McLaughlin, "Can Africa Solve African Problems?" *Christian Science Monitor*, 4 January 2005; Marc Lacey, "Beyond the Bullets and Blades," *New York Times*, 20 March 2005; "World Refugee Day: Testimony of Anne C. Richard, International Rescue Committee," before US House of Representatives Committee on Foreign Affairs Subcommittee on Africa and Global Health, Washington, DC, 20 June 2007.

79. "Afghanistan: The Ignored War," in Christy Harvey, Judd Legum, and Jonathan Baskin, *The Progress Report* (Washington, DC: American

Progress Action Fund, 2005); Fund for Peace and Carnegie Endowment, op. cit. note 71; McLaughlin, op. cit. note 78; "A Failing State: The Himalayan Kingdom Is a Gathering Menace," *The Economist*, 4 December 2004.

80. United Nations, "United Nations Peacekeeping Operations," background note, at www.un.org/Depts/dpko/dpko/bnote.htm, 31 July 2007; "US Official Calls for NATO Flexibility in Afghanistan," *Agence France-Presse*, 6 September 2007; Marc Lacey, "Congo Tribal Killings Create a New Wave of Refugees," *New York Times*, 6 March 2005.

81. U.N. World Food Programme (WFP), "New Operation Provides WFP Food Aid to 550,000 Haitians," news release (Rome: 5 May 2005); WFP, "India Helps WFP Feed Afghan Schoolchildren," news release (Rome: 17 May 2005).

82. Stephanie McCrummen, "In an Eastern Congo Oasis, Blood amid the Greenery," *Washington Post*, 22 July 2007.

83. Roland Ogbonnaya, "Polio Pandemic...Is Nigeria Winning the Fight?" *This Day* (Lagos), 22 July 2007.

84. David Brown, "A Blow to Anti-Polio Campaign," *Washington Post*, 10 May 2005; Donald G. McNeil, Jr., "Muslims' New Tack on Polio: A Vaccine en Route to Mecca," *New York Times*, 20 August 2005; Nigerian polio cases tripling from "Wild Poliovirus 2000–2007," in WHO Global Polio Eradication Initiative, "Wild Poliovirus Weekly Update," at www.polioeradication.org, updated 2 October 2007.

86. "Wild Poliovirus 2000–2007," op. cit. note 84; number of polio-free countries estimated from Celia W. Dugger, "Nigeria and India Cited in Rise of Polio Cases," *New York Times*, 13 October 2006.

Chapter 7. Eradicating Poverty, Stabilizing Population

1. U.N. General Assembly, "United Nations Millennium Declaration," resolution adopted by the General Assembly, 8 September 2000; World Bank, *Global Monitoring Report 2007: Millennium Development Goals* (Washington, DC: 2007), p. 39; International Monetary Fund (IMF), World Economic Outlook, electronic database, www.imf.org, updated March 2007.

2. World Bank, *World Development Report 2005* (New York: Oxford University Press, 2004); Jeffrey D. Sachs, "India Takes the Lead," *Korea Herald*, 4 August 2004.

3. United Nations, "Poverty, Percentage of Population Below $1 (PPP) Per Day, Percentage," *Millennium Development Goals Indicators Database*, updated 27 July 2007; World Bank, op. cit. note 1, pp. 1, 3.

4. U.N. Population Division, *World Population Prospects: The 2006 Revision Population Database*, at esa.un.org/unpp, updated 2007; G-8 leaders, "Gleneagles Communiqué on Africa, Climate Change, Energy and Sustainable Development," document from G-8 Summit, Gleneagles,

Scotland, July 2005; fragile states from World Bank, op. cit. note 1, p. 4.

5. U.N. General Assembly, op. cit. note 1.

6. World Bank, op. cit. note 1, pp. 1–6; U.N. Food and Agriculture Organization (FAO), *Number of Undernourished Persons*, at www.fao.org/faostat/foodsecurity, updated 30 June 2006; UNICEF, *Excluded and Invisible: The State of the World's Children 2006* (New York: 2005), pp. vii, 114–17.

7. All Party Parliamentary Group on Population Development and Reproductive Health, *Return of the Population Growth Factor: Its Impact on the Millennium Development Goals* (London: Her Majesty's Stationery Office, January 2007), pp. 1, 3–9; Martha Campbell et al., "Return of the Population Growth Factor," *Science*, vol. 315 (16 March 2007), pp. 1501–02.

8. Campbell et al., op. cit. note 7; Martha Campbell, discussion with Janet Larsen, Earth Policy Institute, 8 October 2007; All Party Parliamentary Group, op. cit. note 7, p. 4.

9. United Nations, Millennium Development Goals Report 2007 (New York: 2007), p. 11; Hilaire A. Mputu, Literacy and Non-Formal Education in the E-9 Countries (Paris: UNESCO, 2001), p. 5; Polly Curtis, "Lack of Education 'a Greater Threat than Terrorism': Sen," *Guardian* (London), 28 October 2003.

10. Paul Blustein, "Global Education Plan Gains Backing," *Washington Post*, 22 April 2002; World Bank, "World Bank Announces First Group of Countries for 'Education For All' Fast Track," press release (Washington, DC: 12 June 2002); Gene Sperling, "The G-8—Send 104 Million Friends to School," *Bloomberg News*, 20 June 2005.

11. World Bank, op. cit. note 1, pp. 5, 24.

12. Gene Sperling, "Toward Universal Education," *Foreign Affairs*, September/October 2001, pp. 7–13.

13. Gene Sperling, "Educate Them All," *Washington Post*, 20 April 2002.

14. UNESCO, *EFA Global Monitoring Report 2007: Strong Foundations* (Paris: 2006), p.2; U.N. Commission on Population and Development, Thirty-sixth Session, Population, Education, and Development, press releases, 31 March–4 April 2003; UNESCO, "Winners of UNESCO Literacy Prizes 2003," press release, 27 May 2003.

15. U.K. Treasury, *From Commitment to Action: Education* (London: Department for International Development, September 2005).

16. George McGovern, *The Third Freedom: Ending Hunger in Our Time* (New York: Simon & Schuster: 2001), chapter 1.

17. Jeffrey Sachs, "A New Map of the World," *The Economist*, 22 June 2000; George McGovern, "Yes We CAN Feed the World's Hungry," *Parade*, 16 December 2001.

18. McGovern, op. cit. note 17.

19. Ibid.

20. Ibid.

21. Countries with stable or declining populations retrieved from Population Reference Bureau (PRB), *Datafinder*, electronic database, at www.prb.org/DataFind/datafinder7.htm, updated 2007; U.N. Population Division, op. cit. note 4.

22. U.N. Population Division, op. cit. note 4; United Nations, "Total Population (Both Sexes Combined) By Major Area, Region and Country, Annually for 1950–2050," table in *World Population Prospects: The 2006 Revision, Extended Dataset*, CD-ROM (Rome: 15 June 2007).

23. U.N. Population Division, op. cit. note 4.

24. Program for Appropriate Technology in Health (PATH) and U.N. Population Fund (UNFPA), *Meeting the Need: Strengthening Family Planning Programs* (Seattle: 2006), pp. 5–11; quote from All Party Parliamentary Group, op. cit. note 7, p. 22.

25. Janet Larsen, "Iran's Birth Rate Plummeting at Record Pace," in Lester R. Brown, Janet Larsen, and Bernie Fischlowitz-Roberts, *The Earth Policy Reader* (New York: W. W. Norton & Company, 2002), pp. 190–94; see also Homa Hoodfar and Samad Assadpour, "The Politics of Population Policy in the Islamic Republic of Iran," Studies in Family Planning, March 2000, pp. 19–34, and Farzaneh Roudi, "Iran's Family Planning Program: Responding to a Nation's Needs," *MENA Policy Brief*, June 2002; Iran population growth rate from United Nations, *World Population Prospects: The 2004 Revision* (New York: 2005).

26. Larsen, op. cit. note 25.

27. Ibid.

28. Ibid; population growth rates from PRB, *2005 World Population Data Sheet*, wall chart (Washington, DC: August 2005), and from U.N. Population Division, op. cit. note 4.

29. Pamela Polston, "Lowering the Boom: Population Activist Bill Ryerson is Saving the World—One 'Soap' at a Time," *Seven Days*, at www.populationmedia.org/archives/archives2.html, viewed 5 October 2007.

30. Ibid.

31. Ibid.

32. Ibid.

33. Additional spending from J. Joseph Speidel et al., *Family Planning and Reproductive Health: The Link to Environmental Preservation* (San Francisco: Bixby Center for Reproductive Health and Research Policy, University of California, 2007), p. 10, and from J. Joseph Speidel, discussion with J. Matthew Roney, Earth Policy Institute, 16 October 2007.

34. PATH and UNFPA, op. cit. note 24, p. 18.

35. "Bangladesh: National Family Planning Program," *Family Planning Programs: Diverse Solutions for a Global Challenge* (Washington, DC: PRB, 1994); gaps from Speidel et al., op. cit. note 33, p. 10, and from Speidel, op. cit. note 33.

36. World Bank, op. cit. note 1, p. 5.

37. Lack of access to safe water from ibid., p. 13.

38. Mustaque Chowdhury, *Health Workforce for TB Control by DOTS: The BRAC Case, Joint Learning Initiative Working Paper 5-2* (Global Health Trust, 2004).

39. Jeffrey D. Sachs and the Commission on Macroeconomics and Health, *Macroeconomics and Health: Investing in Health for Economic Development* (Geneva: World Health Organization (WHO), 2001); "UNICEF Lists Top Causes of Child Deaths," *Reuters*, 13 September 2007; Ruth Levine and the What Works Working Group, *Millions Saved: Proven Successes in Global Health* (Washington, DC: Center for Global Development, 2004).

40. Bill and Melinda Gates Foundation, "Vaccine-Preventable Diseases," at www.gatesfoundation.org/GlobalHealth, viewed 13 September 2007.

41. John Donnelly, "U.S. Seeks Cuts in Health Programs Abroad," *Boston Globe*, 5 February 2003.

42. Sachs and Commission on Macroeconomics and Health, op. cit. note 39; WHO, "Smallpox," fact sheet at www.who.int, viewed 10 October 2005.

43. WHO, "Polio Eradication: Now More Than Ever, Stop Polio Forever," at www.who.int/features/2004/polio/en, viewed 17 September 2007; Rotary International, "About PolioPlus," at www.rotary.org/foundation/polioplus/index.html, viewed 17 September 2007.

44. Polio cases from "Wild Poliovirus 2000–2007," in WHO Global Polio Eradication Initiative, "Wild Poliovirus Weekly Update," at www.polioeradication.org, updated 2 October 2007; Nigeria from WHO, *Global Polio Eradication Initiative: Annual Report 2006* (Geneva: 2007), p. 6.

45 "Pakistan Polio Drive is Suspended," *BBC News*, 8 August 2007.

46. Michele Barry, M.D., "The Tail of Guinea Worm-Global Eradication Without a Drug or Vaccine," *New England Journal of Medicine*, vol. 356, no. 25 (21 June 2007), pp. 2561–64.

47. Ibid.; country information from "Reported Cases of Dracunculiasis by Country, 1972–2005," in Peter H. Gleick, *The World's Water 2006–2007* (Washington, DC: Pacific Institute, 2006), pp. 293–97.

48. Tobacco deaths from WHO, "Chronic Obstructive Pulmonary Disease (COPD)," fact sheet (Geneva: November 2006); "The Tobacco Epidemic: A Crisis of Startling Dimensions," in Message From the

Director-General of the World Health Organization for World No-Tobacco Day 1998, at www.who.int; air pollution from WHO, "Air Pollution," fact sheet 187 (Geneva: rev. September 2000).

49. Alison Langley, "Anti-Smoking Treaty Is Adopted by 192 Nations," *New York Times*, 22 May 2003; information on WHO Tobacco Free Initiative at www.who.int/tobacco/index.cfm; treaty goals and Bloomberg from Alexi A. Wright and Ingrid T. Katz, "Tobacco Tightrope—Balancing Disease Prevention and Economic Development in China," *New England Journal of Medicine*, vol. 356, no. 15 (12 April 2007), pp. 1493–96.

50. Cigarette consumption from U.S. Department of Agriculture (USDA), *Production, Supply and Distribution*, electronic database, at www.fas.usda.gov/psdonline, updated 31 August 2006, and from Tom Capehart, *Tobacco Outlook* (Washington, DC: USDA Economic Research Service, 24 April 2007); per capita estimates made with population from U.N. Population Division, op. cit. note 4; Daniel Yee, "Smoking Declines in U.S.—Barely," *CBS News*, 10 November 2004.

51. USDA, op. cit. note 50; per capita estimates made using population from U.N. Population Division, op. cit. note 4.

52. Smoking Bans Around the World," *Reuters*, 10 January 2005; "New Zealand Stubs Out Smoking in Bars, Restaurants," *Reuters*, 13 December 2004 ,

53. "Bangladesh Bans Smoking in Many Public Places," *Reuters*, 15 March 2005; Italy from "Europeans Back Public Smoking Ban," *BBC News*, 31 May 2006; "England Smoking Ban Takes Effect," *BBC News*, 1 July 2007; France from Howard K. Koh et al., "Making Smoking History Worldwide," *New England Journal of Medicine*, vol. 356, no. 15 (12 April 2007), pp. 1496–1498.

54. Bernard Wysocki, Jr., "Companies Get Tough With Smokers, Obese to Trim Costs," *Wall Street Journal*, 12 October 2004.

55. Sachs and Commission on Macroeconomics and Health, op. cit. note 39.

56. Joint United Nations Programme on HIV/AIDS (UNAIDS) and WHO, *2006 AIDS Epidemic Update* (Geneva: December 2006), p. 3; total deaths calculated using UNAIDS statistics in Worldwatch Institute, *Signposts 2004*, CD-Rom (Washington, DC: 2004), and in UNAIDS and WHO, *AIDS Epidemic Update* (Geneva: various years).

57. Nita Bhalla, "Teaching Truck Drivers About AIDS," *BBC*, 25 June 2001; C. B. S. Venkataramana and P. V. Sarada, "Extent and Speed of Spread of HIV Infection in India Through the Commercial Sex Networks: A Perspective," *Tropical Medicine and International Health*, vol. 6, no. 12 (December 2001), pp. 1040–61, cited in "HIV Spread Via Female Sex Workers in India Set to Increase Significantly by 2005," *Reuters Health*, 26 December 2001.

58. Mark Covey, "Target Soldiers in Fight Against AIDS Says New Report," press release (London: Panos Institute, 8 July 2002); "Free

Condoms for Soldiers," *South Africa Press Association,* 5 August 2001; HIV prevalence rate from UNAIDS, *2006 Report on the Global AIDS Epidemic* (Geneva: May 2006), p. 421.

59. Condoms needed from UNFPA, *Donor Support for Contraceptives and Condoms for STI/HIV Prevention 2005* (New York: 2005); cost per condom from UNFPA, *Achieving the ICPD Goals: Reproductive Health Commodity Requirements 2000–2015* (New York: 2005); Nada Chaya and Kai-Ahset Amen, with Michael Fox, *Condoms Count: Meeting the Need in the Era of HIV/AIDS* (Washington, DC: Population Action International, 2002).

60. Chaya and Amen, with Fox, op. cit. note 59; cost per condom from UNFPA, *Achieving the ICPD Goals,* op. cit. note 59.

61. "Who Pays for Condoms," in Chaya and Amen, with Fox, op. cit. note 59; Communications Consortium Media Center, "U.N. Special Session on Children Ends in Acrimony," *PLANetWIRE.org,* 14 May 2002; Adam Clymer, "U.S. Revises Sex Information, and a Fight Goes On," *New York Times,* 27 December 2002.

62. UNAIDS, *Report on the Global HIV/AIDS Epidemic* (Geneva: June 2000), pp. 9–11; UNAIDS, op. cit. note 58, pp. 20, 446, 487; UNAIDS, "Uganda: Country Situation Analysis," at www.unaids.org/en/Regions_Countries, viewed 14 September 2007.

63. UNAIDS and WHO, op. cit. note 56, p. 10; treated patients in 2005 from UNAIDS and WHO, *Progress on Global Access to HIV Antiretroviral Therapy: An Update on "3 by 5"* (Geneva: 2005), pp. 7, 13.

64. Clive Bell, Shantayanan Devarajan, and Hans Gersbach, "The Long-run Economic Cost of AIDS: Theory and an Application to South Africa," Policy Research Working Paper Series (Washington, DC: World Bank, 2003); "AIDS Summit: The Economics of Letting People Die," *Star Tribune,* 16 July 2003; Deborah Mitchell, "HIV Treatment: 2 Million Years of Life Saved," *Reuters Health,* 28 February 2005.

65. "AIDS Summit," op. cit. note 64.

66. Organisation for Economic Co-operation and Development (OECD), *Agricultural Policies in OECD Countries: At a Glance 2006* (Paris: 31 July 2006), pp. 18, 19; OECD, "Development Aid from OECD Countries Fell 5.1% in 2006," press release (Paris: 3 April 2007); "The Hypocrisy of Farm Subsidies," *New York Times,* 1 December 2002.

67. European Commission, *General Budget of the European Union for the Financial Year 2007: The Figures* (Brussels: February 2007), p. 4; OECD, Agricultural Policies, op. cit. note 66, pp. 18–22; "The Hypocrisy of Farm Subsidies," op. cit. note 66.

68. OECD, "Development Aid," op. cit. note 66; "South Africa: Weaning States Off Subsidies," *Africa News,* 19 August 2005.

69. See Chapter 2 for further discussion of oil prices and ethanol.

70. Number of farmers from Oxfam International, "Oxfam Dismisses US Cotton Market Access Offer as 'Empty Promise'," press release (Lon-

don: 15 December 2005); Julian Alston et al., *Impacts of Reductions in US Cotton Subsidies on West African Cotton Producers* (Boston: Oxfam America, 2007); OECD, *OECD Statistics,* electronic database, at stats.oecd.org/wbos, updated 25 September 2007; U.N. Population Division, op. cit. note 4.

71. Elizabeth Becker, "Looming Battle Over Cotton Subsidies," *New York Times,* 24 January 2004; Elizabeth Becker, "U.S. Will Cut Farm Subsidies in Trade Deal," *New York Times,* 31 July 2004; Randy Schnepf, *U.S. Agricultural Policy Response to WTO Cotton Decision* (Washington, DC: Congressional Research Service, updated 8 September 2006).

72. Schnepf, op. cit. note 71; Mark Drajem and Carlos Caminada, "WTO Rules Against U.S. in Cotton Dispute With Brazil (Update 1)," *Bloomberg News,* 27 July 2007; Alan Bjerga, "Bush's Opposition to 'Soviet' Farm Bill May Get Plowed Under,"*Bloomberg News,* 23 July 2007.

73. "Ending the Cycle of Debt," *New York Times,* 1 October 2004; debt servicing from World Bank, *Little Data Book on External Debt in Global Development Finance 2007* (Washington, DC: 2007), p. 8; health care spending calculated from IMF, *World Economic and Financial Surveys: Regional Economic Outlook—Sub-Saharan Africa* (Washington, DC: September 2006), pp. 36, 43, from David Goldsbrough, "IMF Programs and Health Spending," presented at Global Conference on Gearing Macroeconomic Policies to Reverse the HIV/AIDS Epidemic, Brasília, Brazil, 20 November 2006, and from U.N. Population Division, op. cit. note 4.

74. "G8 Finance Ministers' Conclusions on Development," Pre Summit Statement by G-8 Finance Ministers, London, 10–11 June 2005; Oxfam International, "Gleneagles: What Really Happened at the G8 Summit?" *Oxfam Briefing Note* (London: 29 July 2005).

75. Oxfam International, "The View From the Summit—Gleneagles G8 One Year On," briefing note (Oxford, U.K.: June 2006).

76. Abid Aslam, "18 Poor Countries to See Debt Slate Wiped Clean, Saving $10 Million Per Week," *One World US,* 26 September 2005; Oxfam International, op. cit. note 75.

77. UNFPA, *The State of World Population 2004* (New York: 2004), pp. 14–15.

78. United Nations, *World Population Prospects: The 2004 Revision* (New York: 2005); UNFPA, op. cit. note 77, p. 39.

79. Costs of meeting social goals in Table 7–1 based on the following sources: universal primary education from U.K. Treasury, op. cit. note 15; adult literacy campaign is author's estimate; school lunch program from McGovern, op. cit. note 17; assistance to preschool children and pregnant women is author's estimate of extending the U.S.'s Women, Infants, and Children program, based on ibid.; reproductive health and family planning from Speidel et al., op. cit. note 33, p. 10, and

from Speidel, op. cit. note 33; universal basic health care from Sachs and Commission on Macroeconomics and Health, op. cit. note 39; closing the condom gap estimated from UNFPA, *Donor Support for Contraceptives and Condoms*, op. cit. note 59, and from UNFPA, *Achieving the ICPD Goals*, op. cit. note 59.

80. Sachs and Commission on Macroeconomics and Health, op. cit. note 39.

81. Ibid.; Wu Xiaoling, "Statement of Madam Wu Xiaoling, Deputy Governor of the People's Bank of China," speech delivered at the 39th Annual Meeting of the Board of Governors of the African Development Bank (Group), Kampala, Uganda, 25–26 May 2004.

Chapter 8. Restoring the Earth

1. Craig A. Cox, "Conservation Can Mean Life or Death," *Journal of Soil and Water Conservation*, November/December 2004.

2. Remaining forests from "Table 2.1. Distribution of Forests by Subregion 2005," in U.N. Food and Agriculture Organization (FAO), *Forest Resources Assessment (FRA) 2005* (Rome: 2006).

3. FAO, *ForesSTAT Statistics Database*, at faostat.fao.org, updated 22 December 2006; U.S. Environmental Protection Agency, *Municipal Solid Waste Generation, Recycling, and Disposal in the United States: Facts and Figures for 2005* (Washington, DC: 2005).

4. Fuelwood as a proportion of total harvested wood from FAO, op. cit. note 3; Daniel M. Kammen, "From Energy Efficiency to Social Utility: Lessons from Cookstove Design, Dissemination, and Use," in José Goldemberg and Thomas B. Johansson, *Energy as an Instrument for Socio-Economic Development* (New York: U.N. Development Programme, 1995).

5. Kevin Porter, "Final Kakuma Evaluation: Solar Cookers Filled a Critical Gap," in Solar Cookers International, *Solar Cooker Review*, vol. 10, no. 2 (November 2004); cost from "Breakthrough in Kenyan Refugee Camps," at solarcooking.org/kakuma-m.htm, viewed 30 July 2007.

6. FAO, *Agriculture: Towards 2015/30, Technical Interim Report* (Geneva: Economic and Social Department, 2000), pp. 156–57.

7. Johanna Son, "Philippines: Row Rages Over Lifting of Ban on Lumber Exports," *InterPress Service*, 17 April 1998; John Aglionby, "Philippines Bans Logging After Fatal Floods," *Guardian* (London), 6 December 2004; Republic of the Philippines, "President Okays Selective Lifting of Log Ban," press release (Manila: 7 March 2005).

8. Alliance for Forest Conservation and Sustainable Use, "WWF/World Bank Forest Alliance Launches Ambitious Program to Reduce Deforestation and Curb Illegal Logging," press release (New York: World Bank/WWF, 25 May 2005); certified area from Alliance for Forest Conservation and Sustainable Use, "World Bank/WWF Alliance for Forest Conservation & Sustainable Use: Questions & Answers,"

World Bank/WWF, at www.worldwildlife.org/alliance, viewed 30 July 2007; new protected area from Alliance for Forest Conservation and Sustainable Use, "WWF/World Bank Alliance Targets," at www.worldwildlife.org/alliance, viewed 30 July 2007.

9. Forest Stewardship Council, *FSC Certified Forests* (Bonn, Germany: 2005), pp. 34, 40, 53; Forest Stewardship Council, "FSC Certification: Maps, Graphs, and Statistics (July 2007)," PowerPoint Presentation, at www.fsc.org/en/whats_new/fsc_certificates/maps, viewed 30 July 2007.

10. A. Del Lungo, J. Ball, and J. Carle, *Global Planted Forests Thematic Study: Results and Analysis* (Rome: FAO Forestry Department, December 2006); grain area from U.S. Department of Agriculture (USDA), *Production Supply and Distribution*, electronic database, at www.fas.usda.gov/psdonline, updated 10 August 2007.

11. R. James and A. Del Lungo, "Comparisons of Estimates of 'High Value' Wood With Estimates of Total Forest Plantation Production," table in *The Potential for Fast-Growing Commercial Forest Plantations to Supply High Value Roundwood* (Rome: FAO Forestry Department, February 2005), p. 24; FAO, op. cit. note 3.

12. Plantation area in "Table 4. Total Planted Forest Area: Productive and Protective—61 Sampled Countries," in Del Lungo, Ball, and Carle, op. cit. note 10, pp. 66–70; Ashley T. Mattoon, "Paper Forests," *World Watch*, March/April 1998, pp. 20–28.

13. Plantation yields from Mattoon, op. cit. note 12; corn yields from USDA, op. cit. note 10.

14. FAO, op. cit. note 6, p. 185; Chris Brown and D. J. Mead, eds., "Future Production from Forest Plantations," *Forest Plantation Thematic Paper* (Rome: FAO, 2001), p. 9.

15. Reed Funk, letter to author, 9 August 2005.

16. M. Davis et al., "New England—Acadian Forests," in Taylor H. Ricketts et al., eds., *Terrestrial Ecoregions of North America: A Conservation Assessment* (Washington, DC: Island Press, 1999); David R. Foster, "Harvard Forest: Addressing Major Issues in Policy Debates and in the Understanding of Ecosystem Process and Pattern," LTER Network News: The Newsletter of the Long Term Ecological Network, spring/summer 1996; U.S. Forest Service, "2006 Forest Health Highlights," various state sheets, at fhm.fs.fed.us, viewed 2 August 2007.

17. C. Csaki, "Agricultural Reforms in Central and Eastern Europe and the Former Soviet Union: Status and Perspectives," Agricultural Economics, vol. 22 (2000), pp. 37–54; Igor Shvytov, *Agriculturally Induced Environmental Problems in Russia*, Discussion Paper No. 17 (Halle, Germany: Institute of Agricultural Development in Central and Eastern Europe, 1998), p. 13.

18. Se-Kyung Chong, "Anmyeon-do Recreation Forest: A Millennium of Management," in Patrick B. Durst et al., *In Search of Excellence:*

Exemplary Forest Management in Asia and the Pacific, Asia-Pacific Forestry Commission (Bangkok: FAO Regional Office for Asia and the Pacific, 2005), pp. 251–59.

19. Ibid.

20. Turkish Foundation for Combating Soil Erosion (TEMA), at english.tema.org.tr, viewed 31 July 2007.

21. U.S. Embassy, Niamey, Niger, "Niger: Greener Now Than 30 Years Ago," reporting cable circulated following national FRAME workshop, October 2006; Chris Reij, "More Success Stories in Africa's Drylands Than Often Assumed," presentation at Network of Farmers' and Agricultural Producers' Organisations of West Africa (ROPPA) Forum on Food Sovereignty, 7–10 November 2006.

22. U.S. Embassy, op. cit. note 21; Reij, op. cit. note 21.

23. Secretariat of the U.N. Convention to Combat Desertification, "The Great North American Dust Bowl: A Cautionary Tale," *Global Alarm Dust and Sandstorms from the World's Drylands* (Bangkok: 2002), pp. 77–121.

24. Jeffrey Zinn, Conservation Reserve Program: Status and Current Issues (Washington, DC: Congressional Research Service, 8 May 2001); USDA, Economic Research Service, *Agri-Environmental Policy at the Crossroads: Guideposts on a Changing Landscape* (Washington, DC: 2001).

25. USDA, Natural Resources Conservation Service, *CORE4 Conservation Practices Training Guide: The Common Sense Approach to Natural Resource Conservation* (Washington, DC: August 1999); Rolf Derpsch, "Frontiers in Conservation Tillage and Advances in Conservation Practice," in D. E. Stott, R. H. Mohtar, and G. C. Steinhardt, eds., *Sustaining the Global Farm*, selected papers from the 10th International Soil Conservation Organization Meeting, at Purdue University and USDA-ARS National Soil Erosion Research Laboratory, 24–29 May 1999 (Washington, DC: 2001), pp. 248–54.

26. Conservation Technology Information Center, Purdue University, "National Tillage Trends (1990–2004)," from the *2004 National Crop Residue Management Survey Data*; FAO, *Intensifying Crop Production with Conservation Agriculture*, at www.fao.org/ag, viewed 20 May 2003; Brazil, Argentina, and Australia from Rolf Derpsch, no-tillage consultant, e-mails to J. Matthew Roney, Earth Policy Institute, 6 and 11 August 2007; Canada from Doug McKell, Soil Conservation Council of Canada, "No-till Census Data-Canada," presented at meeting of Confederation of American Associations for the Production of Sustainable Agriculture, Bella Vista, Paraquay, 12–14 September 2007.

27. FAO, op. cit. note 26.

28. "Algeria to Convert Large Cereal Land to Tree-Planting," *Reuters*, 8 December 2000; Souhail Karam, "Drought-Hit North Africa Seen Hunting for Grains," *Reuters*, 15 July 2005.

29. Godwin Nnanna, "Africa's Message for China," *China Dialogue*, 18 April 2007; International Institute for Sustainable Development, "African Regional Coverage Project," Eighth African Union Summit—Briefing Note, vol. 7, issue 2 (Geneva: 7 February 2007), p. 8; Federal Republic of Nigeria, Ministry of Environment, "Green Wall Sahara Programme," at www.greenwallsahara.org, viewed 17 October 2007.

30. Evan Ratliff, "The Green Wall of China," Wired, April 2003; Wang Yan, "China's Forest Shelter Project Dubbed 'Green Great Wall'," *Xinhua News Agency*, 9 July 2006; Sun Xiufang and Ralph Bean, *China Solid Wood Products Annual Report 2002* (Beijing: USDA, 2002).

31. Author's discussion with officials of Helin County, Inner Mongolia (Nei Monggol), 17 May 2002.

32. Ibid.

33. U.S. Embassy, *Grapes of Wrath in Inner Mongolia* (Beijing: May 2001).

34. India's dairy industry from A. Banerjee, "Dairying Systems in India," *World Animal Review*, vol. 79/2 (Rome: FAO, 1994).

35. Andrew Balmford et al., "The Worldwide Costs of Marine Protected Areas," *Proceedings of the National Academy of Sciences*, vol. 101, no. 26 (29 June 2004), pp. 9694–97; "Costs of a Worldwide System of Marine Parks," press release (York: The University of York, 12 July 2004); current protected area from World Wildlife Fund (WWF), "Problems: Inadequate Protection," at www.panda.org, viewed 9 August 2007.

36. Balmford et al., op. cit. note 35; Tim Radford, "Marine Parks Can Solve Global Fish Crisis, Experts Say," *Guardian* (London), 15 June 2004.

37. Balmford et al., op. cit. note 35; Radford, op. cit. note 36.

38. Radford, op. cit. note 36; Richard Black, "Protection Needed for 'Marine Serengetis,'" *BBC News*, 6 August 2003; Balmford et al., op. cit. note 35.

39. American Association for the Advancement of Science (AAAS), "Leading Marine Scientists Release New Evidence that Marine Reserves Produce Enormous Benefits within Their Boundaries and Beyond," press release (Washington, DC: 12 March 2001); "Scientific Consensus Statement on Marine Reserves and Marine Protected Areas," presented at the AAAS annual meeting, 15–20 February 2001.

40. AAAS, op. cit. note 39; "Scientific Consensus Statement," op. cit. note 39, p. 2.

41. R. J. Diaz, J. Nestlerode, and M. L. Diaz, "A Global Perspective on the Effects of Eutrophication and Hypoxia on Aquatic Biota," in G. L. Rupp and M. D. White, eds., *Proceedings of the 7th Annual Symposium on Fish Physiology, Toxicology and Water Quality, Estonia, 12–15 May 2003* (Athens, GA: U.S. Environmental Protection Agency,

Ecosystems Research Division, 2004); U.N. Environment Programme (UNEP), *GEO Yearbook 2003* (Nairobi: 2004).

42. WWF, *Hard Facts, Hidden Problems: A Review of Current Data on Fishing Subsidies* (Washington, DC: 2001), pp. ii; Balmford et al., op. cit. note 35; Radford, op. cit. note 36; fishery subsidy value includes "bad" subsidies and fuel subsidies as estimated in Fisheries Center University of British Columbia, *Catching More Bait: A Bottom-Up Re-Estimation of Global Fisheries Subsidies* (2nd Version) (Vancouver, BC: The Fisheries Center, 2006), p. 21.

43. U.N. Population Division, *World Population Prospects: The 2006 Revision Population Database*, at esa.un.org/unpp, updated 2007.

44. WWF, op. cit. note 35.

45. Conservation International, "Biodiversity Hotspots," at www.bio diversity hotspots.org, viewed 31 July 2007.

46. U.S. Fish and Wildlife Service, "The Endangered Species Act of 1973," at www.fws.gov/endangered, viewed 31 July 2007; Mark Clayton, "New Tool to Fight Global Warming: Endangered Species Act," *Christian Science Monitor*, 7 September 2007; U.S. Fish and Wildlife S ervice-Alaska, "Polar Bear Conservation Issues," at alaska.fws.gov/ fisheries/mmm/polarbear/issues.htm, updated 5 October 2007.

47. Vattenfall, *Global Mapping of Greenhouse Gas Abatement Opportunities up to 2030: Forestry Sector Deep-Dive* (Stockholm: June 2007), p.1.

48. Ibid., p. 6; World Resources Institute, *Climate Analysis Indicator Tool*, electronic database at cait.wri.org, updated 2007.

49. "Forestry Cuts Down on Logging," *China Daily*, 26 May 1998; Erik Eckholm, "China Admits Ecological Sins Played Role in Flood Disaster," *New York Times*, 26 August 1998; Erik Eckholm, "Stunned by Floods, China Hastens Logging Curbs," *New York Times*, 27 September 1998; Chris Brown, Patrick B. Durst, and Thomas Enters, *Forests Out of Bounds: Impacts and Effectiveness of Logging Bans in Natural Forests in Asia-Pacific* (Bangkok, Thailand: FAO Regional Office for Asia Pacific, 2001); John Aglionby, "Philippines Bans Logging After Fatal Floods," *Guardian* (London), 6 December 2004.

50. Geoffrey Lean, "A Disaster to Take Everyone's Breath Away," *The Independent* (London), 24 July 2006; Daniel Nepstad, "Climate Change and the Forest," *Tomorrow's Amazonia: Using and Abusing the World's Last Great Forests* (Washington, DC: The American Prospect, September 2007); S. S. Saatchi et al., "Distribution of Aboveground Live Biomass in the Amazon Rainforest," *Global Change Biology*, vol. 13, no. 4 (April 2007), pp. 816–37.

51. Vattenfall, op. cit. note 47, p. 16; sequestration per tree calculated assuming 500 trees per hectare, from UNEP Billion Tree Campaign, "Fast Facts," at www.unep.org/billiontreecampaign, viewed 10 October 2007; growing period from Robert N. Stavins and Kenneth R. Richards, *The Cost of U.S. Forest Based Carbon Sequestration* (Arlington, VA: Pew Center on Global Climate Change, January 2005), p. 10.

52. Vattenfall, op. cit. note 47, pp. 1, 16; Dollar to Euro exchange rate of 1.4, from "Benchmark Currency Rates," at www.bloomberg.com/markets, viewed 17 October 2007.

53. UNEP Billion Tree Campaign, at www.unep.org/billiontreecampaign, viewed 12 October 2007; "Mexico Celebrates Día del Arbol with a Commitment to Plant 250 Million Trees," at www.unep.org/billiontreecampaign/CampaignNews, viewed 26 October 2007; Ethiopia pledge from Daniel Wallis, "UN Wins Pledges to Plant a Billion Trees," *Reuters*, 22 May 2007; Senegal pledge from "Global Tree Planting Campaign Puts Down a Billion Roots on International Biological Diversity Day," at www.unep.org/Documents.Multilingual, viewed 12 October 2007.

54. "The State of Parana in Brazil Undertakes a Major Reforestation Project," at www.unep.org/billiontreecampaign/CampaignNews, viewed 12 October 2007; "31 July—The Greenest Day of the Calendar in India and a Tree Planting Record by 600,000 Volunteers," at www.unep.org/Documents.Multilingual, viewed 12 October 2007; carbon sequestration assuming that three fourths of trees will be in tropics and one fourth in temperate regions, using Vattenfall, op. cit. note 47, p. 16.

55. Ministry for the Environment, *New Zealand's Climate Change Solutions: An Overview* (Wellington, New Zealand: September 2007), p. 19; U.N. Population Division, op. cit. note 43; calculations assume a mature stand density of 500 trees per hectare.

56. Chang-Ran Kim, "Tokyo Turns to Rooftop Gardens to Beat the Heat," *Reuters*, 7 August 2002; Washington, D.C., program from Casey Trees, at www.caseytrees.org, viewed 12 October 2007.

57. Kathy Wolf, "Urban Forest Values: Economic Benefits of Trees in Cities," fact sheet (Seattle, WA: Center for Urban Horticulture, November 1998); Greg McPherson et al., "Municipal Forest Benefits and Costs in Five US Cities," *Journal of Forestry*, December 2005, pp. 411–16.

58. Patrick Barta, "Jatropha Plant Gains Steam in Global Race for Biofuels," *Wall Street Journal*, 24 August 2007.

59. Rattan Lal, "Soil Carbon Sequestration Impacts on Global Climate Change and Food Security," *Science*, vol. 304 (11 June 2004), pp. 1623–27.

60. Table 8–1 from the following: planting trees to reduce flooding and conserve soil and protecting topsoil on cropland from Lester R. Brown and Edward C. Wolf, "Reclaiming the Future," in Lester R. Brown et al., *State of the World 1988* (New York: W. W. Norton & Company, 1988), p. 174, using data from FAO, *Fuelwood Supplies in the Developing Countries*, Forestry Paper 42 (Rome: 1983); planting trees to sequester carbon from Vattenfall, op. cit. note 47, p. 16; restoring rangelands from UNEP, *Status of Desertification and Implementation of the United Nations Plan of Action to Combat Desertification*

(Nairobi: 1991), pp. 73–92; restoring fisheries from Balmford et al., op. cit. note 35; protecting biological diversity from World Parks Congress, *Recommendations of the Vth IUCN World Parks Congress* (Durban, South Africa: 2003), pp. 17–19, and from World Parks Congress, "The Durban Accord," at www.iucn.org/themes/wcpa, viewed 19 October 2007; stabilizing water tables is author's estimate.

61. Se-Kyung Chong, "Anmyeon-do Recreation Forest: A Millennium of Management," in Durst et al., op. cit. note 18.

62. Brown and Wolf, op. cit. note 60, p. 175.

63. Runsheng Yin et al., "China's Ecological Rehabilitation: The Unprecedented Efforts and Dramatic Impacts of Reforestation and Slope Protection in Western China," in Woodrow Wilson International Center for Scholars, China Environment Forum, China Environment Series, Issue 7 (Washington, DC: 2005), pp. 17–32.

64. Brown and Wolf, op. cit. note 60, p. 176.

65. Vattenfall, op. cit. note 47, p. 16; Amy Belasco, *The Cost of Iraq, Afghanistan and Other Global War on Terror Operations Since 9/11* (Washington, DC: Congressional Research Service, 16 July 2007).

66. Brown and Wolf, op. cit. note 60, pp. 173–74.

67. Ibid., p. 174.

68. Ibid.

69. Ibid.

70. UNEP, op. cit. note 60, with dollar figures converted from 1990 to 2004 dollars using implicit price deflators from U.S. Department of Commerce, Bureau of Economic Analysis, "Table C.1. GDP and Other Major NIPA Aggregates," in *Survey of Current Business*, September 2005, p. D–48.

71. H. E. Dregne and Nan-Ting Chou, "Global Desertification Dimensions and Costs," in *Degradation and Restoration of Arid Lands* (Lubbock, TX: Texas Tech. University, 1992); UNEP, op. cit. note 60.

72. Balmford et al., op. cit. note 35.

73. World Parks Congress, *Recommendations of the Vth IUCN World Parks Congress*, op. cit. note 60; World Parks Congress, "The Durban Accord," op. cit. note 60.

74. Irrigated cropland from FAO, *FAOSTAT Statistics Database*, at apps.fao.org, land data updated 4 April 2005.

75. Jordan from Tom Gardner-Outlaw and Robert Engelman, *Sustaining Water, Easing Scarcity: A Second Update* (Washington, DC: Population Action International, 1997); Mexico from Sandra Postel, *Last Oasis* (New York: W. W. Norton & Company, 1997), pp. 150–51.

76. Sandra Postel, *Pillar of Sand* (New York: W. W. Norton & Company, 1999), pp. 230–35; Postel, op. cit. note 75, pp. 167–68.

Chapter 9. Feeding Eight Billion Well

1. "Last Food Shipment Signals End of 25-Year WFP Aid to China," *Asian Economic News*, 8 April 2005; U.S. Department of Agriculture (USDA), *Production, Supply and Distribution*, electronic database, at www.fas.usda.gov/psdonline, updated 10 August 2007; U.N. World Food Programme, "China Emerges as World's Third Largest Food Aid Donor," press release (Rome: 20 July 2006).

2. Xie Wei and Christian DeBresson, *China's Progressive Market Reform and Opening* (Geneva: U.N. Industrial Development Organization, 2001); USDA, op. cit. note 1.

3. U.N. Food and Agriculture Organization (FAO), *The State of Food Insecurity in the World 2006* (Rome: 2006), p. 8; Madelene Pearson and Danielle Rossingh, "Wheat Price Rises to Record $9 a Bushel on Global Crop Concerns," *Bloomberg*, 12 September 2007.

4. Thomas R. Sinclair, "Limits to Crop Yield," paper presented at the 1999 National Academy Colloquium, Plants and Populations: Is There Time? Irvine, CA, 5–6 December 1998; Patrick Heffer, *Short-Term Prospects for World Agriculture and Fertilizer Demand 2005/06-2007/08* (Buenos Aires, Argentina: International Fertilizer Industry Association, January 2007); 1950–1960 data from USDA, in Worldwatch Institute, *Signposts 2001*, CD-Rom (Washington, DC: 2001); USDA, op. cit. note 1.

5. U.N. Population Division, *World Population Prospects: The 2006 Revision Population Database*, at esa.un.org/unpp, updated 2007.

6. USDA, op. cit. note 1.

7. Ibid.; Worldwatch Institute, op. cit. note 4.

8. USDA, National Agricultural Statistics Service (NASS), *Crop Production 2006 Summary* (Washington, DC: January 2007); USDA, NASS, *QuickStats*, electronic database, at www.nass.usda.gov/Data _and_Statistics/Quick_Stats, viewed 28 September 2007.

9. USDA, op. cit. note 1; Worldwatch Institute, op. cit. note 4.

10. John Wade, Adam Branson, and Xiang Qing, *China Grain and Feed Annual Report 2002* (Beijing: USDA, 2002); USDA, op. cit. note 1.

11. Double-cropping yields from USDA, *India Grain and Feed Annual Report 2003* (New Delhi: 2003); U.N. Population Division, op. cit. note 5; USDA, op. cit. note 1.

12. Richard Magleby, "Soil Management and Conservation," in USDA, *Agricultural Resources and Environmental Indicators 2003* (Washington, DC: February 2003), Chapter 4.2, p. 14.

13. USDA, op. cit. note 1; Randall D. Schnepf et al., *Agriculture in Brazil and Argentina* (Washington, DC: USDA Economic Research Service (ERS), 2001), pp. 8-10.

14. FAO, *ResourceSTAT*, electronic database, at faostat.fao.org/site/405/default.aspx, updated 30 June 2007; USDA, op. cit. note 1.

15. Pedro Sanchez, "The Climate Change–Soil Fertility–Food Security Nexus," summary note (Bonn: International Food Policy Research Institute, 4 September 2001).

16. Edward Cody, "Chinese Lawmakers Approve Measure to Protect Private Property Rights," *Washington Post*, 17 March 2007; Jim Yardley, "China Nears Passage of Landmark Property Law," *New York Times*, 9 March 2007; Zhu Keliang and Roy Prosterman, "From Land Rights to Economic Boom," *China Business Review*, July–August 2006.

17. Worldwatch Institute, op. cit. note 4; USDA, op. cit. note 1; water use for grain production from FAO, *Crops and Drops* (Rome: 2002), p. 17.

18. Water requirements for grain production from FAO, *Yield Response to Water* (Rome: 1979); water use from I. A. Shiklomanov, "Assessment of Water Resources and Water Availability in the World," *Report for the Comprehensive Assessment of the Freshwater Resources of the World* (St. Petersburg, Russia: State Hydrological Institute, 1998), cited in Peter H. Gleick, *The World's Water 2000–2001* (Washington, DC: Island Press, 2000), p. 53.

19. Sandra Postel and Amy Vickers, "Boosting Water Productivity," in Worldwatch Institute, *State of the World 2004* (New York: W. W. Norton & Company, 2004), pp. 51-52.

20. Wang Shucheng, discussion with author, Beijing, May 2004.

21. FAO, op. cit. note 17, p. 17; Alain Vidal, Aline Comeau, and Hervé Plusquellec, *Case Studies on Water Conservation in the Mediterranean Region* (Rome: FAO, 2001), p. vii.

22. FAO, op. cit. note 17, p. 17; Vidal, Comeau, and Plusquellec, op. cit. note 21, p. vii.

23. Postel and Vickers, op. cit. note 19, p. 53.

24. Sandra Postel et al., "Drip Irrigation for Small Farmers: A New Initiative to Alleviate Hunger and Poverty," *Water International*, March 2001, pp. 3–13.

25. Ibid.

26. "Punjab's Depleting Groundwater Stagnates Agricultural Growth," *Down to Earth*, vol. 16, no. 5 (30 July 2007).

27. For more information on water users associations, see R. Maria Saleth and Arial Dinar, *Water Challenge and Institutional Response: A Cross-Country Perspective* (Washington, DC: World Bank, 1999), p. 26.

28. Ibid., p. 6.

29. World Bank and Swiss Agency for Development and Cooperation, Summary Report, Middle East and North Africa Regional Water Initiative Workshop on Sustainable Groundwater Management, Sana'a, Yemen, 25–28 June 2000, p. 19.

30. Peter Wonacott, "To Save Water, China Lifts Price," *Wall Street*

Journal, 14 June 2004.

31. USDA, op. cit. note 1; USDA, Foreign Agricultural Service (FAS), "Egyptian Rice Acreage Continues to Exceed Government-Designated Limitations," Foreign Countries' Policies and Programs, *FASonline,* viewed 28 September 2007; "Rice Cropped for Water," *China Daily,* 9 January 2002.

32. U.N. Population Division, op. cit. note 5; grain consumption from USDA, op. cit. note 1; water calculation based on 1,000 tons of water for 1 ton of grain from FAO, op. cit. note 18.

33. USDA, op. cit. note 1.

34. FAO, *FAOSTAT,* electronic database at faostat.fao.org, updated 30 June 2007; 1950 data from Worldwatch Institute, op. cit. note 4.

35. Feed-to-poultry conversion ratio derived from data in Robert V. Bishop et al., *The World Poultry Market-Government Intervention and Multilateral Policy Reform* (Washington, DC: USDA, 1990); conversion ratio of grain to beef based on Allen Baker, Feed Situation and Outlook staff, ERS, USDA, discussion with author, 27 April 1992; pork data from Leland Southard, Livestock and Poultry Situation and Outlook staff, ERS, USDA, discussion with author, 27 April 1992; fish from Rosamond L. Naylor et al., "Effect of Aquaculture on World Fish Supplies," *Nature,* vol. 405 (29 June 2000), pp. 1017–24.

36. USDA, op. cit. note 1.

37. FAO, *FishStat Plus,* electronic database, at www.fao.org, updated March 2007; Naylor et al., op. cit. note 35.

38. Naylor et al., op. cit. note 35; FAO, op. cit. note 37; Taija-Riitta Tuominen and Maren Esmark, *Food for Thought: The Use of Marine Resources in Fish Feed* (Oslo: WWF-Norway, 2003).

39. FAO, op. cit. note 37.

40. S. F. Li, "Aquaculture Research and Its Relation to Development in China," in *World Fish Center, Agricultural Development and the Opportunities for Aquatic Resources Research in China* (Penang, Malaysia: 2001), p. 26; FAO, op. cit. note 37.

41. FAO, op. cit. note 37; FAO, op. cit. note 34.

42. Naylor et al., op. cit. note 35; W. C. Nandeesha et al., "Breeding of Carp with Oviprim," in Indian Branch, Asian Fisheries Society, *India, Special Publication No. 4* (Mangalore, India: 1990), p. 1.

43. "Mekong Delta to Become Biggest Aquatic Producer in Vietnam," *Vietnam News Agency,* 3 August 2004; "The Mekong Delta Goes Ahead with the WTO," *Vietnam Economic News Online,* 8 June 2007; FAO, op. cit. note 37.

44. Naylor et al., op. cit. note 35; U.S. catfish production data from USDA, NASS, *Catfish Production* (Washington, DC: February 2003), p. 5.

45. USDA, op. cit. note 1; Suzi Fraser Dominy, "Soy's Growing Impor-

tance," *World Grain*, 13 April 2004.

46. USDA, FAS, *Oilseeds: World Markets and Trade* (Washington, DC: August 2007).

47. USDA, op. cit. note 1.

48. Ibid.

49. Historical statistics in Worldwatch Institute, op. cit. note 4; USDA, op. cit. note 1.

50. FAO, op. cit. note 34.

51. S. C. Dhall and Meena Dhall, "Dairy Industry—India's Strength in Its Livestock," *Business Line*, Internet Edition of *Financial Daily* from The Hindu group of publications, 7 November 1997; see also Surinder Sud, "India Is Now World's Largest Milk Producer," *India Perspectives*, May 1999, pp. 25–26; A. Banerjee, "Dairying Systems in India," *World Animal Review*, vol. 79, no. 2 (1994).

52. USDA, op. cit. note 1; U.N. Population Division, op. cit. note 5.

53. Dhall and Dhall, op. cit. note 51; Banerjee, op. cit. note 51; FAO, op. cit. note 34.

54. Wade, Branson, and Xiang, op. cit. note 10; China's crop residue production and use from Gao Tengyun, "Treatment and Utilization of Crop Straw and Stover in China," *Livestock Research for Rural Development*, February 2000.

55. USDA, ERS, "China's Beef Economy: Production, Marketing, Consumption, and Foreign Trade," *International Agriculture and Trade Reports: China* (Washington, DC: July 1998), p. 28.

56. FAO, op. cit. note 34; U.N. Population Division, op. cit. note 5.

57. China's economic growth from International Monetary Fund (IMF), *World Economic Outlook Database*, at www.imf.org/external/pubs/ft/weo, updated 11 April 2007; U.N. Population Division, op. cit. note 5; FAO, op. cit. note 34.

58. Micronutrient Initiative, *Double Fortification of Salt: A Technical Breakthrough to Alleviate Iron and Iodine Deficiency Disorders Around the World* (Ottawa, Canada: 2005); Alan Berg, former World Bank nutrition program manager, discussion with author, 13 March 2007.

59. Ibid.

60. Author's calculations from USDA, op. cit. note 1; U.N. Population Division, op. cit. note 5.

61. USDA, op. cit. note 1; U.N. Population Division, op. cit. note 5; FAO, op. cit. note 34.

62. Organisation for Economic Co-operation and Development, "Total Expenditure on Health Per Capita, US$ PPP," table, *OECD Health Data 2007-Frequently Requested Data*, at www.oecd.org, July 2007; FAO, op. cit. note 34.

63. Gidon Eshel and Pamela A. Martin, "Diet, Energy, and Global Warming," *Earth Interactions*, vol. 10, no. 9 (April 2006), pp. 1–17; USDA, op. cit. note 1; U.N. Population Division, op. cit. note 5.

64. Pearson and Rossingh, op. cit. note 3; Chicago Board of Trade, "Market Commentaries," at www.cbot.com, various dates; IMF, *International Financial Statistics* (Washington, DC: 2007); Missy Ryan, "Commodity Boom Eats Into Aid for World's Hungry," *Reuters*, 5 September 2007.

65. USDA, ERS, Natural Resources and Environment Division, *Agricultural Resources and Environmental Indicators, 1996–1997*, Agricultural Handbook No. 712 (Washington, DC: 1997).

Chapter 10. Designing Cities for People

1. U.N. Population Division, *World Urbanization Prospects: The 2005 Revision Population Database*, electronic database, at esa.un.org/unup, updated 2006.

2. Urban population in 1900 from Mario Polèse, "Urbanization and Development," Development Express, no. 4, 1997; U.N. Population Fund (UNFPA), *State of World Population 2007* (New York: 2007), p. 1.

3. Molly O'Meara, *Reinventing Cities for People and the Planet*, Worldwatch Paper 147 (Washington, DC: Worldwatch Institute, June 1999), pp. 14–15; U.N. Population Division, *World Population Prospects: The 2006 Revision Population Database*, electronic database, at esa.un.org/unpp, updated 2007; "The 30 Largest Urban Agglomerations Ranked By Population Size," Table A.11, in U.N. Population Division, *World Urbanization Prospects: The 2005 Revision* (New York: October 2006).

4. Christopher Flavin, "Hearing on Asia's Environmental Challenges: Testimony of Christopher Flavin," Committee on International Relations, U.S. House of Representatives, Washington, DC, 22 September 2004; Subir Bhaumik, "Air Pollution Suffocates Calcutta," *BBC News*, 3 May 2007; David Schrank and Tim Lomax, *2005 Urban Mobility Study* (College Station, TX: Texas Transportation Institute, May 2005).

5. Francesca Lyman, "Twelve Gates to the City: A Dozen Ways to Build Strong, Livable, and Sustainable Cities," *Words and Pictures Magazine*, Issue 5 (2007); Lisa Jones, "A Tale of Two Mayors: The Improbable Story of How Bogota, Colombia, Became Somewhere You Might Actually Want To Live," *Grist Magazine*, 4 April 2002.

6. Claudia Nanninga, "Energy Efficient Transport—A Solution for China," *Voices of Grassroots*, November 2004; Enrique Peñalosa, "Parks for Livable Cities: Lessons from a Radical Mayor," keynote address at the Urban Parks Institute's Great Parks/Great Cities Conference, Chicago, 30 July 2001; Susan Ives, "The Politics of Happiness," *Trust for Public Land*, 9 August 2002; Jones, op. cit. note 5.

7. Peñalosa, op. cit. note 6.

8. Jones, op. cit. note 5; O'Meara, op. cit. note 3, p. 47.

9. O'Meara, op. cit. note 3, p. 47; Walter Hook, "Bus Rapid Transit: The Unfolding Story," in Worldwatch Institute, *State of the World 2007* (New York: W. W. Norton & Company, 2007), pp. 80–81; U.N. Population Division, op. cit. note 1.

10. Los Angeles from Sandra Postel, *Last Oasis*, rev. ed. (New York: W. W. Norton & Company, 1997), p. 20; Mexico City from Joel Simon, *Endangered Mexico* (San Francisco: Sierra Club Books, 1997); Chinese Ministry of Water Resources, *Country Report of the People's Republic of China* (Marseilles, France: World Water Council, 2003), pp. 60–61.

11. U.S. Department of Agriculture, Foreign Agricultural Service, *Grain: World Markets and Trade and Oilseeds: World Markets and Trade* (Washington, DC: various issues).

12. Richard Register, "Losing the World, One Environmental Victory at a Time—And a Way to Solve That Problem," essay (Oakland, CA: Ecocity Builders, Inc., 31 August 2005); Richard Register, *Ecocities: Rebuilding Cities in Balance with Nature: Revised Edition* (Gabriola Island, BC: New Society Publishers, 2006).

13. Register, "Losing the World, One Environmental Victory at a Time," op. cit. note 12.

14. Ibid.; population estimate from U.S. Census Bureau, *Population Finder*, electronic database, at factfinder.census.gov, viewed 16 August 2007.

15. Register, "Losing the World, One Environmental Victory at a Time," op. cit. note 12.

16. See Chapter 12 for further discussion of the energy economy.

17. Jay Walljasper, "Unjamming the Future," *Ode*, October 2005, pp. 36–41; Bus Rapid Transit Policy Center, *Transport Innovator* (newsletter), vol. 3, no. 4 (July/August 2007); BRT Information Clearinghouse, "Existing BRT Programs," at path.berkeley.edu/informationclearinghouse/brt/existing.html, viewed 27 September 2007; Yingling Liu, "Bus Rapid Transit: A Step Toward Fairness in China's Urban Transportation," *China Watch* (Washington, DC: Worldwatch Institute, 9 March 2006).

18. Walljasper, op. cit. note 17; Bus Rapid Transit Policy Center, op. cit. note 17; BRT Information Clearinghouse, op. cit. note 17.

19. Molly O'Meara Sheehan, "Making Better Transportation Choices," in Lester R. Brown et al., *State of the World 2001* (New York: W. W. Norton & Company, 2001), p. 116.

20. William D. Eggers, Peter Samuel, and Rune Munk, *Combating Gridlock: How Pricing Road Use Can Ease Congestion* (New York: Deloitte, November 2003); Tom Miles, "London Drivers to Pay UK's

First Congestion Tax," *Reuters*, 28 February 2002; Randy Kennedy, "The Day the Traffic Disappeared," *New York Times Magazine*, 20 April 2003, pp. 42–45; James Savage, "Congestion Charge Returns to Stockholm," *The Local*, 1 August 2007; British sterling to dollars conversion on 16 October 2007, from www.bloomberg.com/invest/ calculators/currency.html.

21. Transport for London, *Central London Congestion Charging: Impacts Monitoring—Second Annual Report* (London: April 2004), pp. 2, 39; Transport for London, *Central London Congestion Charging: Impacts Monitoring—Fifth Annual Report* (London: July 2007), pp. 21, 22, 47.

22. Transport for London, *Fifth Annual Report*, op. cit. note 21, pp. 3, 7.

23. "Milan to Impose 'Pollution Charge' on Cars," *Reuters*, 23 July 2007; "Congestion Charging Sweeps The World—A Rash of Cities Round the Globe is Set to Travel the Same Road as London," *Guardian* (London), 15 February 2004; Aaron O. Patrick, "Life in the Faster Lane: How London Car Curbs Inspired U.S. Cities," *Wall Street Journal*, 20 July 2007.

24. Serge Schmemann, "I Love Paris on a Bus, a Bike, a Train and in Anything but a Car," *New York Times*, 26 July 2007; Katrin Bennhold, "A New French Revolution's Creed: Let Them Ride Bikes," *New York Times*, 16 July 2007.

25. Bennhold, op. cit. note 24; Alexandra Topping, "Free Wheeling: Paris's New Bike System," *Washington Post*, 23 September 2007.

26. Schmemann, op. cit. note 24; La Fédération de Paris du Parti Socialiste, ed., *Ce Que Nous Avons Fait Ensemble* (Paris: Office of Mayor Bertrand Delanoë, 2007), pp. 20-25.

27. John Ritter, "Narrowed Roads Gain Acceptance in Colo., Elsewhere," *USA Today*, 29 July 2007; John Ritter, "'Complete Streets' Program Gives More Room for Pedestrians, Cyclists," *USA Today*, 29 July 2007.

28. National Complete Streets Coalition, "Complete the Streets: Who We Are," at www.completestreets.org/whoweare.html, viewed 16 August 2007; AARP, "AARP: Creating a New Health Care Paradigm," at www.aarp.org/about_aarp/new_paradigm.html, viewed 16 August 2007; Ritter, "Narrowed Roads," op. cit. note 27.

29. Ritter, "Narrowed Roads," op. cit. note 27; Ritter, "'Complete Streets' Program," op. cit. note 27.

30. Car trip reduction is author's estimate.

31. O'Meara, op. cit. note 3, p. 45.

32. Chinese bicycle production compiled from United Nations, *Yearbook of Industrial Statistics* (New York: various years) and from *Industrial Commodity Statistics Yearbook* (New York: various years); "World Players in the Bicycle Market," table in John Crenshaw, *Bicycle Retailer and Industry News*, e-mail to Janet Larsen, Earth Policy

Institute, 8 October 2007; bicycle owners from Song Mo and Wen Chihua, "Turning Full Cycle," *China Daily*, 28 September 2006; cars in China from Ward's Automotive Group, *Ward's World Motor Vehicle Data 2006* (Southfield, MI: 2006), p. 16.

33. Percent of police forces calculated from Matthew Hickman and Brian A. Reaves, *Local Police Departments, 2003* (Washington, DC: U.S. Department of Justice, Bureau of Justice Statistics, May 2006), pp. 3, 13; arrest rate from a member of the Washington, DC, police force, discussion with author.

34. Glenn Collins, "Old Form of Delivery Thrives in New World of E-Commerce," *New York Times*, 24 December 1999.

35. O'Meara, op. cit. note 3, pp. 47–48.

36. Ibid.; Barbara McCann, "Complete the Streets!" *Planning Magazine: Special Transportation Issue*, May 2005.

37. Walljasper, op. cit. note 17; Interface for Cycling Expertise (I-ce), *Locomotives: Annual Report 2006* (Utrecht, The Netherlands: December 2006), pp. 3–4; I-ce, "Locomotives," at www.cycling.nl/frameset.htm, viewed 21 August 2007.

38. O'Meara, op. cit. note 3, pp. 47–48; Japan from author's personal observation.

39. Sunita Narain, "The Flush Toilet is Ecologically Mindless," *Down to Earth*, 28 February 2002, pp. 28–32; dead zones from U.N. Environment Programme, "Further Rise in Number of Marine 'Dead Zones'," press release (Nairobi: 19 October 2006).

40. Narain, op. cit. note 39.

41. Ibid.

42. World Health Organization, *World Health Report 2007* (Geneva: 2007), p. 4; U.N. Food and Agriculture Organization (FAO), *The State of Food Insecurity in the World 2005* (Rome: 2005).

43. U.S. Environmental Protection Agency (EPA), "Water Efficiency Technology Factshee—Composting Toilets," fact sheet (Washington, DC: September 1999); Jack Kieffer, Appalachia—Science in the Public Interest, *Humanure: Preparation of Compost from the Toilet for Use in the Garden* (Mount Vernon, KY: ASPI Publications, 1998).

44. EPA, op. cit. note 43; EPA, "Wastewater Virtual Tradeshow Technologies," at www.epa.gov/region1/assistance/ceitts/wastewater/techs.html, updated 10 September 2007.

45. EcoSanRes (ESR) and Stockholm Environment Institute (SEI), *EcoSanRes Phase 2 Project Document: 2006–2010* (Stockholm: 22 February 2006), p. 14; ESR, "Conferences," at www.ecosanres.org/news-publications.htm, updated 21 September 2007; ESR, "Ecological Sanitation Research," at www.ecosanres.org, updated 21 September 2007.

46. ESR, "China-Sweden Erdos Eco-Town Project, Dong Sheng, Inner Mon-

golia, China," at www.ecosanres.org/asia.htm, updated 21 September 2007; ESR, "Sweden-China Erdos Eco-Town Project, Dongsheng, Inner Mongolia," Fact Sheet 11 (Stockholm: May 2007); nutrients in urine from *Innovative Practices to Enhance Implementation of WSSD Targets-Swedish Initiative for Ecological Sanitation, Water and Sanitation*, Background Paper No. 20, presented at 8th Special Session of the Governing Council/ Global Ministerial Environment Forum, Jeju, South Korea, 29–31 March 2004; people lacking sanitation from U.N. Development Programme, *Human Development Report 2006* (New York: 2006), p. 33.

47. Number of compost toilets from *Innovative Practices*, op. cit. note 46; ESR and SEI, op. cit. note 45.

48. Tony Sitathan, "Bridge Over Troubled Waters," *Asia Times*, 23 August 2002; "Singapore Opens Fourth Recycling Plant to Turn Sewage into Water," *Associated Press*, 12 July 2005.

49. Peter H. Gleick, *The World's Water 2004–2005: The Biennial Report on Freshwater Resources* (Washington, DC: Island Press, 2004), p. 149.

50. Ibid.

51. "Farming in Urban Areas Can Boost Food Security," *FAO Newsroom*, 3 June 2005.

52. Ibid.

53. Jac Smit, "Urban Agriculture's Contribution to Sustainable Urbanisation," *Urban Agriculture*, August 2002, p. 13; Hubert de Bon, "Dry and Aquatic Peri-urban and Urban Horticulture in Hanoi, Vietnam," in René van Veenhuizen, ed., *Cities Farming for the Future—Urban Agriculture for Green and Productive Cities* (Philippines: ETC-Urban Agriculture, 2006), pp. 338–39.

54. Smit, op. cit. note 53, p. 13; pond coverage from Nitai Kundu et al., "Planning for Aquatic Production in East Kolkata Wetlands," in van Veenhuizen, op. cit. note 53, pp. 408–09; fish production from Stuart Bunting et al., "Urban Aquatic Production," in van Veenhuizen, op. cit. note 53, p. 386.

55. Smit, op. cit. note 53, p. 12.

56. "Gardening for the Poor," FAO Newsroom, 2004; P. Bradley and C. Marulanda, "A Study on Microgardens That Help Reduce Global Poverty and Hunger," *Acta Horticulturae (ISHS)*, vol. 742 (2007), pp. 115–23.

57. Katherine H. Brown and Anne Carter, *Urban Agriculture and Community Food Security in the United States: Farming from the City Center to the Urban Fringe* (Venice, CA: Community Food Security Coalition, October 2003), p. 10; U.N. Population Division, *World Urbanization Prospects*, op. cit. note 3.

58. Brown and Carter, op. cit. note 57, p. 7.

59. Ibid.

60. U.S. Department of Agriculture, Agricultural Monitoring Service, "Farmers Market Growth," at www.ams.usda.gov/farmersmarkets/FarmersMarketGrowth.htm, viewed 17 August 2007; 2007 figure based on past growth to 2006.

61. U.N. Population Division, *World Population Prospects*, op. cit. note 3; U.N. Population Division, *World Urbanization Prospects*, op. cit. note 3, pp. 1–5.

62. Hari Srinivas, "Defining Squatter Settlements," Global Development Research Center Web site, www.gdrc.org/uem/define-squatter.html, viewed 9 August 2005.

63. Ibid.

64. O'Meara, op. cit. note 3, p. 49.

65. Rasna Warah, *The Challenge of Slums: Global Report on Human Settlements 2003* (New York: U.N. Human Settlements Programme, 2003).

66. Srinivas, op. cit. note 62.

67. E. O. Wilson, *Biophilia* (Cambridge, MA: Harvard University Press, 1984); S. R. Kellert and E. O. Wilson, eds., *The Biophilia Hypothesis* (Washington, DC: Island Press, 1993).

68. Theodore Roszak, Mary Gomes, and Allen Kanner, eds., *Restoring the Earth, Healing the Mind* (San Francisco: Sierra Club Books, 1995).

69. Public transport ridership growth rate calculated from American Public Transportation Administration, "Unlinked Passenger Trips By Mode, Millions," in *2007 Public Transportation Factbook* (Washington, DC: 2007), p. 12.

70. Ding Guangwei and Li Shishun, "Analysis of Impetuses to Change of Agricultural Land Resources in China," *Bulletin of the Chinese Academy of Sciences*, vol. 13, no. 1 (1999).

71. Molly O'Meara Sheehan, *City Limits: Putting the Breaks on Sprawl*, Worldwatch Paper 156 (Washington, DC: Worldwatch Institute, June 2001), p. 11; Schrank and Lomax, op. cit. note 4.

72. Jim Motavalli, "The High Cost of Free Parking," *E: The Environmental Magazine*, March–April 2005; Donald Shoup, *The High Cost of Free Parking* (Chicago: American Planning Association Planners Press, 2005), p. 591; Daniel B. Klein, "Free Parking Versus Free Markets," *The Independent Review*, vol. XI, no. 2 (Fall 2006), pp. 289-97.

73. O'Meara, op. cit. note 3, p. 49; Donald C. Shoup, "Congress Okays Cash Out," *Access*, Fall 1998, pp. 2-8.

74. "Paris To Cut City Centre Traffic," *BBC News*, 15 March 2005; J. H. Crawford, "Carfree Places," at www.carfree.com, viewed 17 August 2007; see also J. H. Crawford, *Carfree Cities* (Utrecht, Netherlands: International Books, July 2000).

75. Lyndsey Layton, "Mass Transit Popularity Surges in U.S.," *Washing-*

ton Post, 30 April 2000; Bruce Younkin, manager of fleet operations, Penn State University, State College, PA, discussion with Janet Larsen, Earth Policy Institute, 4 December 2000.

Chapter 11. Raising Energy Efficiency

1. Figure of 400 ppm calculated using fossil fuel emissions from G. Marland et al., "Global, Regional, and National CO_2 Emissions," in *Trends: A Compendium of Data on Global Change* (Oak Ridge, TN: Carbon Dioxide Information and Analysis Center, Oak Ridge National Laboratory, 2007), and land use change emissions from R .A. Houghton and J. L. Hackler, "Carbon Flux to the Atmosphere from Land-Use Changes," in *Trends: A Compendium of Data on Global Change* (Oak Ridge, TN: Carbon Dioxide Information and Analysis Center, Oak Ridge National Laboratory, 2002), with decay curve cited in J. Hansen et al., "Dangerous Human-Made Interference with Climate: A GISS ModelE Study," *Atmospheric Chemistry and Physics*, vol. 7 (2007), pp. 2287–312; 384 ppm from Pieter Tans, "Trends in Atmospheric Carbon Dioxide—Mauna Loa," NOAA/ESRL, at www.esrl.noaa.gov/gmd/ccgg/trends, viewed 16 October 2007.

2. International Energy Agency (IEA), *World Energy Outlook 2006* (Paris: 2006), p. 493; electricity consumption per U.S home from U.S. Department of Energy (DOE), Energy Information Administration (EIA), *Regional Energy Profile—U.S. Household Electricity Report* (Washington, DC: July 2005).

3. IEA, op. cit. note 2; coal reduction from DOE, EIA, *International Energy Annual 2005* (Washington, DC: June–October 2007), Table E.4.

4. Bill Moore, "California Bans Future Purchase of Coal-Generated Power," *EV World*, 28 June 2007; Rebecca Smith, "Coal's Doubters Block New Wave of Power Plants," *Wall Street Journal*, 25 July 2007; California Energy Commission, "California's Major Sources of Energy," at www.energy.ca.gov, updated 10 October 2007; Matthew L. Wald, "Citing Global Warming, Kansas Denies Plant Permit," *New York Times*, 20 October 2007.

5. Steven Mufson, "Coal Rush Reverses, Power Firms Follow Plans for New Plants Stalled by Growing Opposition," *Washington Post*, 4 September 2007; James Hansen, "Why We Can't Wait," *The Nation*, 7 May 2007; Martin Griffith, "Reid Opposes New Coal-fired Power Plants Worldwide," *Las Vegas Sun*, 18 August 2007.

6. IEA, *Light's Labour's Lost: Policies for Energy-efficient Lighting* (Paris: 2006), pp. 25, 29; Larry Kinnery, *Lighting Systems in Southwestern Homes: Problems and Opportunities*, prepared for DOE, *Building America Program through the Midwest Research Institute*, National Renewable Energy Laboratory Division (Boulder, CO: Southwest Energy Efficiency Project, June 2005), pp. 4–5.

7. U.S. Environmental Protection Agency (EPA) and DOE, "Energy Star

Change a Light, Change the World: 2006 Campaign Facts and Assumptions Sheet," fact sheet (Washington, DC: 23 April 2007).

8. Ministry for the Environment and Natural Resources, "World First! Australia Slashes Greenhouse Gases from Inefficient Lighting," press release (Canberra, Australia: 20 February 2007); Rob Gillies, "Canada Announces Greenhouse Gas Targets," *Associated Press*, 25 April 2007.

9. "Alliance Calls for Only Energy-Efficient Lighting in U.S. Market By 2016, Joins Coalition Dedicated to Achieving Goal," press release (Washington, DC: Alliance to Save Energy, 14 March 2007).

10. Information on proposed and enacted legislation on light bulbs compiled from state governments by Earth Policy Institute, October 2007.

11. Ian Johnston, "Two Years to Change EU Light Bulbs," *Scotsman* (U.K.), 10 March 2007; Matt Prescott, "Light Bulbs: Not Such a Bright Idea," *BBC News*, 3 February 2006; U.K. Ban the Bulb campaign at www.banthebulb.org; James Kilner, "Moscow Tells Residents to Change Their Light Bulbs," *Reuters*, 28 February 2007.

12. IEA, op. cit. note 6, p. 375; Deborah Zabarenko, "China to Switch to Energy-Efficient Lightbulbs," *Reuters*, 3 October 2007.

13. "Greenpeace Urges India to Ban the Bulb," *Reuters*, 17 April 2007; Greenpeace India, "Greenpeace Launches a Signature Drive Against the Inefficient Bulbs in India," press release (New Delhi: 19 April 2007).

14. Philips, "Philips Calls for Action to Replace Incandescent Bulbs with Energy Saving Lamps," press release (Brussels: 7 December 2006); European Lamp Companies Federation, "European Lamp Industry Commits to a Government Shift to Energy Efficient Lighting in the Home," press release (Brussels: 1 March 2007).

15. Wal-Mart, "With Consumers Facing High Utility Costs and Environmental Challenges, Retailer Offers Simple Solution," press release (Bentonville, AR: 29 November 2006); Wal-Mart as world's biggest retailer from "Sales for World's Top 250 Retailers Show 6 Percent Gain Over Previous Year," press release (New York: Deloitte & Touche USA LLP, 11 January 2007); Hillary Osborne, "Currys to Stop Selling Incandescent Bulbs," *Guardian* (London), 13 March 2006.

16. DOE, "Energy Efficiency of White LEDs," fact sheet (Washington, DC: October 2006).

17. "Company Profile: Expanding LED Possibilities at Samsung Electro-mechanics," *LEDs Magazine*, April 2007; Anthony DePalma, "It Never Sleeps, but It's Learned to Douse the Lights," *New York Times*, 11 December 2005.

18. Energy savings from lighting efficiency calculated using IEA, op. cit. note 6, and IEA, op. cit. note 2; coal-fired power plant equivalents calculated by assuming that an average plant has a 500-megawatt capacity and operates 72 percent of the time, generating 3.15 billion kilowatt-hours of electricity per year.

19. IEA, op. cit. note 6, p. 38.

20. Steven Nadel, *The Federal Energy Policy Act of 2005 and Its Implications for Energy Efficiency Program Efforts* (Washington, DC: American Council for an Energy-Efficient Economy (ACEEE), September 2005).

21. Steven Nadel et al., *Leading the Way: Continued Opportunities for New State Appliance and Equipment Efficiency Standards* (Washington, DC: ACEEE, March 2006), p. v.

22. Jiang Lin, "One Rice-cooker, Two Cell Phones, and Three TVs: Consumer Appliances and the Energy Challenge for China," *BusinessForum China*, November/December 2005, p. 19.

23. Jiang Lin, "Appliance Efficiency Standards and Labeling Programs in China," *Annual Review of Energy and the Environment*, vol. 27 (2002), pp. 349–67.

24. U.N. Population Division, *World Population Prospects: The 2006 Revision Population Database*, at esa.un.org/unpp, updated 2007; Greenpeace, "Your Energy Savings," at www.greenpeace.org/ international/campaigns/climate-change.

25. Marianne Haug et al., *Cool Appliances: Policy Strategies for Energy Efficient Homes* (Paris: IEA, 2003).

26. Ibid.; Alan K. Meier, *A Worldwide Review of Standby Power Use in Homes* (Berkeley, CA: Lawrence Berkeley National Laboratory, 2002).

27. Lloyd Harrington et al., *Standby Energy: Building a Coherent International Policy Framework—Moving to the Next Level* (Stockholm: European Council for an Energy Efficient Economy, March 2007).

28. Meier, op. cit. note 26.

29. Projected coal-fired electricity generation in 2020 is 4,352 billion kilowatt hours more than in 2006, from IEA, op. cit. note 2, p. 493.

30. U.S. Green Building Council (USGBC), "Buildings and Climate Change," fact sheet (Washington, DC: 2007); USGBC, "Green Building Facts," fact sheet (Washington, DC: August 2007).

31. Building lifetime from Edward Mazria, "It's the Architecture, Stupid! Who Really Holds the Key to the Global Thermostat? The Answer Might Surprise You," *World and I*, May/June 2003; retrofit energy savings from Clinton Foundation, "Energy Efficiency Building Retrofit Program," fact sheet (New York: May 2007).

32. Davis Langdon, *The Cost & Benefit of Achieving Green Buildings* (Sydney: 2007).

33. USGBC, "About LEED," fact sheet (Washington, DC: 2007).

34. USGBC, "Green Building Facts," op. cit. note 30; USGBC, "LEED for New Construction" (Washington, DC: 2007).

35. USGBC, *Green Building Rating System for New Construction and Major Renovations*, Version 2.2 (Washington, DC: October 2005).

36. Ibid.

37. USGBC, "Green Building Facts," op. cit. note 30.

38. Ibid.

39. National Renewable Energy Laboratory, "The Philip Merrill Environmental Center—Highlighting High Performance" (Golden, CO: April 2002); "Toyota Seeks Gold for New Green Buildings," *GreenBiz.com*, 23 April 2003; "The Green Stamp of Approval," *Business Week*, 11 September 2006.

40. Nick Carey and Ilaina Jonas, "Feature—Green Buildings Need More Incentives in US," *Reuters*, 15 February 2007; Taryn Holowka, "World Trade Center Going for LEED Gold," *USGBC News*, 12 September 2006.

41. Carey and Jonas, op. cit. note 40.

42. Barnaby J. Feder, "Environmentally Conscious Development," *New York Times*, 25 August 2004.

43. Information on World Green Building Council at www.worldgbc.org; USGBC, op. cit. note 33.

44. Ibid.; "Clinton Unveils $5 Billion Green Makeover for Cities," *Environment News Service*, 16 May 2007.

45. "Clinton Unveils $5 Billion Green Makeover for Cities," op. cit. note 44.

46. Mazria, op. cit. note 31; information on the 2030 Challenge at www.architecture2030.org.

47. Mazria, op. cit. note 31.

48. U.N. Population Division, op. cit. note 24; Ward's Automotive Group, *World Motor Vehicle Data 2006* (Southfield, MI: 2006), p. 202.

49. U.N. Population Division, *World Urbanization Prospects: The 2005 Revision Population Database*, at esa.un.org/unup, updated 2006; Ward's Automotive Group, op. cit. note 48.

50. U.S. Bureau of the Census, "Most of Us Still Drive to Work Alone—Public Transportation Commuters Concentrated in a Handful of Large Cities," press release (Washington, DC: 13 June 2007).

51. Ken Livingstone, "Clear Up the Congestion-Pricing Gridlock," *New York Times*, 2 July 2007; pounds to dollars conversion on 16 October 2007.

52. Sara Kugler, "NYC's Taxi Fleet Going Green by 2012," *Associated Press*, 22 May 2007; City and County of San Francisco, Office of the Mayor, "Mayor Newsom Urges Taxi Commission to Approve Resolution Requiring Taxi Emissions to be Reduced by 50% Over Next Four Years," press release (San Francisco: 12 June 2007).

53. David Schrank et al., *The 2007 Urban Mobility Report* (College Station, TX: Texas Transportation Institute, September 2007).

54. Hiroki Matsumoto, "The Shinkansen: Japan's High Speed Railway,"

testimony before the Subcommittee on Railroads, Pipelines and Materials (Washington, DC: Committee on Transportation and Infrastructure, 19 April 2007).

55. Ibid.

56. Ibid.

57. Inaki Barron, "High Speed Rail: The Big Picture," testimony before the Subcommittee on Railroads, Pipelines and Materials (Washington, DC: Committee on Transportation and Infrastructure, 19 April 2007).

58. Ibid.

59. "A High-Speed Revolution," *The Economist*, 5 July 2007.

60. John L. Mica, "Opening Statement of Rep. Shuster from Today's Hearing on High Speed Rail," press release (Washington, DC: Committee on Transportation and Infrastructure, 19 April 2007.

61. "Bullet Time," *The Economist*, 17 May 2007.

62. "The People's Vote: 100 Documents that Shaped America," *U.S. News and World Report*, 22 September 2003.

63. Gerhard Metschies, "Pain at the Pump," *Foreign Policy*, July/August 2007; Ward's Automotive Group, op. cit. note 48, pp. 202, 244.

64. Fleet average from U.S. Department of Transportation, *Summary of Fuel Economy Performance* (Washington, DC: October 2006), updated to new MPG estimates using EPA, Office of Transportation and Air Quality, "EPA Issues New Test Method for Fuel Economy Window Stickers," regulatory announcement (Washington, DC: December 2006).

65. Ernst Ulrich von Weizsäcker, Amory B. Lovins, and L. Hunter Lovins, *Factor Four: Doubling Wealth, Halving Resource Use* (London: Earthscan, 1997); Friedrich Schmidt-Bleek et al., *Factor 10: Making Sustainability Accountable, Putting Resource Productivity into Praxis* (Carnoules, France: Factor 10 Club, 1998), p. 5.

66. William McDonough and Michael Braungart, *Cradle to Cradle: Remaking the Way We Make Things* (New York: North Point Press, 2002); Rebecca Smith, "Beyond Recycling: Manufacturers Embrace 'C2C' Design," *Wall Street Journal*, 3 March 2005.

67. Claude Mandil et al., *Tracking Industrial Energy Efficiency and CO_2 Emissions* (Paris: IEA, 2007), pp. 39, 59–61.

68. International Iron and Steel Institute (IISI), "Crude Steel Production by Process," World Steel in Figures 2007 at www.worldsteel.org, viewed 16 October 2007; Mandil et al., op. cit. note 67, pp. 95–96.

69. U.S. Geological Survey (USGS), "Iron and Steel Scrap," in *Mineral Commodity Summaries* (Reston, VA: U.S. Department of the Interior, 2007), pp. 86–87; "Steel Recycling Rates at a Glance," fact sheet (Pittsburgh, PA: Steel Recycling Institute, 2007); Mississippi Department of

Environmental Quality, "Recycling Trivia," at www.deq.state.ms.us, viewed 17 October 2007.

70. One fourth the energy from Mandil et al., op. cit. note 67, p. 106; cut in energy use calculated from IISI, op. cit. note 75; McKinsey Global Institute, *Curbing Global Energy Demand Growth: The Energy Productivity Opportunity* (Washington, DC: May 2007).

71. Mandil et al., op. cit. note 67, pp. 139–142; energy savings by adopting Japanese technologies from U.N. Environment Programme, *Buildings and Climate Change: Status, Challenges and Opportunities* (Paris: 2007), p. 19; energy saving from adopting dry-kiln process calculated from Mandil et al., op. cit. note 67.

72. Bus weight from John Shonsey et al., *RTD Bus Transit Facility Design Guidelines and Criteria* (Denver, CO: Regional Transportation District, February 2006); car weight from Stacy C. Davis and Susan W. Diegel, *Transportation Energy Data Book: Edition 26* (Oak Ridge, TN: Oak Ridge National Laboratory, DOE, 2007), p. 415; car-to-bus ratio from American Public Transportation Association, *The Benefits of Public Transportation–An Overview* (Washington, DC: September 2002).

73. Energy savings from using scrap instead of iron ore from Mandil et al., op. cit. note 67, p. 106.

74. "New Hampshire Town Boosts Recycling with Pay-As-You-Throw," *Environment News Service*, 21 March 2007; population data from Town of Lyme Web site, at www.lymenh.gov.

75. "New Hampshire Town Boosts Recycling with Pay-As-You-Throw," op. cit. note 74.

76. Sue McAllister, "Commercial Recycling Centers: Turning Debris into Treasure," *San Jose Mercury News*, 10 April 2007.

77. Ibid.

78. Junko Edahiro, Japan for Sustainability, e-mail to Janet Larsen, Earth Policy Institute, 16 October 2007; Tim Burt, "VW is Set for $500m Recycling Provision," *Financial Times*, 12 February 2001; Mark Magnier, "Disassembly Lines Hum in Japan's New Industry," *Los Angeles Times*, 13 May 2001.

79. Brian Hindo, "Everything Old is New Again," *BusinessWeek Online*, 25 September 2006.

80. Daniel Michaels, "Boeing and Airbus Compete to Destroy What They Built," *Wall Street Journal*, 1 June 2007.

81. Ibid.

82. "FT Report—Waste and the Environment: EU Tackles Gadget Mountain," *Financial Times*, 18 April 2007; Nokia example from Jeremy Faludi, "Pop Goes the Cell Phone," *Worldchanging*, 4 April 2006.

83. Rick Ridgeway, Vice President, Environmental Initiatives and Special Media Projects, Patagonia, Inc., discussion with author, 22 August 2006.

84. Finland in Brenda Platt and Neil Seldman, *Wasting and Recycling in the United States 2000* (Athens, GA: GrassRoots Recycling Network, 2000); Prince Edward Island Government, "PEI Bans the Can," at www.gov.pe.ca, viewed 15 August 2005.

85. Brenda Platt and Doug Rowe, *Reduce, Reuse, Refill!* (Washington, DC: Institute for Local Self-Reliance, 2002); energy in David Saphire, *Case Reopened: Reassessing Refillable Bottles* (New York: INFORM, Inc., 1994).

86. Gold production from USGS, "Gold," in *Mineral Commodity Summaries* (Reston, VA: U.S. Department of the Interior, 2005), pp. 72–73, 84–87; gold ore data calculated from New Jersey Mining Company Reserves & Resources, "Estimated Ore Reserves," at www.newjerseymining.com, updated 31 December 2006; steel ore from Mandil et al., op. cit. note 67, p. 115; CO_2 emissions calculated using Gavin M. Mudd, "Resource Consumption Intensity and the Sustainability of Gold Mining," 2nd International Conference on Sustainability Engineering and Science, Auckland, New Zealand, 20–23 February 2007; USGS, *Mineral Commodity Summaries*, electronic database at minerals.usgs.gov/products/index.html, updated January 2007; EPA, *Emission Facts: Average Annual Emissions and Fuel Consumption for Passenger Cars and Light Trucks* (Washington, DC: April 2000).

87. Catherine Ferrier, *Bottled Water: Understanding a Social Phenomenon* (Surrey, U.K.: WWF, 2001).

88. Charles Fishman, "Message in a Bottle," *Fast Company*, Issue 117 (July 2007), p. 110; Solomon quoted in Paula Hunt, "Why are We Still Guzzling that Bottled Water?" *San Antonio Express*, 8 August 2007.

89. Oil consumption calculated using number of plastic water bottles from Jennifer Gitlitz et al., *Water, Water Everywhere: The Growth of Non-carbonated Beverages in the United States* (Washington, DC: Container Recycling Institute, February 2007), and from Pacific Institute, "Bottled Water and Energy," fact sheet, (Oakland, CA: 2007).

90. Bill Marsh, "A Battle Between the Bottle and the Faucet," *New York Times*, 15 July 2007; Cecilia M. Vega, "Mayor to Cut Off Flow of City Money for Bottled Water," *San Francisco Chronicle*, 22 June 2007; Doug Smeath, "Rocky Wants to Deep-Six H_2O Bottles," *Deseret Morning News*, 22 June 2007; Ross C. Anderson, Salt Lake City Mayor, national press telephone conference, Think Outside the Bottle Campaign, 9 October 2007.

91. IEA, op. cit. note 2, p. 492; IEA, op. cit. note 6.

92. Mandil et al., op. cit. note 67, pp. 39, 59–61, 95–96, 139–42.

Chapter 12. Turning to Renewable Energy

1. Christoph Podewils, "There's a Lot of Water in the Wine: Renewable Energy Lobby Criticizes the EU's Highly Praised Goal for Alternative Energy," *PHOTON International*, April 2007, p. 14; Global Wind

Energy Council (GWEC) and Greenpeace, *Global Wind Energy Outlook 2006* (Brussels: 2006); U.S. Department of Energy (DOE), Energy Information Administration (EIA), *Electric Power 2006* (Washington, DC: October 2007), p. 26.

2. "Texas Decision Could Double Wind Power Capacity in the U.S.," *Renewable Energy Access*, 4 October 2007; coal-fired power plant equivalents calculated by assuming that an average plant has a 500-megawatt capacity and operates 72 percent of the time, generating 3.15 billion kilowatt-hours of electricity per year; an average wind turbine operates 36 percent of the time; Iceland geothermal usage from Iceland National Energy Authority and Ministries of Industry and Commerce, *Geothermal Development and Research in Iceland* (Reykjavik, Iceland: April 2006), p. 16; European per person consumption from European Wind Energy Association (EWEA), "Wind Power on Course to Become Major European Energy Source by the End of the Decade," press release (Brussels: 22 November 2004); China's solar water heaters calculated from Renewable Energy Policy Network for the 21st Century (REN21), *Renewables Global Status Report, 2006 Update* (Washington, DC: Worldwatch Institute, 2006), p. 21, and from Bingham Kennedy, Jr., *Dissecting China's 2000 Census* (Washington, DC: Population Reference Bureau, June 2001); Philippines from Geothermal Energy Association (GEA), "World Geothermal Power Up 50%, New US Boom Possible," press release (Washington, DC: 11 April 2002).

3. International Telecommunications Union, "Mobile Cellular Subscribers per 100 People," *ICT Statistics Database*, at www.itu.int/ITU-D/icteye, updated 2007; Molly O. Sheehan, "Mobile Phone Use Booms," Worldwatch Institute, *Vital Signs 2002* (New York: W. W. Norton & Company, 2002), p. 85.

4. Personal computer data from Computer Industry Almanac Inc, "25-Year PC Anniversary Statistics," press release, at www.c-i-a.com, 14 August 2006; solar cell production (sales) from Worldwatch Institute, *Vital Signs 2005*, CD-Rom (Washington, DC: 2005); Paul Maycock, Prometheus Institute, *Photovoltaic News*, vol. 26, no. 3 (March 2007), p. 6, and previous issues.

5. Cristina L. Archer and Mark Z. Jacobson, "Evaluation of Global Windpower," *Journal of Geophysical Research*, vol. 110 (30 June 2005); Jean Hu et al., "Wind: The Future is Now," *Renewable Energy World*, July–August 2005, p. 212.

6. D. L. Elliott, L. L. Wendell, and G. L. Gower, *An Assessment of the Available Windy Land Area and Wind Energy Potential in the Contiguous United States* (Richland, WA: Pacific Northwest Laboratory, 1991); C. L. Archer and M. Z. Jacobson, "The Spatial and Temporal Distributions of U.S. Winds and Wind Power at 80 m Derived from Measurements," *Journal of Geophysical Research*, 16 May 2003.

7. W. Musial and S. Butterfield, *Future of Offshore Wind Energy in the United States* (Golden, CO: DOE, National Renewable Energy Labo-

ratory (NREL), June 2004); U.S. electricity consumption from DOE, EIA, *Electric Power Annual 2005* (Washington, DC: November 2006); Garrad Hassan and Partners, *Sea Wind Europe* (London: Greenpeace, March 2004).

8. "Wind Market Global Status 2007," *Windpower Monthly,* March 2007, p. 37; GWEC, "Global Wind Energy Markets Continue to Boom—2006 Another Record Year," press release (Brussels: 2 February 2007).

9. GWEC, *Global Wind 2006 Report* (Brussels: 2007), p. 7; share of wind generated electricity in Denmark calculated using BP, *Statistical Review of World Energy 2007* (London: 2007), and GWEC, op. cit. this note, p. 4, with capacity factor from NREL, *Power Technologies Energy Data Book* (Golden, CO: DOE, August 2006); Germany statistics from Janet L. Sawin, "Wind Power Blowing Strong," in Worldwatch Institute, *Vital Signs 2006–2007* (New York: W. W. Norton & Company, 2006).

10. Flemming Hansen, "Denmark to Increase Wind Power to 50% by 2025, Mostly Offshore," *Renewable Energy Access,* 5 December 2006.

11. GWEC, op. cit. note 9.

12. Laurie Jodziewicz, American Wind Energy Association (AWEA), e-mail to author, 16 October 2007; GWEC and Greenpeace, op. cit. note 1.

13. A 2-megawatt wind turbine operating 36 percent of the time generates 6.3 million kilowatt-hours of electricity per year; capacity factor from NREL, op. cit. note 9; wholesale electricity price from DOE, *Wholesale Market Data,* electronic database at www.eia.doe.gov/cneaf/electricity, updated 4 October 2007; wind royalties are author's estimates based on Union of Concerned Scientists, "Farming the Wind: Wind Power and Agriculture," at www.ucsusa.org/clean_energy.

14. Renewable Fuels Association (RFA), *Homegrown for the Homeland: Ethanol Industry Outlook 2005* (Washington, DC: 2005); corn per acre and ethanol per bushel approximated from Allen Baker et al., "Ethanol Reshapes the Corn Market," *Amber Waves,* vol. 4, no. 2 (April 2006), pp. 32, 34.

15. Godfrey Chua, "Wind Power 2005 in Review, Outlook for 2006 and Beyond," *Renewable Energy Access,* 6 January 2006.

16. United States and Spain from GWEC, op. cit. note 9; "Spanish Wind Power Industry Attacks New Rules," *Reuters,* 2 February 2007; "EWEA Aims for 22% of Europe's Electricity by 2030," *Wind Directions* (November/December 2006), p. 34; a 1-megawatt wind turbine operating 36 percent of the time generates 3.15 million kilowatt-hours and the average U.S. home consumes 10,000 kilowatt-hours per year; average energy consumption per U.S. home from DOE, EIA, *Regional Energy Profile—U.S. Household Electricity Report* (Washington, DC: July 2005); capacity factor from NREL, op. cit. note 9.

17. Carl Levesque, "Wind Companies Make $10 Billion Investment Com-

mitment," *Wind Energy Weekly*, vol. 25, no. 1211 (6 October 2006); "Texas Decision Could Double Wind Power Capacity in the U.S.," op. cit. note 2.

18. Paul Klein, Media Relations Group, Southern California Edison, discussion with Jonathan Dorn, Earth Policy Institute, 22 October 2007; Jim Dehlsen, Clipper Wind, discussion with author, 30 May 2001; wind farm proposals from Kathy Belyeu, AWEA, discussion with Jonathan Dorn, Earth Policy Institute, 22 October 2007.

19. "British Columbia," *WT News*, Wind Today, 1st Quarter 2007, p. 30; "UK Plans World's Biggest Offshore Windfarm," *Reuters*, 18 May 2007; Yang Jianxiang, "China Showing All Signs of Major Market Status," *Windpower Monthly*, March 2007, p.38; Germany offshore wind from EWEA, *Wind Force 12* (Brussels: 2002); "China to Build Offshore Wind Complex," *Associated Press*, 15 August 2005.

20. Mike Jacobs, "U.S. States Hatch Solution to Transmission 'Chicken-Egg' Dilemma," *Renewable Energy Access*, 7 May 2007.

21. Ibid.; Leonard Anderson, "Western U.S. States Plan Major Power System," *Reuters*, 5 April 2005; Carl Levesque, "SPP Study Envisions Transmission Project Linking 13,000 MW of Wind with East," *Wind Energy Weekly*, vol. 26, no. 1247 (6 July 2007); Carl Levesque, "Now Proposed at PUC, CAPX 2020 Transmission Project Would Have Big Wind Implications," *Wind Energy Weekly*, vol. 26, no, 1253 (17 August 2007).

22. "Pan-European Wind Energy Grid Proposed," *Renewable Energy Access*, 10 May 2006; "Airtricity and ABB Push for European Offshore Supergrid," *Wind Directions*, July/August 2006, p. 7; Chris Veal, *European Offshore Supergrid Proposal: Vision and Executive Summary* (Dublin: Airtricity, 2006); an average European home consumes 5,000 kilowatt-hours of electricity per year, from *State of the Environment in the South West 2006* (Rotherham, U.K.: Environment Agency, 2006), p. 22.

23. Wind capacity from GWEC, op. cit. note 9, pp. 4, 8; population data from U.N. Population Division, *World Population Prospects: The 2006 Revision Population Database*, at esa.un.org/unpp, updated 2007.

24. Ward's Automotive Group, *World Motor Vehicle Data 2006* (Southfield, MI: Ward's Automotive Group, 2006), p. 218; price of installed wind turbine from Windustry, "How Much Do Wind Turbines Cost?," at www.windustry.org, viewed 21 October 2007; "Trillions in Spending Needed to Meet Global Oil and Gas Demand, Analysis Shows," *International Herald Tribune*, 15 October 2007.

25. Harry Braun, *The Phoenix Project: Shifting from Oil to Hydrogen with Wartime Speed*, prepared for the Renewable Hydrogen Roundtable, World Resources Institute, Washington, DC, 10–11 April 2003, pp. 3–4.

26. Christian Parenti, "Big is Beautiful," *The Nation*, 7 May 2007.

27. Prius mileage based on new Environmental Protection Agency (EPA)

estimates at www.fueleconomy.gov, viewed 23 August 2007; fleet average from Robert M. Heavenrich, *Light Duty Automotive Technology and Fuel Economy Trends: 1975 Through 2007* (Washington, DC: EPA, Office of Transportation and Air Quality, September 2007).

28. Fuel savings are author's estimates updated from Lester R. Brown, "The Short Path to Oil Independence," *Eco-Economy Update* (Washington, DC: Earth Policy Institute, 13 October 2004); Lionel Laurent, "Boeing's Dreamliner, Airbus's Nightmare," *Forbes*, 9 July 2007; cost of electricity equivalent to a gallon of gas from Roger Duncan, "Plug-In Hybrids: Pollution-Free Transport on the Horizon," *Solar Today*, May/June 2007, p. 46.

29. Amory B. Lovins et al., *Winning the Oil Endgame: Innovation for Profits, Jobs, and Security* (Snowmass, CO: Rocky Mountain Institute, 2004), p. 64.

30. Michael Kintner-Meyer et al., *Impacts Assessment of Plug-in Hybrid Vehicles on Electric Utilities and Regional U.S. Power Grids —Part 1: Technical Analysis* (Richland, WA: DOE, Pacific Northwest National Laboratory, 2006).

31. Randy Swisher, AWEA, e-mail to author, 16 October 2007.

32. Joseph Romm and Peter Fox-Penner, *Plugging into the Grid: How Plug-in Hybrid Electric Vehicles Can Help Break America's Oil Addiction and Slow Global Warming* (Washington, DC: Progressive Policy Institute, 2007); Roger Duncan, "Plug-In Hybrids: Pollution-Free Transport on the Horizon," *Solar Today*, May/June 2007, p. 47.

33. Martin Crutsinger, "U.S. Trade Deficit a Record 6.5% of Economy," *Associated Press*, 15 March 2007.

34. Lisa Braithwaite, Plug-In Partners National Campaign, e-mail to Jonathan Dorn, Earth Policy Institute, 19 October 2007.

35. Ben Hewitt, "Plug-in Hybrid Electric Cars. How They'll Solve the Fuel Crunch," *Popular Mechanics*, May 2007; Pacific Gas and Electric Company, *Greening Fleets with New Technologies*, at www.pge.com/about_us/environment, viewed 20 October 2007.

36. General Motors (GM), "Fuel Solutions," at www.chevrolet.com/electriccar, viewed 23 October 2007; percent of Americans who live within 20 miles of their workplace from Plug-In Partners National Campaign, *Building a Market for Gas-Optional Flexible-Fuel Hybrids*, brochure (Austin, TX: 2007).

37. China water heaters calculated from REN21, op. cit. note 2, p. 21; Kennedy, Jr., op. cit. note 2; Ryan Hodum, "Kunming Heats Up as China's 'Solar City'," *China Watch* (Washington, DC: Worldwatch Institute and Global Environmental Institute, 5 June 2007); tripling of solar water heaters from Emma Graham-Harrison, "China Solar Power Firm Sees 25 Percent Growth," *Reuters*, 4 October 2007.

38. Rooftop solar water heaters have a capacity of 0.7 kilowatts per square meter and a capacity factor similar to rooftop photovoltaics

(22 percent); nominal capacity from European Solar Thermal Industry Federation (ESTIF), "Worldwide Capacity of Solar Thermal Energy Greatly Underestimated," *ESTIF News* (10 November 2004); capacity factor from NREL, op. cit. note 9.

39. Ole Pilgaard, *Solar Thermal Action Plan for Europe* (Brussels, Belgium: ESTIF, 2007); Janet L. Sawin, "Solar Industry Stays Hot," in Worldwatch Institute, op. cit. note 9, p. 38.

40. Pilgaard, op. cit. note 39; Sawin, op. cit. note 39.

41. Uwe Brechlin, "Study on Italian Solar Thermal Reveals a Surprisingly High Contribution to EU Market: 130 MWth in 2006," press release (Brussels: ESTIF, 24 April 2007); Sawin, op. cit. note 39; Les Nelson, "Solar-Water Heating Resurgence Ahead?" *Solar Today*, May/June 2007, p. 28; Pilgaard, op. cit. note 39.

42. Nelson, op. cit. note 41, p. 27.

43. Japan solar heating from Sawin, op. cit. note 39; population data from U.N. Population Division, op. cit. note 23.

44. Population data from U.N. Population Division, op. cit. note 23; China calculated from REN21, *Renewables 2005 Global Status Report* (Washington, DC: REN21 Secretariat and Worldwatch Institute, 2006); REN21, op. cit. note 2, p. 21; Turkey from Sawin, op. cit. note 39; nominal capacity from ESTIF, op. cit. note 38.

45. Nelson, op. cit. note 41, p. 26.

46. Ibid., p. 28.

47. Solar cell installations and growth rate calculated from Worldwatch Institute, op. cit. note 4; Maycock, op. cit. note 4; Anne Kreutzmann et al., "Exceeding Expectations: Survey Indicates more than 1 GW Installed in Germany in 2006," *PHOTON International*, April 2007.

48. Travis Bradford, "23rd Annual Data Collection—Final," *PV News*, vol. 26, no. 4 (April 2007), p. 9; Travis Bradford, "World Cell Production Grows 40% in 2006," *PV News*, vol. 26, no. 3 (March 2007), pp. 6–8.

49. International Energy Agency (IEA), *World Energy Outlook 2006* (Paris: 2006); "Power to the Poor," *The Economist*, 10 February 2001, pp. 21–23.

50. "Solar Loans Light Up Rural India," *BBC News*, 29 April 2007.

51. IEA, *Light's Labour's Lost: Policies for Energy-efficient Lighting* (Paris: 2006), pp. 201–02; Kuwait oil production from DOE, EIA, *International Petroleum Monthly*, at www.eia.doe.gov/emeu, updated 12 October 2007.

52. Christoph Podewils, "As Cheap as Brown Coal: By 2010, a kWh of PV Electricity in Spain Will Cost Around 9¢ to Produce," *PHOTON International*, April 2007.

53. Solar cell production (sales) from Worldwatch Institute, op. cit. note

4; Maycock, op. cit. note 4; people who lack electricity from IEA, op. cit. note 49.

54. Sybille de La Hamaide, "Bangladesh Seeks World Bank Loan for Solar Power," *Reuters*, 26 April 2007.

55. Dana Childs, "South Korea Building Largest Solar Installation in World," *Inside Greentech*, 10 May 2007; "Santander and BP Solar Partner in Major Euro Photovoltaic Project," *Green Car Congress*, 24 April 2006; Google, Solar Panel Projects at www.google.com/corporate, updated 20 October 2007; "Google Sets Precedent for Clean Business Practices," *Renewable Energy Access*, 23 October 2006.

56. Sawin, op. cit. note 39; Sara Parker, "Maryland Expands RPS: 1,500 MW Solar by 2022," *Renewable Energy Access*, 12 April 2007.

57. "Largest Solar Thermal Plant in 16 Years Now Online," *Energy Efficiency and Renewable Energy News*, 13 June 2007; Asjylyn Loder et al., "FPL Unveils Plans for a Solar Plant," *St. Petersburg Times*, 27 September 2007.

58. Georg Brakmann et al., *Concentrated Solar Thermal Power—Now!* (Brussels: European Solar Thermal Power Industry Association, 2005).

59. "Algeria Aims to Export Power —Solar Power," *Associated Press*, 11 August 2007; "Algeria Plans to Develop Solar Power for Export," *Reuters*, 19 June 2007.

60. "Algeria Aims to Export Power—Solar Power," op. cit. note 59.

61. Charles F. Kutscher, *Tackling Climate Change in the U.S.—Potential Carbon Emissions Reductions from Energy Efficiency and Renewable Energy by 2030* (Boulder, CO: American Solar Energy Society, 2007).

62. Brakmann et al., op. cit. note 58.

63. Karl Gawell et al., *International Geothermal Development Directory and Resource Guide* (Washington, DC: GEA, 2003); REN21, op. cit. note 2, p. 17.

64. Geothermal growth rate calculated using Eric Martinot, Tsinghua-BP Clean Energy Research and Education Center, e-mail to Joseph Florence, Earth Policy Institute, 12 April 2007, and REN21, op. cit. note 44; Philippines geothermal electricity from "World Geothermal Power Up 50%, New US Boom Possible," press release (Washington, DC: GEA, 11 April 2002); total number of countries with geothermal power from Karl Gawell et al., *2007 Interim Report: Update on World Geothermal Development* (Washington, DC: GEA, 1 May 2007), p. 1; El Salvador geothermal electricity from Ruggero Bertani, "World Geothermal Generation 2001–2005: State of the Art," *Proceeding of the World Geothermal Congress* (Antalya, Turkey: 24–29 April 2005), p. 3.

65. Jefferson Tester et al., *The Future of Geothermal Energy: Impact of Enhanced Geothermal Systems (EGS) on the United States in the 21st Century* (Cambridge, MA: Massachusetts Institute of Technology,

2006); John W. Lund and Derek H. Freeston, "World-Wide Direct Uses of Geothermal Energy 2000," *Geothermics*, vol. 30 (2001), pp. 34, 46, 51, 53.

66. Tester et al., op. cit. note 65.

67. U.S. projects from Gawell et al., op. cit. note 64, p. 11; Japan from Hal Kane, "Geothermal Power Gains," in Lester R. Brown et al., *Vital Signs 1993* (New York: W. W. Norton & Company, 1993), p. 54; DOE, EIA, "Japan," *EIA Country Analysis Brief* (Washington, DC: updated August 2004).

68. Peter Janssen, "The Too Slow Flow: Why Indonesia Could Get All Its Power From Volcanoes—But Doesn't," *Newsweek*, 20 September 2004.

69. World Bank, "Geothermal Energy," prepared under the PB Power and World Bank partnership program, www.worldbank.org, viewed 23 January 2003.

70. Iceland National Energy Authority and Ministries of Industry and Commerce, *Geothermal Development and Research in Iceland* (Reykjavik, Iceland: April 2006), p. 16; World Bank, op. cit. note 69.

71. Lund and Freeston, op. cit. note 65, pp. 34, 51, 53.

72. World Bank, op. cit. note 69.

73. Ibid.

74. Lund and Freeston, op. cit. note 65, pp. 46, 53.

75. U.N. Population Division, op. cit. note 23.

76. Kutscher, op. cit. note 61, p. 118; EIA, "Net Generation by Other Renewables," at www.eia.gov/cneaf, updated 10 October 2007.

77. Swedish Energy Agency, *Energy in Sweden 2005* (Eskilstuna, Sweden: November 2005), p. 37.

78. Population data from U.S. Bureau of the Census, *State & County Quickfacts*, electronic database, at quickfacts.census.gov, updated 31 August 2007; Anders Rydaker, "Biomass for Electricity & Heat Production," presentation at Bioenergy North America 2007, Chicago, IL, 16 April 2007.

79. World Alliance for Decentralized Energy, *Bagasse Cogeneration— Global Review and Potential* (Washington, DC: June 2004), p. 32; sugar production from U.S. Department of Agriculture (USDA), *Commodities and Products*, electronic database, at www.fas .usda.gov/commodities, updated May 2007.

80. Waste to Energy Conference, "Power and Heat for Millions of Europeans," press release, (Bremen, Germany: 20 April 2007).

81. Robin Pence, "AES AgriVerde: An AES-AgCert Joint Venture," fact sheet (Arlington, VA: AES Corporation, May 2006).

82. Ray C. Anderson, presentation at Chicago Climate Exchange, Chica-

go, IL, 14 June 2006.

83. F.O. Licht, "World Fuel Ethanol Production," *World Ethanol and Bio-fuels Report*, vol. 5, no. 17 (8 May 2007), p. 354; F.O. Licht, "World-Biodiesel Production (tonnes)," *World Ethanol and Biofuels Report*, vol. 5, no. 14 (23 March 2007), p. 291.

84. F.O. Licht, "World Fuel Ethanol Production," op. cit. note 83; RFA, *Ethanol Biorefinery Locations*, at www.ethanolrfa.org, updated 28 September 2007.

85. Fiona Harvey et al., "Biofuels Growth Hit by Soaring Price of Grain," *Financial Times*, 22 February 2007; Nigel Hunt, "Biofuel Bandwagon Slows as Feedstock Prices Surge," *Reuters*, 5 October 2007; Bill Guerin, "European Blowback for Asian Biofuels," *Asia Times*, 8 February 2007.

86. USDA, *Biomass as Feedstock for a Bioenergy and Bioproducts Industry: The Technical Feasibility of a Billion-Ton Annual Supply* (Washington, DC: April 2005).

87. Kutscher, op. cit. note 61, p. 127.

88. IEA, op. cit. note 49, pp. 219, 479; IEA, *Member Countries and Countries Beyond the OECD*, electronic database, at www.iea.org/Textbase, viewed 20 October 2007; International Rivers Network, "Frequently Asked Questions about Dams," fact sheet (Berkeley, CA: 2004).

89. "Rural Areas Get Increased Hydro Power Capacity," *Xinhua*, 7 May 2007.

90. Choe Sang-Hun, "South Korea Seeks Cleaner Energy Sources," *International Herald Tribune*, 9 May 2007; Choe Sang-Hun, "As Tides Ebb and Rise, South Korea Prepares to Snare Them," *International Herald Tribune*, 31 May 2007.

91. "China Endorses 300 MW Ocean Energy Project," *Renewable Energy Access*, 2 November 2004, "Company Plans 200-Megawatt Tidal Power Plant in New Zealand," *Energy Efficiency and Renewable Energy News*, 29 November 2006; Sang-Hun, "As Tides Ebb and Rise," op. cit. note 90.

92. Sang-Hun, "As Tides Ebb and Rise," op. cit. note 90; Igor Veletminsky, "Anatoly Chubais Wants Russia to Lead the World in Tidal Power," *FreeEnergy.ca*, 26 February 2007, at www.freeenergy.ca/news.

93. "Company Plans 200-Megawatt Tidal Power Plant in New Zealand," op. cit. note 91; Oceana Energy Company, "Oceana Subsidiary Signs Collaborative Agreement with PG&E, City of San Francisco," press release (Washington, DC: 19 June 2007); Dan Power, Oceana Energy Company, discussion with Jonathan Dorn, Earth Policy Institute, 22 October 2007.

94. Robert Silgardo et al., *Finavera Renewables Inc.: Where There is Wind There is a Wave* (Toronto, ON: Dundee Securities Corporation, 18 June 2007); Federal Energy Regulatory Commission, *Hydrokinet-*

ics— Issued and Pending Permits, electronic database, at www.ferc.gov/industries, updated 6 August 2007.

95. "Wave Hub Names Fourth Developer for Wave Energy Farm," *Renewable Energy Access*, 15 May 2007; European Commission, *Report on the Workshop on Hydropower and Ocean Energy—Part I: Ocean Energy*, 13 June 2007, pp. 1, 3; IEA, op. cit. note 88.

96. Lila Buckley, "Hydropower in China: Participation and Energy Diversity Are Key," *China Watch* (Washington, DC: Worldwatch Institute and Global Environmental Institute, 24 April 2007); "Rural Areas Get Increased Hydro Power Capacity," op. cit. note 89; Pallavi Aiyar, "China: Another Dammed Gorge," *Asia Times*, 3 June 2006; Gary Duffy, "Brazil Gives Amazon Dams Go-Ahead," *BBC News*, 10 July 2007; Patrick McCully, *Before the Deluge: Coping with Floods in a Changing Climate* (Berkeley, CA: International Rivers Network, 2007), pp. 22–23.

97. Table 12–1 by Earth Policy Institute, with 2020 projections cited throughout chapter and with 2006 figures calculated using the following sources: rooftop solar electric systems in Worldwatch Institute, op. cit. note 4, and Maycock, op. cit. note 4; wind from GWEC, op. cit. note 8; geothermal from Gawell et al., op. cit. note 64, and from REN21, op. cit. note 2; biomass from REN21, op. cit. note 2; hydropower, including tidal and wave, from IEA, *Renewables in Global Energy Supply: An IEA Fact Sheet*, pp.13, 25, at www.iea.org/textbase; rooftop solar water and space heaters from IEA, *Solar Heating and Cooling Program, Solar Heat Worldwide: Markets and Contribution to the Energy Supply 2005* (Paris: April 2007); REN21, op. cit. note 2; REN21, op. cit. note 44; geothermal from Tester et al., op. cit. note 65, p. 9.

98. GM, op. cit. note 36.

99. Bureau of Transportation Statistics, *Freight in America: A New National Picture* (Washington, DC: January 2006), pp. 7, 28.

100. Ashlea Ebeling, "What Would You Pay to Stay Cool?" *Forbes*, 15 August 2007.

Chapter 13. The Great Mobilization

1. "New Zealand Commits to 90% Renewable Electricity by 2025," *Renewable Energy Access*, 26 September 2007; carbon sequestration calculated using Vattenfall, *Global Mapping of Greenhouse Gas Abatement Opportunities up to 2030: Forestry Sector Deep-Dive* (Stockholm: June 2007), p. 16.

2. Greenland sea level rise from U.N. Environment Programme, *Global Outlook for Ice and Snow* (Nairobi: 2007), p. 103.

3. Dahle, discussion with author, State of the World Conference, Aspen, CO, 22 July 2001.

4. Redefining Progress, *The Economists' Statement on Climate Change*

(Oakland, CA: 1997).

5. Nicholas Stern, *The Stern Review on the Economics of Climate Change* (London: HM Treasury, 2006), p. 27.

6. Centers for Disease Control and Prevention, *Sustaining State Programs for Tobacco Control: Data Highlights 2006* (Atlanta, GA: 2006).

7. Cigarette death toll from World Health Organization, "Chronic Obstructive Pulmonary Disease (COPD)," fact sheet (Geneva: November 2006); Campaign for Tobacco Free Kids, "Top Combined State-Local Cigarette Tax Rates," fact sheet (Washington, DC: Campaign for Tobacco Free Kids, 1 July 2007); Campaign for Tobacco-Free Kids, "Raising Cigarette Taxes Reduces Smoking, Especially Among Kids (And the Cigarette Companies Know It)," fact sheet (Washington, DC: Campaign for Tobacco Free Kids, 11 June 2007).

8. Carbon content of fuels from Oak Ridge National Laboratory (ORNL), Bioenergy Conversion Factors, at bioenergy.ornl.gov/papers/misc/energy_conv.html, viewed 15 October 2007.

9. Gasoline indirect cost calculated based on International Center for Technology Assessment (ICTA), *The Real Price of Gasoline*, Report No. 3 (Washington, DC: 1998), p. 34, and updated using ICTA, *Gasoline Cost Externalities Associated with Global Climate Change: An Update to CTA's Real Price of Gasoline Report* (Washington, DC: September 2004), ICTA, *Gasoline Cost Externalities: Security and Protection Services: An Update to CTA's Real Price of Gasoline Report* (Washington, DC: January 2005), Terry Tamminen, *Lives Per Gallon: The True Cost of Our Oil Addiction* (Washington, DC: Island Press, 2006), p. 60, and Bureau for Economic Analysis, "Table 3—Price Indices for Gross Domestic Product and Gross Domestic Purchases," *GDP and Other Major Series, 1929–2007* (Washington, DC: August 2007); U.S. Department of Energy (DOE), Energy Information Administration (EIA), *This Week in Petroleum* (Washington, DC: various issues).

10. American Petroleum Institute, *State Gasoline Tax Report* (Washington DC: August 2007); DOE, EIA, "Weekly (Monday) Retail Premium Gasoline Prices, Selected Countries," at www.eia.doe.gov/emeu, updated 9 July 2007; Gerhard Metschies, "Pain at the Pump," *Foreign Policy*, July/August 2007.

11. U.S. Department of Agriculture, Economic Research Service, "Cigarette Price Increase Follows Tobacco Pact," *Agricultural Outlook*, January–February 1999.

12. DOE, op. cit. note 10; carbon tax equivalent calculated using DOE, EIA, *Emissions of Greenhouse Gasses in the United States 2001* (Washington, DC: 2002), p. B–1; DOE EIA, *Annual Energy Review 2006* (Washington, DC: 2007), p. 359.

13. Markus Knigge and Benjamin Gorlach, *Effects of Germany's Ecological Tax Reforms on the Environment, Employment and Technologi-*

cal Innovation: Summary of the Final Report of the Project (Berlin: Ecologic Institute for International and European Environmental Policy, August 2005); German Wind Energy Association, *A Clean Issue— Wind Energy in Germany* (Berlin: May 2006), p. 4; Donald W. Aitken, "Germany Launches its Transition: How One of the Most Advanced Industrial Nations is Moving to 100 Percent Energy from Renewable Sources," *Solar Today*, March/April 1005, pp. 26–29.

14. Estimate of Swedish tax shifting based on Paul Ekins and Stefan Speck, "Environmental Tax Reform in Europe: Energy Tax Rates and Competitiveness," in press, 2007; Ministry of Finance, Sweden, "Taxation and the Environment," press release (Stockholm: 25 May 2005); household size from Target Group Index, "Household Size," Global TGI Barometer (Miami: 2005); population from U.N. Population Division, *World Population Prospects: The 2006 Revision Population Database*, at esa.un.org/unpp, updated 2007; Andrew Hoerner and Benoît Bosquet, *Environmental Tax Reform: The European Experience* (Washington, DC: Center for a Sustainable Economy, 2001); European Environment Agency, *Environmental Taxes: Recent Developments in Tools for Integration*, Environmental Issues Series No. 18 (Copenhagen: 2000); environmental tax support from David Malin Roodman, *The Natural Wealth of Nations* (New York: W. W. Norton & Company, 1998), p. 243.

15. "New Hampshire Town Boosts Recycling with Pay-As-You-Throw," *Environment News Service*, 21 March 2007; Tom Miles, "London Drivers to Pay UK's First Congestion Tax," *Reuters*, 28 February 2002; Energy Council, *Energy Efficiency Policies and Indicators* (London: 2001), Annex 1; Howard W. French, "A City's Traffic Plans Are Snarled by China's Car Culture," *New York Times*, 12 July 2005.

16. N. Gregory Mankiw, "Gas Tax Now!" *Fortune*, 24 May 1999, pp. 60–64.

17. Australia in John Tierney, "A Tale of Two Fisheries," *New York Times Magazine*, 27 August 2000; South Australian Southern Zone Rock Lobster Fishery Management Committee, *Southern Zone Rock Lobster Annual Report 2005–2006* (Adelaide, South Australia: October 2006), p. 2.

18. Edwin Clark, letter to author, 25 July 2001.

19. André de Moor and Peter Calamai, *Subsidizing Unsustainable Development* (San José, Costa Rica: Earth Council, 1997); Barbara Crossette, "Subsidies Hurt Environment, Critics Say Before Talks," *New York Time*, 23 June 1997.

20. World Bank, *World Development Report 2003* (New York: Oxford University Press, 2003), pp. 30, 142; International Energy Agency (IEA), *World Energy Outlook 2006* (Paris: 2006), p. 279.

21. Belgium, France, and Japan from Seth Dunn, "King Coal's Weakening Grip on Power," *World Watch*, September/October 1999, pp. 10–19; coal subsidy reduction in Germany from Robin Pomeroy, "EU Minis-

ters Clear German Coal Subsidies," *Reuters*, 10 June 2002; DOE, EIA, *International Energy Annual 2005* (Washington, DC: June–October 2007), Table E.4; Craig Whitlock, "German Hard-Coal Production to Cease by 2018," *Washington Post*, 30 July 2007; China, Indonesia, and Nigeria subsidy cuts from GTZ Transport Policy Advisory Service, *International Fuel Prices 2007* (Eschborn, Germany: April 2007), p. 3.

22. John Whitelegg and Spencer Fitz-Gibbon, *Aviation's Economic Downside*, 3rd ed. (London: Green Party of England & Wales, 2003); dollar conversion based on August 2007 exchange rate in International Monetary Fund, "Representative Exchange Rates for Selected Currencies in August 2007," *Exchange Rate Archives by Month*, at www.imf.org/external, viewed 16 August 2007; U.N. Population Division, op. cit. note 14.

23. Doug Koplow, *Subsidies in the U.S. Energy Sector: Magnitude, Causes, and Options for Reform* (Cambridge, MA: Earth Track, November 2006).

24. Fishery subsidy value includes "bad" subsidies and fuel subsidies as estimated in Fisheries Center, University of British Columbia, *Catching More Bait: A Bottom-Up Re-Estimation of Global Fisheries Subsidies* (2nd Version) (Vancouver, BC: The Fisheries Center, 2006), p. 21.

25. Table 13–1 calculated with fossil fuel and transport carbon reductions using IEA, op. cit. note 20, p. 493, industry reductions using IEA, *Tracking Industrial Energy Efficiency and CO_2 Emissions* (Paris: IEA, 2007), avoided deforestation and aforestation reductions from Vattenfall, op. cit. note 1, and soil carbon sequestration based on conservative estimates in Rattan Lal, "Soil Carbon Sequestration Impacts on Global Climate Change and Food Security," *Science*, vol. 304 (11 June 2004), pp. 1623–27; deaths from World Health Organization, "Air Pollution," fact sheet 187 (Geneva: revised September 2000).

26. IEA, op. cit. note 20, p. 493.

27. Vattenfall, op. cit. note 1

28. Ibid.

29. Lal, op. cit. note 25.

30. Figure of 400 parts per million calculated using fossil fuel emissions from G. Marland et al., "Global, Regional, and National CO_2 Emissions," in *Trends: A Compendium of Data on Global Change* (Oak Ridge, TN: Carbon Dioxide Information and Analysis Center (CDIAC), ORNL, 2007), and land use change emissions from R. A. Houghton and J. L. Hackler, "Carbon Flux to the Atmosphere from Land-Use Changes," in *Trends: A Compendium of Data on Global Change* (Oak Ridge, TN: CDIAC, ORNL, 2002), with decay curve cited in J. Hansen et al., "Dangerous Human-Made Interference with Climate: A GISS ModelE Study," *Atmospheric Chemistry and Physics*, vol. 7 (2007), pp. 2287–312.

31. "Ditch the Tie Japan Tells Workers as 'Cool Biz' Drive Begins,"

Agence France-Presse, 1 June 2006; U.N. Population Division, op. cit. note 14.

32. Richard Register, e-mail to author, 16 October 2007.

33. Gidon Eshel and Pamela A. Martin, "Diet, Energy, and Global Warming," *Earth Interactions*, vol. 10, no. 9 (2006); USDA, *Production Supply and Distribution*, electronic database, at www.fas.usda.gov/psdonline, updated 12 October 2007; U.N. Population Division, op. cit. note 14.

34. Federal Ministry for the Environment, Nature Conservation and Nuclear Safety, *Renewable Energy-Employment Effects: Impact of the Expansion of Renewable Energy on the German Labor Market* (Berlin: June 2006); "German Plan to Close Coal Mines," *BBC News*, 29 January 2007; Michael Levitin, "Germany Says Auf Wiedersehen to Nuclear Power, Guten Tag to Renewables," *Grist.com*, 12 August 2005.

35. Commission on Weak States and U.S. National Security, *On the Brink: Weak States and U.S. National Security* (Washington, DC: Center for Global Development, 2004), p. 27.

36. The U.S. Commission on National Security in the 21st Century, *Road Map for National Security: Imperative for Change* (Washington, DC: February 2001), p. 53.

37. Commission on Weak States and U.S. National Security, op. cit. note 35, pp. 30–32.

38. "Roosevelt's Tree Army: A History of the Civilian Conservation Corps," at www.cccalumni.org/history1.html, viewed 18 October 2007.

39. For information on mobilization, see Francis Walton, *Miracle of World War II: How American Industry Made Victory Possible* (New York: Macmillan, 1956).

40. Franklin Roosevelt, "State of the Union Address," 6 January 1942, at www.ibiblio.org/pha/7-2-188/188-35.html.

41. Harold G. Vatter, *The US Economy in World War II* (New York: Columbia University Press, 1985), p. 13; Alan L. Gropman, *Mobilizing U.S. Industry in World War II* (Washington, DC: National Defense University Press, August 1996).

42. Doris Kearns Goodwin, *No Ordinary Time—Franklin and Eleanor Roosevelt: The Home Front in World War II* (New York: Simon & Schuster, 1994), p. 316; "Point Rationing Comes of Age," *Business Week*, 19 February 1944.

43. "War Production—The Job 'That Couldn't Be Done'," *Business Week*, 5 May 1945; Donald M. Nelsen, *Arsenal of Democracy: The Story of American War Production* (New York: Harcourt, Brace and Co., 1946), p. 243.

44. Goodwin, op. cit. note 42.

45. Sir Edward Grey quoted in Walton, op. cit. note 39.

46. Jeffrey Sachs, "One Tenth of 1 Percent to Make the World Safer," *Washington Post*, 21 November 2001.

47. Table 13–2 complied from Tables 7–1 and 8–1; see associated discussion in Chapter 7 for more information on social goals and funding.

48. See Table 7–1 and associated discussion in Chapter 7 for more information.

49. See Table 8–1 and associated discussion in Chapter 8 for more information.

50. Table 13–3 compiled from Stockholm International Peace Research Institute (SIPRI), *Military Expenditure Database*, electronic database at www.sipri.org, updated June 2007, with U.S. military expenditure from Center for Arms Control and Non-Proliferation, "Analysis of the Pentagon's Fiscal Year 2006 Supplemental Funding Request," at www.armscontrolcenter.org, viewed 14 September 2007.

51. SIPRI, op. cit. note 50.

52. Amy Belasco, *The Cost of Iraq, Afghanistan, and Other War on Terror Operations Since 9/11* (Washington, DC: Congressional Research Service, 16 July 2007); Linda Bilmes and Joseph Stiglitz, *The Economic Costs of the Iraq War: An Appraisal Three Years After the Beginning of the Conflict* (Cambridge, MA: National Bureau of Economic Research, February 2006).

53. For more information on plug-in hybrids and wind energy, see Chapter 12.

54. SIPRI, op. cit. note 50.

55. Jared Diamond, *Collapse: How Societies Choose to Fail or Succeed* (New York: Penguin Group, 2005); Ronald Wright, *A Short History of Progress* (New York: Carroll and Graf Publishers, 2005).

Index

Acknowledgments

As I have said before, if it takes a village to raise a child, then it takes the entire world to do a book. It begins with the work of thousands of scientists and research teams in many fields whose analyses we draw on. The process ends with the teams who translate the book into other languages. We are indebted to the thousands of researchers, all the translation teams, and countless others.

Our research team, led by Janet Larsen, went through literally thousands of research reports, articles, and books—gathering, organizing, and analyzing information for the book. Janet also helped conceptualize *Plan B 3.0*. In research and writing, Janet is my alter ego, my best critic, and a sounding board for new ideas.

Elizabeth Mygatt and Joseph Florence helped launch the research for *Plan B 3.0*. As Liz and Joe went on to a new job and graduate school, respectively, we were joined by Jonathan G. Dorn, Frances Moore, and J. Matthew Roney. The research team for *Plan B 3.0* of Jonathan, Fran, and Matt, led by Janet, is one of the most talented and hard-working teams I have ever been associated with. I am deeply grateful to each of them.

Some authors write, but this one dictates. Thanks to Gina Mathias who transcribed the early drafts, and Consuela (Sway) Headrick who transcribed the later drafts. Yes, there were many drafts.

Reah Janise Kauffman, our Vice President, not only manages the Institute, thus enabling me to concentrate on research, but she also directs the Institute's outreach effort. This includes, among other things, coordinating our worldwide network of publishers, organizing book tours, and working with the media. Reah Janise's productivity and versatility are keys to the Institute's success. Her value to me is evidenced in our 21 years of working together as a team.

Millicent Johnson, our Manager of Publications Sales, handles our publications department and serves as our office quartermaster and librarian. Millicent, who cheerfully handles the thousands of book orders, takes pride in her one-day turnaround policy.

Reviewers who helped shape the final product include my colleagues at the Earth Policy Institute (EPI), each of whom reviewed the manuscript at least twice, and more than a dozen talented individuals from outside the Institute. Peter Goldmark, for many years publisher of the *International Herald Tribune*, used his rich experience to help us identify the strengths and weaknesses of the manuscript. Peter is simultaneously one of the book's strongest supporters and one of its most able critics.

Edwin (Toby) Clark, an engineer and economist by training, brought his decades of environmental experience as an environmental analyst at the Council on Environmental Quality and as an administrator at the U.S. Environmental Protection Agency to bear on the manuscript, providing both broad structural suggestions and detailed page-by-page commentary.

William Mansfield, a member of the EPI board who has a wealth of environmental experience, including several years as Deputy Director of the United Nations Environment Programme, provided many useful suggestions.

Doug and Debra Baker contributed their wide-ranging scientific knowledge, from physics to meteorology, to chapter-by-chapter critiques that were both constructive and encouraging. Maureen Kuwano Hinkle drew on her 26 years of experience working on agricultural issues with Environmental Defense and the Audubon Society to review the book twice, providing valuable comments and encouragement along the way.

Among those who reviewed particular chapters are energy analyst William Brown, who was particularly helpful with Chapter 2, and Randall Swisher, Executive Director of the American Wind Energy Association, who helped sharpen Chapter 12. Others who reviewed all or part of the manuscript and provided useful comments were Brian Brown, Joseph Florence, Gail Gorham, and Hadan Kauffman.

My thanks also to individuals who were particularly helpful in providing specific information: Alan Berg, Lisa Braithwaite, Colin J. Campbell, Martha M. Campbell, Soh Koon Chng, Ken Creighton, John Crenshaw, Christie R. Dawson, Rolf Derpsch, James Duffield, Junko Edahiro, Mark Ellis, Reed Funk, Nathan Glasgow, Bill Heenan, Ryde James, Dale Kemery, Felix Kramer, Rattan Lal, Marjorie Lallemand, Alberto Del Lungo, Eric Martinot, Mark McHenry, Kyle Nickel, Richard Register, William Ryerson, Adam Schafer, Richard Schimpf, John E. Sheehy, Jonathan Siekmann, J. Joseph Speidel, James Spotila, Jeff Tester, Jasna Tomic, Peter Vanderborght, Martin Vorum, Brian P. Wallace, Wang Tao, Sarah Williams, Robert Wisner, and Walter Youngquist.

As always, we are in debt to our editor, Linda Starke, who brings nearly 30 years of international experience in editing environmental books and reports to the table. She has brought her sure hand to the editing of not only this book, but all my books during this period.

The book was produced in record time thanks to the efforts of Elizabeth Doherty, who prepared the page proofs. The index was ably prepared under a tight deadline by Kate Mertes.

We are supported by a network of dedicated publishers for our books and Plan B Updates in some 23 languages—Arabic, Bulgarian, Catalan, Chinese, Czech, English, Danish, French, Indonesian, Italian, Japanese, Korean, Marathi, Persian (Farsi), Polish, Portuguese, Romanian, Russian, Spanish, Swedish, Thai, Turkish, and Ukrainian. There are three publishers in English (U.S.A./Canada, U.K./Commonwealth, and India/South Asia), two in Spanish (Spain and Latin America), and two in Chinese (mainland and Taiwan).

These translations are often the work of environmentally committed individuals. In Iran, the husband and wife team of Hamid Taravati and Farzaneh Bahar, both medical doctors, head an environmental NGO and translate EPI's publications into Farsi. Their translation of *Plan B* earned them a national book award. The ministries of environment and agriculture regularly purchase copies in bulk for distribution to staff.

In China, Lin Zixin has arranged the publication of my books in Chinese for more than 20 years. Mr. Lin not only personally leads the team of translators, he also arranges outreach. The government of China pays attention to the books. Both Premier Wen Jiabao and Pan Yue, Deputy Minister of the State Environmental Protection Administration, have quoted *Plan B 2.0* in public addresses and articles. The Chinese edition of *Plan B* received a coveted national book award in 2005 from the National Library of China.

In Japan, Soki Oda, who started Worldwatch Japan some 20 years ago, leads our publication efforts and arranges book promotional tours. He is indefatigable in his outreach efforts and is already planning outreach for the Japanese edition *of Plan B 3.0.*

Gianfranco Bologna, with whom I've had a delightful relationship for over 25 years, arranges for publication of our books in Italy. As head of WWF–Italy, he is uniquely positioned to assist in this effort.

In Romania, former President Ion Iliescu, who started publishing our books some 20 years ago when he headed the publishing house Editura Tehnica, not only arranges publication but often manages to publish simultaneously with the English edition. He is ably aided by Roman Chirila at Editura Tehnica.

In Turkey, TEMA, the leading environmental NGO, which works especially on reforesting the countryside, has for many years published my books. They are already planning the outreach for this edition.

In South Korea, Yul Choi, founder of the Korean Federation for Environmental Movement and now head of the Korea Green Foundation, has published my books and oversees their launching through Doyosae publishing.

Most remarkable are the individuals who step forward out of seemingly nowhere to publish and promote Plan B. In Portugal, Antonio Cerveira Pinto, an artist, collaborated with Emanuel Pimenta of the European Environment Tribunal and Julio Sarmento, the mayor of Trancoso, to translate *Plan B 2.0.* They distributed 4,000 free copies to Portuguese government leaders, prominent academics, university libraries, and leaders in other Portuguese-speaking countries.

In France, the publication of *Plan B 2.0* was spearheaded by Pierre-Yves Longaretti, an astrophysicist, in collaboration with

Philippe Vicille, the founder of a biotech company. Pierre-Yves not only translated the book—a huge task in itself—but he added footnotes relating the analysis to the situation in France. Philippe, meanwhile, engaged Calmann-Lévy, one of France's premier publishing houses. In addition, Pierre-Yves and Philippe founded the nonprofit Alternative Planetaire to work on implementing Plan B in France.

Bernd Hamm, a professor at the University of Trier, was so taken with our work that he personally arranged for a German publisher, Kai Homilius Verlag, to publish *Plan B 2.0*.

There are also those who take the Plan B message to another level. For instance, inspired by *Plan B 2.0*, Bill and Dave Mettler of Quiet Riot developed a new performance entitled "One Home, One Family, One Future." This performing partnership uses story, physical comedy, sound effects, music, and audience interaction to awaken communities and organizations to the opportunities, benefits and increased quality of life of the new eco-economy.

Al and Anne Mielen founded Save Our Ship Environmental Institute (SOSE) in order to give presentations to local groups about Plan B. Although they had never been involved in environmental work, after reading *Plan B 2.0* they were inspired to help get the message out. Their goal is to establish branches throughout the United States.

I would also like to thank personally the members of our Plan B team—the 1,600 or so individuals who have purchased five or more copies of *Plan B 2.0* for distribution to friends, colleagues, and opinion leaders. We are particularly grateful to Ted Turner, captain of our Plan B team, who distributed over 3,600 copies to key individuals.

We are also indebted to our funders. Without their support this book would not exist. Among these are the United Nations Population Fund, the Mitsui & Co. Environment Fund, and several foundations including the Appleton, Farview, McBride Family, Laney Thornton, Shenandoah, Summit, and Wallace Genetic foundations. I'd like to especially thank the Lannan Foundation for its generous three-year grant.

Earth Policy is also supported by individual donors. I would like to particularly thank Fred Stanback, Andrew Stevenson, and an anonymous donor through the OppenheimerFunds

Legacy Program for large personal gifts. Other personal donors include Ray Anderson, Doug and Debra Baker, Susan Beck, Junko Edahiro, William Foster, Judith Gradwohl, Paul Growald, Maureen Hinkle, Scott and Hella McVay, Rick Omlor, EcoWorks Foundation, and many others.

Finally, my thanks to the team at W. W. Norton & Company: Amy Cherry, our book manager; Andrew Marasia, who put the book on a fast-track production schedule; Ingsu Liu, Art Director for the book jacket; Bill Rusin, Marketing Director; and Drake McFeely, President, with special thanks for his support. It is a delight to work with such a talented team and to have been published by W. W. Norton for more than 30 years.

And thanks to you, our readers. In the end, the success of this book depends on you and your help in implementing Plan B.

                                Lester R. Brown

About the Author

Lester R. Brown is President of Earth Policy Institute, a non-profit, interdisciplinary research organization based in Washington, D.C., which he founded in May 2001. The purpose of the Earth Policy Institute is to provide a plan for building a sustainable future and a roadmap of how to get from here to there.

Brown has been described as "one of the world's most influential thinkers" by the *Washington Post*. The *Telegraph of Calcutta* called him "the guru of the environmental movement." In 1986, the Library of Congress requested his papers for their archives.

Some 30 years ago, Brown helped pioneer the concept of sustainable development, a concept he uses in his design of an eco-economy. He was the Founder and President of the Worldwatch Institute during its first 26 years. During a career that started with tomato farming, Brown has authored or coauthored over 50 books and been awarded 24 honorary degrees. His books have appeared in more than 40 languages.

Brown is a MacArthur Fellow and the recipient of countless prizes and awards, including the 1987 United Nations Environment Prize, the 1989 World Wide Fund for Nature Gold Medal, and the 1994 Blue Planet Prize for his "exceptional contributions to solving global environmental problems." In 1995, Marquis *Who's Who*, on the occasion of its fiftieth edition, selected Lester Brown as one of 50 Great Americans. Most recently he was awarded the Presidential Medal of Italy and the Borgström Prize by the Royal Swedish Academy of Agriculture and Forestry, and he was appointed an honorary professor of the Chinese Academy of Sciences. He lives in Washington, D.C.

If you have found this book useful and would like to share it with others, consider joining our
Plan B Team.

To do so, order five or more copies at our bulk discount rate at www.earthpolicy.org

This book is not the final word. We will continue to unfold new issues and update the analysis in our
Plan B Updates.
Follow this progress by subscribing to our free, low-volume electronic listserv.
Please sign up at www.earthpolicy.org
to get these four-page Updates by e-mail
as they are released.

Past Plan B Updates and all of the
Earth Policy Institute's research,
including this book, are posted on our Web site
www.earthpolicy.org for free downloading.

EARTH POLICY INSTITUTE
www.earthpolicy.org